Little India

Little India

*Diaspora, Time, and Ethnolinguistic
Belonging in Hindu Mauritius*

Patrick Eisenlohr

UNIVERSITY OF CALIFORNIA PRESS
Berkeley · Los Angeles · London

University of California Press, one of the most distinguished university presses in the United States, enriches lives around the world by advancing scholarship in the humanities, social sciences, and natural sciences. Its activities are supported by the UC Press Foundation and by philanthropic contributions from individuals and institutions. For more information, visit www.ucpress.edu.

University of California Press
Berkeley and Los Angeles, California

University of California Press, Ltd.
London, England

Library of Congress Cataloging-in-Publication Data

Eisenlohr, Patrick, 1967–.
    Little India : diaspora, time, and ethnolinguistic belonging in Hindu Mauritius / Patrick Eisenlohr.
        p.   cm.
    Includes bibliographical references and index.
    ISBN-13: 978-0-520-24879-3 (cloth : alk. paper)
    ISBN-10: 0-520-24879-1 (cloth : alk. paper)
    ISBN-13: 978-0-520-24880-9 (pbk. : alk. paper)
    ISBN-10: 0-520-24880-5 (pbk. : alk. paper)
    1. Anthropological linguistics—Mauritius.
2. Hindus—Mauritius-Ethnic identity.   3. Hindus—
Diaspora.   4. Mauritius—Ethnic relations.   I. Title.
P35.5.M4E57   2006
306.44096982—dc22   2006031439

Manufactured in the United States of America
16 15 14 13 12 11 10 09 08 07
10 9 8 7 6 5 4 3 2 1

This book is printed on New Leaf EcoBook 50, a 100% recycled fiber of which 50% is de-inked post-consumer waste, processed chlorine-free. EcoBook 50 is acid-free and meets the minimum requirements of ANSI/ASTM D5634–01 (*Permanence of Paper*).

Dedicated to the memory of
Richard Burghart (1944–1994)

Contents

Illustrations

Acknowledgments

Fieldwork in Mauritius (June–July 1996, October 1997–December 1998, June–August 2003) was made possible by support from the Wenner-Gren Foundation for Anthropological Research and the University of Chicago Council for Advanced Studies in Peace and International Cooperation (CASPIC) with funds from the John D. and Catherine T. MacArthur Foundation, and Washington University.

In Mauritius, I am grateful to the University of Mauritius, which granted me affiliation during my research, and particularly to Vinesh Hookoomsing for his generous help and many stimulating conversations. The observations on Mauritian society by Farhad Khoyratty, Shawkat Toorawa, and Vidula Nababsing provided vital nourishment for my own ideas. The Centre SYFED-REFER at the University of Mauritius was very kind in allowing me access to its facilities. I want to thank in particular the Centre's director, Altaf Dossa, and also Sushila Naidoo. At the Mauritius Institute of Education I always found a welcoming circle of scholars such as Raj Bhoodoo and Chandra Rungasawmi, who offered copious amounts of their time, as well as intellectual and practical help in many ways. At the Mahatma Gandhi Institute, where I found open doors and encouragement, my thanks go especially to Sanyukta Bhavan, Hossen Edun, Udaye Narain Gangoo, and Pavi Ramhota. The staff members of the Mauritius Archives in Coromandel were always very helpful in providing me access to documents on education in colonial Mauritius. In Mauritius there are other friends and generous persons who went out of their way to aid and support my research. I would especially like to express my thanks to Goolhamid Begum, Marina Carter, Soorajdutt Ghallu, Fauwzee Khodabaccus, and Goswami Sewtohul, as well as the late Cassam Beebeejaum and his family. In London, on my way to Mauritius for the first time, when this project was still in its initial stages, Philip Baker provided encouragement and support.

Without the almost limitless patience and friendship of the Dinand, Chamroo, Bhavan, and Edun families this project would have been utterly impossible. It is difficult to find words to express my gratitude and indebtedness towards all of them. Special thanks also to the Keenoo family, who always kept their door open for me, cheering me up with their good spirit and astute observations of their Mauritian world.

In Heidelberg, the site of my early university education, the encouragement Klaus-Peter Köpping always gave me has proven vital, and I am grateful for the many important conversations we have had. For years I have been intensely aware of the crucial role my former teacher, the late Richard Burghart, played in motivating me to become an anthropologist, and in many ways this book began with him. Ever since his untimely death I have missed listening to him. This book is dedicated to his memory.

At the University of Chicago, my intellectual and other debts to friends and teachers are numerous. My teachers in Chicago are many, and they were all excellent. Here I would like to especially acknowledge the inspiration that Arjun Appadurai, Susan Gal, John Kelly, and Michael Silverstein have given me not only as their student but also ever since. Always generous with their time and pushing me to do my best, without them this work could not have materialized. I wish also to acknowledge the support of a William Rainey Harper Fellowship at the University of Chicago. Finally, I owe a great deal to my colleagues at Washington University, who provided a stimulating and supporting environment for the completion of this book.

Earlier versions of the ideas laid out in this book have been presented before the critical ears of audiences at Washington University, the University of Chicago, New York University, the University of Michigan, the University of Halle, and the Zentrum Moderner Orient in Berlin, and I have greatly benefited from their valuable criticisms and insights. I would especially like to thank Andrew Apter, John Bowen, Dominic Boyer, Katrin Bromber, Lou Brown, Joseph Errington, Ulrike Freitag, Sara Friedman, Thomas Blom Hansen, Adi Hastings, Matthew Hull, Judith Irvine, Aisha Khan, Farina Mir, Viranjini Munasinghe, Joel

Robbins, Bambi Schieffelin, Burkhard Schnepel, Roschanack Shaery-Eisenlohr, and Kathryn Woolard. I am deeply indebted to them for their engagement and comments. Special thanks also to Larry Bowman, Oddvar Hollup, Salikoko Mufwene, and Ellen Schnepel. Needless to say, any shortcomings in this book are my responsibility. Parts of chapter 7 appeared in an earlier version in Eisenlohr 2004, reprinted with the friendly permission of the American Anthropological Association.

My highest gratitude is reserved for my family — my parents, Peter and Stefanie Eisenlohr, as well as my sister, Verena Eisenlohr, and especially my wife, Roschanack Shaery-Eisenlohr, for her patience and critical encouragement.

Except for the discussion of historical material in chapters 1 and 4, in the following pages all names are pseudonyms, with the exception of names of relatively well-known public figures. All resemblances to the names of actual persons are accidental.

Note on Transliteration
and Orthography

In transcribing Indic languages, I have used the standard Devanagari transliteration system for quotations from written Hindi sources only. There is no standard orthography for Mauritian Bhojpuri, which is rarely written, and my transcriptions contain a great deal of ideolectal, generational, and register variation. I have used a modified variant of the Devanagari transliteration system for Mauritian Bhojpuri, without diacritics except for the retroflex plosives *t, th, d, dh* and the retroflex flaps *r* and *rh,* which frequently but not consistently occur in the speech of many older and middle-aged speakers. I have also rendered the voiceless unaspirated palatal plosive represented as *c* in standard Devanagari transliteration as *ch* to minimize confusion for nonspecialist readers.

My transcriptions of Mauritian Creole also show considerable ideolectal and register variations combined with frequent bivalent usage, especially among Mauritian Creole-Mauritian Bhojpuri bilinguals. I have taken the orthography proposed by Baker and Hookoomsing (1987) as an orientation wherever feasible but have not adopted the use of diacritics to indicate nasalization.

Introduction

In February 1999, two months after I had left Mauritius, having concluded my main dissertation fieldwork, riots erupted on the island for
the first time since 1968. The popular singer Kaya had died under suspi-
cious circumstances in police custody, where he had been held on drug
charges. Kaya was a member of the Creole ethnic community of Mauritius, most of whom trace their ancestry to African and Malagasy slaves.
After the news of Kaya's death in the central police headquarters of Port
Louis became known, protesters took to the streets in suburbs of the capital, attacking police stations and other government buildings, torching
vehicles, and destroying and looting businesses. The riots very quickly
acquired an ethnic dimension, since many of the protesters were of poor
Creole background, and some of them viewed the police as a Hindu
force, given the predominance of Hindus in Mauritian state institutions.
In addition, Kaya had been considered a leadership figure among young
Creoles, and while the events were still unfolding, representatives of
Creole organizations publicly claimed that the violence was a reaction
against multiple forms of political and economic exclusion suffered by
members of the Creole community. Fears suddenly spread that groups of
Creoles from suburbs of the capital such as Roche-Bois, where some of
the first outbreaks of violence occurred, were preparing to attack and
loot in the rural, Hindu-dominated north of the island. Driven by these

unfounded rumors, Hindu mobs burned down two Creole neighbor-
hoods in the northern towns of Triolet and Goodlands, minutes from
where I had lived and worked in 1997 and 1998, while a similar event
in the central town of Quatre-Bornes, where armed Hindus had sur-
rounded a Creole *cité*,[1] was only narrowly averted (see also Baptiste
2002, 87–88). When I returned in the winter of 2003 to the predominantly Hindu village where I had lived, my friends told me that wild
rumors about gangs of Creoles from Roche-Bois who were out to smash
their homes *(kraz lakaz)* had prompted the quick formation of vigilante
groups with the assistance of the main local Hindu committee, who kept
watch over the main road, where they expected the imagined attackers to
appear.

Even though the scale of violence was modest compared to recent
episodes of communal violence in some South Asian and African countries — in the end the death toll stood at four and the extent of direct and
indirect economic damage at $50 million[2] — most Mauritians were
deeply shocked by the events in which conflict had become ethnicized in
such a short time. Among scholars of Mauritius as well, the dramatic
turn of February 1999 prompted some reconsideration of Mauritius's
status among observers as a model of a multiethnic society characterized
by harmony and compromise, well on the road to a presumably posteth-
nic future (e.g., Carroll and Carroll 2000a, versus Carroll and Carroll
2000b).

The riots of 1999 should not cause one to lose sight of the record of
relatively nonviolent coexistence in Mauritius. Nor should one downplay
the often successful efforts of many Mauritians, including some in state
institutions, to strive for compromise in addressing conflicts that could
otherwise quickly acquire an ethnic reading. Nevertheless, I suggest that
the events have made more obvious the fragility of the distinction between ethnic and nonethnic solidarities and identifications often pointed
out in the study of Mauritius. This distinction has been fundamental in
recent analyses of Mauritian nationalism and nation-building. Several
scholars of Mauritius have argued that despite a history of colonial plantation capitalism, so often associated with antagonism on the basis of
colonial divisions of labor simultaneously defined as ethnic and racial,
the logic of ethnic competition is becoming less and less relevant for
Mauritian society (Bowman 1991; Eriksen 1998; Srebrnik 2000).
Thomas Eriksen, for example, has emphasized the growing range of
interactional contexts in which nonethnic identifications play a key role,

one result being an emerging sense of shared Mauritian nationhood across the communal boundaries established during colonialism (Eriksen 1993, 118; 1998, 169). Nevertheless, the events of February 1999 made it clear that not all Mauritians feel themselves included in a new Mauritian nation to the same degree (Baptiste 2002; Laville 2000), as they appeared to be evidence of economic and political exclusion on the part of many Creoles.

While overtly ethnic visions of nationhood have been widely discredited in postcolonial Mauritius, it is also misleading to describe this nation as nonethnic. Instead, I suggest that senses of nationhood in Mauritius actually exemplify a "leaking" boundary between what Eriksen has termed the ethnic and the nonethnic (Eriksen 1997, 1998). That is, the nation does not necessarily represent a refuge from and superseding of ethnic antagonism, but in fact is one of its principal battlegrounds as different actors struggle over contrasting definitions of the Mauritian nation.

The main division between competing imaginations of a Mauritian nation is the privileging of traditions understood to be ancestral and diasporic as opposed to those that can be constructed as indigenous, or at least portrayed as locally created.[3] This does not necessarily imply the complete exclusion of one dimension in favor of the other. Rather, there are differences of emphasis in representations concerning which cultural traditions and symbols should play a more central role in the process of postcolonial nation-building, and which are to be relegated to more peripheral positions. Even though both senses of Mauritian nationhood are emphatically portrayed as guarantors of inclusive unity, they nevertheless establish different positions for ethnicities within the nation, often conceived in terms of center and periphery, and serve the material and symbolic interests of some better than others. In short, there is disagreement about precisely what "common denominators" (Eriksen 1998) should provide the base for a new Mauritian nation so it can be portrayed as nonethnic. The nation is one of the main fields of contest for symbolic domination between actors often defined by Mauritians as ethnic.

In 1998, the government of Mauritius decided to launch a new series of bank notes. When in November of that year the first of the new currency bills went in circulation, the focus of public attention was on the fact that the vertical order of the three languages in which the value of the bank note in Mauritian rupees is printed — English, Tamil, and

Hindi — had been altered. English, the official language of Mauritian state institutions, remained on top, but Tamil, placed between English and Hindi on the old series, had been relegated to the lowest place. Within days Tamil ethnic and religious organizations staged protest activities, including road blockades, and Hindu Tamil priests went on hunger strikes in their temples. The island saw large demonstrations by agitated crowds, one of which culminated in the storming of the Bank of Mauritius building in the center of the capital. The minister of education, himself of Tamil background, threatened to step down from his post in protest and warned the "clowns" responsible for the design of the new bank notes that the Tamils were ready "to die for their rights."[4] Two weeks after the protests started, Prime Minister Navin Ramgoolam fired the Governor of the Bank of Mauritius and had the new series of bank notes withdrawn, at a cost of more than two million U.S. dollars. It was promised that future bank notes would leave the old order of languages on the bills untouched.

Even though the conflict was ostensibly between representatives of Hindus of Tamil background and some Hindus of north Indian origin who held senior positions in state institutions, the episode highlighted the wider significance of ancestral language in Mauritius. At first glance, ancestral languages would seem to serve few instrumental purposes. They may not even have been known and used by immigrating ancestors from India, and they are often not well known by Indo-Mauritians, in particular those claiming Tamil origin. Nevertheless, ancestral languages are important emblems of group identification and play a key role in the debates about Mauritian nationality. Language is a crucial field in this struggle, as the two competing senses of Mauritian nationhood mentioned above have coalesced around two different linguistic ideologies of the nation. On one hand, the nearly universally shared practice of Mauritian Creole is often portrayed as evidence of an emerging national culture free from ethnic particularism.[5] Many Mauritians and some foreign academic observers (e.g., Bowman 1991, 164; Eriksen 1992, 123) consider Mauritian Creole a key emblem of a Mauritian nation because its practice transcends ethnic boundaries and because Creole is known to have been created locally. Thus, a sense of Mauritian nationhood emphasizing the cultivation and celebration of cultural traditions conceived as quasi-indigenous has been most powerfully articulated as a Creole linguistic nationalism. On the other hand, those conceiving the Mauritian nation as primarily constituted by traditions having origins elsewhere have placed far more emphasis on the official recognition and cultivation of ancestral languages such as Hindi and Tamil than on the celebration of Mauritian Creole.

"LITTLE INDIA"

"Little India" is what I call a cultural politics in which the performance of diasporic traditions and allegiances to India as a land of origin becomes a hegemonic basis for cultural citizenship in Mauritius. Thus, the term is not meant to imply continuity with an older paradigm of diaspora studies, in which communities of people of Indian origin were described and analyzed in terms of their attenuation or preservation of South Asian cultural traditions in a new environment. Diasporic traditions among Indo-Mauritians cannot be understood as "survivals" from a time before migration to Mauritius. Instead, I seek to show how what are regarded as Indian ancestral cultures and ancestral languages have emerged as central to being Mauritian, indeed, to claiming membership in a Mauritian nation.[6] Mauritius is a former plantation colony with no precolonial population, a fact that has made attempts to envision Mauritian nationhood in terms of indigenousness more arduous. Though relative latecomers in the process of settling the island, Hindu Mauritians, who comprise the largest and politically dominant ethnic community of Mauritius, have legitimized their central place in a Mauritian nation not in terms of an imagined state of indigenousness but by the construction of diasporic ancestral cultures. Enabled by their dominant position in state institutions since the end of colonialism in 1968, they have established the hegemony of a diasporic notion of cultural citizenship according to which Mauritians are primarily defined as subjects having origins in other parts of the world with continuing commitments to putative ancestral traditions. These traditions are portrayed as ancient and glorious and as repositories of cultural values that enable their adherents to lead spiritually and economically productive lives in solidarity with others, thus crucially contributing to the successful economic development and mostly nonviolent coexistence for which Mauritius has come to be known to the outside world. According to this perspective, since ancestral traditions are so germane to the successes of the Mauritian postcolonial experience, full membership in the Mauritian nation is performed through the cultivation of such ancestral traditions with origins elsewhere.

As others have pointed out, the term "overseas Indians" evokes a colonial genealogy (Axel 2001, 15–16). Indeed, cultural traditions among

Mauritians claiming Indian descent are thoroughly shaped by the colonial experience of indenture, and the ethnic boundaries Mauritians consider crucial organizing features of their society have been established by
the practices of the colonial plantation regime (cf. Kelly 1991). My concern here is to show how such colonial genealogies of community have
been reworked as agents of symbolic domination over the nation, legitimizing a central position nowadays held by Hindus. Consequently, the
process of diasporization that accomplishes this recasting of colonial
notions of community has to be understood as rooted in contemporary
politics, and not as self-evidently emerging from the experience of the
first-generation indentured migrants (Hansen 2002).

In this context, ancestral language emerges as a key element in the
invention of official diasporic ancestral cultures because of certain challenges to their hegemony. Such challenges have arisen because some
Mauritians — in particular members of the largest non-Indian ethnic
group, the Creoles — have no recognized claims on ancestral languages
with origins outside Mauritius. Indeed, diasporic constructions of
belonging centered on ancestral traditions are often in tension with constructions of belonging that privilege creolization as a new form of
indigenous Mauritianness. Central to the articulation of Creole versions
of nationhood is the fact that the vast majority of Mauritians use
Mauritian Creole, the French-lexifier Creole language particular to the
country. In the 1970s, language activists began calling for the recognition
of Mauritian Creole, understood as the vernacular language of the "people" regardless of ethnic background, as national language. The practice
of Mauritian Creole in everyday life is often considered one of the few, if
not the only cultural dimension that lends itself to the project of establishing a different kind of nation, one informed by the more uniformizing
tendencies of nation-projects elsewhere and privileging the imagined
indigenousness of certain cultural practices and traditions. In the eyes of
its champions, the nearly universal practice of Mauritian Creole emerges
as perhaps the only available basis for the establishment of what they
consider a "real" nation. In this, Mauritian Creole linguistic nationalists
invoke a sense of nationhood informed by European legacies of cultural
uniformization, vernacular standardization, and the celebration of the
autochthonous. Thus imaginations of nationhood in Mauritius have
taken a distinctly linguistic turn.

Many Indo-Mauritians, in particular Hindus, who base their bid for
symbolic dominance over the nation on the legitimizing powers of diasporic ancestral traditions have resisted the claims of Mauritian Creole

linguistic nationalism, despite the fact that the majority of them use Mauritian Creole as their primary vernacular in everyday life. They have done so by privileging Indian ancestral languages as foci of belonging over those linguistic traditions with a claim to indigenous authenticity. Since the cultivation of such diasporic ancestral languages in Mauritius crucially depends on state support and recognition, in particular, instruction in those languages in state and state-financed schools, access to state power has played an important role in this struggle over defining membership in a Mauritian nation through linguistic ideologies. The failure of the movement to have Creole recognized and supported as the national language in the face of the ongoing massive investment by state institutions in diasporic and above all Indian ancestral languages has important consequences for the kind of nation that Mauritius is becoming. Defining Mauritian nationhood as above all constituted by diasporic traditions, in a situation in which nearly 70 percent of the population is of Indian background, reflects a particular organization of ethnic and linguistic diversity that is shaped by imbalances of power and informed by a logic of exclusion. The politics of "Little India" is a struggle for symbolic dominance over the shaping of Mauritianness in which those who lack claims to institutionalized ancestral cultures and ancestral languages with origins elsewhere are relegated to the margins of the nation.

THE TEMPORALITY OF DIASPORA: LANGUAGE AND CULTURAL HYBRIDITY

Mauritius is unique among Indian diasporas, as nearly 70 percent of the Mauritian population of 1.2 million claim Indian origin. Unlike other Indian diasporas in the Caribbean, the Pacific, Britain, and North America, in Mauritius ideologies of ancestral language play key roles in simultaneously defining a relationship to a "homeland" in India and shaping a sense of nationality in the diaspora. The most important among these Indian ancestral languages is Hindi, locally understood as the ancestral language of Hindus of north Indian origin. Despite its restricted use, Hindi is a principal focus of diasporic belonging among Hindu Mauritians. Its practice, especially in religious contexts, is sometimes even understood to be a way of ritual communion with the Indian ancestors who founded the Hindu community of Mauritius. In contrast, the principal vernacular language, French-lexifier Mauritian Creole, which Mauritian Hindus share with almost all other Mauritians, is less relevant for the construction of a diasporic community, especially because its practice is seen as evidence of spatial and temporal distance from the world of Indian immigrant ancestors.

One question I pursue in this book is: what implications do ideologies of language, that is, representations of social relationships through politically charged images of language and linguistic difference (Silverstein 1979, Woolard and Schieffelin 1994, Irvine and Gal 2000), have in the formation of diasporas? This issue is especially pertinent, since language often plays a central role in the relationships diasporic communities entertain with sometimes changing homelands, thus producing shifting "counter-geographies" (Appadurai 1996b). I propose that among Hindu Mauritians language does so by mediating and shaping the temporal and spatial relationships between Hindu Mauritians and the assumed homeland, making it possible to experience community as diasporic. In this I treat diaspora not as a simple consequence of migration from A to B, but as a form of identification in which some continued relationship or allegiance to a necessarily imagined, and sometimes even invented, homeland is made relevant for such processes of identification. Thus, diaspora is a malleable category, as diasporas are not created by the mere fact of displacement. Displacement does not necessarily imply a continued relationship with a homeland, however imagined.

In addition, my use of the category "diaspora" in this book suggests that in the contemporary world diaspora constitutes a meaningful category only in articulation with national imaginaries in which people with transnational affiliations are situated (van der Veer 1995). In the particular shape this articulation has taken in Mauritius, the claiming of diasporic identities has emerged as a primary way of claiming membership and centrality in the Mauritian nation. Thus, the role of ideologies of language in the formation of diasporas has to be analyzed in terms of how they relate to politically charged ideas about language and linguistic difference constitutive of an imagined national community. In Mauritius, the significance of diasporic ancestral language can only be understood in relation to the key importance considerations of linguistic difference generally have in shaping a sense of Mauritian nationhood.

Mauritius has a Hindu-dominated government that supports the teaching and cultivation of ancestral languages and generally encourages the building of close diasporic relationships with India. In this book I focus on Hindu Mauritians, the largest ethnic group in the country (52 percent of the population, while Muslims of Indian background comprise 17%) and the way Hindus of north Indian origin (approximately 41 percent of the population) cultivate Hindi as their ancestral language.

As I show in detail, the social force most committed to promoting Hindi in Mauritius is comprised of transnationally operating Hindu nationalists, who are well established in Mauritius, having forged strong links with local Hindu organizations and Mauritian state institutions.

In this study I pay particular attention to how the construction of diasporic belonging through Hindi as an ancestral language among Hindu Mauritians articulates with other practices of remembrance of a homeland in India. For example, the large annual Hindu pilgrimage on the occasion of the festival of Shivratri is a privileged context for using Hindi in Mauritius. It is also a performative bridging of a temporal and spatial remove separating Hindu Mauritians from an ancestral homeland in India, while also highlighting the political and economic "progress" and "development" Hindus have undertaken since their migration to Mauritius. In this way, I show that the shaping of diasporic community is crucially based on the mediation between different modes of temporality locating a Hindu diaspora in relation to a homeland.

While this book is an investigation of a Hindu diaspora in Mauritius, it also addresses broader contemporary concerns about transnationalism and diasporic social formations. In anthropology there is an ongoing interest in diasporic practices and identifications and their implications for the study of culture in general. Yet little work has been done on the ways cultural practices centered on language apart from literature are involved in the creation of diasporic communities and identities. I suggest that politically charged representations of language and its use are of central importance for processes of diasporic identification because they shape and modify the theme of spatio-temporal disjuncture, which is so relevant to experiences of diaspora.

Much of the existing literature on language in South Asian diasporas follows an older paradigm of diaspora studies centered on the opposition between cultural retention and attenuation. The continued use of South Asian languages in the diaspora is interpreted as a sign of cultural persistence and preservation of traditions of the homeland. (Siegel 1987, Mesthrie 1991, Barz and Siegel 1988). In contrast, I treat the formation of diasporic community as mediated through language-focused ideologies of ethnic differentiation centered on regimentations of space and time, in particular, the specific form of ancestral languages. There is no direct relationship between the use of a particular language, such as a certain South Asian language, in the diaspora, and forms of belonging. Instead, such links are established through shifting ideologies inhabiting linguistic practice.

A key issue in debates about diasporas and transnational circuits is the question of a link between cosmopolitan, "hybrid" identities and transnational cultural and migratory flows. According to a range of theorists of transnationalism, there are powerful connections between transnational flows of people and cultural forms and the rise of cosmopolitan and transgressive identities (Bhabha 1990, 1994; Clifford 1997; García Canclini 1995; Gilroy 1993; Gupta and Ferguson 1992, 18; Hall 1990, 1991; Lavie and Swedenburg 1996). These authors propose a privileged relationship between diasporic or otherwise transnational situations and hybrid cultures and identities. At the same time, the reconfiguring of experiences of time and space is a central theme in analyses of recent trends of globalization, where those trends are described as "time-space compression" (Harvey 1989), a radical transformation of experiences of spatio-temporal remove and boundaries. In particular, diaspora has been described as a dispersion that "effectively compresses time and space such that it enables the experiences of many places at what would appear to be one moment" (Shukla 2001, 551). This assessment is often linked to the assumption that increased flows of migration and travel in contemporary trends of globalization have dissolved the link between culture and place (Appadurai 1996a; Tomlinson 1999, 141; Hannerz 1996). Ideas about cultural hybridity in the diaspora often derive much of their intuitively compelling force from such reasoning about space and time — the diaspora is culturally hybrid because one can experience several different places and place-indicating traditions and practices at the same time. Diaspora as the paradigmatic case of such "deterritorialization" of cultural practices and identities (Appadurai 1996b) is then also inextricably linked to the issue of temporality, since deterritorialized or diasporic existence is defined by temporal simultaneity in experiencing a diversity of place-bound cultural traditions.

In this book my point is not just to draw attention to the tacit reinscription of ideologies of cultural origins and spatial rootedness of traditions that are often part of discourses of cultural displacement and hybridity. Instead, I problematize the dialectics of place-bound culture and time-space compression by suggesting that language and linguistic practices can intervene to shape and mediate apprehensions of spatio-temporal remove and simultaneity in different ways. In this I build on the insights of Walter Benjamin, who realized that the opposing modes of temporality he called "empty, homogenous" time and "messianic" time have different implications for the creation of political solidarities and communities (Benjamin 1968). Drawing on Benjamin, Benedict

Anderson, in his account of nationalism, made the important point that these temporalities of community are language-mediated, while privileging "empty, homogenous" time over a sacred, "messianic" simultaneity across time (Anderson 1991). In contrast, I suggest that the temporalities of imagining a large-scale ethno-national community are always plural, and that linguistic ideologies play a key role in mediating between them. This is especially evident in the case of diasporic communities, since a dialectics of temporal distance and simultaneity is part of what defines these communities as diasporic.

The problem of temporality can also be approached by a different intellectual route. Following the phenomenological critique of historicism, the experience of duration as also the distinctions between past, present, and future are not to be understood as objective sequences of events. Instead, past and future events emerge as actively constituted and constantly reorganized by subjects inhabiting a continually shifting horizon of the "present" (Husserl 1964). Whether in autobiographical reflection (Dilthey 1958, 199–204; Heidegger 1962)[7] or in the emergence of historical consciousness in a social collective, linguistic practices such as narrative play a key role in reconfiguring the relationships between remembered and anticipated events (Ricoeur 1988). Often this is performed by organizing them into a meaningful storyline, which may change under different circumstances of the "present," and may also be subject to contestation by alternative accounts. These insights into temporal experience, combined with Benjamin's arguments about the different sorts of solidarities and communities projected by different modes of temporality, emphasize the dynamic and creative character of temporality.

An analysis of the multiple temporalities involved in the making of diasporas puts in question Frederic Jameson's thesis of the "end of temporality." Jameson argues that the "postmodern" historical juncture is characterized by a "dramatic and alarming shrinkage of existential time and the reduction to a present that hardly qualifies as such any longer, given the virtual effacement of that past and future that can alone define a present in the first place" (2003: 708). He describes this "reduction to the present" as the symptom of a new cybernetic socioeconomic system, obliterating the sense of "deep time" that was still accessible to those who had experienced the temporality of premodern agricultural villages. However, in a transnational, "postmodern" age, remembered pasts and anticipated futures do continue to be vital resources, as national, diasporic, and religious communities of various sorts are among the key political players. Subjects become part of such communities as different subjective times are mediated through particular narrative and historical times. Moreover, these narrative times may not only be in conflict with each other but may also stand in complex tensions with "messianic" temporalities of sudden simultaneity.[8]

Given this plural character of temporality, a grid of time-space in which cultures are linked to places to be experienced one at a time, unless the culture-place connection is undermined by migration and mass media, should not be presupposed. Instead, the constitution of that grid should be an object of analysis within a study of the malleability of diaspora. Moreover, the time-space dynamics of diasporic displacement are subject to different interpretations in different historical settings. The consequences of diaspora for apprehensions of time, space, and belonging are not uniform; they may manifest differently in different social and historical contexts, and cannot be generalized under the rubric of hybridity.

In the chapters that follow I argue that there is no necessary link between intense cultural circulation across national borders and hybrid identities. Rather, diasporas are shaped by the ways transnational cultural flows are deployed in relation to the experience of spatio-temporal displacement. Linguistic ideologies are one of the central ways in which such concerns about spatio-temporal disjuncture shape ideas of collective belonging, and the resulting forms of diasporic identity do not necessarily foreground the theme of cultural hybridity. I stress that diasporic situations often motivate people to engage in practices intended to overcome the sense of spatio-temporal remove that is at the heart of many diasporic experiences.

The Indo-Mauritian politics of ancestral tradition illustrate how strong transnational cultural flows may actually increase the salience of purist forms of identity, deliberately positioned against practices or other forms of belonging perceived as culturally mixed. This is not to deny the complexity and multilayered quality of Hindu Mauritian cultural practices and identities, which I describe in detail. The specter of mixedness is part of discourses of purity. However, contemporary transnational processes have contributed considerably to the highlighting of the theme of purity in current practices of identification, and above all, in the cultivation of ancestral language. The practice and promotion of ancestral languages have played important roles in turning most Indian migrants and their descendants, despite their diverse regional, religious, and caste backgrounds, into a community of Hindus. An important reason for this is that the theme of linguistic and cultural purity downplays the spatio-temporal distance from the world of the immigrating Indian ancestors, which is vital in defining diasporic existence. Ideologies of Indian ancestral languages draw a link between the "protection" of a pure Hindu identity in the diaspora and the cultivation and dissemination of standardized Indian languages, which represent the ancestors and the homeland, and enable experiences of being one with the ancestors as a response to a diasporic situation.

CREOLIZATION AND DIASPORA

Some researchers consider the linguistic process of creolization a useful metaphor or analogue to transnational cultural processes, capturing the hybridity they see as defining for cultural processes and forms of belonging in the diaspora (Hannerz 1987, Eriksen 2003). Since creolization as a description of cultural processes in the diaspora often draws on reasoning about language, I propose to interrogate creolization with regard to how language reworks processes of cultural deterritorialization.

Although creolization has been a topic of study for linguistic anthropologists (Hymes 1971), it gained currency in the discipline of anthropology mainly through the analysis of culture creation and transformation in the context of colonial plantation capitalism (Mintz and Price 1992 [1976], Troulliot 1998). Creolization as a theoretical frame frequently summons ideas of pure origins that subsequently underwent fusion and mixing. Nevertheless, in the Caribbean context, creolization as a cultural model of diaspora has been understood as both a refuge from the essentialism of a purist search for origins and a central trope in several Caribbean nationalisms striving for local authenticity (e.g., Bernabé, Chamoiseau, and Confiant 1993). For Creole nationalists the inclusion of diverse cultural traditions in the nation is the key legitimizing theme of their national project. At the same time, analysts of South Asian diasporas in the Caribbean have highlighted the exclusionary potential of national ideologies of creoleness, which often put African origins at the center of constructions of belonging while marginalizing people who continue to cultivate their South Asian diasporic origins (Khan 2001, Munasinghe 2002, Puri 2004).

In Mauritius, which in many ways resembles Caribbean societies such as Trinidad and Guyana but with a much stronger Indian diasporic presence, the question of whether creolization is adequate as a description of processes of identity formation is more focused on issues of language. In fact, creolization as a favored concept of contemporary theorists of globalization (Hannerz 1996) has constituted a main target of purist language ideologies spread by Hindu nationalists and their followers in the state apparatus in Mauritius. On the other hand, some francophone writers have described Mauritius as a "Creole country" or "Creole island," since French-lexifier Mauritian Creole is the predominant vernacular used by almost the entire population (Benoist 1985, Bonniol 1985).

I have already mentioned the contest over shaping Mauritian nationhood in terms of Creole indigenousness or diasporic traditions, which ultimately points to the question of what kind of Mauritians are centrally positioned in a Mauritian national imagination and who is relegated to its margins. In addition, I argue that notions of belonging centered on creolization are rejected among the Indo-Mauritian population of Mauritius largely because they highlight the spatio-temporal displacement of a diasporic existence and challenge the relevance of cultivating links with the Indian homeland. Instead, Indo-Mauritians of Hindu background have developed strategies of mitigating the experience of remove from a homeland through religious ritual and linguistic ideologies centered on Indian ancestral languages. While many Hindus are ready to concede the generally "mixed" character of their cultural practices, and of Mauritian society in general, they have reworked this experienced hybridity in particular ways. While the institutionalized practice of ancestral cultures and languages constitutes a particular regimentation of diversity, in which the generally "mixed" character of Mauritius is affirmed, legitimate participation in this mixture is mediated by such ancestral traditions with purist biases. In contrast, transnationally operating Hindu activists equate the polyvalence of Creole culture and creolization, which mingles ideas about language, history and race in the context of its own complex history in Mauritius, with loss of Hindu religion and moral impurity. One important way of articulating this strong concern about diasporic origins has been the promotion and celebration of Indian ancestral languages, above all, Hindi, the language mostly favored by a Hindu transnational activist network. This valorizing of Hindi represents both a denial of and a response to the nearly universal use of Mauritian Creole on the island, and to the fact that the local variety of the only Indian language in active daily use, Bhojpuri, features many Creole elements and differs greatly from Hindi.

In short, in this particular expression of transnationalism centered on the circulation of ideas about language and belonging, cultural forms recognized as creolized are confronted as a threat rather than embraced as expressions of cosmopolitan identity reinforced by increased cultural flows across national boundaries. On the other hand, the mixedness of

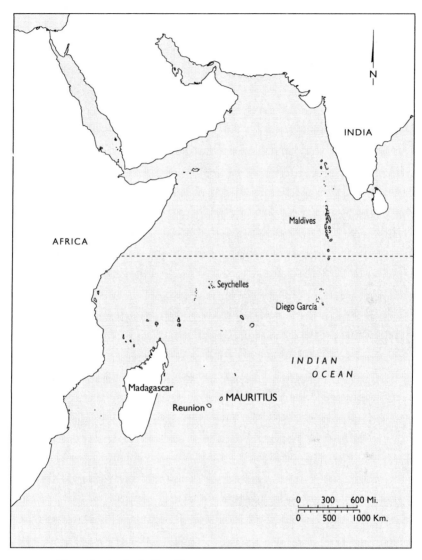

MAP 1. Mauritius in the Indian Ocean

Mauritian society is not rejected as such, but reconfigured into a number of clearly demarcated and officially recognized ancestral traditions. Thus, in this regime of diversity, overall affirmations of "mixture" and projects of homogenization within what are considered ancestral traditions go hand in hand.

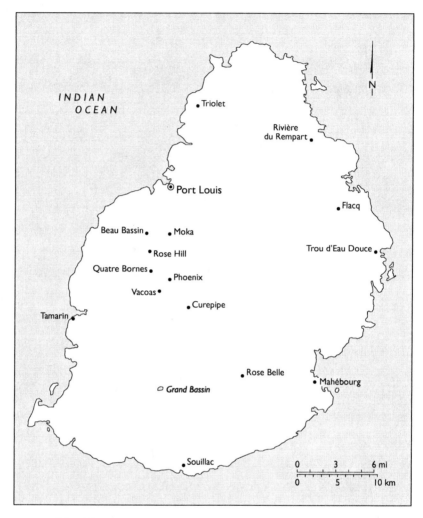

MAP 2. Mauritius

LANGUAGE, IDEOLOGY, AND SEMIOSIS

In contemporary linguistic anthropology, the term "language ideology" is widely used to describe a systemic linkage between ideas about language structure and use, on the one hand, and social and political formations, interests, and conflicts, on the other. Poststructuralist theorists such as Foucault (1980, 118–19) have voiced misgivings about the concept of ideology, as it implies, especially in its more narrowly historical materialist usages, a privileged point of observation from where representations of social reality can be judged as either true or distorted. However, a more "neutral" conception of ideology, one that does not normatively contrast ideology with "true" representations of social worlds (cf. Eagleton 1991, 28–29), is useful in order to situate such ideas about language with respect to their social origins, acknowledging that a dialectic of social positionality, political interests, and knowledge production is pervasive and inescapable in many social contexts. Retaining such a broadened notion of ideology, one without pretensions of claiming a position of unique scientific "truth," seems necessary in order to do justice to the circumstance that some ideas serve the self-understood interests of some better than others and consequently selectively highlight certain aspects of social contexts and historical narrative while eliding others. A Foucauldian analysis of power that seeks to demonstrate how power inscribes itself into the body directly (Foucault 1978, 139–46), bypassing ideology, does little to clarify this problem; moreover, it also elides the fact that the micro-practices of power that are supposed to accomplish this inevitably presuppose legal frameworks and other assumptions that are profoundly ideological (Žižek 1994, 13–15). The notion of ideology I draw on, which is less monolithic and irresistible than Bourdieu's *doxa* appears to be (Bourdieu 1977), also has the advantage of capturing multiplicity and conflict between such forms and practices of knowledge production. A more open usage of the concept of ideology is also receptive to the fact that politically interested ideas and signifying practices are socially productive; that is, they are not simply held or executed by conflicting groups of actors in preexisting social and cultural contexts, they also crucially shape social subjects, their interests, and their historical consciousness. Such an understanding of ideology is comprehensive insofar as it encompasses both ideational representations and embodied practices focused on language. Ideology as a research focus thus highlights the fact that linguistic anthropologists are concerned with the political organization of signifying practices, in particular with language, the most central of signifying practices.

Against this background of debates over the continued utility of the concept of ideology, approaching the issue of linguistic ideology from a semiotic vantage point has a number of advantages. In semiotic analysis of especially the Peircean tradition, the focus is on a multitude of sign relations that is, in principle, changing and bottomless. Thus the issue which have some cast doubt about — the continued validity of ideology as a concept of social analysis — does not really arise in a semiotic approach to ideology, as sign relations cannot be reduced to a relationship between social representations or signifying practices and a social "reality." Further, and more specifically, language ideology as semiosis is a useful tool for understanding the political and social consequences of language structure and use, since it provides a way to describe systematic relationships between linguistic and nonlinguistic signs as they are mobilized at the intersection of language and other social practices.

In this, language ideology can be described as a particular variant of what Michael Silverstein has called metapragmatics (1998, 128–29). Metapragmatics are frames that organize the indexicality of microlevel interaction in such a way that indexical relationships, that is, relationships of contiguity or co-occurrence between signs, linguistic or nonlinguistic (Peirce 1932, 170–72), are recognizable as socially meaningful events and enable the reading of performative acts as indicative of particular socially locatable identities (Silverstein 1976, 1993). For example, metapragmatics may make an unfolding speech event, such as a public address or ritual, recognizable as a token instance or replication of a mythical event, and may assign participants corresponding participation roles and social identities. Metapragmatics are therefore essentially a process of context-making, in which sign-events are connected to other sign-events and social values, thus providing the grounds for social interpretation and evaluation. Certainly, not all metapragmatics need be ideological, but insofar as this process of contextualization sooner or later touches on political and social interests and conflicts, it ends up producing and reproducing ideology. Ideology can be especially effective when particular semiotic resources are deployed to its end. For example, relationships of mere co-occurrence (indexical relations), such as between linguistic signs and other signs signaling social identities, may be cast in terms of iconic relations, that is, as relationships of essential qualitative likeness (Irvine and Gal 2000). Framing relationships of co-occurrence as grounded in inherent sameness has a particular naturalizing effect on the social evaluations involved.

In this book, I not only analyze how social differences among Indo-Mauritians are established and negotiated through such politically charged links between particular features of language in use and social values. I also focus on how temporality, which in semiotic terms is above all an indexical phenomena since indexical relations are relationships of relative spatio-temporal contiguity and co-occurrence, is subject to regimentation by linguistic ideology. Language ideologies are important for an understanding of temporality because they underpin and encode the relationships between different events by framing them in ways that are connected to social and political interests. Inevitably, specification of relationships between events in narrative and ritual representations of the past involves the stipulation of temporal relationships between them. For example, I show how an ideology of ancestral language enacted on ritual occasions positions the world of the ancestors of Hindu Mauritians and their ritual performances in relation to present-day Hindu Mauritians engaged in religious practice. What results is the shaping of a particular kind of diasporic belonging in which language plays a key role, and where the otherwise important social boundaries and differentiations among Hindu Mauritians are downplayed. In turn, a politics of ancestral cultures in which the cultivation of ancestral language is central is one of the most important features of postcolonial Mauritian politics; it places those Mauritians with recognized claims on such ancestral cultures and languages in an advantageous position vis-à-vis those who lack such claims. The Mauritian politics of ancestral language produce a sense of nationhood in which diasporic identities, rather than themes of local origin or indigenousness, become primary. Language is thus present as ideology, enmeshed in conflict and the justification of privileges of some over others, and also subject to challenges from both Mauritians of non-Hindu origin and Hindu Mauritians themselves. Therefore, in this book I pay attention not only to proponents of ancestral languages but also to the lack of consensus and the wide range of stances among Hindu Mauritians regarding the significance of ancestral language for their personal and collective senses of belonging, and consequently for their place in the postcolonial Mauritian nation.

OVERVIEW

I begin by outlining the link between linguistic ideologies and the struggle for symbolic domination over a Mauritian nation. The tension between a politics of "Little India" and a politics of creolization in which different politically charged visions of linguistic differentiation yield contrasting images of the Mauritian nation is the theme of chapter 1. I set out by analyzing the connections between transnationally operating Hindu nationalism and the institutionalization of Hindi as an ancestral language of Hindus in Mauritius. I then compare such Hindu nationalist perspectives to alternative visions of linguistic differentiation in the characterization of Mauritius as a diasporic location, making Mauritius imaginable as a "Creole island." The consequences of these conflicting visions of ethno-linguistic belonging in the diaspora for ethnic relations in Mauritius are also linked to the different temporalities they project onto the Hindu community in Mauritius. Further, in the context of a critical discussion of Benedict Anderson's approach to nationalism and language, I analyze these contrasting ideologies of language as having different implications when it comes to the modularity of ethnolinguistic nationalism.

Chapter 2 describes the main setting of my fieldwork, a predominantly Indo-Mauritian locality in northern Mauritius. I account for the complexity of local stances regarding the "preservation" of Bhojpuri as well as Hindi as an ancestral language as they are informed by class differences and aspirations to social mobility. Further, I focus on how local acts of identifying someone as Hindu articulate with wider internal debates among Mauritian Hindus about the meaning of "Hindu-ness" in the diaspora, experiences of travel to or temporary stays in India, as well as the production of stereotypes of ethnic others. Chapter 3 extends this local perspective by analyzing how linguistic features are linked to social and ethnic values. The shifting between registers and varieties in Creole-Bhojpuri bilingual usage emerges as a key mode of performing interactive stances and identities, in which ethnic and diasporic forms of belonging are negotiated in a way closely shaped by class differences. Again, narrations of travel to India represent an important field in this reworking of diasporic identifications. The ways in which linguistic practices invoke particular regimentations of temporality and thus contribute to experiences of diaspora are also evident in narrative representations of the past. Drawing on the work of Paul Ricoeur (1988), I look at how local historical consciousness emerges through narrative practices that establish temporal relationships between events. My concern here is to draw a link between narrative as creating history and social memory through a reworking of temporal relationships between events and the ways in which linguistic practice otherwise indexes temporality through the use of particular registers in a "discourse of nostalgia." I suggest that the intersection between narrative and temporality as indexed by a range of linguistic features coalescing into recognizable registers is an especially powerful site for the production of diasporic stances and subjectivities through linguistic performance.

Chapter 4 addresses the colonial genealogies of Indian ancestral languages through an analysis of debates surrounding the establishment of a state-sponsored education system under British rule. The focus is on how the idea and institutionalization of Indian ancestral languages emerged at the intersection of colonial discourses on the linguistic identity of "the Indian" in Mauritius and claims of cultural separateness and authenticity forwarded by a rising Indo-Mauritian elite. Evaluations of linguistic difference were crucial in drawing boundaries between communities in colonial Mauritius, while conflicts between those communities in turn drew on discourses of linguistic differentiation. In chapter 5 I turn to the effects of Hindu nationalist ideologies on linguistic practice among Indo-Mauritians, focusing on Mauritian Bhojpuri-language television broadcasts. In particular, I examine how the language shift from Bhojpuri to Mauritian Creole, as well as register differentiation in this bilingual community, are informed by notions of ancestral language, thus enabling the performance of ethno-national purity. This discussion is accompanied by a description of how Mauritian Bhojpuri, previously known as a language of all rural Indians in Mauritius, is re-indexed as a Hindu language. I contextualize this dynamic as part of the growing importance of electronic media for language activism in a politics of recognition.

Chapter 6 looks at the intersection of linguistic and religious performance in creating relationships between diaspora and homeland. I begin with a discussion of the critical implications of the Hindu Mauritian diasporic context for the literature on language and the Indian diaspora, as well as the literature on identities in diaspora in general. The main part of this chapter is dedicated to demonstrating how the practice of Hindi as an ancestral language interacts with other diasporic practices, such as pilgrimage and the creation of sacred landscapes, thereby minimizing the sense of spatio-temporal remove that is at the heart of the diasporic experience. Contrasting notions of temporality turn out to be a salient theme linking an annual Hindu pilgrimage, the imagination of ethnic communities, and the ethnicization of language in Mauritius. I show how the cultivation of Hindi as an ancestral language can be understood as a means of negotiating two contrasting definitions of a diasporic Hindu community through temporal indexicality.

In this study I account for the formation of diaspora as mediated through the cultural phenomenon of Indian ancestral languages in Mauritius. In the process, I intend not only to investigate the intersection of nation and diaspora, but also to offer a reading of the importance of language for the kinds of temporal relationships that enable subjects to experience themselves as belonging to larger communities.

CHAPTER I

Creole Island or Little India?

The Politics of Language and Diaspora

THE MODULARITY OF ETHNOLINGUISTIC NATIONALISM

Reflecting on the spread of nationalism in the colonial world, Partha Chatterjee, in *The Nation and Its Fragments: Colonial and Postcolonial Histories,* asks whether the worldwide spread of the nation form has condemned postcolonial societies to follow "derivative" models of political organization and identification. Engaging with Benedict Anderson's thesis of the modularity of nationalism (Anderson 1991, 4, 87), Chatterjee suggests that postcolonial nationhood does indeed stand in a quasi-dialogic relationship with European models of nationality, yet it nevertheless exhibits irreducible difference from them, since it is crucially shaped by the conditions of the colonial encounter (Chatterjee 1993). Since ethnolinguistic nationalism is one of the central modalities of the Andersonian model (Anderson 1991, 71–77), one might also ask about the modularity of ethnonational community based on language in the postcolonial world, given the continuing relevance of language as an issue in conflicts surrounding postcolonial nationality.

South Asia has provided a rich field for investigation of this question. The way British colonizers engaged in administrative practices and the production of knowledge about Indian languages resulted in a profound transformation of popular and official understandings of language and linguistic differentiation. The creation of standardized vernacular languages, as opposed to sacred (Sanskrit, Arabic) and nonvernacular imperial languages (Persian), possibly represents the most consequential result of this colonial preoccupation with Indian languages (Cohn 1985). This process went hand in hand with the growing impact of European understandings of linguistic ethnicity (Washbrook 1991), that is, the Herderian assumption that the sharing of vernacular linguistic practice constitutes a population as an ethnic group. Even though the understanding of the Indian language situation among colonial scholars as well as Indian intellectuals concerned with language was increasingly informed by the concept of linguistic ethnicity, the domestication of ethnolinguistic nationalism in India frequently led to results that were not intended by colonial scholars and administrators and did not conform to any of the presumably modular European conceptualizations of language and ethnicity. For example, the standardization of Hindustani as a pan-Indian vernacular "language of command" by John Gilchrist and other scholars affiliated with Fort William College in Calcutta provided the base for the Hindi-Urdu conflict in nineteenth-century north India. In the context of this conflict, some of the founding figures of modern Hindu nationalism created sanskritized standard Hindi as the national language of the Hindus (Brass 1974, Dalmia 1997, King 1994, Lelyveld 1993), even if the subsumption of other north Indian vernaculars as "dialects" of Hindi, suggested both by colonial scholars and Hindu nationalists, continued to be challenged by local elites (Burghart 1996, 362–408). In southern India, Tamil nationalists conceived a nationalized Tamil language worshipped as the goddess Tamiltay, represented as both mother and young maiden, in a mode of language-based nationalism better described as language devotionalism. Here language was experienced both through images of parenting, nourishing, and shared substance, and in eroticized forms of devotion to Tamiltay. The focus in this making of political community through language was on a bond of visceral "somatic devotion" between Tamil as a mother and a deity, and Tamil-speakers as her children and devotees, enacted in praise poetry as well as visual practice in iconography as part of a more widely shared ritual practice (Ramaswamy 1997). These scenarios have thrown doubt on the modularity of European models of the nationalization of language, where, according to Anderson, the standardization of vernacular languages occurred in the context of print capitalism, which in turn spurred a "lexicographic revolution" in Europe, a "golden age of vernacularizing lexicographers, grammarians, philologists and litterateurs" (Anderson 1991, 71; see also Hobsbawm 1990, 54–63). Accordingly, the creation of national print vernaculars was crucially informed by an understanding of standardized vernacular languages as key attributes of nationhood. Nevertheless, as the rise of Hindi and the deification of Tamil shows, the articulation between vernacular standardization and the imagination of ethnonational community took rather different turns in colonial and postcolonial South Asia.

The question of the modularity of ethnolinguistic nationalism presents itself still differently in the South Asian diaspora, especially in those overseas communities that were established through the export of labor from colonial India to other parts of the British empire in the context of the indenture system (Carter 1995, Tinker 1974). In these diasporic locations, the developing connection between language and ethnonational community can be understood as doubly refracted by colonialism. In British colonial Mauritius, Indian immigrants became part of a French-dominated plantation society where in the course of the twentieth century two distinct visions of ethnolinguistic community were articulated — Mauritius as a "Creole island," and Mauritius as "Little India," a diasporic location expressed through allegiance to Indian ancestral languages. In espousing very different characterizations of Mauritius as a society, these two ethnolinguistic projects related to European ethnolinguistic "modularity" in quite distinct ways. One important dimension of this tension is that in emphasizing either vernacular or "ancestral" linguistic practice these projects draw on different understandings of what it means for a group to have a linguistic identity.

DIASPORA AND THE INDETERMINACY
OF ETHNOLINGUISTIC IDENTIFICATION

One way to account for the great variability of ethnolinguistic identification in both South Asia and its diaspora while at the same time critically questioning the notion of ethnolinguistic modularity is to understand such processes as informed by varying linguistic ideologies. Such ideologies may differ fundamentally, for example, in how they imagine ethnonational language and the modalities of linkage between a population and a language, in other words, what it means to "have" a language in a socially meaningful way.

Nevertheless, in the study of nationalism, the emergence of group identification based on language has frequently been portrayed as relatively predetermined. For example, Benedict Anderson's account of the rise of nationalism accords supreme importance to preexisting vernacular linguistic boundaries in Europe for determining the boundaries of national communities as these were shaped through the circulation of discourse through print commodities (Anderson 1991, 46–49). Accordingly, the plurality of newly imagined nations was due to the "fatality of human linguistic diversity" (Anderson 1991, 43). In Anderson's view, processes of vernacular linguistic standardization and unification at least partially preceded the rise of national consciousness, generating the nation in their articulation with print capitalism. Thus, following Anderson's model, the choice of, for example, French or German ethnolinguistic identification for the imagined nations of France and Germany was relatively self-evident. Modern print French and German provided the channels of communication through which these nations could be conceived, while a preexisting linguistic boundary between the two languages was responsible for constituting them as separate reading publics, and therefore separate nations. The role of modernized vernaculars in mediating mass communication is also central to Ernest Gellner's approach to nationalism. Here, the connection between language and national community lies in the functional necessity of modern standard vernacular languages for industrial civilization, for which nationalism provided the necessary ingredient of ideological integration (Gellner 1983). Gellner thus pays more attention to the functional role of language as a channel of mass communication in modern societies than to the multiple ways in which constructing nationhood also involved the imagination and ideologization of languages and its speakers.

In contrast, recent work in linguistic anthropology has insisted on the indeterminacy of ethnolinguistic identity, analyzing such processes of identification as shaped by linguistic ideologies (Silverstein 1979, Irvine and Gal 2000, Woolard and Schieffelin 1994). Consequently, it is important to realize that the nationalist imagination is not just confined to the construction of political communities whose relative linguistic homogeneity is presupposed. Contra Anderson, the national vision includes the imagination of not only the nation but frequently also languages and linguistic communities. As Jacqueline Urla's study of Basque nationalism shows (Urla 1988), the construction and imagination of Basque as a modern national language is a vital element in conceiving of a Basque nation especially because many people who identify themselves as Basque co-nationals have little knowledge of the Basque language. While openly admitting that a large part of the population of the territory claimed as belonging to the Basque nation does not speak the national language, nationalists may still strive to refashion and reinforce the imagined community by representing the national language as threatened and in need of support (Urla 1993). In this way, the national language becomes a crucial means of creating national communities, even if the knowledge and use of it are relatively restricted. As is also evident in Urla's discussion, such representations of language-based community and calls for national solidarity need not even be communicated in the national language.

Thus there is nothing self-evident about ethnolinguistic identities. Rather, they are shaped through linguistic ideologies against a range of possible visions. This is especially the case in a situation where alternative understandings of ethnolinguistic belonging are in conflict with each other, as in Mauritius. Categorizations of the country as a Creole island contrast with the building of communities based on Indian ancestral languages highlighting a continuing diasporic link to South Asia. As I will show, these competing notions of community differ not only in the linguistic varieties privileged but also in how they conceive of Mauritians in terms of cultural purity and hybridity, and therefore also how they locate Mauritians in historical time.

HINDUS AND THE NATION IN MAURITIUS

In the remainder of this chapter I describe the politics of language and diaspora among Hindu Mauritians and their implications for constructing a social memory of diasporic belonging. I focus on two principal modes of ethnolinguistic identification — the cultivation of Indian ancestral languages, above all Hindi, and the notion of Mauritius as a Creole island. Despite the fact that French-lexifier Mauritian Creole is known and used by the vast majority of Mauritians in everyday interaction, and despite the impact of a postcolonial campaign to promote a Mauritian nationalism based on the shared status of Mauritian Creole, ideas about ancestral languages play a crucial role for creating communities among Indo-Mauritians, in particular Hindus. I outline the social and historical context of these two modes of conceptualizing Mauritius ethnolinguistically, exploring their consequences for the shaping of the Hindu diaspora. In particular, I suggest that these two perspectives on the Hindu diaspora have very different implications for how to conceive of the relationship between Mauritians and India as the ancestral place for the majority of Mauritians. In thus delineating a Hindu diaspora, they also envision different types of relationships between Hindus and their ethnic others on the island by highlighting the former or the latter's relative importance in imagining a Mauritian nation.

Languages are frequently represented as inhabited by different temporalities. One example of how linguistic ideologies involve a regimenting of temporality (Inoue 2004; Irvine 2004; Woolard 2004) is the way sacred or classical languages are often experienced as literally belonging to another time, as compared to vernaculars (Haeri 2003). Such regimentations play a particularly important role in the creation of diasporas, which are communities defined through spatio-temporal remove from an assumed homeland. Ideologies of Mauritian Creole nationalism and of Hindi as the ancestral language of Hindus locate Mauritian Hindus in different temporal relationships to India. The privileging of ancestral language highlights the diasporic link and thereby minimizes the spatio-temporal remove between Mauritian Hindus and the world of their Indian ancestors, whereas Creole nationalism implies a temporal disjuncture between Mauritian Hindus and their Indian ancestors.

The island of Mauritius, lying in the Indian Ocean 800 kilometers east of Madagascar, had no human population when it was first visited by Portuguese navigators in the sixteenth century. The first settlement, under Dutch rule from 1638 to 1658 and again from 1664 to 1710, failed. Beginning in 1715, from their base on the neighboring island of Bourbon (now the French overseas département Réunion), the French extended their rule over Mauritius, which they named Isle de France. They turned the island into a flourishing trading entrepôt and set up the first sugar plantations, introducing a large slave population brought principally from Madagascar and mainland Africa. The beginnings of Indian migration also fall into this epoch, since a smaller part of the slave population was brought from the French possessions in India. Traders and craftspeople such as stonemasons also migrated to Mauritius from these possessions. In 1810, the British successfully conquered Mauritius from India, ending almost a century of French rule. Under British rule, sugarcane cultivation was greatly expanded and finally became the mainstay of the island's economy. After the abolition of slavery in the British empire in 1834, Indian indentured laborers began to replace the recently freed slaves on sugar plantations. In less than three decades Indian indentured laborers and their descendants constituted the majority of the island's population. At independence in 1968, Mauritius was still economically almost entirely dependent on the sugar industry. The economy, challenged by widespread poverty and unemployment and rapid population growth, was subject to unpredictable fluctuations determined by the weather and the price of sugar on the world market. Beginning in the 1970s, the Mauritian government established an Export Processing Zone to encourage the setup of garment assembly plants. This policy, supported by preferential trade agreements with the European Union and the United States, proved spectacularly successful in the 1980s, when garment factories sprang up all over the island. The standard of living for many Mauritians rose considerably, and the World Bank hailed Mauritius as an "economic miracle." The garment industry remains the most important sector of the island's economy, while the tourist industry, focused on a high-end clientele from Europe, has also grown rapidly since its beginnings in the 1970s. Nevertheless, the former pillar of the island's economy, the sugar industry, remains important, especially because it still employs approximately 7 percent of the workforce.

Mauritius occupies a special place among the numerous countries in which Indian diasporas have been established, since nearly 70 percent of its population of 1.2 million is of South Asian origin. Hindus and Muslims who trace their origins to South Asia constitute 52 and 17 percent of the population, respectively. About 28 percent of Mauritians are Creoles of African and mixed origin, while those of Chinese and French background account for 2 and 1 percent of the population. Unlike other South Asian diasporas established through the indenture system, such as in Guyana, Trinidad, and Fiji, people of South Asian origin in Mauritius are not confronted with a hegemonic national identity tending towards their exclusion. There is no Mauritian counterpart to the challenge posed to people of South Asian background in these other diasporic locations, where Caribbean Afro-Creole nationalisms or assertions of superior indigenous status by ethnic Fijians have denied people and traditions of Indian origin centrality in the imagined community of the nation (Munasinghe 2002, Kelly 1998b). Moreover, in Mauritius, state institutions explicitly encourage the cultivation and public celebration of diasporic links, expending significantly more resources and effort on supporting ethnicized ancestral cultural traditions and ancestral languages than on the promotion of a national public culture transcending ethnic boundaries. The support of religious organizations and festivals with clear communal associations,[1] as well as the building of cultural centers that are presented as the property of a particular ethnic community, absorb much of the state's resources in the fields of arts and culture. Only Independence Day, observed on 12 March, is the occasion of a concentrated and publicized effort to project national cultural forms explicitly designed to include all Mauritians. Yet even the principal performative genre of this national event, the "composite cultural show," demonstrates communal division as a norm. This generic public performance, versions of which are also staged in local community centers in the days preceding the holiday, features a succession of brief separate musical and dance acts by groups overtly recognizable as representatives of a particular ethnic community. Officially presented as a promotion of "unity in diversity," for many spectators the emblematic display of communal and ethnic difference in the composite cultural show confirms their interpretations of Mauritian society as one that clearly stresses ethnic differences and emphasizes official ancestral cultures whose origins are considered to be elsewhere.[2]

At the official celebrations of Independence Day in 1998, a large stage was erected in downtown Port Louis, and the city center was decorated with an almost equal number of Mauritian and Indian national flags. The main celebration of the nation was announced as "Mauritius in all its colors," and was broadcast live on national television. An "African dance" was followed by a troupe performing *séga traditionelle,* whereas an "Indian folk dance" highlighting Hindi film music and aesthetics was coupled with a subsequent "Fusion of Bharatanatyam and Kathak." Finally, after a "Chinese dance from the Tang dynasty" and a French 1950s-style *chanson,* the show ended with a well-known *qawwali* in Urdu by the Pakistani singer Nusrat Fateh Ali Khan, played by a local group. The audience was left with few doubts as to the ethnic identities publicly performed by the respective troupes. Even at a key national event such as the state-organized celebrations of Independence Day, ethnic differences are not temporarily glossed over for the sake of an imagined national unity. Instead, they are publicly highlighted and dramatized.

State policy towards "ancestral," principally Indian, languages in Mauritius reveals a similar perspective, since language-indexed ethnic differences are stressed and encouraged over the nationalization of uniform linguistic practice. Large sums are spent on teaching and promoting these languages, which are universally regarded as the property of specific ethnic communities and, with few exceptions, are of no obvious economic utility in Mauritius. In contrast, Creole, the vernacular language used by nearly all Mauritians regardless of ethnic background and vehemently proposed as the national language by leftist postcolonial nationalists in the 1970s and 1980s, receives hardly any state support at all.[3]

CONTEXTUALIZING ANCESTRAL LANGUAGES

Mauritius is known for its linguistic diversity. However, scholars have pointed out that the actual language situation is less complex than one would expect from the multiplicity of linguistic varieties reported to be in use among the island's population (Stein 1982, 621). For in fact only a few of these languages are actually used in everyday life, and among them Mauritian Creole is by far the most dominant and is known by practically all Mauritians. Mauritian Bhojpuri is known and used in everyday contexts by approximately 20 to 25 percent of the population, though in a bilingual situation with Creole.[4] French is the first language of a small number of Mauritians, almost all of whom also know and use Creole.[5]

English, the language of the former colonial power, Britain, has been retained as the language of state power and administration and as an educational medium since independence in 1968, but it is rarely ever used by Mauritians in everyday conversation. French, however, is dominant in the private sector economy and in the print media; it is also the language most used in television and radio programming originating in Mauritius. Thus scholars have concluded that the language situation is less complicated after all, with Creole featuring in everyday conversation, and English and French used as languages of literacy, state power, business, and mass media. According to Peter Stein, author of the most comprehensive study of the Mauritian language situation to date, "only three languages are of general interest: Creole, French and English." However, English "even though favored in politics and occupying important positions in education, administration and other official institutions, is in reality only of marginal importance, since it is relatively little known and rarely used" (Stein 1982, 621). Besides downplaying the importance of English, this assessment also underestimates the significance of the purported ancestral languages, which even if not used in everyday conversation are important for local understandings of language and belonging.

The role of these Asian languages — or "Oriental" languages as they are also known in Mauritius — referring especially to Hindi, has been described as "emblematic" (de Robillard 1989, 158) and as "rather symbolic" (Stein 1982, 618). Hindi, Tamil, Telugu, Marathi, Urdu, Arabic, and Mandarin are the ancestral languages (referred to as *langues ancestrales* in French, *lang ban anset* in Creole, *purvajõ kī bhāṣāē* in Hindi) claimed by different groups in Mauritian society. Hindi, Urdu, Tamil, Telugu, Marathi, and more recently also Arabic, are considered the ancestral languages of the Indo-Mauritians. The status of an ancestral language does not imply that all members of the Indo-Mauritian ethnic groups claiming those languages as part of their ancestral culture have knowledge of these languages. Linguists have been quick to point out that there are practically no native speakers of these languages in Mauritius, and that they are never used in everyday life (Baker 1969; Moorghen and Domingue 1982).[6] They are nevertheless understood to be signs of ethnic group identification in Mauritius. There are still very small, and dwindling, numbers of speakers of Gujarati, Kutchi, and Hakka on the island, but ironically none of these languages is officially recognized and promoted as an ancestral language.[7] This is also, to a large extent, the case for Bhojpuri, the single Indian linguistic variety actually used by large numbers of Mauritians on a daily basis. Aside from two television shows and some radio programming by the state-controlled Mauritius Broadcasting Corporation (MBC), Bhojpuri is not promoted as an ancestral language by state institutions.[8] It thus seems that for a language to be considered ancestral in Mauritius, it should not only have origins outside Mauritius but should not be used in everyday interaction. Also, as the case of claiming sanskritized standard Hindi as the ancestral language for people whose ancestors were Bhojpuri speakers shows, there is no necessary link between the classification of a language as ancestral and the languages actually used by ancestors at their time of arrival in Mauritius.

Officially recognized ancestral languages are considered the exclusive ethnic property of the particular groups claiming them.[9] They are taught to students in the school system on an ethnic basis and are given airtime on state-controlled television and radio. In a sample of programming during one week in September 1998 on the three channels of the state-run Mauritian Broadcasting Corporation television, 33.7 percent of programming was in French, 32.1 percent was in English, and 32.01 percent of airtime was filled by programming in several Indian languages, 27.7 percent of which were listed as in Hindi and Hindustani.[10]

Indian ancestral languages are further supported by the state through subsidies to religious organizations and ethnically defined cultural centers propagating such languages. In schools, on the primary level and in the first two years of secondary education, ancestral languages constitute a de facto compulsory and automatically assigned subject for students identifiable as members of an ethnic community linked to a particular ancestral language. The use of ancestral languages such as Hindi also turns particular speech events into emblematically ethnic contexts. This is most often the case at religious events, such as discourses in temples or public sermons on festival occasions in a ritual calendar. The use of Hindi by a pandit during a Ramayana chanting and study meeting as he explains or comments on the text, or by the head of a Hindu organization during a live broadcast speech given at the festival and pilgrimage of Shivratri, performatively marks these activities and events as part of the exclusive heritage or ancestral culture of Hindus of north Indian background in Mauritius.

HINDI AND THE MAURITIAN STATE

Of all the ancestral languages claimed by Mauritians, Hindi is by far the most significant — a fact that is to a considerable extent a matter of numbers. Hindi as an ancestral language has more adherents than any other claimed ancestral language, and Hindi is the ancestral language taught to the greatest number of students in the educational system. According to the 1994 statistics of the Ministry of Education, 39.3 percent of all Mauritian primary school students (school years one through six) were enrolled in Hindi classes. The percentages of enrollment for other Asian ancestral languages were significantly lower: Urdu 13.6 percent, Tamil 6.1 percent, Telugu 2.2 percent, Marathi 1.6 percent, Arabic 2.6 percent, and Modern Chinese (Mandarin) 1.1 percent. In total, 66.6 percent of all primary school students received instruction in these languages on an ethnic basis. On the secondary school level (school years seven through thirteen) this figure was 29.8 percent. Even though enrollment numbers were significantly lower for secondary schools, Hindi's predominance over other ancestral languages was even more pronounced, accounting for the enrollment of 22.9 percent of the total student population.[11]

Certainly, other ancestral languages, such as Tamil, Telugu, and Marathi, are championed by people in Mauritius officially classified as Hindus. However, Hindi is regarded as the ancestral property of the largest and politically most powerful subgroup within what the Mauritian constitution describes as the Hindu community, that is, the Hindus of north Indian background.[12] The unequal weight, both numerically and politically, between Hindus with origins in southern and western India and those of north Indian ancestry is also pointed to in the conceptual marked-unmarked pattern common in referring to these different groups. Hindus *(endu)* of north Indian background are felt to be the unmarked "Hindus as such" in Mauritius, as opposed to Hindus of Tamil, Andhra, and Marathi background. In everyday usage, members of these smaller subgroups are referred to not as Hindus but as Tamils *(tamul)*, Telugus *(telegu)*, and Marathis *(marathi)*. Those called Hindu constitute approximately 41 percent of the total population of Mauritius and have dominated Mauritian politics since independence in 1968. With the exception of Paul Béranger, Prime Minister from September 2003 to July 2005, all the Prime Ministers since independence have been members of this group,[13] and most key positions in the state apparatus continue to be held by Hindus of north Indian background. Thus the celebration of Hindi enjoys more political profile than other ancestral languages.

The significant power wielded by members of this Hindu ethnic group in Mauritian state institutions is the key to understanding the promotion of ancestral languages, which in post-independence Mauritius is mainly conducted by the state. This state advancement of an ethnicized Hindu patrimony through ancestral languages such as Hindi, rather than, for example, a nationalized Mauritian Creole, is a way of legitimizing an ethnic perspective on political power sharing in a Mauritius where Hindus dominate. According to this perspective, the Mauritian nation is made up of a number of separate ethnic communities with continuing ties to diasporic homelands rather than by a homogenous citizenry oriented to a locally grounded cultural tradition. Accordingly, the state's role is to support and encourage the performance of diasporic and ethnicized cultural forms, such as ancestral languages. State institutions give a lot of attention to those public cultural manifestations associated with the "majority community,"[14] reflecting both its demographic weight and its powerful position in state institutions.

Another crucial feature of this political vision is that the Creoles, as the second largest ethnic group in Mauritius, do not claim an officially recognized ancestral language as their patrimony. The idea of an official African ancestral culture, which fueled, for instance, the recent creation of a poorly funded African Cultural Center, is only beginning to be formulated and is still very vague compared to the well-established and institutionalized ancestral traditions of Indo-Mauritians and Sino-Mauritians (see also Laville 2000). Moreover, many Creoles themselves hold the negative image of Africa and African cultural traditions common in Mauritius, and, in contrast to Indo-Mauritians, Creoles so far lack powerful institutions that could educate Creoles about African traditions and languages (Baptiste 2002). Further, in marked contrast to indenture, the experience of slavery has made attempts to trace the origins of families to particular places in Africa or Madagascar or to find out about ethnic, linguistic, and religious affiliations of ancestors very difficult.

An additional challenge to Creole participation in the politics of ancestral culture is that the alterity constructed by officially recognized ancestral traditions is primarily defined through religious and linguistic affiliations. No attempts to define an African ancestral language, or languages, for Creoles have been made so far, and there is very little interest in African languages among Creoles — which is again related to the lack of institutions propagating African languages. As to the religious dimensions of officialized ancestral culture, Creoles are Christians, overwhelmingly Catholics, and thus affiliated with an institution historically dominated by Franco-Mauritians in Mauritius. Despite the very important role of Christianity in contemporary Africa, Christian traditions are not associated with Africa and Africans in Mauritius, and thus are unsuitable for a public performance of Africanness. The same is true for the other major African religious tradition, Islam, which, like Christianity, is not locally considered African. Moreover, Islam is already claimed as an ancestral tradition by Muslims of Indian origin, and membership in a Creole community and being Muslim are considered mutually exclusive in Mauritius.[15] Knowledge about other African religious traditions is very limited among Creoles, and there are no organizations propagating it. Creoles are therefore excluded from the legitimizing cultural politics of diasporic ancestry in multiple ways. This is a key characteristic of the reigning political vision, and points to the imbalances of power on which it is based and which it reproduces.

At least since it was initiated after the Second World War (see chapter 4), many Indo-Mauritians have considered the state support of the teaching of primarily Indian ancestral languages indicative of the perceived degree of influence of members of that ethnic group in Mauritian politics. Accordingly, the official respect an ancestral language enjoys is interpreted as a sign of the political power of the community claiming it. A different approach to language policy, conceived in terms of national linguistic unification and emphasizing a public symbolism of transcending ethnic boundaries, would potentially dilute the legitimizing force of ancestral languages for political power sharing in Mauritius. Thus a more nationally uniformizing cultural policy in the promotion of languages could be read as a challenge to the political status quo, and as an invitation for greater participation of the Creole and Muslim minorities in state power and state institutions.[16] Yet the significance of ancestral languages for Hindus in Mauritius is not only a matter of ethnic competition on the island; it also contributes to the production of a diasporic community by encouraging the continuing relationship and links between Indo-Mauritians and India, by reproducing boundaries between

Hindus and other Mauritians, and by privileging a particular vision of diasporic connection to the homeland of immigrant ancestors.

HINDU POLITICS: THE TRANSNATIONAL DIMENSION

What are the forces responsible for state promotion in Mauritius of a language such as Hindi, which is never used in everyday life and, in striking contrast to French and English, is widely regarded as having little economic or other instrumental value? Here it is important to turn our attention to a broad coalition of local Hindu associations, having connections with transnationally operating Hindu organizations, that influence and have links with state institutions in Mauritius. This network of Hindu activists and Hindu nationalists plays a significant role in providing Mauritians of Hindu background with ideas about Hindi as an ancestral language, the cultivation of which is represented as maintaining Hindu identity in the uncertainty of a diasporic setting and as "purifying" for Hindus in an environment often experienced as creolized.

While known as the largest and politically most influential ethnic group in Mauritius, Hindus are also acutely aware of their diasporic status, which implies a spatio-temporal distance from their ancestral homeland. The shaping of diasporic identity engages with this disjuncture in time and space, which frequently functions as a prism through which Hindus in the diaspora appear as spatially peripheral to and also temporally far removed from the world of their ancestors. One response to this sense of diasporic remove in Mauritius has been the cultivation of dense ties to Hindu organizations in India, hand in hand with the promotion of Hindi. The learning and ritual use of Hindi as an ancestral language is a vital part of a larger project of authentication of a Hindu community through minimizing the remove separating the homeland from the diaspora.

The three largest Hindu organizations in Mauritius are the Mauritius Sanatan Dharm Temples Federation, the Hindu Maha Sabha, and the Arya Sabha.[17] They are in charge of the great majority of Hindu temples in Mauritius, function as the umbrella organizations of local temple committees or other Hindu associations, and are the recipients of considerable government subsidies. They support temples, train and pay priests, organize centralized celebrations of major Hindu festivals, and provide for evening and weekend teaching of Hindi in the places of worship under their control. The president of the Mauritius Sanatan Dharm Temples Federation, which is the largest of these three organizations and

controls the most Hindu temples on the island, is usually elected with
regard for his political affiliations and connections to the current government. However, there is another, transnational aspect of Hinduism in
Mauritius that is of political importance and ultimately relevant for the
problem of Hindu ancestral languages.

There is a complex and dense Hindu nationalist network linking
Mauritius and India as well as other diasporic locations such as Kenya,
Britain, and the United States, centered mainly in organizations such as
the Arya Samaj, the Rashtriya Svayamsevak Sangh (RSS), and the Vishva
Hindu Parishad (VHP) (for an overview see Gold 1991). The RSS and the
VHP in particular have been among the main actors in the upsurge of
Hindu nationalist violence and the growing political power of *hindutva*
("Hindu-ness" as a nationalist project) in India since the 1980s. In
Mauritius these organizations have gained members and followers in
local Hindu bodies, which in turn exert influence in the Hindu-dominated
government apparatus, in some cases up to the ministerial level. The RSS
and the VHP are directly connected to three Hindu organizations in
Mauritius: the Hindu House, the Hindu Council, and the Human Service
Trust, and the VHP is also represented through the Chinmaya Ashram,
which is named after the Bombay birthplace of the VHP in 1964 (van der
Veer 1994a, 130–37). The Human Service Trust, a charitable organization running a home for handicapped and elderly people, has also played
a leading role in establishing a *hindutva*-network in Mauritius. Its president, a former Hindi teacher, was advisor in the Prime Minister's office
until 1995. The Hindu House and the Hindu Council were established by
followers of the founder of the Human Service Trust, the Indian Swami
Krishnanand Sarasvati (1900–1992). The swami reportedly used his
influence to obtain from the government the piece of land in Port Louis
on which Hindu House's main building was constructed. In the context
of the worldwide campaign launched by the VHP in 1989, the Hindu
Council sent consecrated bricks (the campaign to collect and consecrate
the bricks known as Ram Shilan Puja) to India for the building of a temple on the deity Ram's purported birthplace in Ayodhya.[18] The leadership
of the Hindu Council also participates in VHP-sponsored all-Africa
Hindu conferences coordinated by the local representative of the VHP
and the head of the Chinmaya Ashram.[19]

The transnational links between Hindu nationalist organizations in
India and Hindu institutions in Mauritius are manifold. The Hindu
House, for example, hosted a talk by RSS supreme chief *(sarsangh-
chalak)* Rajendra Singh during his visit to Mauritius in January 1997,

during which he spoke on "Hindu unity" and met representatives of the major Hindu organizations of Mauritius. Singh also gave a widely covered press conference, and a meeting with the Prime Minister was arranged, as well. The prominent *hindutva* leader Singh offered the support of the RSS to Hindu organizations for the teaching of Hindi in Mauritius, "in order for Hindi to be studied more by Hindus."[20] Singh was also received by the Indian High Commissioner, who posed for a press photo with Singh, at a time when the RSS was still officially banned in India, following the violent events of 1992–1993.[21]

Contacts between top Mauritian state representatives and *hindutva* activists go back to the 1970s. At the Second World Hindu Conference convened by the VHP at Allahabad in 1979, Minister of Commerce and Industry Dayanand Basantrai lead a Mauritian delegation and gave a speech entitled "In Kaliyuga — Organization is Strength." No other foreign state was represented by functionaries of such high rank. Prime Minister Seewoosagur Ramgoolam sent a message to the conference stressing that "in matters of religious faith, social beliefs and cultural relations, the Hindus living in other countries look to India for dynamic guidance."[22] Minister Basantrai was a pivotal figure in Hindu activism in the 1960s and 1970s in Mauritius. A disciple of Swami Krishnanand, he was also president of the Hindu Maha Sabha from 1965 to 1986, as well as one of the leaders of the Mauritius Sanatan Dharma Temples Federation. In addition, Basantrai was the driving force behind consecrating the most important site of Hindu pilgrimage in Mauritius, a mountain lake, as "Ganga Talao" (Ganges lake) in 1972 by having a vessel of flown-in Ganges water ritually emptied into the lake. In his speech addressing the 1979 World Hindu Conference the Mauritian minister and Hindu activist played almost perfectly to the VHP's self-image as the central umbrella organization and provider of "values" for "overseas Hindus":

> I want to make it clear that we Hindu migrants passionately look towards Bharat — our sacred motherland — for gaining the knowledge of high ideas, tenets and traditions and age-old traditional values. If our thirst for knowledge of spiritual, religious and temporal values is satisfied, it may well be presumed that the eternal values of our Dharma and Samskriti will surely be fully recovered. It is a matter of pride for Hindus that even though foreign invaders like Shakas and Huns established their rule here for a while they could not vanquish the Hindu Dharma and culture. The invaders either merged in the society losing their identity or fled to their respective countries. The people of Mauritius can also rejoice in the fact that even after long years of adversities they did not abandon their religion, faith and culture, rather they have strengthened and developed it and now

their descendants are holding high positions in political and other fields of social life.[23]

Basantrai not only expresses his devotion to those Hindu values of the "motherland" the VHP is striving to disseminate among Hindus in India and abroad, he also draws a parallel between the hardships Mauritian Hindus faced under colonialism in diaspora and the powerful Hindu nationalist narrative of Hindu culture in India as constantly being threatened by invading forces. He also presents an image of Mauritius as the home of steadfast diasporic Hindus, ideal disciples who have not only managed to defend their traditions under difficult circumstances, but have even attained positions of respect and power. Delivered several years before the rise of *hindutva* to prominence in Indian politics, Basantrai's address at the 1979 World Hindu Conference ideally combined the themes of Hindu cultural defense and the striving for political power, which are central to the VHP's ideology. A focus on Hindu unity rather than unity of ritual doctrine and practice is a key strategy through which VHP leaders promote political and ideological unity in order to fight perceived weaknesses and divisions among Hindus (van der Veer 1994a). From the beginning, the VHP's promotion of unity by turning India into a modern Hindu nation has had an important transnational dimension. As Peter van der Veer has argued, the marginality experienced by Hindus in the diaspora has been a catalyst for activism at home, by further highlighting perceived threats that Hindus are facing in India (1994a, 114, 117–18; 1994b, 657). Basantrai makes it clear that the common threat lies in the presence and power of "alien" religions and civilizations, both in the diaspora and in India. In this context, he solicits the help of the VHP regarding what he sees as a future threat to the Hindu community of Mauritius:

> Yet, there is a problem in our land, which is a matter of grave concern. Our younger generation is now coming under the influence and impact of the effulgent Western civilization, the present education system and urbanised way of life is fast going away from our religious moorings. This is likely to result in the weakening [of] the very roots of our culture. . . . If Vishva Hindu Parishad gives a little more thought to this aspect of vital importance and evolve [sic] a way out to prevent the growth of materialism and preserve the spiritual ideals it would be highly beneficial and a danger lurking on the horizon will wither away.[24]

On the same occasion when this representative of the Mauritian government expressed the need to keep young Hindus from "losing their cul-

ture" in the diaspora, VHP founder Swami Chinmayananda suggested
an answer to this perceived threat. In an example of what Christophe
Jaffrelot has called the simultaneous stigmatizing and emulation of the
"threatening other" (Jaffrelot 1996 [1993], 11), the swami pointed out
that Christianity and Islam were well organized but "Hindus, on the
other hand were still speaking with different voices and thus had no
voice in their own country. LET US CONVERT HINDUS TO HINDUISM, then
everything would be alright."[25]

Such efforts to simultaneously counter the perceived threats to Hindu
unity and identity at home and in the diaspora were already under way.
Four years earlier, in 1975, the VHP had sent Swami Gangeswarananda
to Mauritius, where Prime Minister Seewoosagur Ramgoolam held a
reception for him, as part of his tour to disseminate the "Vedas in the
West." According to the VHP magazine that reported on the swami's
visit to Mauritius: "The Prime Minister, whose voice was choked with
feelings, expressed his hearty sentiments at the blissful presence of the
Holy Man and the arranged presentations of the sacred Vedas to the
island people. The reception was possibly one of the grandest and [most]
cheerful ones ever witnessed by the elite of all colorful communities of
the island."[26] The tone of the report was otherwise somewhat self-
congratulatory, portraying the VHP representatives as generous deliver-
ers of wisdom to remote "island people." Also printed in the magazine
was a message from Prime Minister Ramgoolam, on official letterhead,
saying that "no doubt God has sent Swamiji to revive and preserve our
Indian culture." This was followed by another affirmative message by
Minister of Economic Planning and Development Kher Jagatsingh.[27]
Swami Gangeswarananda not only toured several temples and headquarters of Hindu associations across Mauritius, he was also invited to
give *darshan* ("viewing" a holy image, person, or deity with respect and
veneration in Hindu contexts, thus gaining spiritual benefit from the act
of "viewing") and be interviewed on national television.

In the 1970s, when contacts and cooperation between the VHP and
top-level representatives of the Mauritian government were initiated, the
VHP was not yet known worldwide as a principal driving force for militant Hindu nationalism, and Mauritius had only recently gained independence. With Mauritius having just emerged from a colonial period
remembered by many Hindus as a period of poverty and frequent
oppression and humiliation, key representatives of the new Hindu-led
government were very receptive to VHP ideology. Emphasizing a "modern" Hinduism and the worldwide unity and organization of Hindus

with a stress on Hindu pride, the vision of the VHP represented a clear break with the subordinate position Hindus in Mauritius had experienced before. Despite being officially known as the majority community on the island, they had occupied a subaltern position not only in economics and politics but also in terms of the perceived lack of prestige and respectability of Hindu cultural practices and forms of belonging in the eyes of the Franco-Mauritian plantocracy and the British colonial government. The sympathies of Hindu activists and politicians such as Basantrai for the global outreach efforts of the VHP have to be understood in the context of this subalternity, which has become central to the Hindu social memory of the colonial encounter.

An indication of the respect representatives of *hindutva* continue to officially enjoy in Mauritius is the visit of Ashok Singhal, the president of the Vishva Hindu Parishad, in August 1998. Singhal was one of the main architects of the Ram Janmabhumi movement that led to the destruction of the Babri Masjid in Ayodhya by *hindutva* activists in December 1992. This event provoked riots in which over two thousand people, most of them Muslims, were killed. Singhal was received not only by the leaders of the principal Mauritian Hindu organizations, but also by Prime Minister Navin Ramgoolam. When he stated that Mauritius owed its present prosperity and political stability to the efforts of the Hindus, Singhal echoed a long-standing argument for legitimizing the politically powerful position members of the Hindu community have held since independence.[28]

Local Hindu nationalist organizations such as the Human Service Trust are skilled at organizing religious events, which provide a public platform for presenting themselves in the company of Mauritian political leaders and prominent chief guests from India, in order to publicly voice their agenda. For example, in October 1998, the Human Service Trust convened an International Ramayana Conference at the Mahatma Gandhi Institute, the Indian chief guest being Murli Manohar Joshi, Minister of Human Resources, Science and Technology, RSS veteran, and at the time number three in the ruling Hindu nationalist party, the BJP (Bharatiya Janata Party). Both Joshi and Prime Minister Navin Ramgoolam gave discourses on the merits and values of the Ramayana, while the president of the Human Service Trust took the opportunity to argue for more state support of Indian ancestral languages.

The promotion of the ancestral language Hindi is frequently at the top of the agenda when *sangh parivar*–affiliated Indian politicians visit Mauritius and are received by local Hindu activists and members of the Mauritian government.[29] On his third visit to Mauritius, in November

2001, Murli Manohar Joshi gave a speech in the presence of several Mauritian government ministers at the groundbreaking ceremony for the World Hindi Secretariat building, a joint venture between the governments of India and Mauritius, during which he commented, "The secretariat has become the symbol of identity, as well as the symbol of the friendship, common tradition and identity of India and Mauritius. We have broken the chains of slavery and dependence. We know the worth of identity."[30] At a later press conference he added that there are two factors unifying India and Mauritius, the Indian Ocean and the Hindi language. The Indian minister and *sangh parivar* leader spent much of his time on the island with local Hindu nationalists. He inaugurated an Indian and Indian-diaspora trade fair organized by the Human Service Trust and was also chief guest at the groundbreaking ceremony for an Ayurvedic hospital to be run by the same Hindu organization.[31]

The boundaries between the "mainstream" government-subsidized Hindu organizations, who control most places of worship, and the organizations with transnational *hindutva* affiliations are often not clearcut in Mauritius. The latter, especially the Human Service Trust, the Hindu Council, and the Hindu House, share some overlap of membership as well as organizational platforms and meeting facilities with the larger established Hindu associations. For example, the Human Service Trust participates with the Hindu Maha Sabha and the Mauritius Sanatan Dharm Temples Federation in the organization of the yearly Shivratri pilgrimage to Grand Bassin, the single most important event in the Hindu calendar of Mauritius. Also, the central building of the Hindu House in Port Louis frequently serves as a central meeting place for all Hindu organizations in Mauritius. Central celebrations of Hindu festivals such as Divali are often hosted by the Hindu House, as in November 2001, when the Prime Minister and other senior state officials were present. The Hindu House also convenes public meetings for determining a common view on current political issues from a "Hindu perspective," often marked by a ritual occasion such as a *maha yaj* (great ritual sacrifice). Shared Hindu nationalist sympathies across Hindu organizations in Mauritius are also evident in events such as the condolence meeting in June 1996 at the headquarters of the Arya Sabha in Port Louis held in memory of the former supreme chief *(sarsanghchalak)* of the RSS Balasahib Deoras, who had died a few days earlier in India.

To take one *hindutva*-affiliated "socio-cultural organization" as an example,[32] the Hindu Council of Mauritius originated in a *hindutva*-inspired initiative to provide a common platform for all Hindu organiza-

tions in Mauritius. On its official letterhead (evidenced in a congratulatory letter printed in 1990 in the souvenir magazine for the eighty-year
anniversary of the Arya Sabha Mauritius) the Council describes itself as
"affiliated to Vishva Hindu Parishad" and lists as members of its
"Executive Committee" all the important Hindu organizations in
Mauritius with the sole exception of the Hindu Maha Sabha. Its president as well as its secretary at the time were disciples of Human Service
Trust founder Swami Krishnanand, and the secretary, a former Hindi
teacher, was simultaneously president of the Mauritius Sanatan Dharm
Temples Federation, which receives the greatest share of state subsidies
for Hindu temples.[33]

The case of the Mauritius Sanatan Dharm Temples Federation is very
instructive for the multiple overlaps and alliances between "mainstream"
Hindu organizations in Mauritius and the transnationally operating
Hindu nationalist network. Such links extend beyond the joint organizing of Hindu religious festivities; they include a continuing overlap of
membership. In addition to the case of joint leadership in the early 1990s
just mentioned, as of 2003 a former president of the Hindu Council was
serving as the president of the Federation, while the federation also provides some financial support for the Human Service Trust and the Hindu
House.[34] While the Federation is not officially affiliated with VHP and
the RSS, according to a former president, contacts are in fact cultivated
with the VHP and also the Gayatri Parivar in India, a VHP affiliate
(McKean 1996, 53) that has its own branch and temple in the north of
the island. The Federation, furthermore, is an umbrella organization for
many temple committees and associations across Mauritius, a number of
which entertain affiliations with Hindu nationalist organizations. For
example, the head of one such temple association in the northeast of the
island, a Hindi teacher and poet, is also a leading representative of the
RSS in Mauritius, publishes a "VHP newsletter," and is active in the
organizing of youth programs, such as camps and extension classes, on
language, culture, and history.

While there is a certain overlap between "mainstream" and *hindutva*-
oriented Hindu organizations in Mauritius, a division of labor is nevertheless apparent. The main government-subsidized Hindu organizations
are principally active in managing temples, organizing Hindu festivals,
and teaching Hindi, while those organizations that are part of the
transnational VHP-RSS network act as public mouthpieces for the Hindu
community whenever they see "Hindu interests" at stake. They also regularly organize "spiritual camps" and "youth camps" for Hindu adoles-

cents from Mauritius and other countries such as India, South Africa, and the Netherlands.

Hindutva-affiliated activists are quick to come forward as defenders of Hindu interests in political conflicts, which in Mauritius are often interpreted as ethnic confrontations, such as when Creoles are perceived to be the opponent. In 1998 on the occasion of the mass of St. Louis, a senior cleric of the Roman Catholic Church in Mauritius denounced the exclusion of Creoles from state jobs in Mauritius, though without going as far as directly blaming Hindus for the problem.[35] The Hindu Council of Mauritius, however, promptly protested. The president of the Hindu Council not only rejected the cleric's claims, stating that it was "normal" that all qualified Hindus who were not hired by the Franco-Mauritian controlled private sector expected to be hired by the state, but also proclaimed that the Catholic priest had "hurt" and insulted the Hindu community of Mauritius.[36] Affiliates of the VHP like the Hindu Council of Mauritius eagerly seize opportunities to present themselves as representatives and protectors of the Hindu community in Mauritius. In this particular case, by pointing to the disadvantages many Hindus think they face in the job market for more qualified positions in the private sector, the president of the Hindu Council managed to draw on a long-standing grievance among Hindus in Mauritius, which in a compensatory logic provided further legitimization for Hindu dominance in the state apparatus. Since Hindus in Mauritius often see themselves as victims of discrimination in the Franco-Mauritian dominated private sector of the economy (a concern I found especially prevalent among young educated Hindus, who complain about a "glass ceiling" in Franco-Mauritian owned companies which only Franco-Mauritians and francophone middle-class Creoles of light-skinned *gens de couleur* racial background can pass), many of them consider broad access to state employment particularly important.[37]

The influence of this Hindu activist network in politics is underscored by the fact that several of the disciples of Swami Krishnanand, who established himself in Mauritius in 1965 and can be regarded as the pioneer of *hindutva* networking in Mauritius, have risen to prominent political positions in the state apparatus of Mauritius, while others have become well-known Hindu activists on the island. One of them was Deputy Prime Minister in 1982–1983, and several others have held ministerial positions, some of them repeatedly. Certainly such Hindu activists do not aim to turn multi-ethnic Mauritius into a Hindu nation, a goal their counterparts hope to accomplish in India, and not even senior *sangh parivar* representatives visiting from India urge them to do so. Instead, the principal goal of Mauritian actors and organizations connected to the transnational Hindu nationalist network is the maintenance and strengthening of a separate Hindu community and group identity — cementing its political dominance in Mauritius and supporting its leaders in their efforts to promote a sense of Mauritianness favorable to Hindu interests. In this, they stress that the cultivation of strong transnational ties in the context of religious identity politics is not at all opposed to the discourse of the nation. On the contrary, in a politics of "Little India," such ties support Hindus in gaining and maintaining a central place in the nation, a dynamic that is familiar in "sectarian" polities elsewhere (compare Shaery-Eisenlohr 2005). A sense of Mauritian identity in which Hindu traditions play a central role legitimizes the dominant position of Hindus of north Indian background in the state apparatus.

The political theme of cultural defense, is significant for Hindu nationalists in India, where it is often combined with discourses about Hindu tolerance as a way to legitimate Hindu political dominance. Similarly, the idea that multi-ethnic Mauritius owes much of its peace, prosperity, and political stability to the patience and "tolerance" of its Hindu majority is not just a theme frequently invoked by local Hindu leaders and visiting *hindutva* dignitaries, but is also present in everyday talk about ethnicity among Hindus, as will become clear in chapter 2.

HINDI AND THE QUESTION OF
DIASPORIC PURITY FOR HINDUS

In the Mauritian context, a main rallying issue and principal political demand of the coalition between local Hindu organizations and the transnational Hindu nationalist activists with connections to Mauritian government and state institutions has been the call for state support for the teaching and status of Indian ancestral languages, above all, Hindi. In taking up the issue of ancestral languages, Hindu nationalists in Mauritius are giving their project a specific form that is language-focused. In fact, they see the promotion of Hindi as one of their main tasks and challenges, combining religious activism with the championing of a particular ethnolinguistic identity. In the words of an Arya Samaji activist:

> Our elders had many problems to protect and preserve our entity *[sic]* and religious practices. . . . In view of this, it is our duty to glorify, as our elders did in the past, our religion and culture. Language is the most important element for ethnic specificity. It is mainly due to the militant efforts of

Arya Samaj that Hindi has survived in the country. This acquisition obtained after long struggle has to be preserved and enriched. It is the duty of every Hindu Youth to learn Hindi and to make use of it, whenever necessary, at all time. Of course we don't mean to neglect of [sic] either English or French. Nevertheless, Hindi remains our cultural and religious language and also the language which symbolizes our ethnic entity [sic].[38]

It has been a long-standing practice of Hindu organizations in Mauritius to support the teaching and spread of Hindi. The Arya Sabha and its Sanatanist counterparts taught Hindi in their temples and *baithka*s, small community-run religious and evening schools, long before Hindi was regularly taught to Hindu children in state schools, and even before formal education became accessible to most Indo-Mauritians. The establishment of Hindi in Mauritius is intimately linked to Hindu reformism and socio-political organization. In 1907, the barrister Manilal Maganlal Doctor arrived from Bombay to work as the first Indian lawyer in Mauritius at the suggestion of Mahatma Gandhi, who himself had visited Mauritius six years earlier. The newspaper he founded, the *Hindusthani,* appeared in English and Hindi. Manilal Doctor was the principal force behind the foundation of the Arya Samaj in Mauritius in 1910, and he donated his Hindi press to the Samaj on his departure from Mauritius in 1911 (Ramyead 1985, 42–46). The reformist Arya Samaj movement was already known for its promotion of Hindi, which it propagated as the true language of the Hindus. Known to the followers of the Arya Samaj as *arya bhasha* (language of the Aryas, that is, the true Hindus), Hindi was also the language of the central text of the movement written by its founder Swami Dayanand (1823–1883), *Satyarth Prakāś.*

Even though Hindi was taught in some state schools in the 1930s (Ramyead 1985, 66), Hindi instruction became more widely available in the school system only after the Second World War, which was also the period when schooling was made available to the majority of the population for the first time. Until then, knowledge of Hindi was mainly available in *baithka*s. In particular, the intense competition between proponents of the Arya Samaj and of Sanatan Dharm Hinduism, who also staged public religious disputations *(shastrarth)* in the language, established standard Hindi as the language of Hindu religious practice and community activism (Bhuckory 1988 [1967]; Ramyead 1985, 53–55). When the missionary Basdeo Bissoondoyal started a Hindu revivalist campaign in the late 1940s, after completing his university education in India, the establishment of community Hindi schools was one of his main activities. Bissoondoyal established a large number of Hindi evening schools across the island where children and adults were taught the language through primers he had written himself (Ramyead 1985, 82–83).[39]

Today, Hindu organizations such as the Arya Sabha are not only active in running their own Hindi classes, they also maintain international contacts in order to invite Hindi literati to Mauritius.[40] The Mauritius Sanatan Dharma Temples Federation has brought prominent Hindi literary figures such as Kamleshvar to Mauritius, in the context of supporting Hindu heritage; it was also one of the organizers of the Fourth World Hindi Conference in Mauritius in 1993. In a conversation with me, a former president of the Mauritius Sanatan Dharma Temples Federation and secretary of the Hindu Council described the goal of such visits and international contacts as the strengthening of a transnational network to support the Hindus all over the world: "The idea was to serve society and to support Hindus in Africa, Fiji, which were in a difficult situation — for them to gather momentum and to unite to fight for political survival; to boost this spirit of Indianness among the Hindu folk; not to be ashamed; and to unite and to organize in order not to be crushed by foreigners like Indians have been in India herself. To organize defense."

From this perspective, the building of a separate group identity and the struggle for political goals go hand in hand. The propagation of Hindi is one of the principal ways activists seek to "boost this spirit of Indianness among the Hindu folk." Cultivating Hindi among Creole-speaking Hindus is thought to turn them into better and more committed Hindus in the diaspora.

Overall, the role of Hindu organizations in pressing for the teaching of Hindi in state schools is far more consequential than their own efforts to teach the language. Their influence is felt in the arenas of language policy and education. Educational policy is often understood to be a province of the nation-state, and the school has even been described by theorists of nationalism as the locus of the production of the *homo nationalis* (Balibar 1991). However, in Mauritius, Hindu organizations have influence in the shaping of educational policies, above all, language policy. They have successfully pressured the government for Indian ancestral languages to be taught as regular subjects in state schools, and in 1995 embarked on a campaign for the ancestral languages to be ranked as subjects in the Certificate of Primary Education (CPE) exams after the sixth school year. These exams are extremely competitive and determine access to the handful of prestigious secondary schools in a system, described as "Indian Ocean Mandarism," that is based on severe inequalities between secondary schools (Miles 2000, 219). Mauritians of non-Indian origin and the Catholic Church, which runs some of the "good" secondary schools, strongly objected to the inclusion of Indian ancestral languages in the CPE exams. They claimed that students of Indian origin would have an unfair advantage if these languages, which only they study, were included in the ranking of students effected through the exams.

In October 1995 when the Mauritian Supreme Court declared the government's plan to include ancestral languages in the CPE ranking unconstitutional, Prime Minister Anerood Jugnauth publicly expressed anger at what he considered a denial of the rights of the Hindu majority by an ethnic minority. Failing to have the constitution amended to get around the judgment, he called for general elections. Although Jugnauth was supported by all the major Hindu organizations during his campaign, which was centered on the issue of "Oriental languages," he was heavily defeated at the polls in December 1995.[41] The new government, however, maintained a policy of reserving seats in the elite secondary schools for students with top results in "Oriental languages," and in 1998 the Privy Council in London overturned the Mauritian Supreme Court's 1995 decision. The proponents of ancestral languages finally attained their goal to have exam results in ancestral languages count towards the overall results of the CPE in 2004, an accomplishment fêted at the official celebration of the Hindu festival of Shivratri in February 2004.[42]

Mauritian state institutions have found the ideology of cultural purity focused on ancestral languages useful as a counterbalance to the ongoing project of economic development. According to Armoogum Parsuraman, Minister of Education from 1984 to 1995, the Mauritian government attempts to combat the negative consequences of economic modernization by the introduction of "human values" and "cultural values" into the school curriculum, which in turn are to be promoted through the study of ancestral languages (Parsuraman 1988, n.d.). This has provided an opportunity for the Hindu activist network and the Mauritian state to collaborate in an area of common interest and has bolstered state support of instruction in Hindi and other "Oriental" languages seen as bearers of cultural values.[43]

GLOBAL HINDUISM, PERIPHERAL LOCATIONS, AND THE "WEAK HINDU"

For Hindu activists in Mauritius, the tension between the ideas of Hinduism as a global force and Hindu nationalism as a territorially

based project in India is especially alive, since it is one expression of inse-
curities about Hindu identity in the diaspora. As the Hindu nationalist
project in India is concerned with turning India into a pure Hindu
nation, against which other localities where Hindus live can be imagined
as a Hindu diaspora, there is a need to negotiate between Hindu nationalism as a territorially defined enterprise and discourses of the globalism
and spiritual universality of Hindu identity. Hindu nationalists in
Mauritius are very explicit about the transnational, global character of
their mission, and there is often a slippage between this aspect of their
project and the idea of spiritual universality. This perceived link between
spiritual universality and the global spread of Hinduism also has implications for understanding Hindu Mauritians as a diaspora, addressing
the tension between global Hinduism and apprehensions about Mauritius as a peripheral location. Again, the tendency is towards downplaying
the experience of spatio-temporal distance between India as the Hindu
homeland and the Mauritian diaspora. Consider for example an Arya
Samaji activist's vision of a "global identity of the Aryan youth": "If the
real meaning of the word 'Arya' is 'noble' then an Arya youth has surely
enshouldered [sic] himself with the responsibility of creating an earth
that is global — an earth that is even very far away from the concept of
'international' existence. In fact 'inter' means 'between,' 'among.' The
Arya identity is noble and if it is noble then it is global."[44] Here the anxieties of being removed from a Hindu homeland, of living in a peripheral
place where maintaining real "Hindu-ness" is a problem, seem resolved
in favor of a model in which territoriality becomes irrelevant because the
Hindu identity cultivated is already global, on the grounds of its inner,
spiritual superiority.

The universality of Hindu identity is sometimes presented in the form
of the argument that Hinduism is not a religion but a civilization. This is
what Ashok Singhal, the president of the VHP, declared on one of his
recent visits to Mauritius: "Hinduism is not a religion. It is a way of life.
Christianity and Islam are religions, but not Hinduism. Hinduism is an
organization, which directs hundreds of religions, but it is not one of
them. There is something to be learned from Hinduism in order to see
how people of different religions manage to live together in one single
country."[45] By claiming for Hinduism a status of universality above mere
"religions," Singhal not only stresses a global significance for Hinduism
that surpasses the same for other religions; he also alludes to the recur-
rent theme of tolerant Hinduism that is so important for Hindu nationalists. Several writers have pointed out the collusion of Orientalism and

Hindu nationalism in the construction of a tolerant Hinduism, which in fact is better understood as a hierarchical relativism.[46] Hinduism is represented as a universal way of life, yet this notion at the same time points back to the hinduization of the Indian nation. Singhal's model implies that Christianity and Islam should be subordinate to the one general "way of life," Hinduism, which is the status that Hindu nationalists in India want Muslims and Christians to accept: adherents of "foreign" religions must be brought into the "Hindu mainstream" and must submit to the rule of the Hindu majority in India (Embree 1994, Fox 1990). There is thus a slippage between the globalism of Hindu identity and the situation in India, where adherents of other religions should be subordinate to Hindus because of the "foreignness" of those religions.

Leaders of the Hindu Council of Mauritius see the globalization of Hinduism as also a practical strategy available to a threatened Hindu community as it preserves its rights in the face of "deculturization," a term often used among Mauritian Hindus to refer to the loss of ancestral culture:

> In this present fast changing world and especially at the threshold of the 21st century, if not checked, the social and cultural background of the Hindu community is bound to undergo profound mutations, principally due to the lack of unity and co-operation among them. We should here not forget those sacrifices made by our forefathers in their adopted countries where they migrated in the early nineteenth century, mostly as indentured laborers. Without their relentless effort to fight for their rights, conversion and deculturisation of the Hindus would have attained irreversible limits. And therefore, regionalisation and globalisation of the Hindu community is a must to fight these coming changes which will no doubt be very detrimental to the Hindus at large.[47]

The ideas expressed here about the urgency of the globalization of Hindu organization echo Anderson's concept of "long-distance nationalism" as a result of the "transnationalization of advanced capitalism" (Anderson 1994). The words quoted here, written by the author on the eve of leading a delegation of Mauritian Hindus to a conference in Nairobi organized by the VHP (attended by the VHP leadership and sponsored by wealthy Gujarati businessmen in Kenya), envision a counter-globalization against the worldwide forces of Westernization, which the author believes are the cause of the "deculturization" of Hindus. Yet the quotation also betrays a deeper insecurity about the possibility of successfully maintaining a Hindu identity outside the Indian subcontinent. Despite the idea of Hinduism and Hindu identity as worldwide and universal, which is so

eagerly championed by Hindu nationalists, the problems of territoriality
and of a center-periphery model of the relationship between India and
other locations are implied here. Hindus in peripheral locations such as
Mauritius and Kenya have to organize in order to ward off threats to
Hindu identity. Hindu activists in Mauritius are constantly arguing for
and against the assumptions of the inherent globalism of Hindu identity
and the relevance of territoriality.

The need for a global organization, so often emphasized by Hindu
nationalists, leads to another issue of debate among Hindu activists in
Mauritius and India alike: the perception of Hinduism and Hindus as
weak. This theme was first systematically articulated in the context of
Indian Hindu nationalism by the Arya Samajist leader Swami Shrad-
dhanand in his manifesto, *Hindu Sangathan: Saviour of a Dying Race*
(1924). The swami argued that *sangathan* (organization, union) is the
key for overcoming the dangers a weakened Hindu community faces,
such as internal caste division, attacks by missionaries of other religions,
and even the imagined possibility of being demographically overtaken by
Muslims in India. Several Hindus I spoke with expressed concern about
what they saw as a persistent disunity in their community because of its
caste divisions, and a laxity in collective religious practice. They saw
Hindu religious practice in Mauritius as offering few opportunities for
social and political mobilization, because much of it is conducted indi-
vidually at home *(puja)* and because Mauritian temples are not much
frequented except during major festivals. They contrasted this apparent
lack of solidarity with what they considered the superior religious organization of Christians and Muslims. In Mauritius, organizations such as
the Arya Samaj exhort their followers to follow the example of Christians and Muslims in this respect: "Every Arya Samajist youth must attend the Sunday Hawan held in the Samaj where he lives. He has to draw
a lesson from his fellow brothers of the Muslim and Christian community who systematically attend their mosque and church. . . . Our Hindu
youth are not born to lag behind."[48]

Such calls for regular attendance of collective religious practice put
more stress on the political and organizational unity of Hindus than on
"correct" religious practice or notions of religious purity. They are more
concerned with forging a united Hindu community rather than with
questions of the standardization or the legitimacy of particular forms of
religious expression among Hindus. But they also provide a focus of
debate about what constitutes "true" Hindus. Arguing and identifying

the "weaknesses" of Hindus thus becomes part of conceiving a Hindu diasporic community in Mauritius.

LANGUAGE AND ANXIETIES ABOUT HINDU-NESS

One of the most important differences between the strategies of Indian Hindu nationalists and their Mauritian counterparts concerns the role of politically loaded ideas about language in Hindu nationalism in relation to the problem of diaspora posed in Mauritius. Language plays a central role in Mauritian imaginations of *hindutva,* or Hindu-ness, though a less prominent part in the project of Indian Hindu nationalists today. This was certainly not always the case. The Hindi-Urdu controversy in late-nineteenth-century northern India was one of the catalysts for the formation of Hindu nationalism in colonial India, and the Nagari Pracharini Sabha of Banaras, devoted to the propagation of modern sanskritized Hindi, was one of its first organizational bodies (King 1989, 1994; Lelyveld 1993; Brass 1974). The chief ideologue of *hindutva* and founder in 1915 of the Hindu Maha Sabha, V. D. Savarkar (1883–1966), considered Hindi the natural language for the Hindu nation (McKean 1996, 83). But since the campaign for Hindi reached its goal after independence with the adoption of sanskritized Hindi as a national language of India, the promotion of Hindi has been among the less salient issues in more recent conflicts engaging Hindu nationalists.

In contrast, in Mauritius the struggle for a higher status for Indian languages, especially Hindi, has remained a political issue. However, the question is not about the national language or the language of administration but about the "preservation" of Hindi as an ancestral language, sometimes dubbed "mother tongue," and about the infrastructure the state should provide for the cultivation of ancestral Hindi. There is less concern about daily linguistic practices among Mauritian Hindus. Creole, the language mainly used in daily life by Hindus in Mauritius, is an issue of contestation only insofar as Hindu nationalists disapprove of the ongoing language shift from Bhojpuri to Creole in rural Mauritius. But much more attention is devoted to Hindi, which has never been used in everyday situations in Mauritius and which people have to learn in schools, either state-run or temple-run.

The rallying for Hindi in order to promote the "Hindu cause" in Mauritius is made possible by identifying Hindi as the "language of our ancestors," regardless of the fact that the vast majority of north Indian immigrant ancestors of present-day Hindus in Mauritius were illiterate Bhojpuri speakers. Moreover, the particular variety of Hindi promoted in Mauritius, sanskritized standard Hindi, only began to be used in the late nineteenth century, in the context of an anti-Muslim and anti-British nationalist struggle.

I suggest that this focus on Hindi as the language of the ancestors is related to the diasporic situation of Hindus in Mauritius, establishing a relationship between Hindus in the diaspora and the homeland. The concern is to demonstrate the continuing relevance of the world of the immigrating ancestors, and in a sense also their copresence, since conceptions of ethnolinguistic belonging are centered more on the purported ancestral language than on the dominant vernacular, Mauritian Creole.

Another way Hindi is linked to Hindu activism in Mauritius is by representing the language in poems and pamphlets as "Mother Hindi" (Hindi Ma), who is in need of protection. Hindi is represented as analogous to a female Hindu deity here, approximated to Bharat Mata, "Mother India." Hindu nationalists in India have staged rituals involving the veneration of statues of Bharat Mata, which are moved in large processions *(yatra)* across India, together with large ritual vessels of Ganges water *(ganga jal)*. In what is often regarded as a major political breakthrough for the VHP, the organization held a series of such Bharat Mata processions crossing India from north to south and east to west in 1983, dubbed Ekatmata Yajna (sacrifice for unity) (McKean 1996, 116–19). Representing Hindi as a deified mother in Mauritius not only alludes to the worship of the goddess in Hinduism but also draws on a particular interpretation of the term "mother tongue," or "mother language," which is taken to mean not the language of childhood socialization, but a language to be thought of as a mother and revered as such:

> Our ancestors came to Mauritius from 1834 on. And when they came they brought with them their religion and sacred scriptures. The foundation of the lives of these ancestors was the Ramcaritmanas [a popular version of the Ramayana composed by Tulsidas]. The language of the Ramcaritmanas is Avadhi and due to this great poem the religion *(dharm)*, culture *(sanskṛti)* has been safeguarded until today.... Sanskrit and Avadhi are similar to Hindi. If Hindi, Tamil, Marathi and Gujarati and other languages were the mothertongues *(matṛbhāṣāē)* of the Indian immigrants, that is, they were the mothers of all of us, then Sanskrit is our grandmother who is protecting her daughters.... Today it is our duty to serve the Sanskrit language which is like our grandmother and the Hindi language which is like our mother so there may be progress in the country.[49]

This statement is very close to V. D. Savarkar's views about the significance of Sanskrit and Hindi for the Hindu nation. For Savarkar, who developed the concept of *hindutva*, Sanskrit is "our mother tongue" and Hindi its "eldest daughter" (quoted in McKean 1996, 83). But very often Hindu nationalists in Mauritius call Hindi simply "our language," and they sometimes maintain that Hindi is widely spoken among Hindus in Mauritius. This is performed by categorizing Bhojpuri as Hindi, erasing the important linguistic and socio-linguistic differences between Hindi and Bhojpuri and thereby appropriating a wide set of linguistic practices for the purposes of Hindu activism (see chapters 5 and 6).

Some Hindu activists and politicians in Mauritius link fears about language loss to fears about the disappearance of the Hindus as a distinct group in the face of "deculturalization," that is. they are concerned about the reproduction of diasporic identity.[50] They project this apprehension onto the language shift from Bhojpuri to Creole, the identification of Mauritian Bhojpuri as Hindi, and the question of the ranking of Indian languages for the CPE exams. . This represents a linking of religious ideology to language ideology as a main focus of nationalist imagination, as well an ideological fusion of linguistic and religious identities, that could not be easily accomplished in the current Indian context by groups such as the VHP and RSS.

"Deculturalization" is also a key term to evoke memories of indenture, when most Hindus lived in poverty under the domination of the Franco-Mauritian plantocracy and the British colonial government. The Franco-Mauritian sugar barons in particular are remembered as having despised the ways of life, languages, and religion of the Hindu laborers in the sugar industry. Versions of Mauritian history told from a Hindu perspective also highlight the attempts to convert Indians to Christianity in colonial times, and the various forms of discrimination non-Christians had to face when they tried to obtain nonmanual jobs in the state apparatus. These events are interpreted as part of a larger design to assimilate the Indians into the Creole ethnic group by suppressing their religion and languages, and so to "deculturize" them, as Ramesh Ramdoyal writes in *The Development of Education in Mauritius 1710–1976:*

> Strenuous efforts were made in the course of time to convert and to deculturize the Indian. Immigration had taken away his freedom, it was depriving him even of the meager material rewards of his hard labor, it was sapping his energy and blighting his humanity, but it could not take away from him his culture and his religion. To the Indian immigrant his culture,

his religion, and his language were an integral whole and under no circumstances would he allow his individuality to be fragmented through the
dissociation of his language from his culture. (Ramdoyal 1977, 90)

The failure of these colonialist efforts is attributed to a heroic resistance
on the part of the Hindus. This social memory of indenture and colonialism downplays the fact that religious practices and ideologies among
Mauritian Hindus underwent considerable change even before the end of
indenture in 1920, and that the language Hindu nationalists are most
concerned about, standard Hindi, was only introduced after 1900
through religious and intellectual contacts with India.

An important aspect of the social memory of these events is that it can
be recontextualized and made relevant to the present political situation
of Mauritius, where Franco-Mauritians are still economically powerful
but the state apparatus is dominated by Hindus. Even though the historical and social contexts of then and now are vastly different, Hindu
activists mobilize memories of past oppression in order to secure advantages, such as having ancestral languages counted for ranking in the CPE
exams.

The controversies around the teaching of Indian languages in
Mauritian schools were from the beginning tied to apprehensions about
what constitutes Hindu identity. When the colonial Director of Education recommended in 1941 that the recently established teaching of
Hindi be discontinued, spokesmen among the Hindu elite protested and
successfully pressed the Legislative Council to appoint a select committee
to look into the matter. The committee later recommended the continuation of the teaching of Hindi in state schools. Seewoosagur Ramgoolam,
a physician educated in England who was the emerging leader of the
Hindu community in 1941 and would become first Prime Minister of
Mauritius after independence in 1968, held that Indians, who at that
time in Mauritius were already largely identified as Hindus, would cease
to be such if Indian languages, of which by far the most important was
Hindi, were not taught in schools:

> The Indian community of this island has a strong attachment for its lan-
> guages. We may spend all our life learning other languages and imbibing
> other cultures, but until we know what is ours we will never become a man
> [sic] in the full sense of the word, nor will we be able to understand and
> cherish our culture. The study of other languages than our own, however
> excellent and useful in itself, must occupy a secondary place in our heart if
> we are to preserve our identity and make a special contribution to the sum

total of the happiness and welfare of the people. The Indians of this island must be taught their languages and that properly and effectively, because that is the only way in which they can preserve their culture, and also because they have not the least intention of being denationalised in the process of time.[51]

According to this view, in order to remain Hindu, religious practices such as daily worship, going on pilgrimages, and visiting temples are not sufficient. Somebody who does not know one of the Indian languages (with the exception of Urdu) cannot claim to be a true Hindu but is "denationalized." More than forty years later the same point is made more strongly by present-day Hindu activists in a postcolonial Mauritius:

If we sit and think deeply over what we are about, we have a lot of ideas coming to open the vistas of our thoughts. The first that strikes our mind is this: we live in a multilingual country where English and French have the precedence so we are bound to study these two languages and be conversant with them. In addition to that we should know the Creole dialect, which is a common link of communication between the different units of the Mauritian community. But we should bear in mind that we should not for any reason sacrifice our mother tongue. As things stand, we note that a large percentage of our young and old have obliterated their mother tongue from the vocabulary of languages at their command. They seem to ignore that if they do not know our mother tongue, they would never be able to understand the philosophy of our religion, culture and civilization. It is commonly said in French "L'example vient d'en haut." What good example could the parents set to their children if they themselves are unable to express themselves in their mother tongue? What pressure could they put on their sons and daughters to learn what they themselves do not know? What could make them feel that they are Hindus if they have no knowledge of Hindi or Bhojpuri? . . . It is indeed shameful on the part of those Hindus who do neither speak their ancestral language nor allow their children to be acquainted with it. These parents should take for granted that people of such mentality would be of little worth as times go.[52]

The knowledge of ancestral languages is a focal point for debate about what constitutes Hindu identity in Mauritius. Hindu nationalist organizations insist on the necessity of knowing Hindi to be a true Hindu. The same understanding is implicit in the Mauritian state's practice of automatically assigning all children with Hindu names to Hindi classes in schools and inferring communal membership from statements of ancestral language in the census.

But the constructed link between ancestral language and Hindu-ness certainly does not go uncontested. Some Hindus in Mauritius think being born Hindu or engaging in certain religious practices is sufficient to be recognized as Hindu. Hindi is also not important for newer Hindu missions in Mauritius such as Hare Krishna and Sai Baba with their middle-class following; they use Creole and sometimes English in their religious activities. While the question of ancestral language remains an issue where anxieties about the shape of Hindu-ness are played out, there are other possibilities for imagining group identifications through language in Mauritius that stand in opposition to those based on ancestral languages.

ALTERNATIVE CONCEPTIONS OF MAURITIUS: THE "CREOLE ISLAND"

Understanding Indian ancestral languages as fundamental to processes of group identification among Hindus in Mauritius runs counter to the ethnolinguistic image of Mauritius in parts of the scholarly literature, where the country is featured as "a franco-creolophone island" (Stein 1982, 622). Several writers have taken the fact that the vast majority of Mauritians, regardless of ethno-religious background, speak French-lexifier Mauritian Creole as their starting point for theorizing a national identity for Mauritius based on that language. Noting that the use of Mauritian Creole transcends ethnic boundaries, some authors have described Creole as a "national cultural bond" (Bowman 1991, 164) between different ethnic communities that supports economic development and political stability in Mauritius. According to Thomas Eriksen, the shared status of Creole facilitates interethnic coexistence and is a key element in the "ethnogenesis of a [Mauritian] nation" (Eriksen 1993. 118). "Kreol- indicates cultural continuity in important fields; it also facilitates inter-ethnic understanding, compromise and cooperation as well as being a basis for an informal national identity" (Eriksen 1992, 123). More particularly, Creole is viewed as partly responsible for the mostly successful and, with the exception of the February 1999 riots, largely nonviolent postcolonial coexistence of Mauritius's ethnic communities. "At first it was just a lingua franca, that is a language for inter-ethnic communication in a plurilingual context. Now it is evolving into a genuine cross-cultural language by its ability to express the different cultural values of different cultural groups, helping the development of inter-cultural understanding and hence of tolerance and peaceful co-existence" (Virah-sawmy and Pudaruth 1984, 576, quoted in Hookoomsing 1987, 140).

Some analysts have gone so far as to interpret the dominance of Creole as the vernacular language as evidence identifying Mauritius as a "Creole island." The anthropologist Jean Benoist, for example, includes Mauritius together with Martinique, Guadeloupe, and Réunion in the category *îles créoles,* forming a "family of societies" and sharing a "common destiny" (Benoist 1985). In this view, the common features uniting these far-flung places are a history of plantation capitalism under French colonial rule, a high degree of cultural hybridity, and the dominance of a French-lexifier Creole language. Similarly, Jean-Luc Bonniol views Mauritius as one among several *îles créoles,* being part of a "Creole sphere" *(aire créole)* named as such "because one speaks Creole there, that is to say a language with a largely French lexical base. . . . This is because these lands have known French colonization at a particular moment of their history" (Bonniol 1985, 77). In other words, Bonniol argues that the Creole identity of Mauritius is due to a combination of conditions: the mixing of cultures and populations under French colonial dominance, and the prominence of a French-lexifier Creole language shared by nearly the entire population.

However, Mauritius differs from the other "Creole islands" listed by Benoist and Bonniol because the majority of its people are of Indian origin. The Indo-Mauritians' insistence on maintaining highly marked ethnic boundaries among themselves and especially between themselves and other ethnic groups in Mauritius, particularly the Creoles, challenges the application of the Creole island model to Mauritius. After all, studies of creolization often take linguistic processes as a starting point for reflecting on perceived mixing in a broad range of cultural fields (Chaudenson 2001). The difference between Mauritius and the other islands of the so-called Creole archipelago is especially evident in the institutionalized and intense nature of the celebration and cultivation of Indian ancestral traditions in Mauritius. The uneasy relationship between discourses of creolization and the powerful presence of an Indian diasporic population is an important issue in the study of Caribbean societies as well. There, the concept of creolization has functioned as a gatekeeping metaphor for anthropological research, defining a central characteristic of Caribbean cultures (Khan 2001). Viranjini Munasinghe's formulation with respect to Indo-Trinidadians is also applicable to visions of Mauritius as a Creole island. Ascribing a Creole identity to Mauritius while suggesting that true Mauritian culture is hybrid and mixed would result in "a narrative that excludes, in this case those people who were thought to embody purity because they never mixed in the first place" (Munasinghe 2002, 685). Thus Indians with strong diasporic connections cannot fully belong because of their "status as *cultural* 'foreigners'" (Khan 2001, 291; emphasis in original).

In Mauritius, Indian cultural traditions have certainly undergone profound transformations, and the image of a unified Hindu community is in conflict with numerous antagonisms based on regional, sectarian, and caste affiliations. Despite this, the imaginings of Indianness that lie behind concerns about ancestral culture emphasize cultural autonomy and separateness and the purity of ancestral traditions, while affirming the centrality of a thus conceived "Indianness" to a Mauritian nation. Benoist (1989) implicitly recognizes the dilemma this poses for the Creole island model, which privileges the field of language as the final criterion for designating Mauritius a Creole island and part of a larger francophone "Creole zone" — that is, the diversity of Mauritian society can be encompassed by the concept of creolization because nearly everybody speaks a Creole language. Nevertheless, in the usage of Bonniol and Benoist, "creoleness" and "creolization" never lose their shifting quality as labels referring to both linguistic and cultural processes of mixing and fusion. At no point do these authors explain possible interrelationships between the linguistic label and other cultural processes otherwise described as evidence for creolization, even though they allude to such relationships in their descriptions of Creole islands and Creole zones. Moreover, the perspective they promote does not address a crucial problem: that many Mauritians of Indian background tend to reject any identity labeled as Creole and do not consider their daily use of Mauritian Creole very significant for processes of group identification.

Another ethno-linguistic perspective on Mauritian identity centered on the idea of Mauritius as a Creole country was formulated soon after independence in 1968. A nationalist movement in the 1970s and the early 1980s sought to overcome the ethno-religious divides of Mauritian society by championing a new national identity centered on the notion that all Mauritians are speakers of Creole. Following the ideas of the linguist, writer, and politician Dev Virahsawmy, the then leftist party Mouvement Militant Mauricien (MMM) sought recognition of Mauritian Creole as the national language of Mauritius. Emphasizing class struggle and postcolonial nationalism against ethno-religious communalism, which it saw as a nefarious colonial legacy, the goal of this movement was to turn Mauritius into a "real" modern nation. The Mauritian linguist Vinesh Hookoomsing described the significance of Mauritian Creole for an emerging Mauritian nationalism, or *mauricianisme,* in the following terms:

> However, following 1968 a new concept has appeared, *mauricianisme.* *Mauricianisme* is conceived as a synthesis and at the same time a superseding of the cultures and traditions of the different ethnic groups consti-

tuting Mauritian society. Of all languages present, precisely the Creole language was in the best position to express the emerging *mauricianisme*, since it lacks any attachment to a particular class or ethnic group. Freed from the old myths and prejudices which are the legacy of colonialism, Creole becomes a weapon of combat and a factor of national unity. (Hookoomsing 1980, 118)

While a main thrust of the MMM was to mobilize what it regarded as a class-specific experience common to the "masses," regardless of ethnic background, the other feature defining a Mauritian national identity from its perspective was the Creole language. The MMM, campaigning under the slogan *en sel lepep en sel nasyon*, intended by the party leadership to mean "one people, one nation,"[53] won the 1982 elections, ousting the Labor Party of Seewoosagur Ramgoolam, who had led the country since independence in 1968. However, the party's plan to establish Mauritian Creole as the national language of Mauritius met with extraordinary resistance and failed the following year, in the context of which the government coalition also dissolved and the MMM lost power.

The collapse of the MMM-led government was triggered by the way it had handled the fifteenth anniversary of independence celebrations in March 1983. Determined to use the celebrations to demonstrate a new Mauritian nationalism, the leader of the MMM, Finance Minister and then acting Prime Minister Paul Bérenger, decided to have the national anthem sung in Creole instead of English, the official language. During the coverage of the event by the government-controlled Mauritius Broadcasting Corporation (MBC), the song was announced as the "national anthem in the national language" (Houbert 1982/83, 255). A storm of protest arose, led by the head of the Hindu faction within the government, Harish Boodhoo. Boodhoo, a follower of Swami Krishnanand, was given the authority to fire the MMM-favored director of the MBC by Prime Minister Anerood Jugnauth, which led to Bérenger's decision to resign and to withdraw the MMM from the government. The MMM then lost the general elections later in the year. Its rhetoric of nationalizing Mauritian postcolonial politics, and thus deemphasizing ethnic solidarities and diasporic connections, was viewed with suspicion by many members of the recently constituted and expanding Hindu state bourgeoisie. Members of this ethnically defined professional group had dominated state institutions since independence in 1968, and they were concerned about the possible loss of power and state employment opportunities to ethnic minorities, such as Creoles and Muslims. The issue of Creole as the national language, deliberately put on the political center stage during the 1983 independence celebrations, was presented by the MMM as emblematic of its policies of promoting a supra-ethnic Mauritian nationalism, thereby largely denying the significance of official diasporic "ancestral cultures." Accordingly, it was interpreted by many Hindus as a threat to their positions in the state apparatus.[54]

Even though Mauritian Creole is spoken by virtually all Mauritians and is emphatically portrayed by its supporters as not associated with a particular group, it is associated with Creoles as an ethnic group in a particular way. African and Malagasy slaves and their descendants, the Creoles, are known as the creators of the Creole language, which was already established as the predominant vernacular in the eighteenth century, long before the beginnings of the indenture system. A Mauritian Creole linguistic nationalism does in fact place in the center of the national imagination those Mauritians who are known to lack any attachment to ancestral traditions with origins elsewhere. Accordingly, the Creole community could have emerged as the unmarked, mainstream Mauritians in the new postcolonial Mauritian nation.[55] If the maximal overlap between Creole ethnic traditions and a Mauritian nation conceived through the lens of Mauritian Creole linguistic nationalism were achieved, Indo-Mauritians would find themselves in a peripheral position of ethnic markedness and difference from a hegemonic national culture, not unlike the experience of Indo-Trinidadians.

Even though it was a political failure, and was rejected by most Mauritians in spite of the fact that Creole is used by nearby all of them, the nationalization of the Creole language offers an alternative vision of Mauritian national identity, one mediated through perceptions of the Creole language as the one cultural element uniting Mauritians. In contrast to the francophone version of Mauritius as a Creole island, this Creole-centered version of "Mauritianism" focuses less on similarities of Mauritian society and history with other locations where French-lexifier Creole languages are predominant, or on shared legacies of French colonization. Indeed, the Creole *militants* of the 1970s and early 1980s saw themselves as combating what they considered French neocolonialism. A territorializing nationalist logic prevailed in their vision, asserting the ideological predominance of the shared vernacular Mauritian Creole over differences in religion, ethnicity, and origin. Nevertheless, despite its inclusivist pathos, Creole linguistic nationalism implies a reversal of the hegemonic order among ethnic groups in Mauritius, and was thus successfully checked as a political project by the Hindu state bourgeoisie.

CREOLIZATION, ANCESTRAL LANGUAGES, AND THE SHAPING OF DIASPORIC BELONGING

The two principal ideologies of ethnolinguistic community discussed, the Creole island vision and the cultivation of Hindi as an ancestral language among Mauritian Hindus, represent conflicting projects in the temporal indexicalities they construct as they locate Mauritian Hindus in relation to India. While the promotion and practice of ancestral language downplays the spatio-temporal remove between Mauritian Hindus and the world of their Indian ancestors, the linguistic ideology of creolization highlights the break with the diasporic homeland and its people. Both in the guise of a complement to *francophonie* and as a Mauritian "anti-communalist" nationalism, Mauritian Creole linguistic ideologies insist on the particularities of Mauritius as a place and its irreducible difference from the Indian homeland, while valuing Mauritian Creole as an indigenous cultural practice. The focus on the local creation of new linguistic practices also emphasizes temporal difference, manifested as the profound cultural change among Indo-Mauritians that has occurred since the arrival of Indian immigrants.

These contrasting approaches to defining Mauritius as a diasporic location through images of linguistic differentiation relate to the question of the modularity of ethnolinguistic nationalism in quite distinct ways. Initially, it would seem that linguistic ideologies of creolization have little in common with European national ideologies, which highlight linguistic purity and homogeneity as part of a larger project of turning impurity and diversity into national purity (Brubaker 1992, Munasinghe 2002). However, the privileging of creolization in assigning ethnolinguistic identity to Mauritians does bear close relationship to European models of the nationalization of language, especially in its assumptions about the relationship between language and groupness. Conceiving of Mauritius as a Creole island and thinking of Mauritian Creole as the national language evoke accounts of the European experience, where political integration through modern forms of communication in a shared standardized vernacular is considered a key factor in producing a sense of nationhood (Anderson 1991, Deutsch 1953, Gellner 1983). This applies in particular to the *mauricianisme* built on Mauritian Creole, which nationalist intellectuals such as Virahsawmy, a linguist by training, sought to standardize and officialize. Further, presenting the predominant vernacular as the crucial and self-evident bond for a nation also recalls the assumptions of

European romanticism, particularly those inspired by a Herderian understanding of an intimate link between vernacular language and the cultural traditions or "spirit" of a people (Herder 1968 [1784–91]). Func-
tionalist and romanticist perspectives on language and ethnonationality
converge in privileging the standardization of a widespread vernacular as
a crucial hallmark of nationhood. Privileging Mauritian Creole in the
conception of Mauritius as a Creole nation is to a large measure reminiscent of these intellectual traditions of nationhood.

However, as the significance of ancestral language among Indo-
Mauritians suggests, there is no inevitable link between languages of
everyday interaction and ethnolinguistic belonging. Many Mauritians of
Indian origin, even though they use Mauritian Creole in their daily lives,
reject the necessity of such a connection. The fact that the dominant language of everyday affairs is Creole does not imply that their ethnolinguistic identity can be described as Creole. Instead, for many among
them the cultivation of Indian ancestral languages presents an alternative
way of ethnolinguistic belonging.

European colonialism in the non-Western world resulted in the spread
of both modernist-functionalist and Herderian ideals of a close relationship between the dominant vernacular language and the "spirit" of a
population. Nevertheless, as mentioned earlier in this chapter, the forms
of ethnolinguistic belonging that emerged from the colonial encounter in
India did not always conform to European models (Washbrook 1991).
The idea that the language of group identification should be pure and not
polluted in everyday usage by common people is of great significance
among Tamil speakers (Schiffman 1996). Many Tamils also imagine
"pure" forms of the Tamil language as a female deity. This particular
manifestation of what Western scholars have termed linguistic nationalism is based on gendered understandings of a "somatic" and inviolable
bond between Tamil and its speakers, which is alternately imagined as a
relationship between deity and devotee and a relationship between
mother and child (Ramaswamy 1997). There is little in such conceptions
of ethnolinguistic belonging to suggest that everyday vernacular usage
necessarily privileges a language's adoption as an emblem of ethnicized
identity. Similarly, in the case of Indian ancestral languages in Mauritius,
it is precisely the relative distance of Hindi from the everyday practice of
speaking Creole that points to the world of the immigrating ancestors,
evoking cultural purity and authenticity, and providing a basis for ethnic
group identification.

In this sense, Hindi as the ancestral language of Mauritian Hindus is the product of a complex history of articulation between European ideals of linguistic ethnicity linked to standardized vernacular languages and South Asian traditions of connecting social and linguistic differentiation. The Hindi movement in nineteenth- and twentieth-century India drew inspiration from modernist assumptions about language, which were effectively combined in the context of the Hindi-Urdu controversy in late-nineteenth-century north India (Brass 1974, King 1994). The supporters of the newly created sanskritized standard Hindi won their case by insisting that the administration of the United Provinces should function in the language of the "majority." Since Hindi was presented by the first generation of Hindu nationalists as the "national language of the Hindus" (Dalmia 1997), and Hindus were, due to the modern census and its forms of categorization, officially known to be the majority, the British colonial government eventually decided to use Hindi instead of Urdu in the local courts and administration of much of north India. The rise of Hindi in India was crucially informed by European ideas of the primacy of standardized vernacular languages for political organization and identification. Nevertheless, the creation and adoption of Hindi as an emblem of Hindu religious nationalism was at odds with the British project of Hindustani as a pan-Indian standard without religious affiliation (Cohn 1985, Lelyveld 1993). Certainly Hindu nationalist "Hindi nationalism" (Rai 2000) cannot be considered a modular extension of the Andersonian model, in which the standardized vernacular provides a vital base for the emergence of the modern, secular nation, filling the void left by crumbling multi-ethnic empires and waning religious worldviews and languages (Anderson 1991). The creation of standard Hindi and its link to an emerging Hindu national identity in colonial India provided the backdrop for its adoption as the ancestral language of Creole-speaking Hindus in Mauritius, most of whose ancestors were actually Bhojpuri speakers. Ideologies of ancestral language reproducing a diasporic link between Mauritian Hindus and an Indian homeland constitute a further articulation of European models of linguistic ethnicity and South Asian sociolinguistic traditions, refracted through the diasporic context of Mauritius. One might conclude that in contrast to linguistic ideologies of creolization, ancestral Hindi in Mauritius provides a powerful case against the modularity of linguistic nationalism.

Finally, the comparison between the two ethnolinguistic projects described in this chapter illustrates the way linguistic ideologies create and justify hierarchical relationships between social and ethnic groups. To begin with, "Creole" is not just the name of the dominant vernacular language but also the designation of the largest non-Indian ethnic group in Mauritius. In contrast to Hindu or Muslim Indo-Mauritians, Creoles are Christians, and overwhelmingly Catholics. Most of them are the descendants of African and Malagasy slaves, but many Creoles also have European and Indian ancestors.[56] Before the recent and still fledgling emergence of an Afro-Creole movement that followed the riots of February 1999, Creoles did not officially claim ancestral cultures and languages based on the memory of their origins outside of Mauritius. In Mauritius, as in many settings of the Caribbean, the label "Creole" is also associated with cultural "mixing" and hybridity. Certainly, given this local background, for many Indo-Mauritians the label "Creole" is loaded with unwelcome indexicality if used to characterize Mauritius in general. It draws a link between Mauritian identity and a minority non-Indian ethnic group that Mauritians of Indian descent often look down upon for its perceived lack of social and economic achievement. Furthermore, as creolization also points to processes of cultural fusion and mixing, the idea of Mauritius as a Creole island stands in direct opposition to ideologies of ancestral cultural and ethnolinguistic purity.

To make matters even more delicate from an Indo-Mauritian perspective, the ideology of creolization also evokes the social memory of attempts to convert Hindus to Christianity under colonial rule. Indo-Mauritian leaders early on regarded these endeavors an attack against Indian ancestral traditions. Consequently, for many Hindus creolization is considered an attempt to make them "like Creoles," that is, turn them into a Christian population presumably without an ancestral culture of their own. Creolization, then, is not only a corruption of Indian traditions, whether cultural, religious, or linguistic, through processes of cultural interchange, but is read as a process of assimilation eventually leading to the disappearance of Indo-Mauritians as a distinct ethnic group.

Indo-Mauritians, resisting notions of creolization as cultural erosion or "progressive acculturation" to an alien norm as described by Singaravelou (1976) with reference to Indians in the French Antilles, have thus for a long time been keenly aware of an issue that is of growing concern in the study of processes of cultural creolization. Creolization is a conflictual, power-laden process in which actors struggle for cultural and political hegemony (Friedman 1994, 208–10; Mintz and Price 1992 [1976]; Price 2001; Trouillot 1998). One way to elucidate this problem is by stressing that discourses of creolization in and about Mauritius are not just about determining and describing the dominant vernacular language. Such discourses, whether by Western or Mauritian academics or activists, constitute instances of language ideology (Silverstein 1979, Woolard and Schieffelin 1994), connecting views about linguistic form and differentiation to several other social and political issues. The slipperiness and shifting quality of the labels "Creole" and "creolization" crucially enable linkages between, on the one hand, interpretations of the language situation in Mauritius and the role and distribution of Mauritian Creole and, on the other, ideas about ethnicity and the national character of Mauritius. Creole in Mauritius functions simultaneously as the name of the dominant language of everyday interaction, as the name of a particular ethnic group, and creolization as a general metaphor for processes of linguistic change and fusion connected to analogous processes of cultural mixing.

The conflict between perspectives on creolization in Mauritius can be read as a struggle over which group is most entitled to represent Mauritianness, since creolization as a way of mapping language and linguistic difference onto social and ethnic differentiation also implies a particular vision of the Mauritius as a nation. The crucial issue here is that concepts of Mauritian identity based on creolization run counter to ideas of diasporic Indianness in Mauritius and the relations to a homeland they construct. Against the background of the politics of language and diaspora described in this chapter, the perceived incompatibility between creolization and Hindu collective self-imaging plays a key role in the struggle over the linguistic culture of Mauritius and its implications for the relationship between Indo-Mauritians and the homeland of their ancestors.

CHAPTER 2

An Indo-Mauritian World

"Ancestral Culture," Hindus, and Their Others

Shortly after my arrival in the village I call La Nicolière, I went with Vinod, a Hindi teacher, to the main village temple *(shivala)* to attend the Tuesday night Ramayan gathering. We walked along the Route Royale, the main street of the village, towards the old banyan tree where the road takes a sharp turn past the oldest and largest shops in the village. Offerings of camphor, candles, cigarettes, and flowers to Dee Baba, a minor guardian deity said to linger near the tree, could be seen as we passed by, continuing on to the Telugu temple and then the small Kalimaye shrine, behind which sugarcane fields open up again. We could hear the steady roar of the immense sugar mill, one of the largest mills on the island, less than two kilometers away. Now, during the harvest season, the mill was running at near full capacity. The *shivala* was just a few hundred meters ahead, near the soccer field and the ruins of the old sugar estate that had given the village its name. The remains of its chimney are still standing. In front of the *shivala*, across from the *boulangerie*, a few men could already be seen gathering and talking to each other, one on his moped with the engine still running. Most homes we had passed on the way had a small shrine for the Hindu deity Hanuman-Mahabir in front of which a small electric lamp was already switched on. Next to the shrine were one or two bamboo stakes with red triangular flags on top, which are replaced in the yearly ceremony of *jhaṇḍa uṟaweke* (the hoisting of the flag). Finally the pandit, a primary school teacher by profession, arrived.

Drawing connections between particular places and people's speech,

Vinod outlined a linguistic geography of Mauritius. Although Creole was spoken all over Mauritius, Vinod explained, Bhojpuri was still widely used in two major regions. Many Bhojpuri speakers could be found in the rural south, another predominantly Indo-Mauritian region of the island. However, he insisted, their Bhojpuri had "suffered." "In the south, the influence of the Creoles on the *endyen* [Hindus] is stronger and their Bhojpuri is much more mixed with Creole.[1] Here in the north the *endyen* have been able to preserve more of their tradition and, because they are more among themselves, speak Bhojpuri more. The Bhojpuri of the north is also less mixed."

Once the chanting of Tulsidas's Ramcaritmanas was over, Vinod introduced me to Pandit Lalbeeharry. The pandit thought I had made a good choice in coming to La Nicolière for my fieldwork. "Most of the people here are Hindus *(endyen)* and still speak pure Bhojpuri." Clearly, Vinod and the pandit considered their village and the surrounding region a Hindu stronghold in Mauritius, where I would be likely to learn about Hindu traditions and their linguistic dimensions. Even though they conceded that people of all ethnic groups can be found in all regions of island, and that a strict geographical separation according to ethnicity does not exist, for them ethnic categories nevertheless served as spatial markers differentiating certain regions of Mauritius. Furthermore, the linguistic geography of Mauritius drawn by the two men was an indication of to how residents of northern Mauritius establish links between ethnic or other designated social groups and linguistic features. In fact, the presence of Bhojpuri speakers is one of the few differentiating features of the Mauritian vernacular linguistic geography. At present, Creole is the predominant language of everyday use all over the island, comprising an important class-indicating register differentiation. Vernacular use of French is only widespread among the small Franco-Mauritian community and middle-class light-skinned Creoles known as *gens de couleur,* who mostly live in the urban zone on the central plateau of the island or in bungalows along the coast. The practice of Bhojpuri alongside Creole is common in rural areas with a great Indo-Mauritian majority, especially the northern and eastern regions of the island, as well as parts of the south. Urban areas, such as the capital and the central urban zone stretching from the town of Beau Bassin to Curepipe, as well as the west coast where the proportion of Indo-Mauritians among the population is lowest and the proportion of Creoles the highest, are home to few regular users of Bhojpuri.

This chapter examines how residents of the rural north of Mauritius engage in processes of group identification, situating themselves vis-à-vis ethnic others while producing a sense of Hindu diasporic belonging, and how they draw on issues of language and linguistic differentiation in doing so. Focusing on the stances people of this region take towards linguistic practices they view as linked to ancestral culture, I show how such language-related aspects of the Hindu tradition in Mauritius are embedded in wider social transformations and processes of ethnic group identification.

SOCIAL MOBILITY

The north of Mauritius is a region covered with sugarcane fields and densely dotted with predominantly Indo-Mauritian towns and villages. Most of these towns and villages, among them La Nicolière, were established in the second half of the nineteenth century, when increasing numbers of Indian indentured laborers moved out of the estate camps set up for them by sugar plantation owners and into rapidly forming villages in the vicinity of the sugar estates. Many villages, including La Nicolière, a rural community of approximately 2,500 inhabitants whose population is over 90 percent Hindu, were named after the nearby Franco-Mauritian-owned sugar estate. Most of these estates became defunct long ago; the ruins of some are still visible. Two interrelated socioeconomic processes that set in during the late nineteenth century have given the landscape of much of rural Mauritius its present look. The sugar industry gradually centralized into fewer yet larger, more economically viable mills. This process, continuing until the present day, caused the number of sugar mills, 303 in 1863, to drop to 188 in 1878 (Allen 1984, 342) and to 9 in 1998. At the same time, the amount of land held by Franco-Mauritian planters, initially owners of nearly all the land in Mauritius, decreased, while the proportion held by Indian immigrants and their descendants increased. These developments, known as the *grand morcellement,* became especially evident in the 1880s. A slump in the global market for sugar forced many of the smaller planters out of business, and most of the larger estates had to sell large parts of their land in order to survive the crisis (Allen 1984, 1999). Most of the land thus available was bought by Indians and Indo-Mauritians, which led to the formation of an Indo-Mauritian class of small planters, who by 1935 owned approximately 39 percent of the cane land in Mauritius (Benedict 1961, 26). This development went hand in hand with the move away from estate camps and the further spread of Indian villages throughout rural Mauritius (Virahsawmy 1984).[2]

The changing appearance of these villages — especially the types of construction of homes, most of which were formerly of wattle-and-daub construction with a thatched roof, later built with corrugated iron sheets, and finally with concrete — is a theme that people in La Nicolière and other nearby rural communities often comment on when narrating their life histories. Sunil is a civil servant in his forties, employed in a government ministry in the capital Port Louis. He commutes to work every day in his new Toyota from the town of Rivière-du-Rempart, where he lives with his extended family. He received a college degree from the University of Baroda, India, where he was sent on an Indian government scholarship.

> My parents had ten children and had never been to school, they were illiterate. My father was a very smart and determined man and had even taught himself French and Hindi. Selling milk, my parents were able to feed the entire family, and also over many years purchase land in his village. I still do not understand fully today how they managed to do it. Together with my brothers and sisters we would help them cut grass and feed the cows in the early morning and after school. Together with them I ran every morning to the Route Royale [the main road passing nearby] to catch a bus to secondary school in Beau Bassin. When I was little, most houses in the village were made of wood and cane straw *(lapay)* with a thatched roof. When a cyclone came, people often lost everything they possessed. Later, houses were made of corrugated iron sheets, but now nearly all the houses you can see are solidly built.

The prevalence of one- and two-story houses constructed with a steel-reinforced concrete frame and roof and walls of masonry blocks painted white fits Sunil's narrative of rapid social mobility. It is a tangible manifestation of the dramatic socio-economic changes of the past two decades.

The experiences and life stories centered on new prosperity and profound economic transformation that people narrated to me were often consonant with the new interest in Mauritius among economists and social scientists. Mauritius has attracted attention as one of the places in the world where "development" seems to have succeeded (Alladin 1993, Bowman 1991), to the point where the World Bank has hailed Mauritius as an economic miracle (World Bank 1989, 1992). In fact, in the context of establishing an Export Processing Zone in the early 1970s, and again more intensely during the 1980s, garment factories were built all over the island. These provided an attractive source of income for many families, compared to working in the sugar industry. Mauritius was transformed from a poor island dependent on a vulnerable monocrop economy into a self-proclaimed economic "tiger in the Indian Ocean." In addition, tourism started to boom, concentrating on a growing high-end European clientele, and hotels and luxury resorts along the coasts became another major resource for jobs and income for Mauritians (Alladin 1993, 131–48).

Every day in the early morning hours, weekends included, the textile companies' buses can be seen cruising the Route Royale of La Nicolière picking up workers, then moving on to the next village and finally the factories. One of the largest garment assembly plants in Mauritius is a mere 15-minute drive away, on the outskirts of Poudre d'Or near the seaside. However, as important as the new jobs in the garment industry are for households in La Nicolière — especially compared to working as a poorly paid *laburer* in the sugar industry — they are certainly not the preferred source of employment, especially for men. The garment industry workforce in Mauritius is 70–75 percent female (Burn 1996, 60), and wages are considerably lower than in the public sector. Hindu men in particular strive for employment in the state apparatus, where their ethnic group dominates, and Hindu women also seek to avoid employment in the sugar and garment industries whenever possible. The sacrifices parents in La Nicolière undertake in order to make the best possible education available to their children are above all aimed at securing a moderately remunerative but eminently secure and also prestigious position as a civil servant.

In my first encounter with Vinod and Pandit Lalbeeharry, the two pointed out what they saw as the virtues of La Nicolière and its surrounding area as a Hindu heartland in Mauritius. They were proud that what they regarded as Indian ancestral traditions were still vibrant and deplored the ongoing language shift from Bhojpuri to Creole, which is very much in evidence in La Nicolière and other nearby towns and villages. "Even here parents do not speak to their children in Bhojpuri any more. They think that their children will be more successful at school if they speak Creole to them. Some even try to speak French at home. The competition for getting into a good secondary school is very intense. Parents see Bhojpuri as a handicap and think the children will have a more difficult time learning French and English. They want their children to have a *head start* in school."

The language shift to Creole began well before the recent times of economic boom. Many rural Indo-Mauritians who are today in their forties and fifties remember school as the place where they learned Creole and had to speak it all the time. Dev, a civil servant in his early fifties who grew up in the rural district of Flacq in the east of the island, about a 20-minute drive from La Nicolière, recalls how his school experience was crucial in turning him into a predominantly Creole speaker:

> This is a thing to remember, although it has improved a lot. There was the feeling of inferiority of the people in La Nicolière, who were mostly labor-ers in the sugarcane fields, toward the townspeople. Earlier there was a clear difference; people in the countryside spoke Bhojpuri and knew little Creole, while you could only speak Creole in the towns. In my primary school, the great majority of the children spoke Bhojpuri, so there was no problem. Once there are a certain number of people who only speak Creole, the Bhojpuri-speaking children learn Creole, and it is taking over more and more. I went to secondary school in Rose Hill [a town in the middle of Mauritius's urban zone], as in those days there were few sec-ondary schools in the villages. There were many people from the towns, and the people of the villages would not speak Bhojpuri, but [would speak] Creole all the time, from morning till evening.

In other words, even before the recent prosperity, Bhojpuri speakers themselves were interpreting the language shift as linked to the spread of formal schooling, and to "development" more generally. They also con-nect it to the decreasing importance of sugarcane cultivation as a liveli-hood for many rural Mauritians. Mr. Faugoonee, a civil servant in his fifties who grew up in a family that had moved from a village in the north to the town of Quatre Bornes when he was a few years old, remembers speaking to his mother in Creole while she spoke in Bhojpuri. "We never made the effort to reply in Bhojpuri." This type of asymmet-rical or nonreciprocal code-switching has been attested in other bilingual settings (e.g., Gal 1979, 110–11). Moreover, he interacted with his father in Creole all the time. Sudesh, who works in a government ministry in Port Louis, to which he commutes daily from his village in northern Mauritius, remembers that before independence, urban middle-class Creoles dominated many branches of the state administration. "They did not respect anybody who spoke Bhojpuri, so one had to speak Creole if one went to the town and needed something from a government office. These people looked down on everything Indian, whether it was speak-ing Bhojpuri, or putting oil on your hair." Even though, according to Sudesh, this attitude lingers on, it changed somewhat when after inde-pendence much of the government bureaucracy was taken over by

Hindus, many of whom had a rural background. Today it is possible to hear Bhojpuri spoken in government offices and, he says, "I sometimes speak to my pals at work in Bhojpuri and I do not care if some people do not like it."

The perceived decline of Bhojpuri in Mauritius has motivated activism on its behalf. Significantly, however, even though there are both Muslim and Hindu Indo-Mauritian users of Bhojpuri, language revitalization activities have only come from Hindu nationalist circles, who view Bhojpuri as an element of Hindu ancestral culture. The most significant attempt to start a movement to "save" Bhojpuri was started by Sarita Boodhoo, the wife of a prominent Hindu politician and former Vice Prime Minister and herself the founder of the Bhojpuri Institute. She has organized cultural events such as Bhojpuri-language stage shows and plays, as well as concerts with Bhojpuri songs. A group of government officials built upon her efforts, using their influence to start Bhojpuri-language television programs on the government-controlled Mauritius Broadcasting Corporation (MBC). The consequences of these attempts to promote and at the same time purify and sanskritize Mauritian Bhojpuri by a group of cultural brokers closely linked to transnational Hindu political activism will be discussed in chapter 5. The most significant feature of such organized language revitalization activities is that they portray Bhojpuri not as part of a widely shared Indian heritage in Mauritius, but as Hindu patrimony. Individuals known for their Bhojpuri activism such as Sarita Boodhoo are also known as champions of Hindi, the official ancestral language of those Hindus claiming north Indian origin. Sarita Boodhoo worked for a long time for the establishment of a World Hindi Secretariat sponsored by the Indian and Mauritian governments in Mauritius.

People in La Nicolière often point out a connection between rapid socio-economic transformations, growing prosperity, and what they see as a loss of tradition, as with the decline of Bhojpuri. However, the state-supported effort to retain traditions through the cultivation of ancestral languages has also proved to be linked with social mobility for some Hindus. This process began in the 1950s, when the first wave of Hindi instructors started teaching in state schools, and gained further strength in the years after independence, when the teaching of Hindi in state schools was rapidly expanding. In order to meet the pressing need for Hindi teachers, the first postcolonial government of Prime Minister Seewoosagur Ramgoolam embarked on a policy of hiring as Hindi teachers young Hindus who had completed secondary school (School Certificate, eleven years of schooling), and in a few cases only primary school. Many of them owed their knowledge of Hindi to instruction in *baithka*s, community-organized village evening schools often attached to a Hindu temple and not under state control. As a consequence, many men and a few women from rural households whose main source of income was either employment as laborers in the sugar industry or growing sugarcane on a small plot of family land, were able to obtain relatively prestigious and very secure employment as civil servants. These Hindus from humble backgrounds and with modest educational credentials now had the opportunity to attain the status of education officer (a middle rank among teachers), and to own a spacious concrete frame house and maybe even an automobile.

Mr. Gungoo's life story is a good example. He grew up a in a house with a mud floor and thatched roof as one of nine children. His father worked as a laborer for the local sugar mill, and his parents together grew vegetables that they sold at nearby markets to supplement their income. In the mid-1950s Mr. Gungoo found employment as a Hindi teacher after finishing secondary school. He initially taught in two different schools and attended additional training sessions at the Teachers Training College (today the Curriculum Development and Research Unit) in Beau Bassin on the weekends. By the time he retired he had attained a position as a deputy head teacher. His home is a rather large concrete frame type; there is a new sofa with matching chairs and a coffee table in the living room. Souvenirs of trips to India adorn the walls, and a large television, as well as a stereo, which is placed in a cabinet with drawers and glass doors, are in evidence, giving the impression of a comfortable middle-class lifestyle. Mr. Gungoo has three sons. One, a primary school teacher, gives private after-hour lessons *(tuition)* to students in the backyard. Another son is a police officer, while the third is studying for a university degree in fine arts in Delhi. Mr. Gungoo's career as a Hindi teacher has clearly been primarily responsible for the family's rise from a humble background to middle-class status.

The career of Pandit Ramkhelawan is another example of upward social mobility through the mastery of Hindi. The pandit grew up in a poor rural family in the south of the island. His father was a *laburer* who was very much engaged in the Hindu religious organizations and activities in the village. Pandit Ramkhelawan used to help his father in market gardening, which the family engaged in to supplement its income, while studying for his School Certificate exams. He had started learning Hindi at the *baithka*, located right next to his parents' house, and soon became proficient enough to give lessons to other students after school. In school, Hindi and Hinduism were his strongest subjects. When he decided to become a full-time pandit, he already had the necessary requirements to start a course with the Mauritius Sanatan Dharma Temples Federation, a School Certificate diploma and the equivalent of the *uttama,* that is, the highest level of the Hindi examinations conducted by the Hindi Pracharini Sabha in collaboration with the Hindi Sahitya Sammelan in Allahabad, India. Some residents who patronize the temple he is attached to say he has made quite a lot of money since moving to their community in the north, and has been able to purchase some land and a car. Most of his income is not the regular pay he receives from the state-subsidized Temples Federation, but the fees and donations for ritual services he performs for individual clients, such as at weddings. The career of this pandit, made possible by a good knowledge of Hindi and the support of the Temples Federation, has resulted in a marked degree of social mobility.

A DIVERSITY OF STANCES REGARDING BHOJPURI

Residents of La Nicolière often expressed regret about the prospect of Bhojpuri falling out of use, as for them it meant the loss of tradition. At the same time they regarded Bhojpuri as the language of the rural poor, of uneducated people of working-class background. This tension between the valuation of Bhojpuri as an ethnicized tradition and its association with poverty and lack of education pervades many of the stances Indo-Mauritians take with regard to what language activists tell them is "their" language. One evening over dinner while Vinod and I were talking about the changing situation of Bhojpuri, he and his wife, Reshmi, pointed out that in contrast to their childhood days, they speak Bhojpuri only in encounters with people they already know as Hindus and speakers of the language. They would never use Bhojpuri with strangers but, in contrast to earlier days, use Creole instead. They commented on the transformation of Bhojpuri from its status as the general language of the Mauritian countryside, reaching beyond ethnoreligious boundaries, to a presupposed in-group language used with social intimates. Vinod, a regular on the temple committee and a Hindi teacher in the primary school of a neighboring village 4 kilometers away, then lamented the impending demise of the language, since children these days rarely hear the language. At this point one of his three sons, Raj, a secondary-school student preparing for his High School Certificate exams, interjected laughingly that Bhojpuri was only for "those poor boys," making a gesture pointing down the road towards the *baithka*, the big banyan tree, and the main village store, where young unemployed men could often be seen spending time and drinking. "But one has to preserve it, it is important," Reshmi retorted, but Raj chose not to answer. Among Indo-Mauritians, Bhojpuri is regarded as both an ethnoreligious "tradition" and a means of creating and justifying internal social differentiation. When the issue of Bhojpuri was raised, Raj had in mind the young men of the village who had failed their School Certificate exams and were unable to find employment with only a primary school education. For Reshmi and Vinod, however, the language constituted an important way of building and maintaining the ethnic distinctness they highly valued.

Mr. Boodhoo, a secondary school teacher in his forties, had traveled with me to a *hardi (haldi)* pre-wedding ceremony in a village some ten kilometers away. When I remarked that at the event I had heard Bhojpuri spoken all night in a way I found rarely the case in La Nicolière, he replied that "there are only *endyen* there, and look at their social background *(zot kuš sosial)*, they are small planters." The dominant use of Bhojpuri indexes low-level employment in the sugar industry — either as a *laburer* employed by one of the big sugar mills, or as an owner of a small parcel of land who sells his sugarcane to the mills — and is construed as standing in opposition to Western-style education and upward social mobility.

According to Bhojpuri speakers, the decline of the language is not confined a reduction in the number of speakers, but also concerns what people see as the "character" of the language itself. Interestingly, it is not so much the obvious use of Creole lexical items in Bhojpuri that is significant in this story of decline, although this is an issue often raised by purist language activists who seek to "protect" Bhojpuri as part of a Hindu heritage in Mauritius, but rather the loss of the honorific register of Mauritian Bhojpuri, whose "correct" use was formerly associated with higher social status and also high-caste membership. The implications of this process of register stripping (Irvine and Gal 2000: 71) will be further explored in chapter 5. Bhojpuri speakers sometimes distinguish between two kinds of Bhojpuri: *motiya* (the coarse one) and *maiya*, or *meya* (the chaste one). *Maiya* Bhojpuri is seen as characterized by the use of honorific verb suffixes and pronouns when addressing senior persons or in speech events defined as formal, such as public addresses or sermons in temples. *Motiya* Bhojpuri lacks these honorific forms and also features the use of the interjections and interpellations *are* and *re*, which is considered disrespectful and uncultivated. These days *maiya* is largely seen as an anachronism, while *motiya* is said to be generally dominant. Goswami, a retired inspector of primary schools of Brahmin background, deplores what he considers the contamination of the "real" Bhojpuri, which for him is *maiya*, by the generalized use of *motiya*. "Even the high castes, even the 'Brahmins' among the Babuji-Maraz now mostly speak *motiya*. But *motiya* is an uncultivated language *(jangali bhasha)*, and more and more people are ashamed to speak it, especially in the city."

While Goswami protrays the differentiation of *maiya* versus *motiya* as an issue of linguistic practices of the Babuji-Maraz, members of the highest caste group among Hindus in Mauritius, compared with those of other Hindus, Ravi, of mid-ranking Vaish caste background, has a different view. He associates the use of *motiya* with the low castes, and considers the roughness of *motiya* iconic of what he sees as the uncultivated nature and moral failings of low-caste people. "You can still distinguish high castes *(gran nasyon)* and low castes *(ti nasyon)*; even if low-caste people manage to get money and education, they still have something rough about them, such as a lack of generosity and politeness."

Even though Bhojpuri speakers entertain different notions of how to link the contrast between obsolescent *maiya* and popular *motiya* to hierarchical social categories, such as castes, they tend to agree that the integrity of Bhojpuri as a respectable language is undermined by the loss of *maiya*. The resulting perceived incompleteness of the language is then seen as further evidence of its decline.[3] This perception is compounded by the observation that rural Muslims also use *motiya* Bhojpuri without the valued honorific forms characteristic of *maiya*, reinforcing the idea that "proper" Bhojpuri is the preserve of the more respectable Hindus, even if people disagree on how to draw a boundary between those and other Hindus.

Vidoor, a secondary school teacher in his forties, recalls as a child often hearing the honorific *maiya* forms when elders were addressed. However, he does not use them today when addressing his mother, who is in her late seventies. Vidoor commented that people rarely use Bhojpuri these days in common situations when they want to convey deference or some degree of formality, such as in addressing strangers and persons of higher social standing. "Today we speak Bhojpuri among intimates, our pals *(ban kamerad)*, and when we joke or swear or use improper *(grossye)* language."

Pandit Mohabeer regrets this development. As a Brahmin he is proud of the way his family cultivates the practice of "proper" *maiya* Bhojpuri.

Having obtained a degree in Hinduism from Banaras Hindu University, he has spent time in a Bhojpuri-speaking region of India. Compared to the Indian varieties of Bhojpuri that he knows, he finds the Bhojpuri current in Mauritian villages rather deficient. In his view, the common code-switching with Creole and the adoption of numerous words of Creole origin have corrupted the language, and the deletion of honorific forms have made it sound "rough" and "rude." In contrast, he feels that the way he and his family speak Bhojpuri measures up to the Bihari varieties, which are "refined" and full of "respect." As to the Bhojpuri of most of his fellow Hindu Mauritians, he can only remark with regret: "They just do not have this Bihari accent." From the pandit's perspective, the current state of Mauritian Bhojpuri is one of severe decline. This is evident not just in the number of speakers and shrinking contexts of use but, most important, in what he considers the deterioration of the language itself, experienced as a compromising of its completeness and integrity.

LIVING WITH AN ANCESTRAL LANGUAGE

So far I have described a contemporary situation in what can be considered the Hindu heartland of north Mauritius characterized by a language shift from Bhojpuri to Creole, Western-style schooling, and widespread and rapid social mobility dependent on knowledge of French and English. Even so, there is a continued desire among Hindus of that region for ethnolinguistic differentiation. Against this overall background, the role of the state-sponsored ancestral languages in the production and reproduction of ethnic boundaries has become more salient. Bhojpuri clearly outweighs Hindi as the "language of forefathers" among Hindus according to the national census, where Bhojpuri has been included among the languages listed in this category since 1983. But the census category "language of forefathers" is not identical with the officially recognized and promoted ancestral languages with origins outside Mauritius. And it is Hindi, not Bhojpuri, that enjoys a monopoly as the ancestral language of Hindus of north Indian background in the educational system and within the framework of activities of Hindu organizations in Mauritius.

Hindus in La Nicolière are confronted with what is officially presented as their ancestral language in contexts of both direct and indirect state sponsorship. Mostly, they experience Hindi through two categories of persons: Hindi teachers and Hindu pandits, who frequently use Hindi in ritual, worship, and sermons and also sometimes teach Hindi on the temple grounds. Occasionally, Hindi teachers also work as Hindu pandits, combining both Hindi-associated professional roles in one person. Either way, the importance of Hindi is clearly mediated by state institutions, which employ Hindi teachers directly or support pandits and their instruction of Hindi indirectly through subsidies to Hindu religious organizations. This fact is significant for understanding local perspectives towards Hindi as the ancestral language, for these perspectives are very much influenced by the positions people in La Nicolière take towards state-sponsored professionals.

People in La Nicolière engage in the cultivation of Hindi as their official ancestral language in several contexts. The *baithka* in the center of the village offers Hindi classes to school students every Sunday morning; in fact, this is its principal function. On a typical Sunday, around twenty-five students, more than two-thirds of them girls, are present. They are divided into two groups, primary and secondary school level. For teaching on the weekends the teacher receives a modest compensation of 500 rupees per month (roughly $22 at the time). He shuttles back and forth between the two groups, keeping them busy with exercises. The textbooks, different from those produced by the Curriculum Development Unit in Beau Bassin in cooperation with the Mahatma Gandhi Institute for use in government schools, are provided by the Hindi Pracharini Sabha. The Sabha periodically sends some of its senior members to La Nicolière to check on the classes. On one occasion, the president of the organization appeared personally to see whether the classes were being held and whether there were any complaints. In comparison with Hindi classes at state schools, the topics covered in the class are more centered on Hinduism, and this was also the case on that day. The teacher, or *guruji,* prompted his students to talk about the Shivratri festival and pilgrimage through most of the session and assigned as homework an essay about the holiday to write for the following Sunday. Classes begin and end with a prayer, with the students standing up and folding their hands, and the *shantipath* prayer is sung to conclude the class, in a manner similar to the Ramayan sessions held in the local *shivala.* The classroom walls are adorned with framed pictures of the deities Shiva and Ram, as well as of Mahatma Gandhi, while the outer walls of the small building feature *om* symbols and a representation of Shiva, next to which is written in English: "Glory to Lord Shiva." Over the entrance the official name of the *baithka* is written in Devanagari script: Lanikolyer Navjīvan Hindī Pāṭhśālā (Hindi school "New Life" La Nicolière).

Residents of La Nicolière see the teaching of Hindi in the *baithka* as only a supplement to Hindi instruction in state schools. In fact, many students are sent to the *baithka* with the goal of improving their grade in Hindi in their regular school. In La Nicolière, as in other parts of Mauritius, Hindi is taught to students of north Indian Hindu background on the basis of ethnic exclusivity from the first grade of primary school onwards. The division into classes for the study of different ancestral languages is often the first unmistakable experience of ethnic separation in children's lives. There is a primary school in La Nicolière, and one state-run and two private secondary schools within a five-kilometer radius. Hindi is taught in all of them.

Although Hindi is widely regarded as a school subject with little practical value unless one opts for a career as a Hindi teacher, many students continue Hindi until the School Certificate level, and even up to the Cambridge High School Certificate. Many students and their parents feel that it is somewhat easier to get high grades in Hindi than in other subjects. A good grade in Hindi can be used to balance a weaker performance in other subjects, an advantage that students of Creole background do not enjoy.

Finally, Hindi occupies a central position in Hindu religious activity in La Nicolière. The pandit usually gives sermons *(pravacan)* on themes such as the deeds of Hindu deities and mythological characters, the significance of particular festivals, and general moral issues of everyday relevance. The last often centers on family problems and concerns about school exams. *Pravacan*s are often delivered at least in part in Hindi, with frequent switches into a purist, hindiized register of Bhojpuri. This is also the case in the *shivala* of La Nicolière during the two weekly evening sessions of worship as well as during festivals, such as Shivratri, Holi, Ganesh Chaturthi, and Divali. Also, ritual events sponsored by particular individuals or families in their homes, such as Durga Puja, are presupposed occasions for the use of Hindi during the ritual and devotional activities. Hindu worshippers in La Nicolière not only listen to these sermons, which most of them largely understand, but even interject questions and comments in Hindi or Bhojpuri at particular points in a pandit's sermon. They also sing Hindi *bhajan*s on these occasions. One particular occasion in which all worshippers engage in the practice of Hindi are the Ramayan sessions held every Tuesday night at the *shivala*. Sections of the Ramcaritmanas are chanted, with the participants holding or sharing individual copies of the printed sacred text. Comments and explanations in modern standard Hindi are printed in the margins of the Ramcaritmanas, an edition of which can found in the great majority of

Hindu households in Mauritius. These often provide the basis for the pandit's comments after each set of lines. The Ramayan sessions consist of a constant back and forth between the worshippers chanting the lines of the main text in chorus, accompanied by harmonium, and the pandit following with comments in Hindi, during which worshippers sometimes ask questions.

There are considerable differences between the "Hindi" of the Ramcaritmanas and the modern standard Hindi taught to Hindus in Mauritius, the former representing a range of regional variants of archaic Avadhi.[4] But in the minds of many people in La Nicolière, the Ramcaritmanas, disseminated through an immense number of print editions since the early nineteenth century (Lutgendorf 1991: 61–63), is one of the obvious expressions of Hindi as part of their "ancestral culture." Hindi is considered the language of the Ramayana, and therefore its connection with Hindu traditions is beyond question for Hindus in Mauritius.

In the view of many Hindus, the decline and possible loss of Bhojpuri highlights the need for cultivation of the more prestigious Hindi as an ancestral language. This means that questions of ethnolinguistic difference become increasingly disconnected from daily linguistic routines. Ms. Ramdin, a Hindi teacher in a primary school in a town near La Nicolière, pointed out that the importance of the ancestral language is really "cultural" *(sanskritik)*: "Because of the rapid economic development we have had here, it is very important that people do not lose their roots, especially for the children. Otherwise, the *social fabric* of our society may fall apart." Ms. Ramdin's comment resonates very much with official government discourse on the promotion of ancestral languages and cultures as a way of supporting "traditional values," and thus counterbalancing the increasing social anomie and conflict that are the assumed consequences of rapid modernization.[5] Ms. Ramdin emphasized the presumably integrative function of traditional values. In fact, these values, seen as embodied in ancestral languages and cultures, are ethnically charged and are deployed in a manner that creates and reproduces ethnic boundaries. The effects on the social fabric of Mauritian society are considerably more complex and contradictory than the promoters of ancestral languages such as Hindi are usually willing to admit.

Among rural Hindus of north Indian background the disjuncture between routine linguistic practice, increasingly dominated by Mauritian Creole, and the maintenance of ethnic boundaries through language is expressed through a strong loyalty to the ancestral language, Hindi. However, the ways this ideological attachment is experienced and justified vary considerably. Organizations with Hindu nationalist connections voice their support for "protecting" the ancestral language most clearly. At a public meeting of the Hindi Pracharini Sabha at its headquarters in Montagne Longue in 1997 on the occasion of the fiftieth anniversary of Indian independence attended by Prime Minister Navin Ramgoolam, the invited speakers stressed that safeguarding Hindi meant safeguarding Hindu religion and traditions in Mauritius. Speaking on a stage whose back wall was adorned with the Hindi Pracharini Sabha's offician slogan in Devanagari — "When the language is gone, the culture is also gone" *(bhāṣā gaī to sanskṛti bhī gaī)* — and an image of the Hindu goddess of learning, Sarasvati, one senior leader stressed that learning and speaking Hindi is important for the "protection of Hindu religion and the Hindu way of life *(dharm ki raksha)*. If you want to wipe out a community, wipe out the language" *(jati miṭa do to bhasha ko miṭa do)*. The links between the propagation of Hindi and the legitimization of Hindu political power in Mauritius were quite obvious to the audience of teenage Hindi students and their parents and relatives when the Prime Minister, speaking in English, assured them of his government's full commitment to the support of Hindi. A member of parliament from the Prime Minister's Labor Party spoke in a more alarmist tone, pointing out that there were enemies of Hindi who were out to destroy the Hindus by undermining the teaching of the ancestral language. He concluded that "destroying the Hindu religion or way of life is equal to destroying life [itself]" *(hindu dharm miṭane jivan miṭane se barabar hai)*.

The same defensive discourse about the necessity of protecting Hindu culture is sometimes taken up when Hindus debate recent social changes in their communities. After visiting a neighbor who had sponsored a celebration on the occasion of Durga Puja, I returned to Vinay's home, where we ate a vegetarian meal served on banana leaves *(set kari)* as appropriate to the ritual occasion, while his mother and his wife were preparing *puri*s in the kitchen. When Vinay's father and one of his cousins joined us, the conversation turned to the relationship between language and Hindu ways of life in Mauritius. Vinay, echoing the official discourse of the Hindi Pracharini Sabha and other Hindu organizations, pointed out: "If one loses Hindi, one slowly loses Hindu culture, and Hindu religion as well. One cannot understand the religion any more, because it needs to be explained though Hindi." His cousin objected, pointing out that Hinduism as a school subject is studied in English, but Vinay would not accept this argument. "People are becoming more and more materialist and Western and only think of profit, and now there are problems in the families that were not there before, when people spoke Bhojpuri most of the time. Look at the ways many girls are dressing today, like the Spice Girls."[6] For Vinay, the ancestral language is associated with conservative ancestral values, which are under attack, and its cultivation can help mitigate the Westernization of Mauritian society, including changes in gender relations that he sees as problematic. Like many Hindu Mauritians, he assesses the erosion of ancestral languages and Hindu tradition in terms of the discourse of gender. Moreover, Hindi and Bhojpuri are closely identified with each other, to the point of being almost interchangeable as holders of tradition, in Vinay's assessment.

Another way of expressing loyalty to the ancestral language is to point out its inherent positive characteristics. A recurring metaphor in this respect is the "sweetness" of Hindi. After completing an engagement ceremony for Mohan's nephew in St. Julien, a *sirdar* (overseer in the sugar industry), a man in his late fifties working as a pandit in his free time, explained why he thought of Hindi as sweet. It received its sweetness from its "mother," Sanskrit, because "when people had stopped understanding Sanskrit they just used Hindi instead." The *fiancailles* was a highly innovative occasion. It combined the European concept of engagement, involving exchange of rings and gifts as well as cake cutting while opening a bottle of (nonalcoholic) champagne, with a *havan* ceremony, during which the pandit instructed the participants in Hindi on what offerings to place in the ritual fire and before the images of deities placed nearby. Hindi film music was playing loudly outside, while most of the men had gathered down the street in front of a neighbor's house to eat nonvegetarian snacks and drink whisky and chat in Creole. Essential attributes of the ancestral language such as its presumed sweetness justify the importance of continuing to cultivate it, especially when the disjuncture between what is considered ancestral language and culture and present-day ritual and linguistic practices is all too obvious. In fact, Hindu Mauritians sometimes explain the link between sweetness and the ancestral language in terms of Hindi being "our mother tongue" *(hamar matribhasha)*. One retired civil servant in his sixties enthusiastically remembered his pilgrimage to a number of sacred Hindu sites across northern India, where, he said, he spoke Hindi all the time: "This is the land of Sanskrit and the sweetness of Hindi comes from Sanskrit. This sweetness is there because Hindi is like a mother to us." These frequently invoked metaphorical ties between sweetness and ancestral language contribute to a naturalizing vision of the connection between Mauritian Hindus and Hindi.

A vision of an inherent link between Hindi and Hindu identity is repeatedly sketched by supporters of Hindi. When I asked Mr. Jeebun, a school inspector, why so many people still study Hindi today since they see little use for it professionally, he answered by posing a counterquestion. "Why should one learn French? English is the official language and French is not strictly necessary. But we love French and this is why we learn it. We are Hindus, and with Hindi we have reached the root of our culture *(hindi se hamari sanskriti ke jhar tak pahunce)*. There are many books in English on Hinduism, but it is not the same; you get further with Hindi. We learn French and English for our material development and Hindi for our spiritual development." Mr. Jeebun's final remark certainly indicates that there is much more at stake in learning French in Mauritius than love for the language. However, he is very clear on his assessment of the role of Hindi — for Hindus, cultivating it is indispensable for living their ancestral culture, because there is an inherent link between Hindi and the Hindu tradition, expressed in the metaphor of roots.[7] Also, in a manner recalling the discourse of early Indian nationalism (Chatterjee 1993), Mr. Jeebun formulates a language ideology portraying Hindu ancestral culture in Mauritius as inhabiting a spiritual realm that is juxtaposed to the material world of the West represented by English and French.

The generous support enjoyed by Hindi as an ancestral language with apparently little instrumental value is a source of pride for many Hindus in northern Mauritius. The valorization and support of Hindi by state or state-subsidized institutions is considered a just reversal of past injustices and a symbolic expression of the political rise of the Hindu community in Mauritius. Mr. Nundlall, a retiree in his late sixties who grew up in a village in the south of the island and worked in a government ministry, spoke of his school days: "At that time most of the teachers were Creoles and many of them preferred the children of the Franco-Mauritian and Creole estate employees to the Indian children. They made us feel that we were not as good, and they made fun of our culture and religion. Some did not really want to teach Indian students. There was even a teacher in a town nearby who smeared grease on the faces of Indian children, so they would not come back and he would not have to teach them. Now nothing like this could happen any more." Criticizing what he sees as a lack of interest in Hindi among the younger generation, he continued: "Earlier they [Creoles and Franco-Mauritians] looked down on our culture and language. But now we are in the government, and we are the majority. We struggled a long time for it, and now Hindi is respected and taught in almost all schools. But I think that young people do not appreciate this. They do not know the value because they have not seen how it is when you and your traditions are being looked down upon in the same way as I have when I was in school."

We can see here that the question of Hindi is mediated by the historical memory of oppression and discrimination of Indo-Mauritians during the colonial period. Also, the people most likely to voice such an interpretation of the role of Hindi — as a sign of compensation for past wrongs, especially with regard to questions of political power and the relationship of Hindus to the state — are precisely those who hold or have held positions in the Hindu-dominated state apparatus. For them, the status of Hindi is part of a historical narrative of redemption, which in turn provides a powerful legitimization for present-day Hindu political power in Mauritius.

Nevertheless, some residents of La Nicolière reject the idea of a necessary link between Hindi and Hindu identity. One secondary school teacher, for instance, mocked this notion. He and I were standing in front of the school in a nearby town with some of his colleagues during a morning break, and he pointed to his back: "There are some who have stuck a label here saying 'Hindu' and tell me that my language is Hindi. But I do not care and what I speak all day is Creole. So what is this business of Hindi about? It is only a matter of politics. It is all fake." Similarly, a neighbor curious about my interest in Hindi dutifully remarked in our first conversation that being Hindu, it was "of course" important for him to learn Hindi, and then changed the subject. During our next conversation some two weeks later, he pointed out that "we speak Creole because we are Mauritians, not Indians. And why spend a lot of time studying Hindi when you are not getting anything for it in return? There are no jobs to be had with Hindi. When my brother went to India two years ago he spoke English to the Indians all the time."

Hindu activists exhort Hindus to take pride in their ancestral language and not be ashamed to speak it in an environment strongly marked by the presence of francophone cultural traditions. The topic of shame comes up in various ways among the residents of La Nicolière, especially when taking stances with regard to Hindi that are not congruent with the promotion of Hindu ancestral languages. Raj, a young policeman, was also among those commending my selection of La Nicolière for my field research. "There is a lot of culture here," he remarked, by which he meant Hindu traditions such as the daily use of Bhojpuri, which he suggested were less in evidence in other parts of the island. "I did Hindi until

Form 5, School Certificate, only to know it a bit, because it is our language. But there is no *scope* for Hindi, no use for Hindi, no reason to learn Hindi. Only it is our language, one has to know it for not being ashamed, so nobody can bother me." Raj revealed that for him studying Hindi was a matter of external pressure, that he did it in order to avoid being looked down upon by fellow Hindus. At least with regard to schoolchildren I witnessed several times a public sanctioning of Hindu students in Hindi classes for their weak performance: "He is a Hindu but does not know Hindi. What is supposed to become of the country?" Another teacher disciplined a student in front of the class in a similar way: "You are a Hindu. Are you afraid to study Hindi? This is not good." But outside the classroom as well, young people occasionally had to worry about being accosted by seniors for their lack of competence in Hindi. On one of my visits to the home of Mr. Bissessur, who is a small planter, we briefly went out to make a purchase at the store around the corner, and when we returned one of his sons was in front of the house with a friend. Obviously motivated by my presence, Mr. Bissessur pointed to his son's friend saying, "Look, he is a Hindu but does not know Bhojpuri or Hindi." The accused looked somewhat embarrassed, smiled, and remained silent. When I spoke to Mr. Bissessur's son a few days after the incident, he said it was not the first time his father had addressed his friend in such a way. Yet, he pointed out, Hindi was of little use after all, and his friend did not take such shaming very seriously.

Some residents of rural northern Mauritius reject the activism for Hindi precisely because they believe it is ultimately linked to motives of economic gain. Such skepticism regarding the significance of the ancestral language is often combined with suspicion towards the politically well-connected organizations propagating Hindi. Senior officials in such bodies are often suspected of using their position to establish connections to politicians for the sake of personal profit. Some people described organizations such as the Mauritius Sanatan Dharma Temples Federation as "mafias" whose leaders are merely out for "business." A civil servant in a one of the towns in the island's central urban zone remarked: "Look at the car battery dealer next door. He got a lot of business when police trucks were sent there. It is useful to know Hindi and to speak in favor of Hindi because this may get you close to politicians. You can make a lot of profit." So, while some young Hindus say Hindi is useless, others consider it to have an instrumental value, which is mediated through Mauritian party politics and ethnic clientelism in which belonging to a Hindu ethnic group plays a central role. Government and other network benefits are sometimes believed to be the result of taking a public stance for Hindi.

Organized community life in La Nicolière revolves around three institutions: the *baithka*, the Telugu Hindu temple, and the local *shivala*, which functions as the Hindu temple patronized by most inhabitants. There is substantial overlap between membership in the associations *(sosiete)* running the *shivala* and the *baithka*, but membership in the Telugu temple association is confined to Hindus of Telugu background. All local associations are in turn members of corresponding national organizations that receive government subsidies that are partially used to support local Hindu associations. The *shivala* association falls under the domain of the Mauritius Sanatan Dharm Temples Federation, the Telugu temple association represents one of the local chapters of the Mauritius Andhra Maha Sabha, and the *baithka* is affiliated with the Hindi Pracharini Sabha.

Two of these village institutions are involved in the propagation of the ancestral language Hindi and one in teaching Telugu as an ancestral language. Hindus of Telugu background in La Nicolière have long ceased to use varieties of Telugu among themselves. As far as their linguistic routines are concerned, they are indistinguishable from their Hindu neighbors of north Indian background in practicing a Creole-Bhojpuri bilingualism that is in the process of language shift. However, they lay claim to a different ancestral language and also patronize a separate temple. Telugus also celebrate different religious holidays, such as Oogadi, and also engage in separate rituals of worship, such as Rambhajan, a veneration of the deity Ram involving singing devotional songs and lighting large multi-armed brass oil lamps supplied by the local association as *arti* (cf. Nirsimloo-Anenden 1990). Rambhajan, whether performed in the local temple or sponsored by a family and performed in a home, is emblematic for the particularity of Telugu Hindu ritual practice in Mauritius. However, Telugus being a small minority in Mauritius, the political stakes involved in the propagation of Telugu "ancestral culture" are less prominent than those connected to the celebration of the north Indian Hindu heritage.

The intersection of party politics and Hindu institutions in the village is a favorite topic of conversation on social occasions, such as visits to neighbors and family members and weddings. The *baithka*, for example, was run by a committee of members known for their loyalty to the MSM *(Mouvement Socialiste Mauricien)*,[8] and former Prime Minister Jugnauth of that party had paid a visit to the La Nicolière *baithka* some time before the 1995 general elections. People in La Nicolière often suspect that leaders of local Hindu organizations offer their political influence in their village to politicians running for office in return for financial or other business favors. For example, it is often assumed that these local leaders seek the attention of a senior politician to gain employment for family members or to import construction materials to sell or use in their own homes duty-free. The local *shivala* association, being under the umbrella of the nation-wide Mauritius Sanatan Dharm Temples Federation, is regarded as a local political ally of the party currently in power, and many expect its leadership to encourage members to vote for the current government. Being the head of a local temple association is widely considered an excellent position from which to seek election to the village council.

The kinds of pressure that leaders of these Hindu village organizations can exert on their fellow citizens are manifold. Vinod complained bitterly about a member of the *baithka* committee who had used his good connections to the MSM, then in power, not only to gain material favors for himself but also to pressure and cause difficulties for neighbors known for their sympathies to the Labor Party, then in the opposition. Since many Hindu men in La Nicolière are state employees of one kind or another, he would report on his neighbors to their superiors in an attempt to block their promotions and pay raises. Also, anyone wanting to build or enlarge a house must obtain a development permit from the district council. La Nicolière has twelve elected village councilors, one of whom is sent to the next administrative level up, the district council. Most people in La Nicolière feel they cannot afford to alienate the councilors, whose political allegiances are well-known, if they are in need of a development permit.

The links between the *shivala* and *baithka* committees and party politics are most visible during election time. Political candidates and those seeking re-election are mindful of the political influence that local Hindu organizations potentially have in rural and predominantly Hindu communities. In a nearby village, the tension was reported to have been particularly high during the 1995 national elections, when the MSM was defeated after thirteen years of rule and the Labor Party was brought to power (an MSM/MMM coalition came to power again in 2000). One village councilor, who helped the Labor Party in its campaign, had to remain barricaded in his home for a few days to protect himself from the MSM supporters of the local *baithka*.

Since promotion of the ancestral language Hindi among Hindus is one of the principal activities of local Hindu bodies like the *baithka*, which is explicitly dedicated to teaching Hindi, and since taking a stance for Hindi within local Hindu institutions can be read as a statement of political loyalty to particular political candidates and parties, Hindi is a politically relevant issue also at the local level. However, mobilizing local Hindu organizations for a political campaign and portraying oneself as a champion of the ancestral language does not guarantee success for a political actor. Trying to please the Hindu electorate, Jugnauth had campaigned for the inclusion of Hindi as a school subject in the ranking of the annual Certificate of Primary Education (CPE) examinations, which determine access to "good" secondary schools. Yet despite the support of the main Hindu organizations nationwide as well as local ones, such as the *baithka* in La Nicolière, Prime Minister Jugnauth and his MSM party were defeated at the 1995 elections. Whatever the actual electoral results of such political cooperation between candidates and local Hindu organizations are in the end, many people in La Nicolière are convinced of the strong connections between committee members of such bodies and political power. For some Hindus, this is an important point to take into account when taking a stand regarding what is supposed to be their ancestral language.

To sum up, Hindus in La Nicolière perceive Hindi as an institutionalized ancestral language to be a key element in Hindu ethnic identity in a variety of ways, but do not agree on the degree of importance of Hindi in this respect. Some even deny altogether the relevance of Hindi for claims to be Hindu. On the whole, the valuation of Hindi as an ancestral language is most pronounced among Hindi teachers, Hindu pandits, and other members of what might be called the Hindu state bourgeoisie in La Nicolière — people who make their living as modest to mid-ranking employees in state institutions. Although they rarely if ever use Hindi outside ritual contexts, they perceive it as an important emblem of Hindu political power in Mauritius and its recognition by the state in the form of an ancestral language as a long overdue compensation for past wrongs during the colonial period.

FINDING THE ANCESTRAL LANGUAGE
IN VERNACULAR PRACTICE

One of the salient features of Hindi activism among Hindus is that the ideology of Hindi as an ancestral language seems disconnected from the actual use of language in their daily lives. However, the plausibility of the relevance of Hindi for ethnolinguistic belonging is reinforced for many by stressing the assumed proximity between Bhojpuri and Hindi, thereby downplaying the disjuncture between routine practice and the cultivation of the ancestral language. In this respect, people in La Nicolière often distinguish between an "ordinary" kind of Bhojpuri, characterized by heavy mixing with Creole lexical items, and a purist form that avoids such recognizably Creole elements and is oriented towards a sanskritized Hindi vocabulary. People in La Nicolière often assert that "Bhojpuri has a large stomach," meaning that it "absorbs" many words from other languages, notably Creole. Like several of his fellow residents in La Nicolière, Suresh talks about everyday Bhojpuri as Bhojpuri *natirel*, which is different from the purist Bhojpuri-Hindi. The latter is closely associated if not downright conflated with Hindi. In a discussion triggered by my inquiries into what might become of Bhojpuri in the current situation of language shift, Suresh suggested that Bhojpuri is to Hindi what Creole is to French. During the course of my field research I heard this recursive logic (Irvine and Gal 2000) restated many times. It enables Mauritians to imagine the relation between these two pairs of languages as diglossic, one being the higher and ultimately "better" version of the other, despite what linguists say about the structural autonomy of Mauritian Creole and the considerable differences between Mauritian Bhojpuri and standard Hindi. According to this view, the relations structuring one of these two linguistic high-low "pairs" explain and illustrate the relations within the other. Ms. Ramdin commented that it was wrong to be so concerned about Bhojpuri, which is just a dialect, when what really mattered for the "survival of Hindu culture" in Mauritius was Hindi. "It is better to substitute bad Hindi with good Hindi," she argued, thereby implicitly subsuming Bhojpuri, whose eventual disappearance would not really constitute a major loss, under the larger category of Hindi.

Mahadev, a Hindi teacher, tacitly identified Bhojpuri with Hindi in a different way. Speaking of his two decades of work as a Hindi teacher in a primary school in a village five kilometers from La Nicolière, he stressed that his job has become progressively more difficult over the years. "Teaching Hindi to these students has become harder because they do not speak it at home any more." By assessing the implications of the language shift from Bhojpuri to Creole in Hindu homes, Mahadev portrays the Mauritian Bhojpuri, spoken less and less commonly in the

countryside around La Nicolière as the local form of Hindi, and its grad-
ual demise is making his task as a teacher of the ancestral language of the
Hindus more arduous.

Another Hindi teacher, Mr. Indranath, agreed with this pessimistic
assessment of the changes that have affected the instruction of Hindi in
Mauritian schools since the 1950s. Pointing through a window of his
home towards the street, he said: "Earlier, Hindi was spoken a lot, everywhere around here. One would walk up and down the entire street and
only hear a few words of Creole spoken. Today Creole is everywhere,
and Hindi is only studied to save the religion and culture *(dharm aur sanskriti bacheke khatir)*. Bhojpuri is the popular form of Hindi, and sadly,
it is fading away." The slippage between Bhojpuri and Hindi, or in Mr.
Indranath's view the subsumption of the former under the latter, enables
some people to conceive of the ancestral language as firmly rooted in
local linguistic practice. Mr. Indranath sees Hindi thus defined — as a
crucial element of what is considered Hindu ancestral culture — as threatened. Nevertheless, according to Ms. Ramdin's view, the possible demise
of the "dialect" Bhojpuri is no real cause for concern as long as Hindus
remain focused on protecting and cultivating Hindi in its standard form.
However, some people who assimilate Bhojpuri to Hindi also envision a
common fate for the two languages. As Mr. Jeebun, the school inspector,
put it: Bhojpuri and Hindi are close/similar to our religion or way of life
(bhojpuri aur hindi hamare dharm se mili juli hain). Here in Mauritius,
Bhojpuri and Hindi are becoming what Sanskrit is in India. Earlier, people in India spoke Sanskrit, and then they stopped speaking it at some
point of time. The same will happen to Bhojpuri and Hindi here." Along
with many other Indo-Mauritians, he expects the fate of the two languages to somehow go hand in hand, with Hindi continuing to be cultivated as an emblem of Hindu identity.

IMAGINING INDIA

Despite the status of India as the undisputed location of Hindu ancestral
culture, the perceptions of India featured in the creation of a sense of
Mauritian Hindu diasporic belonging are multiple and often contradictory, and observed linguistic and religious practices of Indians are far
from uncontested and authoritative models for Hindu Mauritians of how
they should practice and interpret such traditions. To start with, Hindus
in Mauritius are aware that the ancestral language they learn is quite
removed from the varieties of Hindi common in India. This was pointed

out to me by a Hindi teacher who stressed that the Hindi he was teaching to his students is "pure Hindi" *(shuddh Hindi)*, meaning highly sanskritized, unlike the Hindi in India, which he characterized as "mixed." This view is not at all confined to specialists in ancestral language, such as this Hindi teacher. People in La Nicolière are obviously very much aware that the language used in the Hindi-language movies from India watched so avidly in Mauritius is not the *shuddh Hindi* taught in Mauritian schools and Hindu institutions. In fact, the son of an Urdu teacher living in a village a few kilometers from La Nicolière pointed out with satisfaction that the language of the "Bollywood movies" and Indian television sitcoms consumed on a daily basis in rural northern Mauritius would be better described as Urdu than Hindi.

The view that not all Indians, even if Hindus, are shining examples of living ancestral linguistic traditions also applies to Indian spouses of Indo-Mauritians — overwhelmingly, women who have married Indo-Mauritian men studying in India and settled with them in Mauritius. As one Hindi activist in the Arya Sabha told me, "What future for Hindi can we expect here in Mauritius if even Hindi-speaking wives from India speak Creole to their children?" In all the cases I knew of, wives from India had very rapidly learned Creole and spoke Creole and sometimes even English to their children born in Mauritius. One neighbor's cousin had studied in Delhi and married Asha, a fellow student who was originally from Agra. Although I heard them sometimes switching from Creole to conversational (never *shuddh*) Hindi while talking to each other, Asha, also fluent in English, would speak Creole to her children. One evening at their home I asked her jokingly about her Bhojpuri, and she replied, *Ayo! Bhojpuri?* (Oh dear! Bhojpuri?), with a frowning expression on her face.

In contrast to people of Indian origin in other former indenture colonies, such as Guyana, Trinidad, and Fiji, immediate experience of the Indian land of the ancestors is quite accessible to many middle-class Indo-Mauritians. As of 2006, a minimum of ten nonstop flights a week link Mauritius with India, and at the time of my fieldwork roundtrip tickets for the six-hour flight to Mumbai sold for the equivalent of around $600. Numerous Indo-Mauritians have traveled to India to attend university, or for pilgrimage, business, shopping, or tourism, which are often combined. Sunil, who is employed in a government ministry, studied at the University of Baroda, while his brother, who works for a state-owned enterprise, obtained a degree from the University of Kanpur and married an Indian woman who was a fellow student there.

Both brothers had obtained scholarships for university study offered by the Government of India. Their sister Sushila obtained a Ph.D. in Hindi literature from Banaras Hindu University and follows a guru who resides in India, to whom she has visited repeatedly. Other family members have made trips to India on which they combined visits to Hindu pilgrimage sites across India with sightseeing and extensive shopping. Pictures from various visits fill several photo albums, and their home features many handicrafts and other souvenirs from India.

Despite the popularity of traveling to India, returnees often report ambiguous experiences. Exuberant accounts of visiting major Hindu pilgrimage sites and satisfaction at finding largely familiar and tasty food and extremely attractive shopping opportunities contrast with complaints about sanitary conditions and safety concerns. Instead of experiencing familiarity with the land of the ancestors, many Indo-Mauritians felt alienated by the confrontation with the "real" India.[9] "Now I know how different we live from the Indians," Mahadev says about the trip he had taken to India two years earlier. "In Delhi, we went to the cinema, and there were metal detectors at the door and people searching us. Imagine you are sitting in there in this cinema full of people and someone carries some dynamite in there. I was really afraid." Prem, a secondary school teacher, told about his colleague's stay in a north Indian city for further training. His colleague returned early because he could not stand the smell, dirt, and noise of the neighborhood he was staying in. Another neighbor described a bus trip he took in south India. The bus broke down in a forest in the middle of the night, and he was warned to staying close to the site because of wild animals. Rikesh, another resident of La Nicolière, described his arrival in Delhi on his first visit to India: "When we got out of the airport, it seemed as [if] I was unable to breathe because of the air pollution. All these crowds and many people sleeping on the street on gunny sacks. I immediately wanted to return home, but you slowly get used to it." I was sometimes struck by how Indo-Mauritians portrayed the India they visited as an exotic place, often combining themes of fascination and adventure with those of fear and disgust. Most Indo-Mauritian visitors to India I met were at pains to stress what they saw as vast differences between their Mauritian world and the aspects of India they had experienced, rather than developing the theme of communality and familiarity due to ancestral, cultural, and religious ties.

However, I never encountered anyone who, on the basis of such vast "rediscovered" differences, concluded that the ties to India were no longer meaningful. Visitors to India often reworked the emphasis on perceived differences into a more complex account of the relationship between Indo-Mauritians and Indians. Suresh, a civil servant, drew on a particular discourse of culture to accomplish this: "I am not Indian but I follow Indian culture. Our way of life is different — our clothes, our food, language, and way of thinking. Our culture in Mauritius is a mix, a *masala*. But the preserving of our religion is very strong; this is transmitted, and it is even stronger than in India." Here Suresh's perspective on the concept of culture is very much influenced by the official discourse on ancestral culture in Mauritius, which, as Suresh suggests, is understood to consist largely of religious traditions. Interestingly, however, while interpreting his encounter with India, Suresh employed this notion to mark boundaries rather than to stress the links between India and Indo-Mauritians. This is evident even in his assessment of religious traditions, which according to Suresh are more avidly "preserved" in Mauritius than in India.

Nevertheless, some who had traveled to India emphatically stressed sentiments of attachment to the India they had seen. When Sunil was in Delhi a few years preceding our conversation, he met a young man from Bihar who worked in the kitchen of the educational institution where Sunil had been sent for further training. Sunil shared: "Normally we don't say we are from Bihar, but because he told me, I said to him I am also from Bihar, and he became very emotional. Do you know what he said to me? *kaun janta hai, ho sakta hai ap hamare parivar se hain* (Who knows, maybe you are from our family). He said that right away — I believe you are family." While Sunil's description of arriving in India for the first time more than twenty years earlier for his college education — "I felt like coming home, like going back to the source of where my forefathers came" — was not very typical compared to those of others I spent many evenings with hearing about their travel or study experiences in India, several others also recalled their first arrival in India as a major moment in their life, often because they were the first person in their family to have set foot in India since the immigrant ancestors departed for Mauritius.

Some travelers were quite critical of other Indo-Mauritians who, as they saw it, focused excessively on the unpleasant aspects of their visit. Shankar, for example, pointed out the vast size and diversity of India, which defied any final judgment: "My first impression was the diversity there. In every different place I went to I found a new lifestyle, new food, way of dressing; it was, so to say, as if the world itself had changed. I felt like [I was] traveling through different countries." He went on distancing

himself from other Mauritians who had returned with a sense of
Mauritius being the better place:

> Everyone said be careful, watch your money, don't trust anyone, there are
> so many thieves and crooks, but I never had any of this there. Every time I
> go to India, I develop new contacts. I have made friends. India is a wonder
> I enjoy. . . . Mauritians have developed in their culture a tendency of being
> too European, a superiority complex. They think [we] are superior to
> Indians in our ways of eating, dressing, our lifestyle, because we have this
> European influence. We have a tendency to compare ourselves with this
> guy who sleeps in the street; we do not compare ourselves to this other
> class of people who are twice as educated as we are, richer, more refined,
> but we underestimate them.

Those who have gone to India repeatedly over a longer period of time
and those who have visited again years after they studied there also frequently remarked on the positive changes they saw, especially how
"developed" the large Indian cities have become. As Sunil put it: "The
poverty, the people sleeping and children begging in the street, they are
still there. But in Bombay there are so many new buildings and roads, new
cars, flyovers, and in Delhi there is now an underground train." This rel-
ativizes one of the principal themes of boundary-making in many Indo-
Mauritians' travel narratives — the widespread poverty and poor sanitary
conditions they witnessed in India — presenting India in a more attractive
light and as more suitable as a focus for ancestral identification.

Finally, many are attracted to the opportunities for higher education in
India, which are much more affordable for Mauritians than studying at
universities in Europe, Australia, or even South Africa, and the Government of India also offers the largest numbers of scholarships for Mauritians to study abroad. Several Indo-Mauritians also compared not only
the quality of education obtained but also the experience of being a student at Indian universities favorably to institutions of higher learning in
Mauritius. Mr. Ramlall, who studied at Panjab University in Chandi-
garh, fondly spoke of the welcome and sympathy he had received from
his teachers as a student of Indian background from Mauritius. He also
made the larger point that the opportunity to study at Indian universities
played a pivotal role in the formation of an Indo-Mauritian middle class
in a population the great majority of whom had until relatively recently
lived as laborers or small planters in the sugar industry: "India has made
a very big contribution to education in Mauritius. If the Indian government had not offered all these facilities to study there, our country, espe-

cially the people of Indian origin, the immigrants, the generations that came after them, would not have progressed so much." Mr. Ramlall also missed the "love for learning for its own sake" and the "challenging intellectual environment" he witnessed as a student in India. The fact that India is the most important foreign destination for higher education, enabling the kind of social mobility and middle-class standard of living that many Mauritians have recently come to expect, features as a counterweight to the widespread narrative representation of India as a backward country, above all marked by the poverty of many of its citizens.

At the well-maintained Mauritius immigration archives housed as national heritage at the Mahatma Gandhi Institute, many Indo-Mauritians are able to trace their immigrant ancestors. The immigration archives are a pleasant and up-to-date facility, contrasting markedly with the state of the National Archives, which are housed in a dilapidated former factory building in the industrial zone of Coromandel. In the immigration archives, Indo-Mauritians can readily obtain information about ancestors' names, date of arrival, place of birth, district of origin, and port of embarkation in India, and even declared caste identity. One prominent high-caste Hindu family in particular still maintains relations of intermarriage with members of their caste group in Bihar, from where their ancestors departed for Mauritius, but their case is quite exceptional. In the vicinity of La Nicolière I met only one person (whose grandfather had arrived in Mauritius around 1905) who had actually established contact with distant relatives living in India on the basis of archival information. He had gone to eastern Uttar Pradesh to see them. To many others, the thought of doing so was unappealing, or even just amusing, primarily because Indo-Mauritians are very much aware of the humble social background of the majority of indentured immigrants and are therefore doubtful about how any traceable distant relatives in India would be and what they might be doing today. As Ms. Rambhuruth, who obtained a college degree in India, put it pointedly while laughing about my question: "Imagine you are going to some town in Bihar and find out that your relatives are beggars at the train station." One evening at a neighbor's house in La Nicolière, I told about my visit earlier in the day to a retired schoolteacher of upper-middle-class background in Quatre Bornes who has employed an elderly Creole woman of humble background, Mireille, as a housekeeper for decades. As it turned out, Mireille was recently able to trace relatives on the neighboring French island of Réunion, and as a result one of her daughters is now married there and able to financially assist the rest of the family in Mauritius. My neighbor joked, "She has won the La Réunion lottery! If we did such a thing, going to Bihar to look for relatives — *ayo* (oh dear), poverty over poverty, I am not interested!" while everybody burst into laughter. Many Indo-Mauritians who are able to travel to India or pursue studies there prefer to maintain relationships and friendships, or even ties of inter-marriage, with Indians who they regard as their equals in wealth, educa-tion, and social status.

Also, these days, many Indo-Mauritians have firsthand experience with people from India in Mauritius. While the number of tourists from India is still relatively small, people in La Nicolière encounter some Indians through the garment industry. Although most of the foreign workers in the Mauritian garment industry are from China and Sri Lanka, Indians make up some of the imported work force, staying in Mauritius for a few years under special contracts for lower pay and longer work hours as compared to local employees. They usually live in poor housing provided by their employers, separate from the local Mauritian population.[10] People in La Nicolière often resent these Indians because of their willingness to work longer hours for lower wages than the locals, while looking down on them because of the kind of accom-modation they live in. Far from providing a model of ancestral authen-ticity, these Indians command little respect among people in La Nicolière.

A second group of Indians in Mauritius is small in number but well-known and highly visible to people in and around La Nicolière: Hindu pandits from India. It is easy to assume that this category of Indians, coming to Mauritius as religious experts, would be invested with consid-erable authority vis-à-vis local Hindu Mauritians in matters of ancestral traditions. In fact, some Indian pandits have come to Mauritius on invi-tation from Hindu societies who maintain links to Hindu organizations in India. For example, the pandit in residence at the Vishvanath Temple at Grand Bassin / Ganga Talao is from India, brought from Banaras to Mauritius by the Hindu Maha Sabha, the organization controlling most of the temples at this key Hindu pilgrimage site.

Hindu ritual specialists from India are also not uncommon in the rural north of Mauritius. Through the mediation of a former president of the Mauritius Sanatan Dharm Temples Federation, who lives in a village nearby, an Indian pandit from Panjab was brought to a town near La Nicolière in the mid-1990s. However, soon after his arrival, tension developed between the local pandit of the main *shivala* and his Indian colleague. As he was losing clients to the Panjabi ritual specialist, the local pandit begun to resent his presence and used his own influence to ensure that the pandit from India was banned from staying in the temple. The latter then became a guest in several households in the town, including Sunil's family, who had dense ties to India. The Panjabi pandit is said to have made a handsome profit during his stay selling clothes, other textiles, and *puja* utensils from India — an additional thorn in the side of the local pandit, since the latter also operated a small store selling Hindu ritual items. In 1998, the Indian pandit returned to Mauritius for an extended visit, again being hosted by a local family. Several people who commented on his repeated presence concluded that business was the real motivation of his trips to Mauritius.

On the other hand, several residents of the rural north of Mauritius are convinced that pandits from India are more competent and their knowledge is more authentic. Shankar, a major sugarcane planter of the area around La Nicolière, for example, has more confidence in the abilities of pandits from India:

> Pandits in Mauritius do not show people how to do *puja*, so they accept anything. For example, this morning I went to the temple [the temple on the street where he lives and where he is a prominent member of the temple committee, and where a pandit from India lives] I bought a coconut. But the coconut normally has 'three eyes,' and the pandit opens them. But the pandit there who is from India, he says that this coconut is not good, you cannot do *puja* with it, it has to be covered with its fiber like this. Why? He explains that the coconut represents Shiv, like Shiv has three eyes. Normally Shiv does not open his eyes, if he opens them he is a destroyer, he is angry, it has to be covered. The pandits from there, they are better informed, they know everything. There are some things in Mauritius we do out of ignorance, by habit. Fortunately, the pandits from India explain it. For example, a pandit asked me, where in the whole world do you see Mahabir Swami outside the house? Here. But in India, go and look whether you will see a Mahabir Swami outside anyone's home, you do not see it there at all. Mauritians invented it.

For Shankar there is little question about the superior authority of Indian pandits, while practices particular to the diaspora, such as the ubiquitous small shelters in front of Hindu homes marked by red triangular flags on bamboo poles with a *murti* of the deity Hanuman-Mahabir Swami inside, are a sign of deviation and ignorance if it can be demonstrated that they are not as common in India.

Yet many people in the rural north of Mauritius have ambivalent views about pandits from India in their communities. On the one hand, they are willing to engage their services and appreciate their expertise, and some even host them in their homes. On the other hand, they suspect that the Indian pandits' ultimate motive for staying in Mauritius is the good money they appear to be making. What some Hindus in the north of the island view as an undue preoccupation with the accumulation of material wealth certainly does undermine the status of Indian pandits as representatives of authentic ancestral heritage, which in the minds of many is aligned with spiritual and ethical values opposed to the self-interested striving for material gain.

Such skepticism vis-à-vis the practices of Indian pandits turns into widespread rejection among their Hindu-Mauritian colleagues. While several people in La Nicolière quickly explained this antagonism as a matter of economic competition, some local pandits question the authenticity and appropriateness of the ritual practices Indian pandits are introducing. For example, high castes in Mauritius, the Babuji-Maraz (corresponding to the Brahmin and Kshatriya *varna*s) perform an extra ceremony known as *tilak* before weddings. This consists of a visit by members of the bride's family to the house of the bridegroom during which the brother of the bride presents the bridegroom with gifts, principally clothes and a sum of cash, up to 1,000 Mauritian rupees, in a brass vessel *(lota)* (see also Hollup 1994, 302). Yet some Indian pandits in Mauritius have stated that the *tilak* is not necessary for anyone. A Mauritian pandit of high-caste background who describes himself as a "full-time spiritual advisor" (using the English term) expressed the conflict in the following way: "The Indian pandits have become a real problem. They preach differently and conduct different rituals, and even say that what we Mauritian pandits do is incorrect. We really have to work against this, because we follow the principles of *lok achar, kul achar,* and *desh achar* [customs of the people, customs of the descent group, and customs of the country]. Every country has its particularities in ritual, and what is valid in India does not need to be correct here." The local pandit undermines the Indian pandits' claims of superior authenticity for their practices by pointing to the particularities of Mauritians and their supposedly different needs, while not denying his own link to ancestral authority. Similar to the case of travel experiences in India, for the local pandit the confrontation with Indians leads to the "discovery" of and emphasis on the perceived differences between Indians and Indo-Mauritians.

Finally, high-caste Hindu religious specialists such as the pandit just quoted resent the role Indian pandits have played in opening up to persons of non-high-caste background official recognition to practice as a pandit in a registered temple that receives government subsidies. Members of the mid-ranking and politically and numerically dominant Vaish caste had long opposed the monopoly of the Babuji-Maraz over the official priesthood among "orthodox" Sanatanis (as opposed to the followers of the Arya Samaj) in Mauritius, which the latter previously enforced by their control over the Mauritius Sanatan Dharm Temples Federation. Already in the 1970s a few Indian pandits were active in Mauritius, training Hindus of Vaish background for the priesthood, and one of them was even deported by the government of Seewoosagur Ramgoolam, which was widely reputed to favor Hindus of Babuji-Maraz background in government positions. However, the subsequent government of Anerood Jugnauth, who took power in 1982, lost interest in protecting the monopoly of the Babuji-Maraz over orthodox Hindu priesthood and in 1986 did nothing to prevent a "coup" within the Mauritius Sanatan Dharm Temples Federation. Vaish members took over control from Babuji-Maraz leaders and removed the caste bars to priesthood. After the "coup," pandits from India initially played an important role in the training of pandits of Vaish background. During that period, for example, a man who eventually became the pandit at one of the two main *shivalas* in Rivière-du-Rempart, underwent a three-year training course by the Mauritius Sanatan Dharm Temples Federation. This course of one day per week was conducted by an *acharya* from India, and the certificate obtained at the end of the course authorizing the trainees as pandits was issued by the Devani Parishad in Delhi. However, the pandits from India were resented as troublemakers by the established Mauritian pandits.

Far from constituting a universally respected and authoritative presence as far as Hindu ancestral traditions are concerned, Indian pandits in Mauritius, while gaining the following of some local Hindus, have provoked ambiguous attitudes and even hostility in a few Hindu Mauritians. Rather than uniting local Hindus behind an authentic model of living ancestral traditions, their authority is often questioned as they have been drawn into internal debates about religious authority among Hindus in Mauritius.

ANCESTRAL CULTURE AND ETHNIC OTHERS

The importance many Hindus in rural north Mauritius attach to what they consider ancestral traditions shapes their self-image in the multiethnic society of Mauritius while also tending to both create and draw upon stereotypes of ethnic others. As mentioned before, Mauritian Hindus regard the recent history of their community as one of rapid and sometimes spectacular upward social mobility, and they are proudly aware of "their" community's dominant position in Mauritian politics and in most state institutions. Because the time before independence is remembered as one of economic hardship, political marginalization, and inadequate representation in state institutions, the recent changes are felt to be all the more striking. In the view of many Hindu-Mauritians, the themes of economic transformation and the development of Hindu political power combine to constitute a powerfully redemptive narrative of the "rise" of the Hindus in Mauritius.

Known as the largest ethnoreligious community of Mauritius, and cultivating a social memory of the sufferings of the colonial period, many Hindus think their group's political preeminence in contemporary Mauritius is entirely legitimate. Moreover, many rural Hindus in north Mauritius offer an explanation for the rise of their community that resonates with ideologies of ancestral culture. According to this view, Hindus in Mauritius have in the end been redeemed by their steadfast attachment to ancestral traditions and values, which are responsible for their economic success and climb upward from a previously inferior position in the political system. These ancestral traditions are also imagined to be a source of legitimate political power, besides being primarily responsible for the differences many Hindus perceive between themselves and other Mauritians.

That is, the importance of what is perceived as ancestral culture is linked to historical memory as a form of collective remembering (Wertsch 2002). Pandit Mohabeer's father vividly recalls the colonial period and the time around the Second World War when he was a young man: "We were very poor and I was working in road construction. One day, I still remember it, a white overseer kicked me with his foot. These were bad times, there was misery and oppression. We were not allowed to vote, even though we are the majority." Sitting in the well-furnished living room of his son's house, he emphasized the positive changes that happened after independence, especially that "we are now in the government." The memory of the Hindu electorate voting overwhelmingly for independence in the last elections under colonial rule in 1967, in opposition to voters from all other communities, who were overwhelmingly against decolonization and in favor of a continued association with Great Britain, is also turned into a legitimatization of current Hindu dominance over the state apparatus.[11] Hindu political power is not the only current compensation for past wrongs; the respect and official valorization that Hindu ancestral traditions now enjoy is weighed in a similar way. "I was sitting in the train reading a Hindi book," Indranath told me, relating an event from pre-independence days to make clear how drastically the prestige of "Indian things" has increased compared to those times. (Mauritius had a railway network until the 1950s.) "The other people in the compartment were *endyen* too, but when a Christian couple also entered the compartment, they quickly gestured to me to close and put away the book." In particular, older rural Hindus' memories of trips during their youth to Port Louis or other towns are sometimes associated with humiliating experiences. Members of the politically and economically dominant groups at the time, the Franco-Mauritians and middle-class Creoles, are remembered for their hostile stares and disparaging remarks about the *malbar bitasyon* ("estate barracks Indians," *malbar* being an ethnic slur directed against Hindus). This was especially the case if one wore Indian clothes, treated one's hair with coconut oil, or spoke Bhojpuri. Against this history, state support for celebrating official Hindu ancestral culture, including the ancestral language, Hindi, is considered an entirely justified compensation.

Many Hindus, whether urban or rural, draw a link between the recent social mobility and increasing prosperity of the north Mauritian countryside and Hindu ancestral traditions by pointing to a particular economic ethos as responsible for the rise of the Hindu community. An image of a Hindu propensity for thrift, sacrifice, and home ownership is not infrequently constructed and then illustrated by contrasting it with its perceived opposite, a negative image of Creole social and economic behavior. As Vijay, a civil servant, put it: "Our ancestors worked very hard, and even though they were very poor. Little by little they managed to save some money to buy land or to send their children to school. Among ourselves, somebody who does not work and save and own his own house, *dernye kategori dimun sa* (these are the lowest types of people). But not for the Creoles. For them, having nice furniture, clothes, and a stereo are more important. They do not care whether they live as renters." He laughs. "For us it is like this: When a father wants his daughter to marry, he first looks if the boy has a steady job and a house, and then he looks at the background of his family." Vijay's cousin Suren attributes what he sees as the superiority of a Hindu lifestyle over Creole ways to the different origins and traditions of these two groups: "The Creoles are Africans, and they do not like to work or think about the future, and they are above all interested in music." Alluding to the public housing projects, or *cités*, mostly located in the urban zone of Mauritius and associated with the mostly poor Creoles living there (though some residents are actually from other communities, including Hindu), he points out that "this is why our government has to take care of them and provide them with a place to live."

Ramoo, who is a Hindu Tamil in his late forties and lives in Rose-Hill, talks about the changes in the relations between Creoles and Tamils of Christian background, who are often considered part of the Creole community by Hindus and Hindu Tamils:

> During my childhood in Rose Hill, before independence, I remember the Hindus, the *endyen*s, and we, the *tamul*s, were at the very bottom. One of our neighbors was Christian, and my father always addressed him with *Missye*, but he always called my father using his last name only, even though at work his rank was below my father. People looked down on us *tamul*s and the *endyen*s. Today things have changed. Christian Tamil girls now marry Hindu Tamils and see it as a step upwards. Their own families have no money and no education. Men have no work, drink at the *butik*, and borrow money from you. Then the girls see what kind of respect *endyen* women enjoy. The girls move up and join the Indian mainstream.

However, some people in La Nicolière differentiate between urban Creoles, who they see as mostly living in *cités* and certain poor suburbs of Port Louis such as Roche-Bois, and the Creole families living in their community. Although there is little socializing between the few Creoles living in La Nicolière and local Hindus, the latter generally consider the Creoles good neighbors and different from the urban Creoles. One Creole man was even popular enough to be elected to the village council of this overwhelmingly Hindu locality. While some neighbors considered this evidence of their tolerance towards ethnic others, stressing that it showed they had nothing against Creoles, they also figured that there were few tensions with the local Creoles because the latter were influenced by living in a predominantly Hindu environment. Several residents of La Nicolière noted with approval that the family of the Creole village councilor would decorate their home with strings of electric lights on the festival of Divali, in the manner of their Hindu neighbors. A lawyer who is active in a Hindu organization in a nearby town holds the Creoles' African heritage responsible for what many Mauritians call *misère Creole* and their perceived lack of economic achievement compared to other ethnic groups, including Hindus. The local Creoles he knows, however, are different. "If they live in another environment, like here, it is good for them and they can live decently. They have work, and their houses. But the Creoles in the *cités* — forget it."

However, according to some, this imagined relationship of interethnic influences can also work inversely. One day when one of the larger Hindu landowners in the area took me to see some of his sugarcane fields several kilometers away, we passed a small village on the coast mainly inhabited by Creoles who worked as fishermen or were employed in the extraction of sand from the lagoon. Driving slowly in his air-conditioned late-model Toyota 4x4 truck,[12] he pointed at what he considered the negative aspects of the local social life. "See how they live here. They are always on the street, drinking. Some of them have affairs with the wives of others and there are a lot of fights here. There are also bastards and squatters, who later got the land from the state. The Hindus who live here are also affected by this lifestyle." He suggests that the Creoles of this coastal village lead a lifestyle opposed to what he sees as appropriate for Hindus, and that Hindus risk being influenced accordingly by their Creole neighbors. Moreover, he criticizes the Creoles of this particular locality not just for their supposed idleness and wrong spending patterns. In his view, they also lack family cohesion and sexual morality, which are also important features of what Hindus in Mauritius see as their ancestral heritage.[13]

Creating a Hindu group identity by drawing on presumed features of Hindu ancestral traditions often involves moral discourses about having superior economic and family ethics as compared to those of other groups. Moreover, people in La Nicolière do not think that the propensity for social and economic achievement made possible through the Hindu cultural ethos is limited to Hindus in Mauritius. They eagerly seize on examples of Hindu achievement in India or Western countries to vindicate the positive characteristics of their self-image vis-à-vis other groups in Mauritius. For example, in September 1998, the visit of Lord Meghnad Desai, economist, member of the British House of Lords, and Director of the Center for Global Governance at the London School of Economics, was widely covered on state-run television. For people in La Nicolière who followed the event, the fact that he was Indian and Hindu was by far the most noteworthy aspect of Desai's visit, and prompted expressions of pride among them. They were very impressed by this example of a Hindu having attained such a preeminent and prestigious position even in a European country, all the more, the country that had ruled Mauritius until 1968. Sitting in front of the television, one of the neighbors contrasted this instance of what he considered a specifically "Hindu success" with what he saw as the typical Creole lifestyle in Mauritius. "They [Creoles] just want to party and have fun *(maja karo)*, and they will not able to get where he [Desai] is the way they live." The powerful image of the stellar professional career of a Hindu in Britain was recontextualized to reproduce ethnic boundaries, using the Hindu visitor from Britain as an example for distinguishing the superior moral characteristics possessed by Hindus in contrast to Creoles in Mauritius.

However, Creoles certainly do not represent the only ethnic other for rural Hindus in north Mauritius. In comparison to other former indenture colonies, where tensions between people of Indian origin and people of a non-Indian ethnic group, such as Afro-Creoles in the Caribbean or indigenous Fijians in Fiji are often prominent, in Mauritius the internal Indo-Mauritian antagonisms appear to be more important for the construction of ethnic boundaries and images.[14] Thus Hindus in La Nicolière define what they consider the essential characteristics of their ancestral traditions in contrast to those of Muslims of Indian origin. Even though in the past most Muslims and Hindus in Mauritius largely shared similar experiences of indenture and originated from the same districts of India, nowadays many Hindus, while thinking of themselves as tolerant and striving to live in harmony with all other ethnic groups in Mauritius, often stereotype Muslims as "fanatic."

One theme brought up many times in the conversations I had with Hindus was a comparison of the way Muslims and Hindus engage with ancestral traditions. This was framed in terms of a perceived Hindu weakness vis-à-vis a smaller but presumably better organized and more unified Muslim community. As the principal of a secondary school in eastern Mauritius put it:

> There is racial harmony and peace in Mauritius because Hindus are so patient and long-suffering. They never rebel, like the Muslims. Once there was an article in a newspaper about the prophet Mohammad, which the Muslims did not like. The same day there was a huge demonstration in Port Louis and they attacked the office of the paper.[15] You can do anything to the Hindus but they do not rebel. It is the same in India; look at what is happening in Kashmir. It has to be our culture. Muslims are much better organized, because in the mosque people not only pray together but they can also be organized for politics. When we pray and worship, we do it at home, or we just do *puja* in the temple and there are no political speeches. Only the Arya Samajis used to do something similar, but since the 1960s and 1970s they have also started to go to temples.

In this view, the perceived weakness of Hindus is seen as a threat, yet the peacefulness and tolerance that supposedly distinguishes Hindus from Muslims also legitimates their political dominance in Mauritius and their hold on the civil service.[16] In a similar vein, two civil servants told me how offended they were by the title of a well-known English language novel by the South African–born Mauritian writer Lindsay Collen, *The Rape of Sita,* yet they also took this as an opportunity to take credit for the positive effects of the large Hindu presence in Mauritius. Commenting on the fact that the book has not been banned and that there were no large-scale protests against it, one of them pointed out that "we Hindus are tolerant, after all, and this is why everything is peaceful here and Mauritius has developed so well." Such narratives and comments serve to construct a vision of Mauritius in which Hindus emerge as ideal citizens and members of the nation, while the claims of ethnic others to a central position in the nation are delegitimized — for instance, by pointing to the supposedly deficient work ethic of Creoles or the presumably intolerant spirit of Muslims.

One remarkable aspect of these instances of identity construction by contrast with an ethnic other is that personal experience in Mauritius is sometimes related to perceptions of Hindu-Muslim relations in India, as evident in the comment concerning Kashmir quoted earlier. When the largely Muslim supporters of the Scouts soccer team allegedly set fire to sugarcane fields around the main sports stadium in the north of the island, located not too far away from La Nicolière, after a major match, a young Hindu man from a nearby village commented on these events in a way in terms of political events in India. Referring to Muslims from the Port Louis neighborhood of Plaine Verte, who reputedly form the backbone of the soccer team's fans, he said: "They are a really savage 'race'/community *(sa ras la zot mari sovaz)*," adding that "this has to do with their religion."[17] He then drew a connection with India: "Muslims always cause problems in India, too, Hindus cannot live in Kashmir any more, but Muslims from Kashmir are everywhere in India." Some people when defining Hindus as tolerant and Muslims as fanatics refer to events in India only and do not draw on Mauritian Muslims or events in Mauritius as evidence at all. One high-ranking member of a Hindu organization not normally known for *hindutva* ties who was living in a town close by remarked to me: "Hindus are tolerant, indifferent, and disunited, but Muslims are spreading everywhere in the world. In Bombay Muslims have caused so much trouble, but now the Shiv Sena has done something and the Muslims are quiet." From such a perspective, Hindu-Muslim riots in India, even those of 1992–1993 after the destruction of the Babri Masjid in Ayodhya by Hindu nationalists, which in Bombay turned into deadly pogroms against Muslims, are made relevant in assessing differences between Hindus and Muslims in Mauritius as a matter of tolerance versus fanaticism.

Hindu nationalist interpretations of the history of India and the role of Muslims in it are well-known among Hindus in northern Mauritius, and they sometimes color the perceptions of local Muslims. According to Hindu nationalist historiography, a pre-Islamic golden age in an essentially Hindu India was brought to a cruel end during the Middle Ages by Muslim conquerors, under whose rule India declined and Hindus were brutally oppressed. If it had not been for the arrival of Islam and the presence of Muslims in India, the country would have maintained its greatness and splendor.[18] A sugarcane planter from a village near La Nicolière, for example, thought that Muslims in Mauritius were dangerous because "the entire drug trade in Mauritius is controlled by them. If you go to Plaine Verte you will see what I mean." He then drew a link to Indian history, saying that Muslims had also ruined India; before the Muslims' arrival in India, Afghanistan and Burma had belonged to India, but Muslim "pirates" had destroyed India's trade. The planter said that he had studied the history of India by reading a book in Hindi, *Bharatvarṣ kā itihās* (History of India) given to him years ago by his Hindi teacher in the *baithka* of the village where he grew up. The Hindi teacher, who presumably had helped him study this book, in turn had been trained by the Hindu activist and missionary Basdeo Bissoondoyal, who had established a large number of Hindi schools throughout the island in the 1940s and 1950s. The two-volume *Bharatvarṣ kā itihās*, published by Arya Samaj educator and activist Ramdev in 1910 and 1914, is one of the earlier classical Hindu nationalist treatises redefining the Indian past from an anti-Muslim perspective (Fischer-Tiné 2003).

Such negative rhetoric about Muslims, which often exceeds the stereotyping of Creoles in degrees of suspicion expressed, is nearly always directed at an impersonal, undifferentiated Muslim other, and rarely against those Muslims known personally as colleagues at work or neighbors. Gyan, a secondary school teacher living in La Nicolière, was on very good terms with Salim, a Muslim colleague, and repeatedly spoke of him as "a good friend" *(en bon kamerad)*. Also, at his sister's daughter's wedding in another village of the north, he saw Muslim neighbors helping in the preparations, carrying chairs and tables and preparing some of the food. The large rented tent pitched to shelter the many guests was reaching across into the neighbor's lot. The next day, during the main rituals, the crowd under the tent was visibly diminishing as many of the male guests gathered at a *butik* down the street drinking whiskey and rum, while the women had continued to attend. Commenting on this, one of the uncles of the bride said jokingly, "They just went to the 'other temple,'" making a drinking movement with his hand, and then continued, "We Hindus are liberal, see, many people are not attending temples and ceremonies. Not like the Muslims, who are fanatics and all go to the mosque together." However, he commented that the Muslim neighbors next door who had helped with the wedding were friendly and open-minded.

Nevertheless, when personal conflicts between Hindus and Muslims do arise, they are readily recontextualized into the rhetoric of ethnic stereotyping. A health officer at a local hospital who teaches Hindi to primary school students in a *baithka* on Sundays told me how dissatisfied he was with his job. He was looking for other work and attributed the difficulties at his workplace to the differences he had with a particular Muslim superior. "In Mauritius when Hindus and Muslims work together, there are always problems. Muslims stick together and try to dominate Hindus." The difficulties at work were explained by recourse to ethnic stereotypes, without much consideration of the particularities of the situation and the persons involved. Similarly, Sitaram, who works in a government ministry in the capital, made the following observation regarding the relations between Hindu and Muslim colleagues: "If there is only one Muslim in an office, everything is fine. He will be nice and a good *kamerad*. But if there is just one more Muslim coming in, the two will join and form a power center. A Muslim will be friendly to you on the surface, but in the end they always stick together and work against you."

The image of debilitating disunity among Hindus in contrast to a presumed Muslim group unity and coherence is built on the acute awareness of caste and sectarian differences among Hindus in Mauritius, but denies the existence of similar divisions among Mauritian Muslims. While there is some recognition of the vast differences between the Muslim Gujarati trading communities in Mauritius and Muslims of indenture background, Hindus (and non-Muslim Mauritians in general) are largely unaware of the marked antagonism between supporters of different South Asian Sunni traditions in Mauritius, especially the Barelwi and Deobandi schools (Eisenlohr 2006a, 2006b), and very rarely know about the sectarian differences between Sunni and Shi'ite groups in Mauritius (the latter are Musta'li Ismaeli Bohras—a Bohra family who owns the biggest non-Franco-Mauritian controlled business enterprise on the island—and Shia Khoja Ithna 'Ashari). One Hindu neighbor said he had heard that Muslims also had internal disputes and that the presence of more than one mosque in numerous villages across Mauritius was related to religious divisions among Muslims. However, alluding to the importance of caste categories and rivalry among Hindus for Mauritian party and electoral politics, he concluded: "But it is not the same as with us Hindus. You can read about our problems and divisions every day in the newspaper."

Some Hindus also generalize about the differences between the economic ethos they see as embedded in their own ancestral heritage and the ways they perceive Muslims organizing their livelihoods. Since the early 1980s, numerous Muslims, considering themselves victims of discrimination in the Hindu-dominated state institutions and civil service, have opted for establishing private businesses, especially in the import-export and retail sectors.[19] Several Muslim families of indenture background have prospered considerably in these ventures, clearly having obtained wealth beyond the reach of even the more senior civil servants. Yet many Hindus, used to the economic dominance and great wealth of a small number of Franco-Mauritian families in Mauritius, are uncomfortable with the recent prosperity of some local Muslim families. Not always accepting the legitimacy of their success in business, some even suspect that such profits in private ventures were obtained through illegal means, such as incorrect customs declarations of imported goods. They apparently feel left behind and fear the possibility of their Muslim neighbors gaining greater economic power than themselves. Anil explained the differences between Hindus and Muslims in the economic field in the following way: "For Hindus a good post with the government has more prestige than business. *endu li kontan so ti travay kot guvernman* (the Hindu likes his little post with the government). He does not like to take risks. He buys a house and land and pays it back little by little with his secure salary. But he would never take a large loan for business like the Muslims do. Many Hindus are in the small retail business now and have shops, but most of them are for additional income and are not real, important businesses." Here Anil paints a rather positive image of Hindu economic strategies, but at the same time voices uncertainty about whether what he describes as the Hindu economic ethos is really the most successful path to economic success.

However, other Hindus in rural northern Mauritius are less committed to emphasizing sharp contrasts between themselves and ethnic others by drawing on exclusive ancestral traditions. Followers of Sai Baba, a neo-Hindu movement that is also very active in Western countries and has numerous followers in Europe and North America, see themselves as not identifying with a particular official ancestral culture but instead engaged in a "universal" form of worship, potentially open to anyone, in which Westerners also participate. A town near La Nicolière has a temple and center of worship where *satsang* gatherings are held, which include the singing of *bhajan*s and *puja* before images of Satya Sai Baba. Devotees place great emphasis on the miracles attributed to Sai Baba. One civil servant, who attends *satsang* regularly, told how a child in Rivière-du-Rempart, severely ill with cancer, was miraculously cured by the intervention of Sai Baba. Followers of Sai Baba, although clearly drawing on a wide array of Hindu imagery and traditions in their practices of worship, are less likely to describe themselves as Hindus in opposition to Creoles and Muslims.[20] Ms. Dayal, a regular devotee, explained that she disliked the entanglement of the local *shivala* she had patronized before in local politics and caste-based rivalry. The latter was especially important for her since she, being of Vaish background, had married a man of low-caste origin. She felt that fellow worshippers in the Vaish-dominated *shivala* had stopped respecting her, whereas caste background was not an issue among Sai Baba devotees. Sitting in the local Sai Baba community center, she pointed out how all the devotees sit in orderly rows to chant *bhajan*s. "If a minister comes here, it does not matter, they are all equal. But in the *shivala* they would all run after him. There is too much politics." While Ms. Dayal's representation of the community center as a politics-free space is reminiscent of ideologies of religious authenticity based on a putative separation of the spiritual from the political, her point that followers of Sai Baba in rural northern Mauritius are much less part of the institutional nexus of party politics, with their caste and patronage dimensions, state institutions, and the official promotion of Hindu ancestral culture, is important.

Followers of Sai Baba in northern Mauritius are often of a middle-class background with high levels of education. At a *kirtan,* a worship session of singing Hindi *bhajan*s, led by a Sai Baba pandit at a neighbor's relative's home in Rivière-du-Rempart on the occasion of a son of the family's departure for college studies in Britain, the pandit's exclusive use of Creole was one of the most striking features. Devotees of Sai Baba, though they are overwhelmingly of Hindu background and engage in ritual practices in which chanting Hindi *bhajan*s is a central part, place little importance on the cultivation of Hindi as an ancestral language since they view it as unnecessarily dividing them from other potential devotees. However, there is no clear boundary between followers of Sai Baba in rural northern Mauritius and other Hindus because some followers of

Sai Baba also patronize Hindu *shivala*s where they live, and nowadays the worship of images of Sai Baba is also accepted in many *shivala*s throughout Mauritius.[21]

In this chapter I have offered an ethnographic description of how ideas about ancestral traditions among Hindus in rural northern Mauritius contribute to the everyday practices of historical memory, diasporic relations, and the production of ethnicity. Ancestral language as a key element in what is locally understood to be ancestral culture provides a crucial link between these different dimensions of identity production and debates about what it means to be a Hindu in Mauritius. In the following chapter I examine some of these practices as they shape and rework the sense of a diasporic community, including cultivation of a particular historical memory, reproduction of ethnic stereotypes, and engagement with India and people from India, from the vantage point of linguistic performance. Drawing on an understanding of performance as a creative force in social life, I take a closer look at how the shaping of ethnic and diasporic belonging is mediated by linguistic difference.

CHAPTER 3

Social Semiotics of Language

Shifting Registers, Narrative, and Performance

Hindu Mauritians make use of a wide repertoire of registers and styles of language in order to construct and inhabit interactional stances and claim ethnic and diasporic identities, which raises the issue of performance and its role in establishing social relationships and distinctions.[1] Building on John Austin's theory of performance, Judith Butler (1990) has conceptualized social identities as created and reproduced through acts of performance, which in turn depend on the citationality of conventional signs recognized by others. Focusing on these qualities of performance, in this chapter I explore the multiple ways in which Hindu Mauritians both construct and align themselves to modes of belonging through linguistic performance, making use of a wide array of linguistic and other semiotic resources while doing so. The interactions I discuss touch upon the power of acts of performance in creating and claiming identities, which has been the focus of attention from a variety of disciplinary perspectives, such as anthropology, gender studies, and philosophy. A key theme in these approaches is the performative production of interactional stances and social identities based on what Derrida has called the iterability of language (Butler 1997, Derrida 1991), that is, the potentially limitless replication of meaningful signs by others. Predating gender theory's interest in linguistic performance, semiotics and linguistic anthropology have described this double quality of the performativity inherent in linguistic practice in terms of a presupposed versus a creative or entailing indexicality (Silverstein 1976). Presupposed indexicality in linguistic performance, that is, the expected co-occurrence of particular linguistic signs with certain social relationships, stances, or identities, describes the condition of possibility for the meaningful replication and recognition of acts of signification, whether in linguistic or other modes of cultural practice. For example, in using honorific pronouns of address, such as French *vous,* presupposed knowledge about the relationship indexed between speaker and addressee by using *vous* rather than *tu* is required for use of this pair of second-person pronouns of address to be meaningful. However, the repeated performance of these acts of address can also break with presupposed notions of co-occurrence of linguistic signs and social identities and relationships, such as by shifting from the respect-indicating to the familiarity-indicating pronoun of address, or vice versa, in the course of an interaction (Friedrich 1972). Such creative uses of indexicality effectively transform social relationships and identities within the framework of the interaction, though this function is dependent on the availability of knowledge about presupposed uses of these pronouns of address.

Thus, the construction of identities and situational stances through linguistic performance is necessarily based on the recognizable replication of culturally meaningful signs indexing particular social values and modes of belonging. The signs I pay attention to in this chapter are the different linguistic varieties and registers linked to social and cultural values and forms of identification that are part of the linguistic repertoire of rural Hindu Mauritians. While the use of these linguistic resources is embedded in presupposed ideas of expected co-occurrence of certain forms of linguistic variation and the interactional stances and social identities claimed, Hindu Mauritians at the same time often employ them in creative and innovative ways. In other words, the citationality of indexical signs with their presupposed values enables the creation of new stances and identities in new contexts of performance. This is because identities, such as diasporic forms of belonging among Hindu Mauritians, are not necessarily preexisting entities expressed in linguistic interaction but rather emerge as the effect of linguistic practices. "Indeed to understand identity as a *practice,* and as a signifying practice, is to understand culturally intelligible subjects as the resulting effects of a rule-bound discourse that inserts itself in the pervasive and mundane signifying acts of linguistic life" (Butler 1990, 145). Such performative drawing on linguistic resources can also result in particular effects of "stylization," that is, the production of stances and identifications not normally associated with the acting subjects in question (Coupland 2001, Rampton 1999). My goal in this chapter is to closely examine signifying practices among Hindu Mauritians, showing how they are grounded in presupposed indexical values attributed to linguistic varieties and registers, yet at the same time can be creatively redeployed to reinforce or subvert claims of diasporic identity.

Finally, while explaining how linguistic registers index and create social identities in Mauritius, it is useful to draw a parallel with Mikhail Bakhtin's concept of voicing in literary language. In his analysis of the realist novel, Bakhtin explains voicing as the way in which the narrator represents and positions the characters in relation to the narrating world of the text (Bakhtin 1981). The indexical component of language that links forms of speech with socio-cultural valuations can be understood as functioning in an analogous manner. Thus Bakhtin's model can be fruitfully applied to the analysis of social worlds of discursive interaction, which can be understood as polyphonic in the sense that participants in linguistic interaction draw on a narrated world of cultural values and social voices. Subjects in social interaction draw upon cultural values and social images through linguistic practice, that is, they use language in order to position identities and interests vis-à-vis cultural and social values. Bakhtinian voicing therefore directs our attention to how particularities of linguistic practice can evoke social images and link them to actors in a social situation. In the present context, the focus is on how the use of certain linguistic registers is conceptually linked to particular cultural and social images. It is from this perspective that I treat the registers and speech styles discussed here as especially potent forms of voicing and performing social identities when employed in discursive interaction.

There is a wide repertoire of varieties and registers available to rural Hindu Mauritians that is only inadequately captured by the label "Creole-Bhojpuri bilingualism." Seeking to do justice to this linguistic diversity, I not only examine the use of Creole and Bhojpuri as different linguistic varieties; I also focus on two particular registers: *Creole fransise*, that is, Creole with numerous elements evaluated as French, and purist Bhojpuri, in which Creole loans in Bhojpuri are maximally avoided and replaced by Hindi lexical items instead. While *Creole fransise* has historically been linked to urban and middle-class identities in Mauritius, indicating formal education and at least some knowledge of French, purist Bhojpuri evokes Hindu ritual contexts and the performance of Hindu ancestral authority. I examine how rural Hindu Mauritians employ shifts within this repertoire to index interactional stances and claims to group identity. Quite often, linguistic forms as indexes of ethnic group boundaries simultaneously function as indexes of internal social differentiation among Hindus in rural Mauritius. In the description of how the inhabiting of interactional stances and claims of belonging can be accomplished through creative use of sociocultural valuations of linguistic forms, the interplay between the indexing of ethnic and diasporic belonging and other forms of social differentiation plays an important role.

The linguistic crossover phenomena that appear as rural Hindu Mauritians use their multilingual and multiregister repertoire are important as a way for them to position themselves vis-à-vis models of belonging couched in discourses of ethnic and diasporic community. Here a distinction similar to that between "nationalism" and "nationness" proposed by Katherine Verdery (1993), drawing on John Bornemann (1992), is useful to account for how such group identifications are inhabited and perpetuated. This distinction is important because ethnic group identifications are not explicitly invoked in most interactive encounters. According to Verdery, "the former refer[s] to conscious sentiments that take the nation as an object of active devotion, the latter to daily interaction and practices that produce an inherent and often unarticulated feeling of belonging" (Verdery 1993, 41). I suggest that linguistic practice in a complex environment where some linguistic forms and registers clearly function as indexes of ethnic belonging, while others do so to a lesser degree, can articulate a form of belonging operating on the same level as "nationness." Without requiring an overtly expressed invocation of ethnic community, for instance, through explicit discourse or ritual practice, the use of such ethnic pointers can achieve a placement of selves within the framework of an ethnic community.

Certainly, using language loaded with ethnonational values does not always imply an affirmative stance towards such ethnolinguistic identities. On the contrary, as I show, Hindu Mauritians occasionally take an ironic and distanced position towards ethnicized language and the identities it indicates. In contrast, on other occasions ethnicized language is used to make hierarchical distinctions among Hindus while nevertheless incorporating them into discourses of authority. Diversity and contestation in language ideologies (Gal 1993) are very much part of Hindu Mauritian practices of identity. However, the significance of linguistically performing in certain registers for the construction of a Hindu diasporic community is highlighted even in those instances of use, thus betraying an ambiguous stance with regard to ideologies of diasporic community.

The principal themes of the following examples fall into two general categories: the performance of authority and distinction, and interactive positioning vis-à-vis forms of belonging conceived as ethnic and diasporic relationships. As I intend to show, the performative constructions of these stances and identities are closely connected. The presupposed links between linguistic forms and social stances or identities with respect to the creating of authority and social distinction among Hindu Mauritians often function as the background knowledge necessary for the linguistic construction of social identities, such as diasporic forms of belonging.

LINGUISTIC CROSSOVERS: ANIMATING
CHARACTERS AND COMPETING FOR DISTINCTION

I start with an example illustrating how several stances and identities, drawing on the diverse linguistic resources available to rural Indo-Mauritians, can be inhabited over the course of a single interaction. "Intermediate" or sometimes even bivalent language that blurs the boundaries between Mauritian Creole and French is one way such shifting between interactionally indexed identities can occur. This follows a pattern also known in other locations where a French-lexifier Creole coexists with standard French, such as Haiti, Martinique, and Guadeloupe in the Caribbean and La Réunion in the Indian Ocean. However, in Mauritius such multilingual phenomena that challenge the notion of clear linguistic boundaries often take even more complex forms, since nearly one-quarter of the population is also bilingual in Creole and Mauritian Bhojpuri. Mauritian Bhojpuri is perceived by its speakers to be very much "mixed" with Creole tokens, raising the question of whether we can speak of intermediate bilingual practices among Creole-Bhojpuri bilinguals, and in a way recalling the juxtaposition and blending of French and Creole elements in what Mauritians call *Creole fransise*. Sometimes these two kinds of bilingualism are brought together in the same linguistic interaction. Consider the following example, which features a maximal range of shifts between registers current among Hindu Mauritians from Bhojpuri to *Creole fransise*. This is an excerpt from a conversation between three middle-class government employees of Indo-Mauritian background — Ramesh, Bikram, and Suresh — who are on their way to work together in the morning. They often share the thirty-minute commute from their rural community to Port Louis, traveling by car, and I sometimes joined them when I traveled to the capital or other towns beyond. This episode was recorded in the later months of my fieldwork. I had gotten to know these men over the course of almost one year, visiting their homes and also meeting each of them at weddings and other ritual occasions. The speakers' middle-class status is significant because working-class Hindus usually have a very limited command of *Creole fransise,* while the conversation among these three men spans a wide range of registers and styles, including some features characteristic of *Creole fransise.* All three grew up in rural bilingual Bhojpuri-Creole households.

EXAMPLE 3.1*

A: Eta to konne kombien kas pu kute pu fer sa zansman larzan la? Mo krwar en ven-senk miyon passe sa. Pa bizin paye sa bug dehor ki pe imprime sa ban biye la? Mazin twa kan biye ver ven rupee ti pu trwa miyon wi san mil rupi to paye en dehor pu fer emprime sa. Be otan miyar so biye.

B: Fer li apre kan posisyon Moris bon. Posisyon . . . larzan Moris to kone rupi kombyen fin vini?

R: Ha ha ha.

B: Rupi pena valer-la, banla, banla onte pu fer devale . . . devaler. Rupi pena valer.

R: Non, li pa fasil sa, pa fasil sa.

B: Banla, banla koz menti tro boku. Mo dir politisyen bizin koz menti, WAI, politisyen bizin kokin, WAI. Moi mo dir WAI. Bizin kokin, non? Eh, bizin develope osi, apre kokin osi. Mwa mo dir kumsa.

R: To konne kot moi en sekreter minis ki dir, dir lot banla, zot ti pe kokin lotte banla, sa banla pe met lamen lor koko mem zot pe pran.
[all are laughing]
. . . .

1 A: Oh my, do you know how much money it will cost to do that change of money [banknotes]? I believe it has gone over 25 million. Don't you have to pay 5 that guy abroad who is printing these banknotes? Imagine you would have to pay 3.8 million abroad to make the green twenty rupee note. Well, that is so many 10 billions for the notes.

B: Go for it when Mauritius is doing well. As for the Mauritian currency, do you know how much the rupee is?

15 R: Ha ha ha.

B: The rupee has no value, they, they are ashamed to devalue it. The rupee has no value.

R: Well, it is not easy, not easy.

20 B: They, they lie too much. I say that politicians have to lie, YES, politicians have to steal, YES. I say YES. They have to steal, no? Eh, they also have to do public 25 projects, and after that they also have to steal. That is what I say.

R: You know, at my [work]place there is a secretary of a minister who says, he says they over there, 30 they were stealing, even if they put their hand on their head, still they are stealing.
[all are laughing]
. . . .

*Creole is unmarked; **Bhojpuri is boldfaced;** *Creole fransise* is underlined. All-uppercase indicates vocal emphasis.

B: La bank mondyal, la bank mondyal emprimeri pe dikte guvernman travayist. Be sa, sa trez banane la labank mondyal lemprimeri pa fin gajn lokkasion dikte. Ta ti dimun **kaha** kompran **hola** politik? **Khali aake thoṛa batya dewelansa.** Be lemprimeri bank mondyal dan soz . . . en pe zour li pu empose li.

S: Wi, pu to gayn devis ar li li pu empose li. [2-second pause] Li en pey demokratik me pa konne . . . .

R: **Chokar-wa abri hala, abri baris okar** lexamen ka rahi?
B: Wi, wi, sa dernye lanne ki pa krwar.
R: Sa mem dernye lanne sa, non?
B: Oui, dernye, wai. Li koNNE li.

R: Li konne, non?
B: Wi. . . .
[laughter]
R: Be pu mwa la ti fer byen dernye lanne <u>lüniversite</u> moris, li ti parmi, mo krwar ban best si ki ti ena.
B: Non, do, ban zenfan kapav travay.
R: Non, zot bizin travay. Pu mwa li en kas-tet sa mo dir twa frank si guvernman pa pu ede enfen zot pe explor tu ban possibilite dapre F. zot gayn lafrans, zot pe rode lostralie kot zot kapav envoye sa ban zenfan la. Liniversite osi pa pe krwas lebra pe assize, u pe kompran.

B: Non be fodre eh eh politik guvernman.
R: Non be pa pe krwas lebra pa pe assize me li pa fasil.

B: The World Bank, the World Bank and the note press are dictating to the Labor government. Well, during those thirteen years the World Bank and note press did not get the opportunity to dictate. **So how can** poor, humble people understand politics? **They just come and talk a little.** Well, the note press and the World Bank in a few days will impose [its (sic) policies].

S: Yes, in order for you to get hard currency from them, they will impose. [2-second pause] It is a democratic country, but you never know . . . .

R: **That boy, what will be with his** exam **the coming year?**
B: Yes, yes, last year he did not believe it.
R: Just last year, no?
B: Yes, last year, yeah. He really knows.

R: He knows, no?
B: Yes. . . .
[laughter]
R: Well, for me he did well last year at the <u>University</u> of Mauritius, he was among, I think among the best.
B: These kids can work.
R: They have to work. For me it is a worry, I tell you frankly, if the government will not help, finally they are exploring all possibil-ities, according to F. they get to France, they are seeking out Australia, wherever it is possible to send these kids. The university is also not sitting there doing nothing, you know.

B: Well, a government policy is necessary.
R: No, they are not sitting there doing nothing but it is not easy.

B: Lüniversite pa kapav fer tu.

B: The university cannot do everything.

R: Parski li konne de miyon rupi apre pu sa trwa an la pur en zenfan, pur en parent pu envoye li angleter li pa fasil sa, non?

85 R: Because they know two million rupees afterwards for these three years for one child, for the parents to send him to England, that is not easy, no?

S: De miyon?

90 S: Two million?

R: Trwas an li fer otan. Non, be, en kur medisin in large üniversite Moris la, oui. Fer trwa an Moris, trwa an u al fer li Newcastle, Manchester. . . .

R: Three years he studies, that much. For an education in medicine when he has left the University of Mauritius, yes. Do three years in Mauritius, you go and do three years in Newcastle, Manchester. . . .

95

N: Kot pu al gayne de miyon?
. . . .

N: How do get two million [rupees]?
. . . .

R: Mo garson in gayn laburs.

100 R: My son got a scholarship.

S: Ki kote?

S: From where?

R: Ban laburs pu al fer medisin li pa gayne. Ban laburs pu al fer enženyer ti gaygne, enženyer, BSc tu sala. Be li lin dir li envi fer sa kur medisin la. Kuman pu dir li non?

R: He did not get one of the scholarships to go and do medicine. He got one of those to go and study engineer, engineer, BSc and all this. Well, he said that he likes to study medicine. How could I tell him no?

105

B: Nu pran en risk nu met en lipie divan nu gette ki arrive.

B: We take a risk, take a step forward and see what happens.

110

S: Wi si li pu ale li osi bizin pens so lavenir.

S: Yes, when he goes, he also has to think about his future.

R: Wai, medisin-la ena boku appran sa — ayo — pa fasil sa. Si mo dir ou ban zenfan ki lir li pu konne ena boku pu appran.

R: Yeah, in medicine there is a lot to learn — oh dear — it is not easy. If I say [this to] your kids who study they know that there is a lot to learn.

115

B: Ban enženyer mem ki in kit lüniversite Moris.

B: Even for the engineers who left the University of Mauritius.

R: Wai eh.

120 R: Yeah.

B: Pa kapav mem suiv pa kapav pa kapav mem suiv a fors, tough.

B: They were not able to even follow it, even with great effort, [it is] tough.

R: Wi li pa fasil sa.

R: Yes it is not easy.

B: Tro tough.

B: Too tough.

R: Üniverste Moris so enženyer la cumsa mem sa.

125 R: Even for the engineers of the University of Mauritius it is the same.

N: En kamerad li ti gayn laburs zon don li la burs la, banla in don li

N: A friend got a scholarship, they gave him that scholarship, they

en laburs lend, be minis pa paye, 130
wi, wi, be ti gayne de san mil
rupi. Banla don li en laburs pur
al kot sa, lin fer premier, banla
in don li en laburs lend lin al fer
soz, li en enziniye en dan soz . . . 135
eromekanik. . . .

B: Non ena lüniversite bien bien 140
tough laba, ena ban lüniversite
ki pa bon OSI bizin dakor sa,
mo kamerad.

R: Wi.
R: Ena, ena de, trwa iniversite, 145
lüniversite ki konne. Angleter
sa priority sa.

gave him a scholarship to go to
India, well the minister did not
pay, well, he got two hundred
thousand rupees. They gave him
a scholarship to go there, he was
classed first, they gave him a
scholarship to go to India, he
went and did engineer in, what
was it . . . aeromechanics. . . .

B: No, there are really demanding
universities there, there are also
universities which are not good
EITHER, [you] have to agree, my
friend.

R: Yes.

R: There are two, three universities
which are well-known. England
is leading in this.

The conversation starts with a discussion of political events in Mauritius, and the participants voice agreement that something is wrong with the politics of the current government. The issue raised here is monetary policy. On the one hand, the three government employees disapprove of the decision to withdraw, at great cost, a new series of banknotes just printed for the Bank of Mauritius in Britain. The government made this decision in late 1998 because of protests by the Tamil community, who vehemently objected to the placement of the Tamil language labels on the banknotes in the third and lowest position, below both English and Hindi, and not in the middle position, under English but above Hindi, as on the old series. The participants then pass from this subject to the considerable loss of value of the Mauritian rupee against the major Western currencies in 1998 — clearly exaggerating the problem.

In the process they interactively construct a collective stance as "ordinary people" who are different from the "politicians" and at the mercy of their decisions. Ramesh's joke about politicians being so corrupt and bent on "stealing" in a way the politicians themselves are unable to control invites the other participants to join in this stance of solidarity against "those above" in sympathy. The linguistic variety used by all is "ordinary" Mauritian Creole without indications of an intermediate, French-influenced register. This changes, however, in the next section of this interaction.

The three men, approaching the capital, are still criticizing the government's monetary policy. The World Bank is conflated with the company in London that manufactures Mauritian paper currency in the context of the recent fiasco with the new banknotes (lines 35–36). Bikram compares the current Labor Party government's performance unfavorably with that of the previous government, which had been in power for thirteen years. He then engages in code-switching from Creole to Bhojpuri (lines 40–42). This turns out to be another way of contrasting the collaboratively established and shared interactive stance of membership among the "people" with the powerful politicians far removed from them and their concerns. But by switching to Bhojpuri in this fashion, the solidarity of the people against the government is voiced somewhat differently, compared to the joke on lines 29–31. In fact, by code-switching to Bhojpuri, Bikram animates a character (Goffman 1974) somewhat different from himself and those present. Leading solidly middle-class lives, the three men are not the *ti dimun* ("little people," meaning people of humble background) at the bottom of society whose underprivileged position and lack of education is indexed by Bhojpuri. This is also clear from the propositional content of the two phrases, which portray the *ti dimun* as innocent people who lack the sophistication necessary to see through politics — an ability, however, that the three men talking implicitly claim for themselves. The two social voices and identities performed by juxtaposing Creole and Bhojpuri are also intermingled to produce an effect of consonance; they are not employed to indicate opposed values and identities. On the contrary, the three speakers seem to voice solidarity with the *ti dimun,* even though some distance is created between the voice of the *ti dimun* and the participants' own identities.

The further unfolding of this conversation introduces another set of distinctions, indicating the activation of a different social voice. Another switch to Bhojpuri in lines 52–53 is linked to an inquiry by Ramesh about family issues, here the educational plans of one of Bikram's sons. Once this topic is embarked upon, the common front of solidarity of "us" against "them" *(ban-la)*, that is, the politicians, becomes less relevant, even though the participants continue to criticize the government and seek the other speakers' approval of their criticism. The participants also start to praise the educational achievements and talents of their children, especially Ramesh, who apparently inquires about Bikram's son in order to create an opportunity to talk about his own son, who he says is "among the best" at the local university (lines 64–65). Later he announces that his son has won a scholarship (line 100). No more code switches to Bhojpuri and playing the role of the *ti dimun* occur. The collective egalitarian stance inhabited vis-à vis the politicians is modified by a hierarchical element when the educational successes of sons are highlighted and implicitly compared. In this context, the participants draw on another bivalent resource, French phonological elements, which are employed in two salient and repeated lexical items that are prominent in this stretch of the conversation: "university" and "engineer,". The contrast between [ü] and [i] as well as [ž] and [z] plays a key role. *Lüniversite* is practically identical to the French *l'université*, as opposed to "ordinary" Creole *liniversite*. Similarly, *enženyer* corresponds to French *ingénieur* and contrasts with Creole *enzenyer*. These elements are used in the part of the conversation when the three men highlight their expertise in educational matters. The use of these variants seems to be a device to subtly indicate the knowledge and education of the speaker, while not creating an overly great interactional distance from the other participants — as would doubtlessly have been the case if the speaker had completely switched codes from Creole to French.

To sum up, this interaction as a whole is an informal conversation in Creole between participants with similar first-order demographic identities. However, the speakers employ two other sets of linguistic distinctions to transform interactional stances and introduce different social voices and messages of distinction while not directly departing from the overall script of an encounter between social equals in solidarity. In this way, a multilingual situation in Mauritius offers speakers ample resources to construct interactional strategies based on the manipulation of multiple linguistic boundaries.

Studies of code-switching have identified reported speech as one of the reasons for shifts to another language within a conversation (Gumperz 1982, 75–76; McClure and McClure 1988, 35–37). The perceived contrast between two linguistic varieties enables a speaker to emphasize differentiation between one's own speech and that of others within an utterance. This can also function as a distancing device, allowing a speaker to effectively deny responsibility for what is being said, by "othering" the reported voice through use of an alternate linguistic code (Hill 1995). However, by marking reported speech through use of another code the characters quoted can also be invested with social qualities that may or may not have been salient to the reported speech event as it actually unfolded. This point is at the center of what Mikhail Bakhtin analyzed as the polyphonic character of discourse, which is particularly evident in reported speech (Bakhtin 1981). Similar to the "animating" of the character of the *ti dimun* through shifting from Creole to Bhojpuri in example 3.1, other people's speech may be reported by giving it a particular valuation implied by the shift in the linguistic or stylistic repertoire. Investing the words of others with particular social meanings by such uses of linguistic variation effectively signals a particular interactional stance that the narrator takes towards the voices and events narrated. Consider the following extract from a conversation between three schoolteachers, Dilip, Vijay, and Mahen, concerning a scandal that reportedly occurred during a government-sponsored Bhojpuri and Hindi drama competition. Here, Vijay and Dilip switch between Bhojpuri and Creole but they use Hindi to mark the reported speech of other people known to them.

EXAMPLE 3.2*

V: Han, okar **manier** hi aisne ha janila ham

D: **En fwa la ki li ti fer, ti boycott pri pur drama la,** haw **pri** leke aise pri leke bolata yeh tofa meri or se Mohan, Mohan Maharishi ko de de . . . [all are laughing] . . . **piblik ke samne. Eh! Final** ke din — han. **Nu si nu ti kum sa dan sa lepok la me kontmem ki to pu fer, malartic pran alle, don grup alle.** . . .

[all are laughing]
Ita nai boli ki nai lele bate na, **ayo.**

M: **U konne ki ti arrive?** Ciz hol okar **klas men.**

V: **U likela selman.**

M: Suna, elog, **zot represesan en pies apel "Bakri"** . . . "Bakri."

V: Nay Hindi, Bhojpuri sab rahal. Sunna ego **joli,** ego **pies** rahal. Han. Ih ego athi rahal, ban **satir** sa. Han-han, ban . . . ab **presente** karlansa, **banla fini swazire pu final.**

1 V: Yes, that is just the **way** he is, I know.

D: **Once, what did he do, he boycotted the prize for this drama,** he took this **prize,** taking this prize he said give this gift to Mohan, Mohan Maharishi on my behalf . . . [all are laughing] . . . in front of the **audience. Eh! On the day of the final —** yes. **We also we were like this at that time, but nevertheless what can you do, do it like Malartic[2] take it and leave, give it to the group, and off you are.** . . .

[all are laughing]
You are not going to say you are not going to take it, **oh dear.**

M: **Do you know what happened?** Something happened in his **class.**

V: **He just writes.**

M: Listen, these people, **they presented a piece called "Bakri"** . . . "Bakri" [goat].

V: No, it was all in Hindi, Bhojpuri. Listen, it was a **beautiful piece.** Yes. It was, like, one of those **satires.** Yes, yes, they . . . now they **played it, they got chosen for the final.**

*Bhojpuri is unmarked; Creole is boldfaced; Hindi is underlined.

D: Ou chal gailansa.
V: Semi-final swazire ho gal ba. En lot grup fer full length "Bakri."

D: Uhi pies-wa, hawe pies-wa, ban in fer full length "Bakri," ke ... han-han. Senser ki in fer, in rezet sa pies la mem fini swazir pur semi-final kisanla pu pran sa aster, han, lamerdman hoi lagal ab.

V: Sa osi, mokwar ti en apepre en mwa, de mwa ke bad hol rahla semi final, final.

D: 'Accha.
M: Han aise chalata.
V: Han, sa mem lepok la premier fwa ti alle final, non?
D: Ta do semi final men gal ta okra ego prize dehle rahlan sa.
V: Han.
M: A bon!
D: Ta bollak prize Mohan ...... Mohan Maharishi ko de do.
 [all are laughing]
Ta bug-wa lal-piar ho gal hoi.

V: Ta Mohan sikhaile rahli apan drama men.
D: Han.
V: Mo osi mo ti pe fer ban pies absurd company.
D: Han.
V: Drama within drama, han. Haw ab Hindi ke artist rahla aur boli, aur batlab enla dir kumsa ... yeh nirnayak mandal sadasya sabhi murkha hain, kya.
D: Accha, accha.
V: To inhen kyon dosh dete ho, bhai? To, eh, nyay karta kaun hai ... hai ek girgit jo rang badalta rahta hai.
[all are laughing]

30 D: They went there.
V: It got chosen for the semi-finals. Another group played "Bakri" at full length.
D: Just this piece, this piece, they
35 played full-length "Bakri," that ... yes, yes. The juror what did he do, he rejected this piece even when it was cho-sen for the semi-finals, who is
40 going to take it now, yes, now this started to become a real annoyance.
V: This too, I think it was after about one month, after two
45 months the semi-finals and finals.
D: Right.
M: Yes, like this.
V: Yes, at that time he went to the
50 final for the first time, no?
D: So he got into two semi-finals, they gave him a prize.
V: Yes.
M: All right!
55 D: So he said give the prize to Mohan ... Mohan Maharishi. [all are laughing] Then this guy goes red and yel-low [with anger].
60 V: So Mohan taught a bit about his drama.
D: Yes.
V: I too did absurd pieces.
65 D: Yes.
V: A drama within a drama, yes. Now there was this Hindi artist and he would say, one of them said this ... the members of the
70 jury are all fools.
D: All right, really?
V: Why do you blame them, brother? So who is making the decision ... it is a lizard who
75 keeps on changing his colors.
[all are laughing]

. . . Han, essan essan. . . .   . . . Yes, these these. . . .
D: Eh sab sach ha, bhai athi Gopal,   D: Eh, it is all true, brother, this
ekriven, u. . . .   Gopal, **the writer**, he, . . .
V: Ta u jannat rahal sab pathar-wa   80 V: So he knew that all this trouble
okre par giri. . . .   would fall on him. . . .

The three men collaborate in telling a story about a scandal at a public event involving people they personally know. Their exchange highlights an evaluative disjuncture between the acts and utterances reported and the reported use of Hindi by the characters reanimated. The ancestral language Hindi is commonly considered appropriate for formal, even solemn, events and displays of conformity to religious and ancestral tradition that illuminate Hindu ethnicity and values, for example, a sermon *(pravacan)* by a pandit in a temple. In Mauritius one very rarely comes across the use of the ancestral language Hindi as a medium for dispute or expression of anger. The narrative about the argument at the prize-giving ceremony is particularly amusing to the speakers, because participants in the ceremony expressed their anger and even publicly insulted each other in Hindi, as reported by Vijay (lines 69–70). Thus the example not only reveals valuations of the ancestral language, achieved indirectly by pointing to the discrepancy between presupposed values and lines of actions associated with the use of Hindi, on the one hand, and the actual unfolding of the event, on the other. It also demonstrates how the three men creatively use such presupposed valuations in commenting on an event while inhabiting the distanced perspective of amused bystanders. Furthermore, contrasts between the linguistic varieties available to many Hindu Mauritians can be deployed as interactional devices in situations of conflict. Let us have a more detailed look at the role of such shifts in linguistic practice in disputes.

ARGUMENTS, DISPUTES, AND CREOLE-BHOJPURI BILINGUALISM

Arguments are situations in which perceived oppositions between codes and their valuations are often foregrounded in the conversational strategies (Gal 1979, 114–116; Heller 1988). In Mauritius, such shifts in interactional stances in the course of an argument are frequently based on contrasts between presupposed valuations of Creole and Bhojpuri. Even so, the use of value-laden oppositions mapped onto two different linguistic varieties does not invariably mean the reproduction of such presupposed valuations. These different possibilities are explored in the following examples. The first excerpt is an exchange that took place in the back room and kitchen of a Hindu temple between two bilingual male members of the local temple association who were busy with preparations for a festival. The relative sharpening of the dispute between the two men is accompanied by a shift from Bhojpuri, in which their conversation was conducted to that point, to Creole.

EXAMPLE 3.3*

M: Parsadi bani?	1 M: Is the parsadi ready?
R: Ta are! Konti khai, adamiya?	R: You bet! What will they eat, the people?
M: Khali khaike ke bina maryansa, khali khai khatin? Parsadi nai charaybe kahe?	M: They will just die without eating, just for eating? Why will you not serve the parsadi?
R: Nai, parsadi banayeke. . . .	R: No, preparing parsadi. . . .
M: Han, **donk** kahe nai . . . ketna lek **de-trwa liv**?	M: Yes, **so** why not . . . around how much, **two-three pounds**?
R: Ego **dis** liv lek.	R: Around ten pounds.
M: Eta chup-re!	M: Goddamn, what are you saying!
R: **Nu get posisyon.**	R: **We will wait and make an analysis.**
M: **To pu get posisyon depi dis her to pu attan, kwi li en trwa liv si pa kat liv, kommien ena, nu pu partaze li tigin tigin ena laddu, tu!**	M: **You are waiting and seeing since ten o'clock, just cook it with two-three, maybe four pounds, however much is there, we will divide it in small portions, there are laddu, everything!**
. . . .	. . . .
R: Ba, u **krase** ba, **krase** ba.	R: Oh, it is **crushed, crushed.**
M: Laiti wa chini.	M: Cardamom with sugar.
R: Eh **set lit** we daleke na pani, nai **senk lit** dalde.	R: Eh, pour **seven liters** water, no, pour **five liters.**
M: Chini wa.	M: That sugar.
R: Alle **sis** dal de, chini.	R: Go on, pour **six,** and sugar.
M: Hai dal.	M: Pour like this.
R: Ka re . . . pakar ta. . . .	R: What . . . lift it. . . .
M: **Sa ve dir tu seki vini pran bartan alle.** . . .	M: **That is, all who are coming take a pot and go.** . . .

This example seems to follow a well-studied pattern, evident in other bilingual settings, in which local valuations of language can frequently

*Bhojpuri is unmarked; Creole is boldfaced.

be mapped onto an axis of power versus solidarity (Labov 1972, Trudgill 1983). For example, according to sociolinguistic research in Western urban contexts, a middle-class standard variety of speech can often be used to express social distance and hierarchy, whereas a working-class vernacular frequently appears associated with values of solidarity and social equality. A somewhat similar contrast is described as a distinction between a "we-code" and "they-code," the latter ideologically linked to outsiders and state institutions (Gumperz 1982). Although it would be wrong to describe Creole as a language variety Hindu Mauritians evaluate as not "their own," shifts from Bhojpuri to Creole are nevertheless effectively employed in example 3.3 to mark a change in the interactional relationship between the actors reminiscent of the contrasts foregrounded in the analyses of code-switching just mentioned. Mohan is pressing Rikesh to prepare *parsadi* (Hindi: *prasād*) for distribution to worshippers in the main Hindu temple of La Nicolière. Rikesh becomes fed up with Mohan's insistence, and, feeling challenged, he switches to Creole to fend off what he sees as Mohan's attempt to impose his authority. Mohan intensifies his challenge by continuing his pressuring critique of Rikesh's handling of the preparations, also in Creole. A few moments later in the conversation, he again seeks to take on the stance of a leader by switching to Creole while uttering a directive, telling the others present that they should carry pots of *parsadi* away. Presupposed valuations of Bhojpuri in relation to Creole in the dimension of relative socioeconomic prestige are thus put to use in situations of interpersonal struggle. A change of code to this effect is a stylistic device akin to what John Gumperz has termed metaphorical code-switching, which in Silverstein's terms represents a phenomenon of creative indexicality, in opposition to situational code-switching. The latter indicates a major change from one type of speech situation or speech event to another (Blom and Gumperz 1972), thus following a logic of presupposed indexicality. Code-switching of the kind described in example 3.3 is not confined to middle-aged or young bilinguals, but is also common among members of the older generation, who grew up when bilingualism and a good knowledge of Creole were not yet established as the norm among rural Hindu Mauritians. The following example is an exchange between Indradev, an eighty-year-old former *sirdar* on a sugar estate, and his nephew Sandip, who is visiting to invite Indradev to his brother's wedding. As much as the young man is pressing Indradev to accept the invitation, his paternal uncle is reluctant to do so. First, the old man reminds his nephew that the brother and other family members have not visited him in a long time; therefore he declares that he also does not want to visit them.

EXAMPLE 3.4*

S: Accha, din se nai gale hawe.

I: Ilog lage, na? Ha, ta ilogo, accha, dinse nai alba. **Sa ve dir** duno ke duno. **Li preske parei.**

S: **Parei.**

I: **Banla pa gayn letan, nu osi nu pa gayn letan.** . . . **Mo, mo gayn letan si u pa vin kot mwa.** . . .

S: **Mwa osi pa pu vin kot u.** . . . [laughing]

I: **Sa ve dir, gaspias.** Ek, do hala ham gayn haye.

---

1 S: Well, you have not gone for a long time.

I: To their place, no? Well, these people have not come [here] for a long time. **That is to say,** both of us. **It is nearly the same.**

S: **The same.**

I: **They have no time, then we also have no time.** . . . **I, I have the time, if you do not come to me.** . . .

S: **I will also not come to you.** . . . [laughing]

I: **That is to say, a waste.** Once or twice I went.

Indradev, who like many rural Hindu Mauritians of his generation is more comfortable speaking Bhojpuri, switches to Creole first while announcing his retaliatory refusal to visit his nephew's household. His nephew, as is evident on line 11, does not take the elderly man's refusal very seriously.

Later, after Indradev's wife has entered the room, the conversation continues with the nephew insisting on his uncle's attending his brother's wedding.

EXAMPLE 3.5†

S: Bon, chacha, chachi, ego choṭa bhai rah gal ba, dernye unkar sadi karat haija hamni. Ham aur buṛhiya, men mil-mila ke **enfen** sab koi.

I's wife: Ha, accha ba.

S: Ta gal dafe aisne hi sadi kar lianja, na. **Sa ve dir** athi ke

---

1 S: Well, uncle, auntie, there is one younger brother left [to be married], the last for us to organize his wedding. With my wife and me, let us all meet, **finally.**

I's wife: Yes, all right.

S: So they will have a wedding like the one last time. **That**

---

*Bhojpuri is unmarked; Creole is boldfaced.
†Bhojpuri is unmarked; Creole is boldfaced; Hindi elements of purist Bhojpuri are underlined.

le nef ut ke sa ve dir le hwit   10
ke samdi hawan ba sis her,
aur le nef ke, le nef ke
baryat nikli ghar se. Ta
palivar sath-sath nimantran
ba, suk se lendi lek.   15

is, something like, on the
ninth of August, that is, on
Saturday the eighth, there
will be the havan [sacrificial
fire central to the wedding
ceremony] at six o'clock,
and on the ninth, on the
ninth the baryat [Hindi:
barāt, the bridegroom's
marriage procession party]
will leave the house. So   20
there is an invitation to the
whole family, from Friday to
Monday.

I: Han, han. . . .

I: Yes, yes. . . .

S: Ta, chacho, dekh, ham toke   25
forse naiy karab. Sadi men
barabar ayebe, lendi ke
dekhabsa kaise ba swastra
nimantran hoi ta hamar
sange chaliye.   30

S: Well, uncle, look, I am not
going to force you. Come
also to the wedding, on
Monday we will see how
things are, there is an
auspicious invitation, so
please come with us.

I: Nai sakab jaye, hamar ego
laika pagli ba jon u jaha jai
ta boli "chal ghare, chal
ghare" nai sakba rahe.   35

I: I will not be able to come,
one of my children is crazy
[mentally handicapped],
when she will go, she will
say "let's go home, let's go
home" she will not be able
to stay there.

S: Nai ta lendi ke hamar sath
phursat mili jayeke   40
chowtari?

S: No, so will you be free on
Monday to come with me to
the chowtari [the concluding
wedding feast]?

I: Nai, dekhya, chowtari u ta
manze-bwar ka mamla ha.
Mwa mo pu alle nek gette u   45
pe bwar u pe manze soz me
mo pe manz en tigit, mo pu
assiz dan kwa, sa gaspias
sa. . . .
                                          50

I: No, look, the chowtari
is a matter of eating and
drinking. I would only go to
look around, while you are
eating and drinking and so
on, but I will just eat a little
and sit in the corner, this is
a waste. . . .

S: Naiy, enfen gette okasion.

S: No, just see the event.

This segment of the conversation occurs after Sandip has already made attempts to have his uncle agree to come to the wedding and the elderly man has already shown his reluctance to do so. Note the use of honorific Bhojpuri verbal suffixes (-*ja*) on lines 4 and 9, underlining the formality and seriousness of the request. In line 28, Sandip turns to Hindi to suggest the formal register in his request, even using a formal Hindi phrase, *swastra nimantran* (auspicious invitation), and the honorific imperative of the Hindi verb *calnā* to underscore the seriousness of his invitation. Finally, the uncle shifts to Creole as he again rejects the invitation and starts to give reasons for not coming to the wedding, which will stretch over four days. This conversational strategy, like the one in example 3.3, makes use of the different valuations Creole and Bhojpuri carry in relation to each other, Creole being considered an effective form in which to signal personal assertiveness.

However, the perceived contrast between Bhojpuri and Creole is not inevitably connected to what could be described as a power-solidarity, or "in-group" versus "out-group" (Gumperz 1982), opposition. In interpersonal dispute situations where shifting between Bhojpuri and Creole appears to be a part of the conversational strategies adopted by the contestants the shift to Bhojpuri does not always index a stance of solidarity and narrowing of social distance. On the contrary, values of shared background and social experience that the use of Bhojpuri evokes among rural Indo-Mauritians can also be employed to "score" points in a dispute. Let us look at the following example, in which two middle-aged men discuss the possibility of obtaining plastic chairs at a discounted price from a Hindu religious organization.

EXAMPLE 3.6*

B:	Kaissan ba?	1	B: What are they like?
A:	**Plastik**-wa, **blan** wa.		A: Made of **plastic, white.**
B:	Le lie hamar das go, are, sau go leke **san-dis** lebe hamar leliye.		B: Take ten for me, if you are taking one hundred, take
		5	**one hundred ten** for us.
A:	**Sa depan.**		A: **That depends.**
B:	Kaunci **depan?**		B: What **does it depend on?**
A:	Kaise ham tohra boli. Nai sakab bolle abhi . . . **kuma kapav dir**		A: How should I tell you. I cannot tell you now . . . **how can I tell**
	twa.	10	**you?**
B:	Haaye tor . . . **to pran san, matlot, pran san-dis.** Mo donn twa en ti larsan pu dis.		B: Well your . . . **if you take one hundred, man, then take one hundred ten. I give you some money for ten.**

6. Bhojpuri is unmarked; Creole is boldfaced.

A: Li pe refer kommand la.

B: Han.

A: Li pe refer kommand la, nu fini fer applikasion pu san-la. Kuma explike non? To bizin fer applikasion de san trwa san, kompran, to fer trwa san. Kompran hoile, na? Mem pri mem. Sa kapav fer. Depan, depan kouma to fer applikasion. Ab sau go applikasion karbe, san dis mangbe, ta tora naiy dei.

B: Nai, applikasion-we fer san-dis, to bizin san-dis!

A: Kar dele ba . . . nai, bolhom. . . .

B: Nai ab, ab sau go applikasion kar? To fer san-dis! Aster to kapav fer swa. De-san. Aster-la sosiete pran li.
   . . . .

A: Ena case ladan . . . chek, zaffer audit. Parski to pe tir en check. Si en zur vini kontrol, to ban ses . . . si to gaijn en sel tet brile, to fini gaijn beze. Band ke mamla ha. Ti zafer katin.

15 A: He is redoing that order.

B: Yes.

A: He is redoing that order, we have made an application for one hundred. How can I explain?
20 You have to make an application for two hundred, three hundred, you understand, you do it for three hundred. Got it? All for the same price. You can do that. It depends, it depends on how you do the application. Now if you do an application for one hundred, and then ask for a hundred ten, then they will not
30 give it to you.

B: No, make an application for one hundred ten, you have to do it for one hundred ten!

A: It has already been made . . . no,
35 my friend. . . .

B: No, now, now you are applying for a hundred? You apply for one hundred ten! Now you can do whatever. Two hundred. Now then the association will take it.
40 . . . .

A: This can turn into a [legal] case . . . a check, auditing. Because you are drawing a check. When one day there
45 is a check of your chairs . . . if there is a single airhead, you are screwed. It is a matter of jail. For a small thing.

In the first part of the interaction, which begins in Bhojpuri, Bhojpuri and Creole seem to be employed in the familiar roles outlined before. B presses A to order a few chairs more than originally requested for the temple in order to put them to other uses. A, uncomfortable with the request, switches to Creole at line 6 to fend off the risky proposition. In line 31, B also turns to Creole in order to voice his plan in a more urgent manner, using bald directives to try to get A to agree. But A keeps on resisting. In the final part of the exchange, conducted primarily in Creole by both protagonists, A creatively uses a shift to Bhojpuri (line 46) as a means to finally refuse the deal proposed by B. The gravity of his argument: "It's a matter of jail. For a small thing." is intensified in the switch to Bhojpuri, here giving the serious risk outlined the air of shared, self-evident insider knowledge. In this example the two presupposed roles of Bhojpuri and Creole as solidarity versus instrument to win an argument are, it seems, switched around, with Bhojpuri employed to make the final point of refusal to an unwelcome request. This shows that there is no inevitable connection between overall valuations of linguistic varieties and registers and their immediate use by bilingual actors. As demonstrated in example 3.6, there is always the possibility of skillful manipulation of such valuations for purposes that may appear to contradict patterns of indexicality commonly assumed by members of bilingual speech communities.

CREOLE FRANSISE AND
BIVALENT CONVERSATIONAL STRATEGIES

A major contrast in varieties of Mauritian Creole is the distinction between "ordinary" Creole and *Creole fransise,* which features linguistic "traces" representing French elements and is regarded as a more refined type of Creole. Because of the institutional connection between schooling and competence in French, speaking Creole with some French-influenced features is held to be typical of educated middle-class persons, who are also generally considered more refined than those with little formal education. There is thus an iconic correspondence between the characteristics ascribed to the register of *Creole fransise* and the presumed qualities of those persons considered its typical users.

In Mauritius, the legacy of political and economic domination by a Franco-Mauritian plantocracy even under British colonial rule, along with the continuing dominance of French in the private sector economy as well as the role of French in the educational system, have cast French in the role of a language of economic and political power. In contrast, Mauritian Creole is not an official language recognized by the Mauritian state, nor does it play a formally recognized role in the educational system — though its use is officially tolerated for facilitating the explanation of topics during the first years of primary school. Therefore, the indexical link between French features in Mauritian Creole and ideas of refinement and power is rather well-established. The use of *Creole fransise* in Mauritius recalls similar practices in other settings where a French-lexifier Creole is used alongside a dominant European language, such as St. Lucia (Garrett 2000), Réunion (Chaudenson 2001, 30), and Guadeloupe (Hazaël-

Massieux 1996, Managan 2004). Such intermediate or "acrolectal" varieties occupy a middle position on what is known in Creole linguistics as a Creole continuum (Rickford 1987) between basilectal Creole varieties on the one end and the European superstrate language on the other.[3]

Arguing from a different perspective, such "in-between" manifestations of linguistic practice have recently given cause to questioning the normativity of linguistic boundaries in research on language in its social context. Pointing to the widespread occurrence of bivalent usages straddling boundaries between languages, Kathryn Woolard (1998) has called for treating bilingual phenomena as prototypical in linguistic anthropological and sociolinguistic research. Analyzing Spanish-Catalan bilingualism in Catalonia, Woolard suggests that practices of bivalency, interference, and code-switching in bilingual discourse can accomplish both a simultaneous voicing of two social identities, and a weakening of the linguistic boundaries between the two languages.

Creole fransise can be described as an intermediate register between French and Creole, activating a particular social voice. While *Creole fransise* is often described as a French-influenced Creole, based on a distinction between elements considered normal Creole and those experienced as French-sounding, some of the linguistic forms typical of this register rely on a blurring of linguistic distinctions between Creole and French. In several ways, some features of *Creole fransise* can also be understood as a bivalent bilingual phenomenon in Woolard's sense, albeit in a situation where the speakers' competence in one of the two languages at issue (French) is very unevenly distributed and quite minimal among many Mauritians. Nevertheless, awareness of French qualities and linguistic elements in this intermediate variety of Mauritian Creole is very widespread even among Mauritians with little competence in French. Let us look at the following example in which Sushila, a student, explains why she thinks many Mauritians wish to see the ancestral languages preserved.

EXAMPLE 3.7*

L'importans, **wai, komman že t'entan, donk** on n'a pa envi ki li disparet, nu pa ena envi ki li vinn en "dead language" . . . a Moris, parski	1	The importance, **as I understand you,** is that **one does not** like it to disappear, we do not like it to become a "dead language" . . . in Mauritius,

*Creole is unmarked; French is boldfaced; *Creole fransise* is underlined.

bon . . . šak komünote ki isi enkor ena ban lien avek **le pay** kot zot ban anset fin vini, <u>donk</u> mo panse li pu interessan, li pu <u>enriši</u> <u>lakültür</u>, li donn en pe plis **de variete**, nu ban zenfant petet pu benefisie, zot konn en, en, **le fe** ki nu en pei . . . eh . . . mültirasial . . . <u>donk</u> li pu interessan si nu arriv preserv . . . tu sa <u>ban</u> <u>kültür-la</u> e transmet li a ban <u>nuvo</u> <u>ženerasion</u>.

5 because, well every community which is here still has links to **the country** where their ancestors came from, <u>so</u> I think that it will be interesting, it <u>will enrich the culture,</u> 10 it gives a little more **variety,** our children will maybe benefit, they know a, a, **the fact** that we are . . . eh . . . a <u>multiracial</u> country, <u>therefore</u> it will be interesting if we 15 manage to preserve all <u>these cultures</u> and transmit it [sic] to <u>the new generations.</u>

This segment, taken from a discussion among university students about the "language issue" in Mauritius, is a good example of *Creole fransise*, featuring multiple instances of bivalency. On one hand, code-switching from Creole to French is evident, as in lines 1–2 and 6–11. These switches appear to be of such routine quality that it is difficult to assign a particular conversational function to any of them. Rather they seem to constitute an unmarked norm which, along with the Spanish-Catalan case analyzed by Woolard, recalls similar usages among Puerto Ricans in New York (Urciuoli 1996) and Hindi-English bilinguals in Delhi (Pandit 1986), as well as in various bilingual scenarios involving Swahili in Kenya (Myers-Scotton 1993). Furthermore, the speaker, a university student, chooses Creole items that already exhibit a certain bivalent quality, insofar as their phonetic shape very closely resembles corresponding French lexical items and differs from what Mauritians consider "normal" Creole. A striking instance of this is the substitution of [s] with [š] in *šak*, "every" (line 5), now almost identical with the French *chaque* in contrast to the Creole *sak*. Another bivalent phonetic variation in Mauritian Creole is the use of [ü] instead of [i], giving a perceived French quality to *komünote* (line 5) and evoking the French *communauté*, in contrast to the Creole *kominote*, and *mültirasial* (line 12) as distinct from *miltirasial*, as well as *lakültür* (line 8) resembling French *la culture*, differing from *lakiltir*. A similar relationship obtains between [z] and [ž], the former being replaced by the latter in *ženerasion* (line 15), identical with the French *genération*, as compared to the Creole *zenerasion*. An example of bilingual interference (Woolard 1998, 14–15) is on lines 13–14. Here the phonetic shape of *kültür* follows French usage, making it practically identical to the French version of this word, but is pluralized by using the Mauritian Creole plural marker *ban,* and also suffixed with the Creole definitive marker *-la.* To sum up, the underlined *(Creole fransise)* forms in this example sound French to Mauritian Creole speakers, and are indeed hard to distinguish from French, while still being indentifiable as Creole. That is, they cannot be clearly attributed to only one of the two languages in question. Let us consider the following example, in which one of the students who participated in the discussion from which example 3.7 was taken talks about the social significance of Creole, using a combination of Creole, French, and *Creole fransise:*

EXAMPLE 3.8*

Eh, eh, se leka pur <u>lamažorite</u> ban dimun **de mon až** kot zot paren tu letan fin kumadir truv **la lang** kreol kum en lang, eh . . . ba, en lang ki pena valer zot pu dir twa beh . . . to pe al lekol, to pe koz angle to pe koz franse, kifer to pe koz kreol en lakaz, kontinye koz angle ou byen franse.

    La lang kreol li pa importan pu nangien pa capav gayn en degre avek **la lang** kreol to kompran, to pa kapav arive avek **la lang** kreol, li en lang ki la, ki tu dimun servi **lironi dü sor** se ki pa all pli lwan ki sa . . . to kompran.

    Ena en espes <u>lieraši</u> ki dan ban lang ki nu servi isi, kot kreol **retruv** li **o ba de lešell** to pe kompran *set* en lang ki mo ena lempression . . . ki ban dimun zot gayn en pe. . . <u>žene,</u> petet mem. Li en lang kom tu lezot lang me <u>lakültür</u> in fer li ki angle franse domine.

1 This is the case for <u>the majority</u> of people **of my age** whose parents all the time, so to say, find that the Creole **language** is . . . low, a
5 language that does not have value they will say to you . . . you are going to school, you speak English, you speak French, why do you speak Creole at home, continue to speak
10 English or French.

    The Creole language is not important for anything, it is not possible to get a degree with the Creole **language**, you understand,
15 you are unable to get anywhere with the Creole language, it is a language which is there, which all people use, but **the irony of all** is that it does not go further than this . . . you
20 understand.

    There is a kind of <u>hierarchy</u> in the languages that we use here, where Creole **finds** itself **at the bottom of the scale** you understand, <u>it is</u> a lan-
25 guage that I have the impression . . . people maybe get a little <u>ill at ease</u> with. It is a language like all other languages but <u>culture</u> is the reason that English and French dominate.

*Creole is unmarked; French is boldfaced; *Creole fransise* is underlined.

TABLE 1 Main features of *Creole fransise*

Phonology	Substitution of [š] for [s], [ž] for [z], [ü] for [i] where French usage would prescribe it
Lexicon	Use of French vocabulary *(Maison* for *lakaz, magasin* for *labutik, parle* for *koze)* and discursive markers such as *en fait*
Grammar/morphology	Occasional use of French verb morphology *(disons)* Occasional use of French plural article *les* for Creole plural marker *ban*
	Occasional use of French possessive marker *de* as in *ban paran de Suren* for *ban paran Suren* ("Suren's parents")

The French and Creole elements in example 3.8 were identified by playing the recorded speech to several research assistants who were Creole first-language speakers, who pointed out what they considered the particularly French-sounding elements. Continuing with phonetic variation, the substitution of [ž] for [z] is evident in lines 1, 2, and 25, *lamažorite* (majority), *až* (age), and *žene* (to inconvenience, to make someone ill at ease), approximating French pronunciation in contrast with what most people agree are the "ordinary" Creole terms *lamazorite, az,* and *zene.* The consonant [š] is used instead of [s] in lines 16 and 23, resulting in the "French" *lieraši* (hierarchy) and *lešell* (scale) as opposed to the Creole *lierarsi* and *lesell.* The speaker, a twenty-four-year-old Indo-Mauritian female university student, talks of *lakültür* instead of *lakiltir* (culture) in line 27, again producing a token my research assistants readily recognized as not only French-influenced but also difficult to distinguish from French usage.

Just as striking to my informants were the numerous instances of adoption of words and whole expressions classifiable as "French." *Retruv,* recognized as French *retrouver* ("to find again," line 22), is not known as a Creole lexical item. We also encounter *l'ironi dü sor,* following the French *l'ironie du sort* ("the irony of it all," line 15), and *o ba de lešell,* intended to resemble the (ungrammatical) French *au bas de l'échelle* ("at the bottom of the scale," line 23). The last example is particularly illustrative of a conscious striving to integrate French elements into one's speech by a non-native French speaker.

Examples 3.7 and 3.8, as I analyzed them with the help of my native-speaker consultants, highlight the varying importance of different types of linguistic phenomena for speakers' evaluations of their own and others' speech. In comparison to, for example, syntactic patterns, lexical items can function as referential and easily segmentable and reproduceable elements in language that a speaker's metapragmatic awareness can readily access (Silverstein 2001). Indexical components of meaning in language are more likely to be consciously remarked upon and described by speakers when they manifest as segmentable surface items, such as words. From this perspective, then, it is not too surprising that French words and expressions should be singled out by speakers as hallmarks of *Creole fransise*. Other common examples are the use of *mentnan* in the place of the Creole *aster* (now), *magasin* instead of *labutik* (store), *larb* instead of *pye* (tree), *utiliz* or *utilize* instead of *servi* (to use), *parle* instead of *koze* (to speak), and *vwar* instead of *gete* (to see). Further, the use of certain French discursive markers not common in Creole, such as *en fait* (in fact), function as obvious features of this register.

The intermediary register straddling the boundary between Creole and French provides an opportunity to examine how Hindu Mauritians manipulate linguistic boundaries in order to construct and inhabit stances of distinction in interaction, creatively drawing on the range of social and cultural values and differences indexed by linguistic signs and coalescing these into recognizably distinct and labeled linguistic registers and varieties. Nevertheless, indexicality is not the only semiotic process of importance in linking social values and forms of identification to linguistic forms in performance, thus creating various forms of belonging, class, ethnicity, and diaspora being central among them. Iconicity as another significant semiotic process is explored in the following section.

ICONICITY AND INTERMEDIATE REGISTERS

What makes some instances of intermediate and sometimes bivalent usage more salient than others? How do such apparently subtle shifts along the boundaries between languages indicate particular social identities? I would like to address these issues by considering some features of *Creole fransise*. For many speakers of Mauritian Creole, the alveopalatal fricatives ([š], [ž]) as well as the high fronted and rounded vowel [ü] represent emblematic features of "clarity," a quality apparently not shared by their counterparts, the alveolar fricatives ([s], [z]) and the high fronted and unrounded vowel [i] typically used in what is considered vernacular Creole. In example 3.7 this distinction is evident in contrasting *šak* (line 5) with *sak*, *ženerasion* (line 15) with *zenerasion*, and *komünote*

and *lakültür* (lines 5 and 8) with *kominote* and *lakiltir.* These sounds
evoke linguistic images of "clear" (*kler*) and "refined" (*rafine, devlope*)
expression, corresponding to a particular social image considered characteristic of educated, middle-class persons.

Iconic correspondences between linguistic features and social or ethnic
identities have been analyzed as one of the central ways of ideologically
linking languages to certain social or ethnic groups in a variety of ethnographic contexts (Irvine and Gal 2000). Yet the question remains: how
exactly are such links established? One clue in the Mauritian context is
that many users of Mauritian Creole, including Hindu Mauritians,
ascribe a metaphoric quality to the production of the sounds [š] and [ž],
which involves a "pointing," or slight fronting and tightening, of the lips.
According to many speakers, this enables one to speak with more clarity
and precision. While assisting in analyzing my fieldwork tapes, native-
speaker consultants pointed out that in contrast to what they evaluated
as "careless" *(neglize)* speech, the use of [š] and [ž] in certain words
make thems "clear" *(kler)* and "beautiful" *(zoli)*. They also associated
this positive quality of speech with the same formation of the lips in a
certain buccal hexis for the production of vowels. For example, the [i]
versus [ü] contrast, evaluated as significant in distinguishing *lakiltir* from
the French-sounding *lakültür* in examples 3.7 and 3.8, involves a similar
"pointing" of the lips that is associated with ideas of clarity. While assisting me with the transcripts, one native-speaker assistant said the following about this bivalent phenomenon: "They pronounce words more
clearly and fluently. From the way they speak you can tell they have this
French accent. They have read a lot and this is why they can speak in a
more elevated manner. Their mouth is more at ease with this. That's why
they do not sound careless." Others repeatedly said that this bilingual
phenomenon simply sounded "beautiful" *(zoli)*.

In Mauritius there is a long tradition of assigning values of clarity and
subtlety to French and contrasting these with the qualities supposedly
inhabiting Creole. Early discourse among language experts highlighted
the apparent lack of grammatical complexity of Mauritian Creole compared to French, drawing an iconic link between the language's perceived
simplicity and the presumed simplicity and lack of civilized qualities of its
speakers. One of the first systematic descriptions of the Creole language,
Charles Baissac's *Étude sur le patois créole mauricien* (1880), is an elaborate and classic formulation of this hierarchizing ideology,[4] drawing
directly on ideas about French in Europe (Swiggers 1990).[5] The meta-

phorical features of clarity, beauty, and orderliness Baissac ascribes to French iconically correspond to the social qualities of sophistication, refinement, and orderliness considered characteristic of educated middle-class speakers.

For Creole speakers, the contrasts between the voiceless alveo-palatal fricative [š] and voiceless alveolar fricative [s] and between the voiced alveo-palatal fricative [ž] and voiced alveolar fricative [z] in the linguistic environments discussed represent an emblematic distinction characteristic of the difference between the registers of *Creole fransise* and "ordinary" Creole. For Bhojpuri-Creole bilinguals, the contrast between [s] and [š] in these two forms of Creole carries even greater significance, because the same contrast applies to the differentiation of Bhojpuri from standard Hindi. Examples include: *sadi* versus Hindi *šadi* (wedding), *santi* as opposed to Hindi *šanti* (peace,), *sarir* versus Hindi *šarir* (body), *sarab* as against Hindi *šarab* (alcoholic drink), and *sahar* compared with Hindi *šeher* (town, city). That is, for Bhojpuri-Creole bilinguals this particular alternation represents the relationship of a subordinate linguistic variety to a standard language in a double way.

Since many Mauritians of different ethnic and linguistic backgrounds are highly conscious of these phonetic differences, speakers aspiring to a middle-class identity sometimes engage in hypercorrection, using [š] and [ž] instead of [s] and [z] in their realizations of French or French-derived Creole words where these sounds would not normally occur in either standard or Mauritian varieties of French. Frequent examples of these hypercorrections are: *en faš* instead of *en fas* ("opposite"; French: *en face*), *šerf* for *serf* ("deer"; French: *cerf*), *appprešie* for *appresie* ("appreciate"; French: *apprécier*), *širtu* instead of *sirtu* ("above all"; French: *surtout*), and even *morišyen* instead of *morisyen* ("Mauritian"; French: *mauricien*).

Consider this example from a conversation between Bharatee, a garment-factory worker in her early twenties, and one of my research assistants, a university student of similar age. Bharatee completed her secondary school education with the School Certificate (eleven years of schooling), and considers herself overqualified for her job but found no alternative employment. While Bharatee talks about her job she is aware of the my research assistant's higher education, as well as the fact that the conversation is being recorded. She uses Creole, and sometimes shifts to French pronunciations of certain lexical items, mostly speaking what would be recognized as "ordinary" Mauritian Creole. Sometimes, however, these French realizations turn out to be hypercorrections.

EXAMPLE 3.9*

Bis compaynie vin sers nu, eh sis her
kens, o pli tar sis her ven. Nu bizin
fini vin dan šemen pu kapav al dan
lisin-la. Tu lezur . . . nu fini rant
ladan set her.

. . . .

Me non selman ban **morišyen** ki
travay laba, ena ban sinwa kin vin
depi lašin, banla travay kuma lanwi,
lezur zot travay mem, gramatin sis
her, set her e demi pe rantre, eh, nef
her parfwa onze her di swar zot
travay. Zot travay tro boku, kuman
bef.

. . . .

Mo pa kontan travay dan lisin me,
ki a fer, a kos problem famiy mon al
travay, lemplwa byen difisil pu gayn
pu **morišyen**. Mon fer form senk me
mo, mo travay avek ban, ban
etidian si ki in fer **sižiem**. Mo pa
kontan travay dan lisin mwa,
"loading" li byen fatigan.

1 The company bus comes to pick
us up, at six fifteen, or later at six
twenty. We have to be ready waiting
on the street to get to that factory.
5 Everyday . . . we get there at seven.

. . . .

But there are not only **Mauritians**
who work there, there are Chinese,
who have come from China, they
10 work day and night, they are just
working. From six, half past seven
in the morning, until nine or sometimes eleven at night they work. They
work very much, like cattle.

15 . . . .

I don't like to work in the factory,
but what to do, because of a family
problem I have gone to work. For
Mauritians it is pretty difficult to get
20 jobs. I have done Form 5, but I work
with students who have completed
the sixth grade [of primary school].
I don't like to work in the factory,
the "loading" is really tiring.

Compare *sers* and *šemen* in lines 1 and 3. While the first follows Creole
phonology, as different from *šerš* ("to look for"; French: *chercher*), the
second appears to be *Creole fransise*, compared with Creole *simen* (way,
street). Similarly, *sinwa* and *lašin* in lines 8 and 9 show a similar pattern
of alternating between ordinary and French-influenced speech. However, *morišien* in lines 7 and 19 and *sižiem* in line 21 are clearly hypercorrections, indicating that Bharatee is striving to sound more sophisticated. Similar to Bharatee's articulation of *sižiem* for *sisiem* ("sixth";
French: *sixième*), *trožiem* for *trosiem* ("third"; French: *troisième*) is an
analogous and frequently heard hypercorrection, involving the substitution of [z] with [ž].

Such semiotic processes may help explain the relative salience of certain models of linguistic authority over others in a given interaction. In

*Creole is unmarked; *Creole fransise* is underlined; hypercorrections in *Creole fransise* are
underlined and boldfaced.

the complex sociolinguistic situation in Mauritius, French is certainly not the only "legitimate" linguistic norm available to speakers, who navigate a plurality of models of language-based authority and authenticity, and may use bivalent discourse to simultaneously voice multiple interactional stances and social identities. The simple dichotomous model of overt prestige oriented to French as a power code as opposed to Creole inhabited by covert values of prestige such as solidarity and egalitarianism is not sufficient either. Beginning in the 1970s, Creole was promoted by leftist postcolonial nationalists who saw themselves combating the colonial legacies of French domination and communalism as an everyday political reality by promoting Creole as the proper and legitimate national language. Even though these efforts failed politically in the early 1980s and were viewed with suspicion by many Mauritians, they to some degree changed the sociolinguistic valuations of Creole, which is now seen as an appropriate linguistic variety for many public and even formal contexts, such as political oratory. Also, Mauritius experienced multiple colonial regimes that left the Mauritian state with English as the official language, even though French has persisted in a dominant role since the change of colonial powers in 1810. Finally, for Mauritians of Indian background, especially bilingual Creole-Bhojpuri-speaking Hindus of north Indian origin, Indian ancestral languages represent an additional model of "legitimate language" manifested in another kind of bivalent discourse, purist, "Hindiized" Bhojpuri.[6] Iconic relationships such as those discussed above may contribute to the relevance and attraction of one model of linguistic authority over the others available as an interaction unfolds.

Further, such bivalent discourse straddling the limits of two or more languages stands in indeterminate relation to the continuing salience of linguistic boundaries. The effects such bilingual phenomena may have on linguistic boundaries are not universal and do not necessarily involve a blurring and weakening of such boundaries from the perspective of speakers. Even though Bhojpuri is widely talked about as thoroughly mixed with Creole, and rapid code-switching back and forth is expected among bilinguals, the idea that Creole and Bhojpuri are entirely different linguistic varieties remains uncontested. However, the same cannot always be said about the way Creole fransise as a bilingual phenomenon mediates ideas about the relationship between French and Creole. While nobody in Mauritius argues that French and Creole are literally the same, the bilingual and bivalent linguistic practices discussed above reinforce the idea that French and Creole are not only closely related, but also stand in a relationship of hierarchical subsumption. However passionately Creole linguists and language activists have been fighting the notion that Creole is a substandard or corrupt variety of French, a *patois* and not a "real language," the ethnographic observation of social valuations shows that this view continues to be widely held in Mauritius.

TEMPORALITY, NARRATIVE, AND REGISTER: NARRATIONS OF *DUKH* AND NOSTALGIA

Reflecting on the ways their villages and their lives have changed in recent decades, rural Hindu Mauritians frequently stress the theme of radical transformation. They view the present economic and political situation as a great improvement over the colonial past. Most Hindu Mauritians have been able to escape poverty, which was the common fate of the majority before independence. Now secure government jobs are available to many. Most significantly, within a few decades, the great majority of rural Hindu Mauritians were able to move out of the *habitations* on the sugar estates (cramped and very basic housing in subdivisions comprised of long, flat barracks) or straw-thatched or corrugated iron homes into solid, concrete-frame houses with furniture. Formal schooling became available to all and contributed to unprecedented social mobility. The changes in housing and educational opportunity are transformations that rural Indo-Mauritians highlight most often in personal life stories.

Transformations over time are not only a key theme in Hindu Mauritians' reflections on their lives; their narratives are also a prime means for positioning themselves as diasporic subjects in relationship to an imagined homeland and the different sets of sociocultural values implied by the evocation of India. Here it is useful to recall the phenomenological argument that temporality is not reduceable to a uniform and linearly progressing standard of cosmic time on which a sequence of events can be located. On the contrary, the experiences of present, past, and future are intimately interdependent and dynamic constructs. This is because a "temporal object" such as an event can only be experienced against the shifting horizons of anticipated futures and remembered pasts, inhabited by other events (Husserl 1964). Thus the experience of duration cannot be understood as a continuing series of "nows" in an objective sequence of events.

Narrative has been recognized as a key practice in structuring and transforming the temporality that is at the heart of both subjectivities and

social memories (Carr 1986, Ricoeur 1988). Narrative as a social practice establishes relationships between subjects and events that have been
experienced by many, mediating the intersection between subjectively
lived time and cosmic time, and thus producing the historical consciousness of a social collective (Ricoeur 1988, Koselleck 1985). By establishing
and organizing relationships between subjects and lived events in time
narrative has the power to link subjects into experienced communities,
creating a "narrative identity," a sense of collective being and location in
history (Ricoeur 1988, 246–47). Such social forms of temporal regimentation through narrative not only frequently diverge sharply from, if not
contradict, one another across social groups but also become foci of contestation within self-defined communities (Wertsch 2002, Zerubavel
2003) over what appear to be the "same" events and historical processes.
Thus we might say that the life stories of Hindu Mauritians can be read
as different ways of building relationships of experienced closeness and
distance between remembered events and places and the narrator's self.
This narrative constitution of lived temporality often works through
tying remembered events together in plots and story lines, establishing
relationships of valuation and relevance between these events and the
narrator's self. At the same time, following the phenomenological argument of the radical interdependence and co-constructedness of experienced pasts, presents, and futures, the practice of narrative remembering
also shapes different senses of inhabiting the present and also necessarily
involves distinct modes of anticipation of events to come.

My concern here is to link these insights about the crucial role of narrative in establishing a sense of history to forms of temporality indexed
by differences in linguistic form, and thus to elucidate the diasporic
stances and subjectivities created and inhabited by rural Hindu-
Mauritians through linguistic practice. One way of doing this is to analyze the intersection of such narrative reflections and particular linguistic
registers, with their indexical loadings and their embeddedness in ideological visions of social difference and belonging.

As mentioned, the difficulties and hardships most Indo-Mauritians
endured under colonial plantation capitalism are well remembered.
Older people in particular, who witnessed firsthand the dramatic historical transformations, sometimes perform vivid narratives of the suffering
they experienced in the past and the positive changes that have taken
place since then. When remembering the earlier part of their lives, *dukh*
(pain, suffering) is a prominent theme under which past events are inter-

preted. Example 3.10 is an excerpt from the life narration of Anjali, a sixty-eight-year-old widow, who is talking to her granddaughter Reshmi.

EXAMPLE 3.10*

A: Hamni paile ke **tan** men bahut dukh **passe** karle haisa ge beti, bahut dukh, bahut dukh, habhi etna laika rahal, sab laika ke posli choṭa se sabke poske saadi biyaan karli, paisa bahut **miser**, bahut dukh, hamar sab. Hamar **missye** mar gal, **afin** bahut bahut **miser**. **Mayok** khailasa, **mayok buye** karlasa, nai milal ba uha khaike niman se, tani tani dele hai, posli sab ke, sab ke tigin, tigin, tani, tani dele hai, posli sabke, sab ke saadi karli. **Miser-we**, **miser**-we chal jata hamar ta ab ka karabsa? Bahut dukh **passe** karle hai ham bahut dukh **passe** karli hai kochi karab? Chaugo, chaugo laika rahal sabke posli, ta athi **lapai** ke ghar hamar rahal, **lapai** ke ghar men se poste poste sab laika log ke tab ego **tol** ke ghar banaili chota sun tab souru karli ab sab laika log ke saadi karleke, sab ke *laika-oika* ke *saadi-oudi* kar deli ta ab **miser** men **miser**-we chal jata. Ab sab laika log apan apan ba egbagal egbagal men **selman** ham apan dukh hi **passe** karila, ka karab.
. . . .

R: Ka sochela habhi ke laika log, apan maa baap ke respekte karela?

1 A: We **went through** a lot of pain in the past like this, my daughter, a lot of pain, a lot of pain, then there were so many children which had to be raised from little 5 on, they had to be married, no money and much **poverty**, a lot of suffering for all of us. My **husband** died, and then there was a lot of **misery**. We ate **manioc, boiled manioc**, we did 10 not get proper food to eat, little by little, to raise all of them, little by little I was able to provide for them, to get them all married. We went through a lot of **misery**, 15 **misery**, what could we do? We **went through** a lot of pain, **went through** a lot of pain, what could we do? There were four, four children and all had to be raised, 20 we lived in our **straw**-house, in the **straw**-house they were brought up, until we built a small **corrugated iron sheet** house, then I started to marry 25 off all the children. All the children and the like, I had them married and such, and we went through **misery, misery**. Now all children live separately, but I 30 **went through** all this pain, what could I do.
. . . .

R: What do you think, do today's 35 young people **respect** their parents?

*Bhojpuri is unmarked; Bhojpuri echo-word constructions are in italics, Creole is bold-faced; Hindi or hindiized elements are underlined.

A: Han, apan, apan maa baap ke laika log apan maa baap ke athi mein rahela adab men, maa baap. Ab paṛhawata likhata apan maa, habhi ta hamre natin log ba oke paṛhailak likhailak okar maa, okar maa ta laike we ke chahela ego samajhleke ki oke okar maa ke ego **lede** kareke chahi. [40][45]

R: Kon **differans** ba paile ke laika log aur habhi ke laika log men?

A: Laika **kumadir** paṛhata likhata paṛhai ba han ta **selman** mehengi dher ba aur paile ke laika ta konon tani mani paṛhe ta [unclear] chayansa, habhi ke laikwa ta paṛhata han **selman defans double** ba defans bahut ba. [50][55]

. . . .

R: Ta ka sochela paile ke **lepok** me sange sab koi jaise bolat rahlansa <u>sanyukt</u> <u>parivaar</u> aur habhi ke jaise beta log apan apan rahela, sab beta log, ta kaun men jasti **lavantaz** rahal age ke ya habhi ke? [60][65]

A: Habhi ke habhi apan apan ba, ta sab olog ke hath men ba na?

R: Ta paile ke nai, nai sochat rahla jasti pyar mhabat rahal apan men? [70]

A: Han, han sab koi **kumadir**, sab koi hamar sange rahal tab **ale ale ale** sab **ale** sab koi apna sab laika-phaika baṛeh lagal, ta hamar sathe nai rahi koi rahi, ta na apan *laika phaika* ke dekhi na. . . . [75]

R: Ta ab. . . . [80]

A: Apan sab koi apan apan rahela.

R: Apan akele rahela ta tohra nai nai mehes . . . sochela nai **pense**

A: Yes, young people do hold their, their parents in respect. They are now educated, now there are my grandchildren, they are educated, they understand that they should **help** their mother.

R: What **difference** is there between yesterday's and today's youth?

A: The young people are, **that is,** educated, **only** everything is expensive today and in earlier times children knew how to read a little, so they want [unclear], now young people are educated **only expenses** have **doubled,** there are a lot of **expenses** [instead of defans she means to say depans, "expense"].

. . . .

R: So what do you think, in earlier **times,** when all were together in what they call <u>joint</u> <u>family</u>, and now it is like children live apart, all children, so what is **better,** the way it used to be or the way it is now?

A: Now all are living by themselves, so it is up to them, no?

R: So you do not think that before there was more affection and love between parents and children?

A: Yes, yes, everybody, **like,** all were living with me, then they **went, went, went,** all of them, all **went** by themselves, became grown up, so no one stayed with me, no one, so I do not see my children and such, nor. . . .

R: So now. . . .

A: All are living by themselves.

R: Living by yourself, do you not feel . . . think, don't you **think,**

karela, toke accha lagela din
bhar akelewe raheke nai sochta   85
je koi koi tor sangue rahata ta
jasti accha se accha se rahta?
A: Nai ham khusi rahela akele
raheke. Jab **malad** ho jab ta olog
dekhbe kari laika ha ta dekhbe   90
kari na aur **lopital**-upital le jaibe
kari ki kani [unclear] men mar
gaila ta olog ta aur ego **maler**
ho gal ta dekhe kari na sahaita
karbe kari na? Apan laika ha ta   95
nai kari, ta dusar koi kari.

do you like being by yourself the
whole day, don't you think if you
lived with someone it would be
better?
A: No, I like to live by myself. If I
fall **sick**, then the children will
look after me, will take me to the
hospital and such, when someone dies in [unclear], so they, so
if there is a **calamity**, then they
will look, one will give support,
no? If one's child will not do it
then somebody else will.

Anjali paints a grim picture of her past experiences. Memories of grinding poverty, the early loss of her husband, and the pressures of raising her children without significant help from others do not result in a nostalgic image of the past. On the contrary, she views her present circumstances as preferable to the earlier part of her life and seems glad that her life has changed. Asked by her granddaughter, she concedes that she spends more time on her own than in earlier years, because joint-family residence for extended families has become uncommon. However, she says that she prefers living on her own, and besides, as she states in another part of the conversation, two of her four sons have their homes right next to her house, on what was formerly a single plot of family-owned land.[7]

Anjali grew up speaking Bhojpuri and never went to school. As her confusion of *depans* (expense) with *defans* (defense) in line 55 suggests, her command of Creole is hardly equivalent to her Bhojpuri, which she speaks as her first language. However, Anjali makes regular use of Creole loans, which are very common in Mauritian Bhojpuri. They are so integrated into her speech that they are even subject to echo-word constructions, such as in line 91, *lopital-upital,* echo-word constructions being a salient feature across Indian languages, including Bhojpuri and Hindi. Sometimes Anjali also integrates Creole loans morphologically into Bhojpuri, as in lines 13–14 and 26, where the Creole loan *miser* (poverty, misery) carries the Bhojpuri noun suffix *–welwa*, with which the "redundant" form of the Bhojpuri noun is formed (Tiwari 1960, 104).[8] Significantly, the Creole elements appear only as referential, glossable forms. She uses none of the purist Hindi elements that replace many of the commonly used Creole items in, for example, the speech of Hindu pandits, who almost always have undergone some training in Hindi. In many ways she appears to be an almost prototypical speaker of the Bhojpuri of the older generation, which proponents of official Hindu ancestral culture otherwise point to as emblematic of tradition. Nevertheless, Anjali's narration of her life's events, besides reflecting no nostalgia for the past, conveys no concern for what Hindu activists would consider the erosion of the ways of the ancestors.

I compare this excerpt to an account by Prakash, a Hindi teacher in his mid-forties, with respect to narrative representations of past and present and characteristics of speech. Anjali's and Prakash's narrations constitute an interesting contrast because both contain either explicit or implicit representations of the past, highlighted in terms of the social changes that have brought about the situation of the present. They accomplish this from different horizons of the present, shaped by their very different social vantage points within the Hindu community of Mauritius. In this regard, I link what I describe as Prakash's linguistic purism to his membership in a group of professional guardians of ancestral culture and the fact that he completed his higher education. In contrast, I link Anjali's narration of *dukh*, which features many Creole loans, to her social standing as a poor widow who never went to school. In a conversation with Aparna, a student who is one of his neighbors and who started with talking about the wedding of Prakash's son, Prakash draws a picture of the past and its relationship to the present that can be characterized as a discourse of nostalgia. He views present-day life in Mauritius in far less positive terms than Anjali, contrasting it with what he sees as the superior moral values of earlier generations of Indo-Mauritians.

EXAMPLE 3.11*

A: Ta ab guruji, ta ab apan beta ke   1   A: So, Guruji, haven't you made
    saadi ke taiyari nai karba?   preparations for your son's
P: Ta beṭa ke shaadi ke bare men   wedding?
    habhi ego tij ba ki beṭa ke chahi   P: There is one thing about the
    khud apan <u>pair</u> par khara hoike.   5   wedding of a son, the son should
    Ham beṭa ke saadi tab tak   be able to stand on his own <u>feet</u>.
    kareke taiyar nai ha ki jab tak u   I am not prepared to arrange for
    apan <u>paira</u> par nai khara hoi, u   my son's wedding as long as he is
    aaj, aajkal janela aajkal jon **zenes**   not standing on his own <u>feet</u>, he

*Bhojpuri is unmarked; Creole loans and other elements are boldfaced; Hindi or hindiized elements are underlined; English terms are boldfaced and italicized.

ba olog bahut <u>behekh</u> gal ba,   10
ulog maa-bap ke kadar nai
karata, izzat nai karata, ghar
men ego **su** nai dewata ta kaise
saadi karba olog ke? Aur olog
<u>chahta</u> ke maa bap hi sab kuch   15
olog khatir karke *ghar-dwar*
mati zamin sab kuch karke dei.
Ta ham osan baap ha jon ki
tolere nai karela aur ih khatir jab
ham **tolere** nai karila laika ke aur   20
<u>khaskar</u> beṭa laika ke ta beṭa
accha nai laukata.

Ta beṭa tanikun apan **lesan** ba
lekin ek din yadi apan <u>pair</u> par
khara hoi, kamai dekhab ki hon   25
ab saki koi ke posse ta ham
sakab okar saadi kar dewe okar
parski ego baap ke ta pharz ha
okar laika log ke saadi kareke
lekin laika log ke bhi koi pharz   30
rahela, baṛah <u>ke prati</u> apan farz,
apan <u>kartavya</u> nai <u>nibhaila</u>, ta
baṛa dukh howela.

A: Aajkal ke naujawan par tohar
     kaun <u>vichar</u> ba?

P: Ajkal ke naujawan baṛa hi
     hamra laukata ki olog hi ego
     dunyia chal al ba, olog aisan ego   40
     dunyia men jiyata apan dunyia
     kree karata jaha par <u>josh</u> ba
     lekin <u>hosh</u> nai ba. Hamni ab
     olog sochela ki olog apan baṛa
     admi se jyada janelansa aur olog   45
     apan baṛah adamyia ke apan
     fason men ane lekin ih galat ba.
     Baṛah admi men olog men <u>hosh</u>
     bhi ba, <u>josh</u> bhi ba lekin
     naujawan men khali <u>josh</u> hi <u>josh</u>   50
     ba olog <u>josh</u> men aake ta okar
     galat <u>parinam</u> niklata. Aaj
     dekhbe <u>sarvatra</u> nawjawan log
     sigaret piyata, **ladrog** men
     hawanja u **la plipar** chori karata,   55
     prison men jaata ih tarah hamra

knows that now, today's **youth**
have become very <u>spoiled</u>, they
do not value their parents, do
not honor them, they do not
contribute a **penny** to the
household, so how can one
arrange for their marriage? And
these people <u>want</u> that their
parents do everything for them,
give them a *house and such* and
land, everything. So I am one of
those fathers who do not **tolerate**
this and I am not **tolerating** this
because <u>especially</u> from a son, it
is not seemly for a son.

So with a son it has a particular **sense**, but if one day he stands
on his own <u>feet</u>, and I will see his
income so he is able to raise someone, then I can arrange for his
marriage, because it is the duty of
a father to have one's children get
married, but children also have
duties, if they do not <u>fulfill</u> their
duty, their <u>duty</u> <u>toward</u> the elders,
then this is very sad.

A: What is your <u>view</u> on today's
     youth?

P: It seems to me that today's
     youngsters have moved to
     another world, they live in such a
     world, they have **created** their
     own world in which there is
     <u>amusement</u> but no <u>spirit</u>. We
     think that now these people know
     more than their parents, and that
     this also shows in their own **way**
     to live in comparison to their
     parents, but this is wrong. Among
     the parents, there is <u>spirit</u>, and
     also <u>amusement</u>, but among the
     young people there is just
     <u>amusement</u>, only <u>amusement</u>,
     just living for <u>amusement</u> so the
     bad <u>consequences</u> are showing.
     Now you will see that young
     people <u>everywhere</u> smoke

kul milake laukata ki aaj ke jon
nauwjawan ba olog barah hi
galat raasta mein jaata aur olog
ke roke khatir bahut **enstitision**   60
ke chahela samne aweke bahut
sangathan, samaj ke chahela
samne aweke jon ki saki olog ke
ego sahi raasta men aneke olog
men dharmik pravriti chahela,   65
sanskar chahela jagaike. Aaj ke
naujawan jaha puja path, saadi
biyah howata dekhba olog ego
mantra nai janata, jab pandit, eh,
purohit jab biyah karawat   70
hawan ta olog ke malum nai ba,
ta ih tarah se bahut aisan
shabdha ba jon ki aaj ke
naujawan olog dekhta ki pandit
kaise phale olog ke batlay kaha   75
pari kaise pani chirke ke tab olog
kari ta ih tarah se dekhba ta ha
bhasha ki taraf olog ke prem-rah
gal ba, olog ke ta bas olog ke ta   80
ego disco, olog ke khali git
bajana haiye olog ke ego dunyia
ho gal ba aur bahut kam ham nai
bolat ha sab aise ba, lekin bahut
kam aisan naujawan ba jonki   85
maata pita ke prati apan
kartavya, bhai bahin ke prati
apan kartavya ghar ke prati apan
kartivya nibhawata. Do kori ka
olog ke paisa mil jata olog   90
sochata ki olog duniya saki
kharid lewe bhau se olog ke
petha men khaike bhojan nai ba
lekin dekh ba eh eh niman niman
juta, niman niman kapra sab   95
bahri, *show, show* karat hawanja
lekin bhitar se sab khokhla
howal jata.

100

A: Ka **panse** karelan hai ghar
parivar men, sadasya men,
kahe algaw, duri aa gal ba?

cigarettes, are into **drugs**, and
most of them steal, go to **prison**,
this way we can see very well that
today's youth have taken a very
wrong path, and to stop them one
needs a lot of **institutions**,
associations have to come
forward, [religious] societies have
to come forward who can get
these people on a true path, a
religious mentality is necessary
for these people, one has to
awaken rituals. When there is a
puja or a wedding one sees that
these people do not even know a
single mantra, when the pandit,
eh, the priest conducts the
weddings rituals, then they do not
know, and there are some such
words that, if you look at today's
young people, like the pandit tells
them before where one has to
sprinkle the water so they do it,
so in this way people take the
path of the [Hindi] language,
they take the path of love, but
these people just do disco, they
just sing songs, they have made
this world, and very few, I do not
say all are like this, but there are
very few such youngsters who
toward their parents do their
duty, toward their brothers and
sisters do their duty, toward their
household fulfill their duty. They
get two times twenty [plenty] of
money, and they think they can
buy the world, they can eat whatever they fancy, if it is not a feast,
then look, neat shoes, neat
clothes, it is all a superficial
show, they make a *show*, but
on the inside it is all hollow.

A: What do you **think**, among
family members, why has
there developed isolation
and distance?

P: Algaw aur duri har ghar ke ego kahani ho gal ba, ghar-ghar ke kahani ho gal ba ekar sab se bara karan ihi ba ki hai athi hai bara aur chota ke bic men koi **dialog** nai ba, koi samvaad nai ba olog ke bic men, aur bara jon ba ou lakh samjah we khojata par hai nuvo generation ke, ta hai **nuvo zenerasion** jon ba u behak gal ba u u bara ke u sunbe hi nai karata u kadar nai karata u izzat nai karata aur bara bhi bolte bolte thak gal ba. Aur ihlog apan ego duniya **kree** karata jon men ki ta, **prison** ba, **ladrog** ba, aur hamra ta ekar se jyada kuch nai laukata ki aaj ke naujawan khaskar kuch *creative* **work** karata bahut kam ba ki jon *par* likhke chala ego *degree*, ego *certificate* prapt karata, koi naukri ke talash men ba, lekin **en mazorite** dekh ba ta sab bhramil ba, ki ta samundar men jake khali nahat ta, macchi marata hawe okal jivan ho gal ba, maa-bap se alag aur ghar men ego **su** jaise ki ham boli nai diyansa. . . .

A: Hamni bolilasa ki desh ke pragati okar **developman** sab ki naujawan log par jyada nirbhar karela ta agar olog ke gati naujawan ke gati esne chalita ka sochela desh pragati kari?

P: Eih, nishchai ba ki desh pragati nai kari. Ham jaise boli ha ki kuch jaha par susanskrit maa-baap ba, jekar ghar men accha sanskar ba, ulog lage ih **problem**-wa nai ba, olog saki ih desh ke rajniti men, desh ke samajikta mein sakyansa haath barhawe, desh ke okar **ekonomi** men, okar arthtantra men sakyansa hath

105 P: Isolation and distance has become the story of every household, in every household, and its most important reason is that there is no **dialogue** between old and young, there is no 110 dialogue between them, and the old search for a hundred thousand ways of understanding, while the **new generation** has gone astray, they do not even 115 listen to the elders, do not value them, do not honor them, so the elders while talking have become tired. And the world these people are **creating**, what is in it, **prison**, 120 **drugs**, and besides this I do not see much, and today's youth especially do not do much *creative* **work**, very few go and write about this or acquire a 125 *degree* or *certificate* in this, or look for job in this field, but if you look **at the majority** they are all misguided, they go to the 135 seaside, swim, catch and eat fish, so their life goes, separate from their parents and as I said not giving a **penny** for the household. . . .

140 A: We have said that the progress of the country and its **development** are fulfilled mostly by the young people, but if they are in this condition, the young people, do 145 you this the country will progress?

P: Well it is certain that the country will not progress. As I said, where there are cultured parents, 150 in whose home there are good rites and rituals, in their house there is not this **problem**, they can support the politics of the country, the society of the 155 country, and the country's **economy**, they can support its

barhawe lekin jon ghar men koi
<u>disha</u> hi nai ba jon ghar men hai
koi <u>ankush</u> jon ghar men koi
disiplin nai ba u sab ketnon kuch 160
karba u sab laika <u>desh</u> ke <u>pragati</u>
khatir kuch nai saki kare, balki
uolg <u>desh</u> <u>ke</u> <u>liye</u> ego bojha ban
jai aur ketne koi dekhba aaj
<u>sarkar</u> ke parata ketna karata   165
pansion dewe ke ketna ke parata
jon *rehabilitation center* men
ladrog ke <u>shikar</u> ho gal ba,
sigaret ke *cancer* ke <u>shikar</u> ho gal
ba, sab **lopital** men kekra kharch   170
parata. . . .

A: Ta jon <u>bigar</u> gal hawansa, haw
sab haw jawan wa ke sidha rasta
men aane khatir maa-bap log ke
koti chahela kareke?   175

P: Maa-bap log khudh behsahara
ho gal ba, maa bap ta khudh
<u>niradhar</u> ho gal ba. Bahut dukhi
ba, maa-bap ta hamesha chahela
ki olog ke laika ego niman rasta   180
par chali, han, ta olog ke ta ghar
ke ghar bhi olog niman se chalai
ta <u>desh</u> bhi niman se chali. Ghar
ghar hi ta jake <u>desh</u> banela aur ih
roop men maa-bap aaj bahut   185
dukhi ba ham ihi sakab bole
lekin olog <u>koshish</u> mein lagal ba
ki olog ke laika jon ba ki ego **ku
pravriti** [unclear] ke ego niman
<u>sanskar</u> olog ke mili har maa-   190
bap ke bat ba ki laika log
naujawan log ajkal maa-bap ke
bahut dukhi aur tur-<u>tiraskrit</u>
karata.

<u>economy</u>, but those households
where there is no <u>direction</u>, no
<u>control</u>, no **discipline**, they can
do whatever, their children
cannot do anything for the
<u>progress</u> of the <u>country</u>, but they
will become a burden <u>for the</u>
<u>country</u>, and how much, look
how much does the <u>government</u>
have to spend for **pensions**, for
those who <u>chase</u> **drugs** in the
rehabilitation centers, <u>chase</u> the
cancer of the cigarette, how
many expenses this will cause in
all the **hospitals**. . . .

A: What should parents do to bring
those youngsters who have been
spoiled back on the straight
path?

P: The parents themselves have
become helpless, the parents
themselves have become
<u>humiliated</u>, today's sons and
daughters. It is very sad, parents
always want that their children
go along a correct path, yes, so
when households also guide them
well, the <u>country</u> moves on well,
too. In every household the
<u>country</u> is shaped and in this way
parents are very sad today, I can
say that, but they keep on <u>trying</u>
so their children's <u>mentality</u>
suddenly [unclear], so they
receive a correct <u>ritual</u>, all parents
say that today the children,
young people cause the parents a
lot of pain and <u>disrespect</u> them.

In this conversation Prakash evokes an image of the past characterized
by adherence to standards of morality, something that he thinks has been
lost among the younger generation. He presents a dramatic and exaggerated picture of what he views as the moral decline of today's adolescents,
saying they are prone to criminality and drug abuse and fail to pay
proper respect to their parents. According to Prakash, many of them are

TABLE 2 Comparison of Creole and Hindi tokens
in Anjali's and Prakash's narrations

	Total number of tokens	Creole tokens	Hindi or hindiized tokens
Anjali's narration of *dukh* in example 3.10	382	30 (7.9%)	0
Prakash's discourse of nostalgia in example 3.11	974	27 (2.8%)	72 (7.4%)

spoiled and unwilling to become self-reliant, and are used to their parents providing for them. He sees the restoration of the moral values of the past as the only solution to the problem and as a task falling especially on religious leaders and associations. His own professional investment in the teaching of official ancestral culture certainly plays a part in this assessment, and his portrayal of contemporary Indo-Mauritian adolescents legitimizes his own role in instilling the values of "tradition" into today's youth. In many ways, Prakash's representation of the past and present is the exact opposite of the experiences expressed by Anjali, whose characterization of the past is one of suffering and whose opinion of young people today is generally positive.

Comparing Anjali's narrative of *dukh* with the teacher's discourse of nostalgia is also very instructive in terms of the different linguistic resources employed. Not only is Prakash a fully fluent Creole speaker, his Bhojpuri is also strikingly at variance with Anjali's. He uses few Creole loans, and only one of them (*problem-wa,* lines 150–51) shows the morphological integration of the "redundant" noun suffix frequently heard in Anjali's speech. However, purist Hindi elements, which are rarely used by most Bhojpuri speakers, are common in his speech. As in Anjali's narrative, the Creole elements used by Prakash are all referential, glossable forms: nominal, verbal, or adjectival. This is also mostly the case for the Hindi or Hindiized elements, though not exclusively so. Exceptions are the compound postpostions *ke prati* (to, toward) and *ke liye* (for), as well as the gendered Hindi possession marker *ki* in line 79, replacing Bhojpuri *ke.*

Table 2 compares the contrasting discourses of *dukh* and nostalgia, showing that the differences between Anjali's and Prakash's narrations lie in the relative frequency of Creole elements and, above all, in the presence of Hindi or hindiized tokens in Prakash's speech. Since all the Creole tokens used by both speakers and most Hindi tokens in example 3.11 are referential, glossable forms, the percentages in the table would be even higher if the number of Creole and Hindi or hindiized tokens were compared to only the total number of referential tokens in both examples.

Example 3.11 reveals an interesting relationship between Creole and Hindi elements. Prakash at times uses a pattern in which a Creole token is followed by a Hindi synonym or cognate, or vice versa. In lines 109–10, *dialog* is followed by its Hindi synonym *samvaad*; in lines 155–60, *ekonomi* is followed by its Hindi synonym, *arthtantra*, and the semantically related Hindi terms *disha* and *ankush* are lined up with *disiplin*. The overall effect is not only the reinforcement of a statement but also, from a purist point of view, the "correction" of the use of the Creole loan by immediately adding an equivalent Hindi term.

In Prakash's narrative a close relationship is evident between a certain mode of narrative organization concerning temporality and social memory and the use of a particular register. The purist register of Bhojpuri indicates a particular stance towards the past, present, and future, in this case, a narrative of nostalgia and decline that intersects with a narrative organization according to which a golden age of ancestral values has given way to moral decay and highlights the desirability of a return to the superior conditions of the past. The narrative organization and the register-based indexicality thus reinforce each other in constructing the particular temporal relationship Hindu Mauritians entertain towards the world of ancestral values according to the narrator.

This kind of conservative invoking of an idealized past has been called by Jane Hill a "purist discourse of nostalgia" (Hill 1998). As in Hill's analysis of linguistic purism among Mexicano (Nahuatl)–Spanish bilinguals in central Mexico, a discourse of nostalgia as a narrative mode of regimenting temporality is combined with linguistic purism, reinforcing the discursive stance adopted. By hindiizing his Bhojpuri, Prakash also gives his discourse an ethnic quality, since it incorporates numerous elements of the Hindu ancestral language Hindi.

Prakash's purist discourse of nostalgia nicely shows the interplay between community-internal social distinctions and the construction of community boundaries. He makes a distinction between morally inferior and superior members of the Hindu community within a discourse of tradition which assumes that modernity leads to moral decline. The purism of tradition, linguistically marked by the use of purist, hindiized Bhojpuri, embodies a claim of authority over those who have gone astray from tradition. Prakash explicitly suggests that those young Hindus who have become morally weak should accept the leadership of professional guardians of tradition, like himself as a Hindi teacher and other representatives of Hindu traditions in religious organizations. At the same time, he is engaged in a performance of Hindu identity in which a discourse of morality and linguistic images of purity reinforce each other. The construction of community goes hand in hand with the mapping of hierarchical distinctions among Hindus.

This creation of ethnic meanings through linguistic variation appears in conjunction with a discursive insistence on moral values, which are not only held to be representative of the Indo-Mauritians' past but also feature prominently in Hindu discourses of morality. Prakash does not take a distancing stance towards the Hindi elements in his speech; in his performance of nostalgia, he clearly inhabits an affirmative position vis-à-vis the ancestral language. His narration provides an example of how language can be ethnicized. Social meanings created through the use of purist, hindiized styles of Bhojpuri combine with the discursive invocation of moral values, such as respecting one's parents, abstinence from intoxicating substances, and sacrifice on behalf of family and kin, which are considered typical of an ideal Hindu self and thus indirectly indicate ethnic belonging. Together they constitute an image of Hindu identity in Mauritius.

Prakash's membership in a group of professional guardians of ancestral culture under state sponsorship is an important part of the context and sets his perspective on Hindu tradition apart from that of persons often considered typical bearers of that tradition, like Anjali. His use of purist Bhojpuri very much supports his discursive stance, as the Hindi elements in his speech index official Hindu ancestral culture. That is, a link can be drawn between his interest in a nostalgic take on the past, which is evoked in both the register he uses and the temporal organization of his narrative, and his socio-economic position in rural north Mauritius. In this social milieu, which was dominated by poverty and dependence on employment in the sugar industry only a generation ago, a career as a Hindi teacher joins concerns about ancestral culture with social mobility.

The link between the use of purist Bhojpuri — avoiding common Creole loans and using Hindi elements instead — and the indexing of Hindu ethnic values is also evident in another type of purist discourse: pandits' sermons in temples. Consider the following excerpt from a sermon *(pravacan)* at a festival celebrating the birth of the Hindu deity Ganesh (Ganesh Chaturthi, a national holiday in Mauritius) delivered by Pandit Mohabeer at a *shivala:*

EXAMPLE 3.12*

Bhagwan Ganesh ke janam hoi.
Sabhi log jan jayelan ki ego bahut
sundar balak paida hol ba. Bhu lok
men yeh samachar chali gai jaise
naya naya dulhin sadi karke awelan
ta sab koi dwagke jalanja dekhe
dulhan-wa kaisse ba, waise hi trilok
men sab devtaon Gauri Ma ke yaha
pahunch gaye us balak ko dekhne ke
lie. Ki wo kitna sundar balak hai, aur
sabhi devtaon ke sath-sath shani bhi
aye the. Sabhi devta us ballak ki
prashansa kar rahe the, parantu
shani nahi dekh rahe the. Tab Gauri
Maya ko accha nahi laga, pucha he,
sanichar tu mere ballak ko nahi
dekhe rahe, kya bat hai? Tab Shani
ne kaha nahi maya aisi bat nahi
tumhara balak to bahut sundar hai
parantu mujhe shaap hai ki mein jis
par drishti rakhunga us ka amangal
hi hoga.
  Yeh shani dekhiyan okar amangal
hoye. Haw bolinasa shani gran ha,
shani ke drishti parti hai to amangal
hi amangal hi hota hai.
  Ta us samay Gauri Ma ne kaha
aisi koi bat nahin hai, jo honi hai wo
to hokar hi rahega. Jon hoike ba u
hoibe kari, devta ke agya bina kuch
nai hola. To nisandeh ha, bina
sankoch hamar balak ke dekha.
. . . .

Gajendra so raha hai aur kaise soya
tha, uska mukh uttar ki disha men
tha, okar muh **lenor** danai rahal. Aur
bhali bhati jante the ki jo bhi prani
uttar disha ki or mukh karke soye
hue hein unka vad kiya kar sakta hai.

1 Bhagwan Ganesh was born. All
people got to know that a very
beautiful child had been born.
Among the people of the earth the
news went around like when a new
5 bride comes to get married, so
everybody comes running to see what
the bride is like, in this way all deities
in the three worlds came to Gauri
Ma's place to see this child. It was
10 such a beautiful child and with all
deities Shani [the planet Saturn,
represented as a deity in Hindu
traditions] also came along. All
deities praised the child, but Shani
15 was not looking. So Gauri Ma did
not like this, she asked, Sanichar, you
are not looking at my child, what is
the matter? Then Shani said, no
mother, nothing like this, your child
20 is very beautiful but I carry a curse
that whoever I cast my glance on, he
will suffer misfortune.
  Whoever is looked at by Shani,
will suffer misfortune. They say that
25 Shani is a planet, when his glance
strikes, only misfortune will occur.
  Then Gauri Ma said this does not
matter, what has to happen, will just
happen. What has to happen will
30 happen, without the permission of
the gods nothing can occur. So without a doubt, without hesitation have
a look at my child.
. . . .

35 Gajendra was sleeping, and how was
he sleeping, his face was in northern
direction, his face was in **northern**
direction. And he knew only too well
that a living being sleeping with the
40 face in northern direction can be

*Bhojpuri is unmarked; Creole loan is boldfaced; Hindi is underlined.

Jon **lenor** danai muh karke sutal
hawan unkar vad hoye saki. Hawe
khatir dekhilasa koye bhi prani uttar
men mu karke nai sutelansa.

killed. Whoever sleeps with his face
in **northern** direction can be killed.
Therefore you see that living beings
do not sleep with their face to the
45 north.

Drawing on puranic traditions about the birth of Ganesha, son of Shiva
and his divine wife, Parvati or Gauri Maa, Pandit Mohabeer tells the story
of how the infant Ganesh is introduced to the other deities who have gathered after his birth. Gauri Maa does not want to exclude the planet Shani
(Saturn) from beholding the infant deity, even though his glance is normally regarded as inauspicious. While delivering the sermon, the pandit
alternates between standard Hindi and purist Bhojpuri. In contrast to the
pattern in example 3.11, the pandit not only makes frequent use of Hindi
lexical items but completely switches to Hindi for entire stretches of his
discourse. His use of Bhojpuri shows maximal avoidance of Creole words,
the only exception being *lenor* (north) in lines 37 and 41. *Lenor* is juxtaposed with the Hindi synonym *uttar* on line 36, in a manner similar to
Prakash's lining up of synonyms or semantically closely related Creole
and Hindi terms in 3.11. In contrast, sanskritized Hindi terms, unfamiliar
in everyday Bhojpuri, are frequent in the pandit's discourse. The setting is
of course one dominated by Hindu religious practice, where the use of the
ancestral language Hindi is expected from a pandit. The shifts from Hindi
to Bhojpuri seem to have no inherent relation to the moments when they
occur. They are, for example, not associated with particular thematic shifts
or with reported speech or with changing narrative or interactional
stances. They appear to be a regular, unmarked practice by the speaker,
who besides alternating between the two languages is also introducing
numerous Hindi items into his use of Bhojpuri. The overall effect of this
shifting back and forth between Hindi and Bhojpuri and hindiizing of
Bhojpuri is to invest Bhojpuri with Hindu ethnic meanings, that is, to eth-
nicize Mauritian vernacular Bhojpuri by ideologically minimizing its distance from the ancestral language, Hindi. This process is further fostered
by the setting, a Hindu religious festival, and by the discursive content of
the sermon, which focuses on Hindu deities and moral values.

The same observations largely apply to example 3.13, where again an
affirmative stance towards Hindu values and tradition co-occurs with the
use of purist Bhojpuri with Hindi elements and the avoidance of Creole
words.

EXAMPLE 3.13*

Bhagavadgita hamni ki aisan pustak   1   The Bhagavadgita is such a book of
ha jon ki manushya ke, insan ke,   ours, which provides education for
admi ke siksha dewela, aisan siksha   man, man, man, gives such education
dewela ke kaise jiyeke chahi apan   like how one should live with oneself,
sange kaise jiyeke chahi apan parivar   how one should live with one's family,
sange kaise jiyeke chahi log sange.   5 how one should live with people.
    Eh, bhagavadgita jon bhagvan   Well, the Bhagavadgita gives
krishna sandes dewelan, jo aj se   a message by Lord Krishna, who
bahut pehele, jo jug kahelwan Dwar-   long ago, in a cosmic age called
parjug, u jug dwaren awelan . . .   Dwarparjug, in this age he came . . .
dharti me, gyan ke prachar ke de. . . . 10 entered the earth, in order to spread
                                          knowledge. . . .

Similar to example 3.12, the speaker in 3.13 is a pandit explaining the significance of a central sacred Hindu text during a sermon in a temple. The purist character of the pandit's Bhojpuri is underscored by the honorific verbal suffixes — rare in everyday speech — that he uses when referring to the deity Krishna, as in lines 7 and 9 (italicized in this excerpt). These together with the addition of Hindi elements and the avoidance of Creole lexical items reinforces the purist quality of the discourse, which is centered on Hindu values.

In contrast, more ambiguous stances with regard to Hindu tradition are often established in a register rather distant from such linguistic purism. A controversial topic in Hindu circles in Mauritius is the role of pandits and the pay they are asking for services such as performing a wedding. In the following discussion with me, Shankar, a well-to-do sugarcane planter who owns a fair amount of land, draws a distinction between the pandits of the Arya Samaj and those affiliated with the Sanatanist tradition. Even though Shankar's family is Sanatani, he views the Arya Samaj pandits as more reasonable in their demands, and criticizes Sanatani pandits for their exaggerated financial expectations.

EXAMPLE 3.14*

    S: Eh vedic men esan problem nai   1   S: Among the Arya Samajis this
       ba — kahe ke parski huwa ego   problem does not exist — why,

---

*Bhojpuri is unmarked; Creole loans and other elements are boldfaced; *Creole fransise* is boldfaced and underlined; English loans and other elements are boldfaced and italicized.

athi ha, kaise ego **liv** ba, **etabli**,
okar ego *rules and regulations*
etabli ho gal ba **ziskale** okar
pandit ke **sippose** ego pandit
ai saadi karai, ego acharya
athi ke pandit ta okar rate
fixe ha. Olog ke *rate*, olog ke
assosiasion fixe karela saadi
ke etna, marni ke etna, katha,
hawan ke etna ta jab panditwa
ai ta u kari aur ego **resit** dei
athi aur sab ta tora **par examp**
saadi ke daam **fixe** ho gal ba
senk san rupi ta tu sakba apan
se khushi se **mil** rupi dei, **de mil**
rupi dei. Ih **problem** nai ba
selman selman fixe karal ba, ih
sosiete fixe karleba.

Me **tandik** ke hamni men ta
pandit-wa **fixe** karela ta ou
tohra dekhi hai adamiya tani
baṛa ghar ba, tani athi ba, ta
ekar daam etna dalab okar
daam otna daalab, u apan par
fixe karela, apan se apan **pri**
fixe karela.

P.E.: Ta bahut mangela. . . .

S: Egzažere, egzažere, habhi kaise
hiya par ego pandit ba, u janela
kochi karle rahal, u jaiba oke
ego athi ke dekhe, ego kaam ke
dekhe ta u jab awela **lalist**
samaan kineke ta u **lalist**-wa
men dale. Apan daam wo daal
dewela, daal dewela apan, apan
pujari fees, pujari fees etna
daal dewela tah ih sab **normal**
nai ha **parski** ego pujari jab *fees*
mangata, *fees* — han — ta hai
valer cültürel-wa kuman ne pli
respecte karata, ta **komersialise**
karata oke okar ego ta

because there is a thing, like a
book, which is established, its
rules and regulations have
become established, up to when
their pandit, let's assume a
pandit has come to conduct a
wedding ceremony, a preacher,
pandit, so his *rate* is fixed.
Their *rate*, their association
fixes how much for a marriage,
how much for last rites, how
much for a katha, a hawan
ceremony, so when this pandit
comes, he will give you a
receipt and everything, so for
example the price of your
marriage ceremony is fixed,
five hundred rupees, then you
can by yourself, if you like, give
a thousand rupees, or two
thousand rupees. This problem
is not there, it is just fixed, and
that association sets it.

However, among us [Sana-
tanis] that pandit determines
[the price], so he will look at
you, if the people have a house
which is a little big, a little so
and so, so he will just set the
price, he sets it by himself, by
himself he sets the price.

P.E.: So he asks a lot. . . .

S: Excessive, excessive, now here
is a pandit, do you know what
he did, he went to prepare for
a service, so when he came
having bought a list of utensils,
he just put his own prices into
the list, just puts it in, for his
pujari fees, pujari fees he
charged so much, all of this
was not normal, because when
a priest asks for *fees, fees* —
yes — then he does *not* respect
this cultural value any more,
then he commercializes it, its,
with a *commercial aspect*,

commercial aspect se tandik   50
ego pandit ke ham sochila u
chahe kuch bhi konon kaam
karai ta chahi chor deike
jajmaan ke koi ke ketna
mankari deike u dei apan khusi   55
se me jab daam dale lagbe etna
chahela hamra **senk san**
chahela hai puja ta hawke ta
okar **valer commersialise** ho
jala.   60

meanwhile I think a pandit,
whatever service he does, he
should stop demanding this
and that from the patron, the
patron should give whatever
he likes, but if you set a price,
you want this much, you want
five hundred from us for this
puja, then its **value** becomes
commercialized.

At first glance, the language in which Shankar voices his approval of some pandits and critique of others resembles the nonpurist Bhojpuri most often used in everyday life, which is characterized by frequent use of Creole words. However, Shankar draws on other linguistic elements to lend authority to his perspective. But rather than inserting the sanskritized Hindi elements characteristic of the purist register of Bhojpuri, as in examples 3.11, 3.12, and 3.13, he uses *Creole fransise* (lines 35 and 47) and even English lexical items. This is especially the case the second time he speaks, when he criticizes Sanatani pandits for making unreasonable financial demands and suggests that financial profit has overshadowed "cultural values." Shankar's choice to deploy alternative linguistic indexes of authority in talking about Hindu religious practices underscores the distanced position he is taking with regard to ancestral traditions.

SITUATING INDIA: ETHNIC BELONGING AND DIASPORIC ORIENTATION

Patterns of shifting between registers and languages also offer interesting perspectives on how Hindu Mauritians conceive of the diasporic relationship to the land of their ancestors, India. The most obvious instance is the use of Indian ancestral languages in contexts such as religious settings and practices. Most interpret the cultivation of such languages as a sign of appreciation and respect for the ancestral land and its cultural and religious traditions. However, stances with regard to the land of the ancestors are far more complex and contradictory than those stressing the value of ancestral culture like to admit. This becomes evident among those who have had firsthand experience of India or have listened to others' accounts of travel or temporary stays there. While many Mauritians who have visited India narrate pleasant experiences, such as long-desired visits to important religious sites, highly attractive shopping and educational opportunities, and a sense of adventure in a vast land, others returned with more ambivalent views. In both cases, the great differences between Mauritius and India as places and societies are "rediscovered" and very often put at the center of travel narratives. The performance of travel narratives negotiate the complex relationships of experienced closeness and distance, identification and difference that Hindu Mauritians maintain with regard to India as homeland.

As in the life stories and narrations of the past discussed earlier in this chapter, the intersection between the semiotics of language-indexed difference and the narrative organization of contrasts between events, places, and states of affairs is of key interest here. In particular, Hindu Mauritians often highlight value-laden differences between life in Mauritius and the aspects of India experienced in travel through shifts in register and code. Talking about travel to India establishes some of these experienced contrasts between Mauritius and the India, reinforcing them with shifts between Bhojpuri and Creole as well as creative deployment of the ancestral language Hindi.

For example, Hindu Mauritians in La Nicolière frequently employ Bhojpuri in bilingual conversations to animate Indian characters, whether located in Mauritius or in India, thereby sometimes suggesting that they are rustic or very "traditional" types. The following is an excerpt from a conversation about *tilak*, the Hindu prenuptial gift-giving ritual associated with higher castes in Mauritius. In a conversation with Sandip and me, Rajesh animates two men who are negotiating the sum of money expected. The shift from Creole to Bhojpuri marks Rajesh's portrayal of the two men as Hindu Mauritians engaged in a very traditional activity, which in this narrative is also located in the past, approximately two generations ago.

EXAMPLE 3.15*

R:	Fin vini dan tilak, li dir, bon, mo pu don senk san rupi, letan pu lepok lontan mo pe dir la eh, dan tilak ketna janna aibah tilak men? La pu dimande, par examp, par examp mo, mo kote garson, twa to kote tifi, wai, ta	1 5	Someone came to the tilak, he would say, well I will give five hundred rupees, long ago, I would say, how many people will come to the tilak? He would ask, for example, for example I am the boy's side, you are the

*Bhojpuri is unmarked; Creole is boldfaced; English terms are boldfaced and italicized.

accha, tilak, tilak men, ta tu tilak
men ketna charhaiba? Ta tu
bolba accha, panch sau charha   10
dab. Ta tilak, ab jab aaiy tilak,
tilak charhar gal, tah **senk san**
nai ba, char sau ba, hahaha. . . .
    Tah ab saadi nai hoi, *cancel.*
Parski u ti dir senk san, saadi   15
cancel, pa pu fer saadi, hahaha,
fin ena, wai wai, fin ena, ayo, a
kaus sa tilak-la maryaz in *cancel,*
fin refis. . . .

                                    20

girl's side, well, for the tilak,
tilak, how much will you give?
Then you would say, well, I will
give five hundred. Then when
they come for the tilak, the tilak
is presented, there are not **five
hundred**, there are four hundred,
hahaha. . . .
    So there will be no wedding,
it is *canceled,* Because you said
five hundred, the wedding is *canceled,* there will be no wedding,
hahaha, this happened, yes, yes,
it happened, oh dear, because
of this tilak the wedding was
canceled, refused. . . .

S: Akoz san rupi, problem san
   rupi. . . .   25

R: Sa lepok ti boku kas sa. . . .

S: Non, san rupi ti boku kas sa
   lepok-la.   30

R: Ti boku kas! En arpan later ti pe
   vande sa lepok-la pu san senkant
   rupi, de san rupi. Beh, senk san
   rupi kan dimun donne ti boku
   kas.   35

S: Because of a hundred rupees,
   because of a problem of a
   hundred rupees. . . .

R: At that time it was a lot of
   money. . . .

S: Really, it was a lot of money at
   that time.

R: It was a lot of money! One arpent
   [0.85 acres, or 0.4 hectares] land
   at the time sold for one hundred
   fifty, two hundred rupees. Well,
   if someone gave five hundred
   rupees it was a lot of money.

Some people in La Nicolière extend this usage of Bhojpuri in reported
speech to the momentary performance of an Indian character in a narrative about travel in India. Here the effect is to highlight the difference
between the voices of Mauritian travelers and those of certain Indians
they encounter. Notably, the Indians thus animated in narration may not
have spoken in Bhojpuri at all, as in the following example, where the
actual conversation was in Hindi or Hindustani, but the reported voice
of an Indian interlocutor is partly rendered in Bhojpuri. Ajay and his
wife, Meera, had been on a tour of India with two other couples the year
before. With Ajay, their daughter, Kavita, and myself present, Meera tells
about Vishnu, the driver of the minivan they had hired in Delhi for their
tourist excursions, and reports Vishnu's words in a mix of Hindi and
Bhojpuri.

EXAMPLE 3.16*

A: Apre, lematen u leve en pe tar,   1 A: In the morning you would get
    set her, set her e demi, manz en   up a little late, at seven, half past
    tigit, bwar en pe dite tu sala,   seven, eat a little, drink some tea
    apre re, apre pe alle, transpor-la   and the like, then you would
    li ensam, ensam li, transpor ki   5   leave, traveling all together,
    nu ti pran la, li res ensam ensam,   the way we traveled it was all
    lematen veye, kumans promene,   together, in the morning we
    fer tu . . . .   would start touring, do
                                                   everything. . . .

M: Aster lor simen, rule rule, si in   10 M: Now on the road, traveling,
    gayn swaf-la . . . dhabba, hauja   traveling, when one gets
    dhabba <u>hai</u>. Visnu pyas lagal <u>hai</u>.   thirsty . . . a stall, there <u>is</u> a stall.
    <u>Chaliye</u>, <u>mataji</u>, <u>wahan par mein</u>   Vishnu <u>is</u> thirsty. <u>Come along</u>,
    <u>ek thar karunga</u>, <u>aap chaa piye</u>,   <u>lady</u>, <u>I</u> <u>will</u> <u>make</u> <u>a</u> <u>stop there</u>,
    <u>dhabe men</u>, <u>dhaba</u>. **Bwar dite.**   15   <u>you</u> <u>drink tea</u>, <u>at</u> <u>the stall</u>. **Drink**
                                                   tea.

A: Non . . . **malprop.**   A: No . . . it is dirty.
K: Nai ta tora kaise bollata. . . .   K: No, how should I tell you. . . .
A: **Pena, pena lizien.**   A: There is no, there is no hygiene.
M: **La u ou pe bwar dite, sa soz la,**   20 M: Where you drink tea, this thing,
    divan la vini, sa lapussier la . . .   the wind comes, this dust . . .
    huuuuh [making a sound like   huuuuh [making a sound like
    wind] . . . **u pe bwar dite?** . . .   wind] . . . you are drinking
    Oblize, oblize bwar.   tea? . . . You have to, you have
                                           25   to drink.

Some La Nicolière residents who have traveled to India use the same social voices animated by Bhojpuri and Creole in the two previous examples to construct overall differences between Mauritius and India in travel narratives, and to place the narrator and other characters in a particular position vis-à-vis the two places, which are portrayed as vastly different. In the following excerpt from another narrative, shifts in register and language are part of the performative distancing and difference-marking vis-à-vis experiences in India related by two men of La Nicolière. Raj, a civil servant in his forties, performs a vivid account of his recent visit to India with his family for tourism and shopping. Prem, a secondary-school teacher of about the same age, has never been to India but has already formed an opinion about the country by listening

---

*Bhojpuri is unmarked; Creole is boldfaced; Hindi is underlined.

to friends' travel stories. Ashvin, a neighbor of Raj's, is also present. Raj
and Prem collaboratively construct a common stance as inhabitants of a
Mauritius starkly different from India. Raj begins by telling about their
final train ride from Delhi back to Mumbai, from where he and his family intended to depart for Mauritius. However, the train derailed, leaving
them stranded in the countryside with almost no money, and they had to
take a bus the rest of the way to Mumbai.

EXAMPLE 3.17*

R: Ab konchi hoi ab? Ek mahina
lek? Kapṛa kinnail ha, kinnail . . .
paisa kalass ho gal.
[P. and others present are
laughing]
Aisa khalass ho gal ba. Hola, na?
Apan **bize** kareke, aweke. **Tren**
men paisa **fini** ho gal, ab **bis**
lelisa. Rat din hoige, do din do
rat, **rule mem**. . . .

1 R: Now, what now? One month has
passed. You have bought clothes,
bought . . . the money is totally
finished.
5 [P. and others present are
laughing]
So it is totally finished, no? You
have exhausted your **budget** and
then you go back. The money
10 ran out while on the **train**, now
we took a **bus**. Day and night,
two days, two nights, **just
driving**. . . .

A: Dehli se Bombay tak.
R: **Wai**, do rat do din.
A: Bahut **fatigan** ba.
R: Bahut **fatigan**. . . .
P: **Sa, bap**. . . .
R: Ham hause **la pir zurnee**.
[all are laughing]
Ham ta batiae dekhe. . . .
P: **En gran lexperians, selman,
lend**.
[all are laughing]
Ton pa enjoy li.
R: Ah, mon dezi, dezi, mon pa
contan. *I'm not happy with*. . . .

A: **From Delhi to Bombay**.
15 R: **Yeah**, two days and two nights.
A: This is very **tiring**.
R: Very **tiring**. . . .
P: **This, good heavens**. . . .
R: That was my **worst day**.
20 [all are laughing]
I will tell and you will see. . . .
P: **It is just a great experience,
India**.
[all are laughing]
25 **You have not enjoyed it**.
R: Oh, I was disappointed,
disappointed, I did not like it.
I'm not happy with. . . .

A: Hm.
R: **Wai, bez, to bizin**. . . . **Lend so
lenvironman** accha nai ba, okar
latmosfer. . . .

A: Hm.
30 R: **Yes, damn, you have to**. . . .
India's environment is no good,
its **atmosphere**. . . .

*Bhojpuri is unmarked; Creole and Creole loans are boldfaced; English is boldfaced and
italicized.

P: Ižien nai ba.

R: Ižien nai ba.

P: Mem en pei, mem li miser. . . .

R: Delhi . . . ba, Bombay nai. . . .
    Bombay men bahut **pollusion** ba,
    santi nai ba, hauwa **trankilite** nai
    ba.   40

P: To konne lend so problem . . .
    mass illiteracy. Dimun la illetre,
    zot pa konn so valer, so valer
    soz-la.   45

R: Non, non, non zot pa . . . kont
    its very normal in Mauritius. . . .

P: Non, mo pe dir twa en zafer.   50
    Ližien li deman. . . .

R: Oui, sa sa.

P: Li deman *literacy.*

R: Partu puhar, malang, na. Sa . . .
    hauw **voyas**-wa. . . . Ootee se   55
    awat rahlisa, rat ke. **Katrer** hauja
    pahunchlisa. **Fini fer visite.** Jab
    awat rahlisa. . . .

A: Bahut baṛa des ba.   60

R: Bahut baṛa. Jab awat rahlisa, ta
    kai baje awelansa char baje. . . .

P: Me lend, ena so plas, ena so plas,
    ban-la alle ban endien e tusala,
    ban-la alle zot ena so kontakt-la.   65
    Zot all dan plas prop byen. To
    compran-la?

R: Wi ena plas pu enjoy. Me bizin
    konne boku.
                                                70
P: Par kont, Gunessee lin alle. Lin
    bizin rest enferme. Me ki arrive,
    sa plas lin alle la, partu malang!
    Lin pa kapav sorti mem. Lin rest
    dan lakaz. Ban-la dir lin res mo   75
    kwar en trwa semen. Si donk lin
    gayn degu. Mon ublie kot lin
    alle-la.
                                                80

P: There is no **hygiene**.

R: There is no **hygiene**.

P: Even if a country, even if it is
    poor. . . .

R: This is . . . Delhi, not Bombay. . . .
    In Bombay there is a lot of
    pollution, there is no quiet and
    peace, you do not find this
    tranquility.

P: You know what India's problem
    is . . . *mass illiteracy.* The people
    there are illiterate, they do not
    know its value, the value of this
    thing there.

R: No, no, they do not . . . on the
    other hand *it is very normal in
    Mauritius.* . . .

P: No, I will tell you one thing.
    Hygiene needs. . . .

R: Yes, this this.

P: It needs *literacy.*

R: Everywhere filth, it is **dirty**.
    This . . . this **journey**. . . . We
    were coming from Ootee, at
    night. We got there at **four**. We
    completed the visit. When we
    were coming. . . .

A: It is a very large country.

R: Very large. We we got there, at
    what time, at four. . . .

P: But India, there are places, there
    are places, they, the Indians and
    so on, they go there and have
    their contacts. They go to nice
    clean places. You understand?

R: Yes there are places to enjoy. But
    you really have to know your
    way around.

P: On the other hand, Gunessee
    went there. He had to remain
    locked up. What happened, that
    place where he went, everywhere
    filth! He wasn't able to even go
    out. He stayed inside. They said
    that he stayed about three weeks.
    As if he had become disgusted. I
    forgot where he went there.

R: Nu, nun voyaz boku. Kuma nun
   desan Bombay nunres kat zur
   [unclear] nun al, nun al
   Bangalore. De Bangalore nun
   al. . . .   85

P: Lin all en plas kot, kumadir, tu
   ban dimun malang. Zot pe fer
   zot bizin natirel-la . . . *in the
   open!* Ehh, pe kras partu. Lin   90
   gayn en degu.

R: Wai. Sa ena sa. Sa ena boku
   sa. . . .

A: Sa ena, salte partu. . . .
                                              95

P: Partu, li normal.

R: Ena so scavenging, tu. Kamion
   passe kumsa mem, me ena tro
   boku dimun.
                                              100

P: Tro boku, taaa. . . .

R: Sa pollusion nwar la, sa baap, pa
   fasil sa. Sa lesiel ble-la zame truv
   sa.

P: Purtan lend, li pa en pei   105
   endistrialise. So pollusion ki to
   pe dir-la.

R: So pollusion, eh, ban vehikil ki
   ena.   110

P: Ban vehikil, vehikil boku.
   Me pans ki pu ete en pei
   endistrialise. Lamor sa.
   Lamor.

R: We, we traveled a lot. When we
   went down to Bombay we stayed
   four days [unclear] we went,
   we went to Bangalore. From
   Bangalore we went. . . .

P: He went to a place where, like,
   all the people are dirty. They
   relieve themselves . . . *in
   the open!* Eh, and they spit
   everywhere. He became
   disgusted.

R: Yeah, you find this there, there is
   a lot of it. . . .

A: That is what you find, dirtyness
   everywhere. . . .

P: Everywhere, it's normal.

R: They have scavengers and
   everything. The truck passes
   like this, but there are too many
   people.

P: Too many, oh my. . . .

R: With this black pollution, it's not
   easy. You will never see a blue
   sky like this.

P: Even though India, it is not an
   industrialized country. [If it was]
   what would you have to say
   about the pollution.

R: The pollution, and all the
   vehicles that there are.

P: Vehicles, many vehicles.
   But imagine if it was an
   industrialized country. Like
   death. Death.

The shift of the conversation from Bhojpuri to Creole is initiated by Prem, in his ironic remark in lines 22–23, after which he discusses the backwardness of India compared to Mauritius. The shift is quickly taken up by Raj, who in reporting the negative aspects of his travel experience joins Prem in constructing a value-laden contrast between India and Mauritius. The theme of lack of hygiene in India is brought up, and then the conversation shifts entirely to Creole when illiteracy is identified as a problem in India and then connected to the experienced lack of hygiene. As in examples 3.7 and 3.8, *ližien* (hygiene) in lines 33–34 and 51 can be characterized as *Creole fransise*, corresponding to French *hygiène*, as compared to Creole *lizien*, and the indexical loading and interactive stance signaled by its use in this context can be compared to the use of *enženyer* (engineer) instead of "ordinary" Creole *enzenyer* in example 3.1. Note also the salient use of the English terms *mass illiteracy* and *literacy* by the teacher Prem in characterizing India, which he has never visited. Raj seeks to keep up with Prem's token displays of education in line 48, education being presented in this particular conversation as generally lacking in India, thereby further highlighting the contrast between Indians and Mauritians already established. While collaboratively constructing a stance of alienation and distance from the diasporic homeland, the two men draw on *Creole fransise* and English elements as alternative indices of authority. Prem further intensifies the opposition between the two places by interrupting Raj's narrative and retelling the experiences of a colleague whose accommodations on a work-related trip to India were reportedly in a neighborhood with open sewers and overpowering smells, which are not common in Mauritius. Further references are made to the great multitudes of people in India and the intense urban pollution, again implicitly contrasted with more amenable conditions in Mauritius. The patterns of shift between Bhojpuri and Creole in this conversation clearly draw on presupposed valuations of the two languages, Bhojpuri often considered "backward" in the sense of being both "traditional" and evidence of little or no education. This value-laden linguistic contrast is in turn employed in a recursive manner to construct differences between a perceived India and Mauritius. The shift to Creole in the course of the interaction signals the speakers' distancing themselves from perceived backwardness, ignorance, and lack of cleanliness, and thus the place momentarily presented as typifying these qualities, India.

A few moments later, Raj continues with his detailed description of the trip to India.

EXAMPLE 3.18*

R:	Ler ke nu pe desann depi Ootee,	1	R:	When we were going down to
	ver minuit, laru klate, derier, laru			Ootee, near midnight, the tire
	derier. Laru divan klate, tombe			burst, the rear one, on the rear
	en ba, lamor . . . right . . . aster			wheel. If the front tire had burst,
	sanse. Bahut dan bwa . . . gayn	5		we would have fallen down,

*Creole is boldfaced; Bhojpuri is unmarked; Hindi and hindiized terms are underlined.

per. Apre, apre truve gardien, pe
allim dife. Mon diman kifer u
allim dife. Li dir li pu zanimo
laba. Gayn per!

dead . . . right . . . now wheel
change. Deep in the forest . . . I
became afraid. Then, then I saw
the guardian, he is lighting a fire.
10 I asked why do you light a fire?
He says it's because of the
animals down there. I was
frightened!

A: Haha, ban zanimo sovaz. . . .
R: Na pa vini. Aster nu pe vini vini.
Laru'n sanze. Nu pe vini vini, de
gro lelefan lor sime! Les li
trankil. Les li buze par li mem,
lerla. . . .

A: Haha, wild animals. . . .
15 R: Could not go on. Now we are
driving on. The wheel has been
changed. We are driving, two big
elephants on the road! Leave
them in peace. Let them move by
20 themselves, then. . . .

A: En lelefan?
R: En elefan! Asterla li lor sime.
Kan lin avanse ler la li rule,
asterla. . . .

A: An elephant?
R: An elephant! Now he is on the
road. When he moves, the bus
moves on, now. . . .

P: To pa kapav avans li la.

25 P: You are not able to move it
aside.

R: Kot pu kapav fer sa? Li sovaz
li . . . li sovaz li. Lelefan sovaz.
Dan bwa ke ba. Pa konne,
trankil, li bon ban sofer la
konne.

R: How are you supposed to do
this? It is wild . . . it is wild. A
wild elephant. It is in the forest.
30 Don't know, be quiet, it is good
that the drivers know about this.

P: Li bon, ton fer en bon yatra ton
vini. [laughs]

P: Good, you have made a good
journey, and you are back.
[laughs]

R: Move yatra. En yatra "sok
samachaar."

35 R: A mean journey. A "frightful
journey."

Again, Raj emphasizes the contrast between India and Mauritius in
relating his travel observations. In this extract his representation of India
shifts towards the exotic, the fascinating, and the dangerous. Wild animals in a dense forest and elephants blocking the road are unknown
experiences in Mauritius, further underscoring the differences between
the two places. It is, however, the ironic use of the Indian "ancestral language" Hindi by both Raj and Prem on lines 32 and 35–36 that is most
remarkable in this excerpt. Raj almost sarcastically uses the sanskritized
Hindi term *yatra*, denoting primarily Hindu pilgrimage and secondarily
journey in a wider sense, to refer to Raj's trip. Prem replies in an equally
ironic hybrid Creole-Hindi phrase, characterizing his trip as *sok samachaar*, alliteratively combining the Creole *sok* (shock) with the sanskrit-

ized Hindi *samacaar* (news, information), translatable as "shocking news" or more loosely, "frightful experience."[9] The creative use of the ancestral language, normally employed to express an affirmative and respectful stance towards the land of the forefathers, now functions as an ironic distancing device, further stressing the alienation and the sense of difference the men performatively construct, and reinforcing the stance of Mauritians towards an India portrayed as strange and foreign. It also demonstrates the creative deployment of presupposed valuations of Hindi in order to express ambivalence about Hindi as ancestral language and even estrangement. Such a use, however, would not be imaginable without the speakers' awareness of presupposed uses of Hindi in Mauritius. In a wider sense, this dialogue points to the complexity of Hindu Mauritian stances toward a diasporic homeland, negotiating the tension between a presupposed and institutionalized relationship to India through state-sponsored ancestral culture and language that Hindus draw on to justify their central position in a Mauritian nation, on the one hand, and the experiences of difference and even alienation travelers often report concerning their encounters with India and Indians, on the other.

In this chapter I have discussed a range of examples demonstrating how interactive stances and social identities among Hindus in rural northern Mauritius are created in linguistic performance. While diasporic Hindu subjects are shaped through linguistic practice, the marking of distinction, authority, and class intersects in complex ways with the performance of ethnicity and diasporic belonging. At the same time, language functions as a powerful means of establishing varying relationships of temporality experienced with respect to events and places. Linguistic practice and performance thus locate Hindu Mauritians in time through both narrative structuring, as in life stories and narrative representations of social changes, and invocation of the world of the ancestors by using particular registers and language varieties: purist Bhojpuri and Hindi.

Colonial Education, Ethnolinguistic Identifications, and the Origins of Ancestral Languages

NATIONALISM, COLONIALISM, AND LANGUAGE

This chapter addresses the intersection of colonialism, nationalism, and language, in particular, it analyzes how the construction of communities in a colonial context was mediated by ideas about language. I show how debates surrounding the establishment of an educational system and educational language policy in colonial Mauritius became a privileged site for contesting hegemonic claims in the form of negotiating the relationships of different groups in a colonial plantation setting. Conflicting approaches to language in education also informed debates about the role and significance of Indo-Mauritians in ascribing an identity to Mauritius with its lack of a precolonial population. At the same time, the contesting ideas about language and linguistic differentiation highlighted in debates about education were also important in shaping Indo-Mauritians' notions of identity and community, which later emerged as key elements of a postcolonial politics privileging diasporic ancestral languages and cultural traditions over those with claims to indigenousness.

One of the origins of the prominent role that questions of language have played in the creation of notions of nationality and ethnic belonging in Mauritius compared to other colonial plantation settings is the early strategy of the Franco-Mauritians, who after the British conquest of Mauritius in 1810 sought to justify the continuation of their political and economic hegemony in discourses about the primacy of French in Mauritius. Debates on the relative prevalence of certain languages in Mauritius and on classifications of local linguistic practices under the labels of certain standardized languages, such as Creole under French and Bhojpuri under Hindi, turned out to be closely linked to struggles about the entitlements of particular groups to political rights and privileges on the island. The shaping of a Mauritian identity in these contexts often took place through a process of ideologically linking the island to sources of ethnolinguistic authenticity beyond Mauritius, such as the French heritage invoked by Franco-Mauritians and Indian ancestral languages later championed by Hindu activists.

In examining colonialism in India, anthropologists have emphasized how modern techniques of control and rule such as the census resulted in the construction and reification of communal identities (Appadurai 1996a, Cohn 1987). An important dimension of these administrative practices of colonialism was the surveying, classifying, and counting of languages and speakers. These contributed to an objectification of Indian social identifications, whose explosive consequences are especially apparent in contemporary ethnonationalism and religious communalism. As scholarship on South Asia has amply documented, the production of knowledge about Indian languages was an inseparable part of this process, resulting in attempts to define, objectify, and standardize Indian languages (Cohn 1985, Lelyveld 1993). Similarly, the role of colonial linguistics in producing "representations of languages as powerful icons of spiritual, territorial, and historical hierarchies" (Errington 2001, 19) that justified colonial rule has been demonstrated by researchers working on other parts of the colonial world (Harries 1988, Irvine 1993, Meeuwis 1999, Rafael 1988). Nevertheless, the agency of colonial scholars such as George Grierson, the director of the monumental Linguistic Survey of India, has often been overestimated, considering the crucial role their local elite interlocutors played in the process of language construction and standardization (Burghart 1996, 376–78).

Theorists of nationalism such as Benedict Anderson have also paid attention to the role of language in the formation of ethnonational identities in colonial contexts. However, in explaining the spread of nationalism under colonialism, Anderson mainly stresses projects of linguistic homogenization imposed by a state bureaucracy. This model of "Russification" in the context of what he describes as state-driven "official nationalism" is presented as a scenario characteristic of nineteenth-century empires, whether the Czarist empire or colonial empires. Anderson portrays this type of linguistic nationalism "from above" as instrumental in the process of modern state-building and centralization, as well as enhancing the legitimacy of imperial rule. Regarding the intersection of nationalism, colonialism, and language in India, he is mainly concerned with the rise of an English-educated elite along the lines of "Macaulayism" (Anderson 1991, 91). In contrast to Anderson's account, which stresses the instrumentalities of communication for the functioning of imperial state apparatuses, Partha Chatterjee has shown how language emerges as one of the cultural sites for the imagination of ethno-national identity under colonialism (Chatterjee 1993). Nineteenth-century bilingual Bengali elites constructed a newly standardized Bengali as a central component of what was perceived as a "spiritual, inner" sphere, conceived in marked contrast to the world of the European colonizer.[1] In contrast to Anderson's approach, Chatterjee develops a theory of "reactive" anticolonial and postcolonial nationalism in which a nationalized language features prominently in the definition of an ethnonational essence. The role of language as a means of communication for spreading national consciousness is of lesser consequence compared to the ideological field it provides for the imagination of the nation. In this way, Chatterjee's perspective brings us to an understanding of how so-called ancestral languages could play a role in shaping ethnonational identities in Mauritius.

The Mauritian situation confirms many of the points made about the colonial bureaucratic creation and objectification of linguistic ethnicity in India. However, the formation of ethnolinguistic communities among Indo-Mauritians cannot be characterized as a mere imposition of such identifications by a colonial apparatus of knowledge production.[2] Instead, especially starting in the 1930s, the process took on the character of an ideological struggle between different groups of colonizers and various factions among the Indo-Mauritians over the definition of ethnolinguistic identities, resembling a scenario of conflictual colonial "dialogics" (Kaplan and Kelly 1994) rather than a successful imposition of colonial knowledge.[3]

Also, the notion of linguistic ethnicity was already very much in evidence among the Franco-Mauritian population by 1834 when indentured laborers started to arrive in Mauritius from India, and was further brought to the forefront in the context of the Franco-Mauritians' initially uneasy relations with the British colonial administration. The ethnicization of language in colonial Mauritius resulted in the eventual construction of ethnonational communities among Indo-Mauritians based not on vernaculars but on presumed ancestral languages, such as Hindi. In contrast with Anderson's model of linguistic nationalism in colonial contexts, neither the imperial languages nor, following a European model, "shared" vernaculars of everyday communication became the focus of ethnonational mobilization among Indo-Mauritians. The languages of empire and dominant print languages (English and French) as well as the dominant languages of routine verbal interaction (Creole and Bhojpuri), remained on the periphery of such constructions of community. Instead, Indo-Mauritians advocated the recognition of standardized Indian languages that were unknown to most immigrating ancestors and were initially mastered only by a small minority of religious specialists and activists.

The rise of ancestral languages in Mauritius also defies instrumentalist approaches to linguistic nationalism that seek to explain political mobilization and conflict around language as the reaction to blocked social mobility for members of a given ethnolinguistic group within a modern state (DeVotta 2004, Inglehart and Woodward 1972 [1967]). The importance of these ancestral languages has been above all their role in shaping boundaries between what came to be known as ethnic communities and in providing ideological support for them as legitimate claimants of political rights and privileges. In comparison, their role in providing access to material resources and employment was less consequential, even though new opportunities for employment as teachers and administrators were created when ancestral languages were eventually taught in state or state-supported schools. At issue here is the highlighting of a source of ethnolinguistic authenticity connected with a diasporic homeland in India, employed as a legitimizing principle in the struggle for political power in post–Second World War Mauritius.

LANGUAGE AND EDUCATION
IN THE BRITISH COLONIAL PERIOD

The way language emerged as a primary focus for the creation of ethnic communities in colonial Mauritius is nowhere as apparent as in the debates surrounding education. Two different phases can be distinguished in the development of the education system in colonial Mauritius as it contributed to shaping Indo-Mauritian ethnolinguistic identifications. The first spans the period of British colonial rule up to the Second World War, a period marked by rivalries between the Franco-Mauritian plantocracy and the British colonial administration centered partly on their different perspectives on the Indian population in Mauritius. My discussion starts with the establishment of a system of education in the second half of the nineteenth century, when the colonial state first attempted to provide formal education for Indians in Mauritius. These beginnings of state-supported schooling resulted in the formulation of a colonial educational language policy in which French and English predominated. In its basic principles this policy has remained in effect until today. During this period of colonial rule, the shape of the educational system, especially its language policies, was the outcome of conflicts and compromises between the different groups of colonizers present in Mauritius. I draw attention to the fact that just as the colonial subject population of Mauritius was marked by striking diversity and later reworked into a plurality of "communities," the colonizers also represented a collection of different groups with conflicting interests (Comaroff and Comaroff 1991, Cooper and Stoler 1997). This was the case not only with regard to the perspectives on education in general held by the local British administration, the Colonial Office in London, the Franco-Mauritian plantocracy, the Catholic Church, and Protestant missionaries, but also when it came to their varying approaches to language in schools. Analyzing the larger part of the colonial period, I show how different ideas about language in Mauritian education were integral parts of wider ideologies through which members of the groups exercising colonial power identified Mauritius and the roles they thought they should play in the colonization of the island.

During much of the nineteenth century, language policy in Mauritian education was dominated by an antagonism between the Franco-Mauritian plantocracy and the Catholic Church on one hand, and the British administration and Protestant missionaries on the other. The points of contention were whether Indians and Indo-Mauritians should be provided with access to schooling at all, and whether the dominant language in education should be French or English. The question of Indian languages was raised several times in the context of British proposals for "vernacular" or "Anglo-vernacular" education for Indians. The Catholic Church and the Franco-Mauritians viewed these proposals as supporting British policies of anglicization. Towards the end of the century the predominating linguistic arrangements in Mauritian education emerged as a compromise between the two principal competing colonizing groups in Mauritius. English and French were made compulsory on all levels, English being the official medium of instruction beyond the first years of primary school. The role of Indian languages became marginal.

The second phase in the establishment of an education system begins with the Second World War. During the war Indo-Mauritians asserted themselves politically in the context of changes that were moving Mauritius towards decolonization in the British Empire. Indo-Mauritian leaders demanded that Indian languages be taught to Indo-Mauritian students, though they did not question the overall dominance of French and English in schooling. In contrast to the debates of the nineteenth century, when the issue was the introduction of Indian languages as medium of schooling, in the second phase the point of debate was the teaching of Indian languages as ancestral traditions in order to valorize and "protect" Indian cultural traditions in Mauritius. The grounds for this proposal had been laid in the early part of the twentieth century by the establishment of Hindu organizations with close links to India who considered the teaching and cultivation of Indian ancestral languages one of their objectives. I describe how such claims and their realization in the institutionalization of the teaching of ancestral languages led to a growing ethnoreligious "communalization" of debates about language in Mauritius, which continued after independence in 1968. As I will show, an important reason for this is that the positions of ancestral languages in the school system came to be viewed as iconic of the power relations of the ethnoreligious communities claiming them. The recognition of ancestral languages in education with their strong links to ethnoreligious group formation demonstrates how perceptions of linguistic diversity and differentiation lead to imaginations of ethnic and national boundaries through a series of semiotic mediations (Irvine and Gal 2000). In the scenario analyzed here, claims related to language policy in education are part of wider power struggles between simultaneously emerging communities in Mauritius, finally becoming part of debates over which group most clearly represents the postcolonial Mauritian nation.

DETERMINING THE LINGUISTIC IDENTITY OF THE "INDIAN": SCHOOLING AND COLONIAL CONTROL

During much of the nineteenth century, the approach of the British colonial administration to the question of education for Indo-Mauritians was very different from that of the Franco-Mauritians and the local Catholic Church, which was closely tied to the Franco-Mauritians and their political and economic interests. In general, the Franco-Mauritians, and consequently the Catholic Church, were at first reluctant to provide any sort of formal education for Indo-Mauritians, due to the Franco-Mauritian sugarcane planters' need for a large, educationally unenlightened and unskilled labor force. In the British colonial administration, however, the idea of providing basic schooling to children of Indian background in order to turn them into "civilized," disciplined, and loyal subjects predominated. The provisions for the schooling of Indo-Mauritians that were the outcome of this British colonial project turned out to be a compromise among the powerful Franco-Mauritian settlers and plantocrats, who were then dominating the island's economy, the Legislative Council of the colony, and the local British administration. The Court of Directors of the East India Company and the Colonial Office in London also intervened at crucial moments. Thus language policy in education was a field in which the different ideologies and interests of the various colonial groups and factions were manifested in a particularly clear way.

While there had been an Indian presence in Mauritius even under French colonial rule, the year 1834 marked the beginning of large-scale indentured Indian immigration to Mauritius. Out of concerns to solidify their control over the Indian immigrants, who already by the end of the 1850s constituted the majority of the Mauritian population, and regarding them as heathens in want of morality, some British colonial administrators in collaboration with Protestant missionaries wanted to use the presumably civilizing effects of schooling in order to create more loyal and orderly colonial subjects. From the outset, they recognized the "language question" as one of the most difficult problems in educating Indo-Mauritians, who they knew were linguistically diverse. They were aware that "two entirely different languages spoken by the Bengal, and by the Coast Indians,"[4] presumably Bhojpuri and Tamil, predominated among them.

The first systematic attempt to provide Indian immigrants and their children with schooling took place under Governor Higginson in the 1850s, culminating in the 1857 ordinance for compulsory education, which was highly controversial in Mauritius and was ultimately canceled by the Court of Directors of the East India Company in London. The medium of education was at the forefront of debate, since Governor Higginson was an advocate of "vernacular education" for Indians, and the British were at the time also pursuing a policy of attempted anglicization in this colony where francophone traditions dominated.

Before assuming office as Governor of Mauritius, Higginson had had a long and successful career in the Indian Army, based in Agra. Early in his term as governor, Higginson provided for a government grant to set up an experimental Indian vernacular school, run by a teacher from India, in the south of the island, since he was convinced that Indian vernaculars should be the medium of instruction for Indian indentured immigrants in Mauritius. Although the experiment was later judged a failure, Higginson pressed on with his original plan of compulsory vernacular education for Indians. Higginson's concerns for Indian education in Mauritius have to be understood against the background of wider developments in education in India and Britain (Kalla 1984). The time of his early career in India saw the well-known debates on education in colonial India between the "Orientalists" of Fort William College in Calcutta and the "Anglicists" led by Thomas Macaulay. The position of the latter, expressed in Macaulay's famous Minute of 1835, calling for the primacy of English in Indian education and the creation of a "class of persons Indian in blood and colour, but English in tastes, in opinions, in morals and intellect," (cited in Sharp 1965, 116), initially prevailed. However, while Higginson was governor in Mauritius, Governor General of India Sir Charles Woods approved the institutionalization of vernacular education in India in his Educational Dispatch of 1854, finally reversing the pro-English policy in education. Further, Higginson was aware that Protestant missionaries in India strongly favored use of the vernacular in education to facilitate their project of proselytizing through "plain teaching" (Kalla 1984, 123). Finally, Higginson's ideas of compulsory education for the laboring classes were influenced by contemporary developments in Britain, where employers were being pressured to pay for half-time education for the children working in their factories and other enterprises.

Higginson was in favor of separate schools for children of Indian immigrants in Port Louis, "one for children from Madras, in the Tamil language; the other for Calcutta children, in the Hindoo dialect" (quoted in Ramdoyal 1977, 83). In 1854, Higginson pressed for the establishment of a school in the colonial capital Port Louis with Tamil as the medium of instruction and English as a second language. The school would be run by Protestant missionary Reverend Hardy, who "from his long sojourn" in India "must be conversant with the Tamil languages" and "familiar with methods of instruction" (quoted in Kalla 1984, 124). This project was resisted by the Franco-Mauritian-dominated Council of Government, and a special committee advised that Indian children should receive the same French-medium instruction as Creole children (Ramdoyal 1977, 83), meaning locally born children of Christian families who were not Franco-Mauritians but were at least partly of African ancestry.

It is important to realize that the resistance to Indian vernacular education by the Franco-Mauritian plantocracy was part of an attempt to reverse the 1847 decision to make English instead of French the language of the Supreme Court of Mauritius (Kalla 1984, Toussaint 1969, Tirvassen 1989). Franco-Mauritians at the time were mobilizing against what they perceived to be a British policy of anglicization of the colony. They considered the plans for compulsory education in Indian vernaculars with English as a second language for the majority of the island's population a measure directed against the status of French. The decision was ultimately left to the Colonial Office in London, and the main official in charge of the issue, Secretary of State for the Colonies Henry Labouchère (later Lord Taunton), sided with the Franco-Mauritians against the governor and his local administration. Writing to Governor Higginson, Labouchère remarked:

> On the question whether the Indian children should be educated as Creoles or as Indians, i.e. in the dialect of the part of India from which they come, or in the dialect in use in Mauritius . . . much should depend on the question whether the greater portion of the Indian children are likely to remain in Mauritius, or to return to India, much also on the wishes of their parents. If the children are likely to remain through life in the Colony, I am of the opinion that a French dialect would be far better for them in every way than the language of the country of their extraction, and I should hope that their parents would be sensible of the advantages they would derive from it. It is also to be borne in mind that the education is to be given at the cost of the people of Mauritius, who must naturally wish to encourage the Indians to remain, and with that view, to educate them in that dialect which is spoken by the majority of the taxpaying classes of the colony. If, therefore, you should find it expedient to cooperate with the Council in adopting a scheme for conducting the education in the dialect of Mauritius, I should be quite prepared to give it my sanction.[5]

There are several striking points in this assessment from London. First, despite the fact that recent Indian immigrants already comprised half of the population, Creole was understood to be the dominant language of Mauritius. According to the Secretary of State, if Indians were to settle permanently there, it would be natural to educate them in the local language. Further, following one of the standard arguments of the Franco-Mauritian plantocracy in their rejection of anglicization, this predominant local language is portrayed as a French dialect and then further associated with the "taxpaying classes" of the colony. That is, the Secretary of State recognized the French linguistic hegemony over Mauritius. This was in contrast to the governor's perspective, formed during his long years of service in India. Higginson viewed the recent immigrants as the "Indians" he knew, to whom educational practices common in colonial India could naturally be extended.

In the end, fundamentally different perspectives about Mauritius clashed in this debate about the medium of instruction in Mauritian schools. While the Colonial Office followed the Franco-Mauritian notion that Mauritius is a French-dominated colony, and that immigrants from India should adapt to this by being submitted to a process of creolization, Governor Higginson thought that at least as far as the education of the large and rapidly growing Indian immigrant population was concerned, Mauritius could be treated as a "little India." He was supported by the Protestant missionaries working among Indians in Mauritius, who reckoned that the success of the Church of England schools among this population was because of the use of Indian vernaculars as mediums of instruction (Kalla 1984, 127).

Governor Higginson was able to have an ordinance for compulsory education passed in 1857, but in the face of the combined opposition of the Franco-Mauritian-dominated Legislative Council of the colony and the Colonial Office in London, he had to give in on the language issue. Ordinance 21 of 1857 stated that all boys between ages six and ten in Mauritius residing within one and half miles of a school were obliged to attend school and that "the French language was to be the medium of instruction; but in every school English was to be taught" (Ramdoyal 1977, 83).

However, despite the fact that the compulsory education ordinance received royal confirmation, it was brought down in the end. The year 1857 also saw a major uprising against colonial rule in India. The Court of Directors of the East India Company, made extremely nervous in their administrative dealings with Indian subjects after the experience of the rebellion, which had only narrowly failed, objected to the ordinance and advised the Colonial Office to stop it. The reason given was that the "right of the colony to force a system of education from which their mother tongue was excluded" was questioned (quoted in Kalla 1984, 130; see also Ramdoyal 1977: 84). This caused Lord Stanley, Secretary of State for India, to render the school attendance of Indian children in Mauritius optional instead of compulsory. With this, the project of compulsory education had failed.

The most noteworthy feature of these developments was that the Court of Directors of the East India Company brought down the ordinance because the Court, in marked contrast to the Colonial Office, shared Governor Higginson's views on Indian vernacular education. The

Court, like Higginson, viewed the Indian immigrants in Mauritius in the same terms as Indians in India and assumed that similar administrative measures could be applied to them. The idea that Mauritius was under French hegemony and that Indians were supposed to adapt to this situation linguistically and culturally through creolization and obtaining education through French was far from the minds of the members of the Court of Directors. Higginson, of course, was more than aware of the local political and economic dominance of the Franco-Mauritian plantocracy as well as their view that Mauritius had really never ceased to be the Île de France. His plans for vernacular and Anglo-vernacular schools for Indians grew out of both his perspective on the Indian immigrants as an extension of India, and his desire to bring the island closer to anglicization.

Despite the defeat of the 1857 compulsory education ordinance, the British administration in Mauritius continued to pursue plans for the schooling of Indo-Mauritians, whose enrollment continued to be at a very low level, the vast majority of Indo-Mauritian children on the sugar estates never receiving any sort of formal schooling. From 1862 until 1880, schooling in Mauritius was crucially influenced by Superintendent of Schools J. Comber Browne (later Esquire). Browne was a stern advocate of Victorian moral ideals, which he sought to spread among Indian immigrants and Indo-Mauritians through the schooling of their children. Having a dim view of the customs and habits of the Indian immigrants, especially the "Hindoo type, among whom the grossest ideas of morality prevail,"[6] he nevertheless recognized the promising "mental abilities" of Indian children in a racialized understanding of ethnic stereotypes while comparing Creoles and Indians.[7] His vision of the moral transformation of Indians through education was one of panoptic supervision, which would yield more controllable and loyal colonial subjects,[8] and he viewed the school as a "preventive institution."[9] Browne's perspective was also influenced by European developments in mass education at the time, namely, the "part-time" school of Victorian Britain,[10] which combined child labor with after-hour schooling supported financially by the employers, and especially the model of the "reformatory school." In Mauritius, he established one such school, mainly for Indo-Mauritian children, which was connected to a "vagrant depot."[11] In the 1860s, Browne left Mauritius for a long trip to Europe, during which he visited three such reformatory schools in Britain, France, and Belgium. His enthusiastic account of visiting these schools took up almost half of the annual report on elementary schools of 1868.[12] According to him, the main benefit of this kind of institution, in which students could be placed under total supervision and "sound moral discipline," isolated from any "corrupting" influences, was that it provided a "refuge from crime" and immorality.[13] It was clearly his favorite project in Mauritius. At the same time, Browne was anxious to avoid the "over-education" of Indians, who were seen as a manual labor force by all colonial groups. Still, it was clear that Browne represented the influential faction among the British administrators who saw in education a valuable disciplinary tool that was crucial for the consolidation of colonial rule.[14]

Browne was very much in favor of the general trends of British policy in Mauritius at the time, which were marked by attempts at anglicization and Protestant proselytizing, and he sought to make these the base of his educational plans, to which he added his particular obsession with disciplining the Indian. He saw value in "vernacular schools" for Indians insofar as vernacular Indian languages could be a transitional medium to English. For this reason, and also in combination with his generally negative view of "Hindoo morality," he regarded with suspicion the *baithka*s, the vernacular schools set up by the Indians themselves in conjunction with non-Christian religious instruction and "connected more or less with the idol temples erected on, or near sugar estates."[15]

The plans of the British administration to provide vernacular education to Indians within the framework of a wider policy of anglicization were in direct contrast to the ideas of schooling pursued by the Catholic Church, one of the main representatives of Franco-Mauritian interests in Mauritius. The Franco-Mauritian plantocracy and the Catholic Church were determined to resist British policies of anglicization and saw French as the language of the country, despite the fact that only a small part of the population had any competence in French. One of their central arguments was that French was actually spoken by most of the population in the form of the *patois créole*, which they considered merely a degenerate form of French. Advocates of this position never failed to point out the importance of Creole also among children of Indian background, for they would speak it among themselves.[16] They stressed how difficult it would be for Creole-speaking children to learn English, a language they would hardly ever use in their lives as plantation workers, all the while assuming that the acquisition of French would come about much more "naturally" for Creole-speaking students.

Consequently, Catholic schools, subsidized by the colonial state under a grant-in-aid scheme, were French-medium, although English was also usually taught, since this was a condition imposed by the colonial administration in order to be eligible for a government grant. The number of these schools increased considerably after the middle of the century, partially in response to Protestant missionary schools' targeting of Indian children and the British attempts to anglicize the island.

Nevertheless, the British administration did not abandon plans to combine vernacular language education for Indians with its project of anglicization. In 1878, under the governorship of Sir Arthur Phayre, three new vernacular schools became operational.[17] In 1883, based on his experience as Director of Education in Ceylon,[18] Colonial Secretary Sir Charles Bruce took a strongly provernacular stance regarding Indian education, again intended to lead to an Anglo-vernacular system of education, which, for the sake of the island's colonial plantation economy, was limited to primary schools.[19] But in the search for a suitable scheme of vernacular education for Indians, the evident multiplicity of Indian languages was seen as a major problem. As early as 1874, in a Minute addressed to Colonial Secretary Edward Newton, Acting Superintendent and Inspector of Schools W. H. Ashley suggested that among the four Indian languages he identified as current in the colony, "Hindi, Bengalee, Tamil and Telugu," Hindi and Tamil were "the most commonly in use here." He concluded that "in face of these difficulties I am fully of the opinion that any attempt to teach so many Indian languages would meet with entire failure, and therefore urge that English should be the language taught to all, through the medium of their own respective dialect, as far as teachers would be found to speak such dialect, or failing that, by Creole-Indian [Mauritian-born Indians] teachers through the Creole."[20] That is, both the issue of Indian vernacular education as such and the difficulties encountered with it due to linguistic diversity among Indo-Mauritians were used by the British administration as arguments in favor of a privileged place for English in Mauritian education. This stance for the anglicization of education was ultimately directed against the educational preponderance of French due to the strong position of Catholic schools in the educational system of the island. It was further based on the assumption that the spread of English would turn Mauritius into a colony more loyal to the British crown, all the while having a "civilizing" effect on its Indo-Mauritian subjects.

A crucial point overlooked by the British in their assessment of the linguistic situation in Mauritius and its implications for Indian education was that a single Indian vernacular used by most Indo-Mauritians was already available in the latter part of the nineteenth century. The Mauritian variety of Bhojpuri was rapidly learned and used by Indo-Mauritians of the most diverse backgrounds, including south Indians. This language, commonly called *endyen* even nowadays and more widely known as Bhojpuri in Mauritius after independence in 1968, was invisible to the British colonial administration, most likely because it was perceived and labeled as "Hindi" or "Hindustanee," which south Indians claimed they did not know.

A COMBINED FAILURE: INDIAN VERNACULAR EDUCATION AND THE BRITISH PROJECT OF ANGLICIZING MAURITIUS

The attempts by the local British administration to introduce Indian vernacular education had no lasting success against the continuous resistance of the Franco-Mauritian establishment and their allies. By 1882 the experimental vernacular Indian schools in Grand Port district in the south of the island had been turned into Anglo-vernacular schools — though one of these schools, the one on Plaisance Estate, was moved to a different building off the estate because its Franco-Mauritian owner objected to the teaching of English on his premises.[21] And in 1885, the Indian language departments in "Indian" schools disappeared.

The 1880s were characterized by debate between the advocates of English and the Franco-Mauritian promoters of French in Mauritian schooling, the pro-French faction claiming that French was simply the language of Mauritius, spoken by everyone in either its "pure" form or its "corrupted" version as *patois créole*. This argument continued to be repeated during the next hundred years, up to the debates concerning the official recognition of Creole in the 1970s and early 1980s. The crucial conceptual moves behind this argument are Creole's erasure as a "language" and subsumption under French, and its devaluation as "corrupt." Contemporary studies of Mauritian Creole such as Charles Baissac's *Étude sur le patois créole mauricien* (1880), propounded this view. In this way, the simultaneous devaluation of Creole and its subsumption under French can be read as a response to the British attempts to anglicize Mauritius.

Another point highlighted by the defenders of the supremacy of French in education was that learning English was not only a severe handicap to Creole-speaking students, it also "estranged" the masses from the "high classes," who naturally would be French-speaking.[22] Here again, the greater proximity of Creole to French as compared to English was the main argument. But the power of this particular claim lay in representing a presumed greater linguistic distance as iconic of an increased social distancing that would be detrimental to the social and political fabric of the colony (compare Irvine and Gal 2000). Questions of linguistic differentiation and the relationship between different linguistic varieties became a prominent frame through which the structure of colonial society was conceived. That is, perceptions of linguistic differentiation not only mediated views of ethnic differentiation, as evident in discourses about vernacular education and, later, ancestral languages; they were also constitutive of relations of class hierarchy and political domination.

Throughout the 1880s another major debate about the medium of instruction was underway in the Council of Education, leading to the Education Code of 1890. The new ordinance, which raised protests from the Anglican bishop and other Protestant clergymen, stipulated that both French and English should be taught on a compulsory basis in schools supported or run by the government. This new rule was a major victory for the Franco-Mauritian-led pro-French faction and effectively meant the end of Indian vernacular education, since Indian languages were relegated to optional subjects. In the Council of Education debates, one of the members, Dr. C. Meldrum, had argued in vain for a model that left the choice of a single compulsory language to the school managers. In this way, he proposed, English, French, and Indian languages would be placed on a "footing of equality." He specifically pointed out the importance of Indian languages for education in a colony in which two-thirds of the population were Indian immigrants and their descendants: "But as fully two thirds of the population are Indians, and as they contribute largely to the public revenue, it is but just that no obstacles should be put in the way of those of them who wish their children to learn an Indian language."[23]

However, the position held by the President of the Council of Education, the Franco-Mauritian George Guibert, prevailed in the formulation of the code. He left no doubt that according to him French was the language of Mauritius and therefore had to be compulsory in all schools. English should be taught as well, since Mauritius was a British colony, but French was the language of the country: "Mauritius is a French speaking country. French is I may say universally spoken here. All children brought up in this place come naturally to speak it, whatever their origin. It is true that young children of all classes and grown up persons who have not received any education, speak French in the form of the Creole patois, *but the Creole patois is nothing but French badly pronounced and free from the ordinary rules of grammar.*"[24]

Once again, the declaration of Creole as "bad French" provided the crucial argument in claiming that Mauritius is a francophone country. As in the debates over the failed 1857 compulsory education ordinance, the competing positions in this debate about language in Mauritian education revealed fundamentally different perspectives on Mauritian society and which groups should dominate it. The Franco-Mauritians' view of Mauritius as a naturally francophone country was intimately linked to their self-perception as the original Mauritians and thus entitled to dominate the island. The position of the local British community of administrators and businessmen was colored by the experiences many of them had had in India. The fact that Mauritius clearly had an Indian majority population in their view justified treating Mauritius in certain respects as an extension of India, and there was no reason why Indians should not be educated in Indian languages, especially when combined with the teaching of English.

In the end, the 1890 ordinance can be seen as a compromise between the British administration and the Franco-Mauritians, and as symptomatic of the failure of the British project of anglicizing the island. Even though the British had succeeded in establishing English as the official language of their colony, they completely failed to break the dominance of French in education, in the island's economy, in the print media, and in what the British themselves referred to as "cultured society."[25] Insofar as the 1890 code did not provide for compulsory education, despite long-standing British plans to this end, as evident in the failed ordinance of 1857, it also represented a victory for Franco-Mauritian interests in child labor on plantations over British projects to "civilize" and control Indo-Mauritians through schooling. At the turn of the century, the participation of Indo-Mauritian students in the colony's school system remained very low. Out of sixty thousand Indo-Mauritian children of schooling age in 1908, only seven thousand attended school (Bunwaree 1994, 87). The proportion of school-going children increased, however, after the passing of a new labor ordinance of 1908 that declared a minimum age of thirteen years for employment.[26]

By 1908, however, the basic order of languages in Mauritian education had become established, as stated in the Education Code B of 1903. Any language could function as a medium of education until Standard III, and more French than English should be taught in the lower classes of primary school, on the assumption that most students would know more French than English to begin with.[27] English would ideally function as a medium of instruction from Standard IV onwards, but other languages could be used if necessary. This arrangement was confirmed in the Education Code of 1916.[28] The question of Indian vernacular education was not raised again, and the position of Indian languages in Mauritian education was marginal. As the British lost interest in anglicizing the colony, based on the futility of their earlier attempts, they also abandoned schemes for Anglo-vernacular education. In contrast to earlier British views on the necessity of "civilizing" Indo-Mauritians through education in Indian languages, leading to a knowledge of English, the 1913 Memorandum of Education was more pragmatic:

> The number of Indian languages in the colony is numerous. They include Hindi, Tamil, Urdu and Telegu [sic]. The pedagogical difficulties that arise from this circumstance are, however, far smaller than may be supposed. Nearly all the children that attend the schools were born in the colony and speak the corrupt French dialect or Creole patois of the place, even if they know some Indian language as well. The general desire of the children and their parents is that they should learn English and French. There is hardly any demand for the teaching of Indian languages in the schools. A few of the better class Indians say that they like their children to learn Indian languages, but they prefer to have that done at home. In a few schools in the most populous centres Indian languages are taught by special teachers as extra subjects in addition to the ordinary subjects of the curriculum, including English and French. Probably in no case would an Indian child or his parents desire to have an Indian language substituted for either English or French. The reason for this state of things is probably that the Indian children who grow up in Mauritius, even those of the agricultural immigrants, nearly always settle in the Island, where they succeed in agricultural, commercial and other pursuits.[29]

Two aspects of this quote are striking. First, Creole is now officially acknowledged as a substandard French dialect and accepted as the language "of the place," a point long emphasized by the Franco-Mauritian establishment. The long-deplored multiplicity of Indian languages is no longer seen as a problem for schooling because children born in Mauritius are likely to know Creole, which is available as a de facto medium of primary education. Second, Indians in Mauritius are represented as having little interest in education through Indian languages or even in studying them at school for reasons of socio-economic achievement. The *baithkas*, village or temple schools organized by Indo-Mauritians themselves where children received basic religious instruction and learned Indian languages, mostly a variety of Hindi through studying the Ramayana, are not mentioned at all. This is in striking contrast to the fact that these Indian community schools play a great role in Indo-Mauritian his-

torical memory today. Moreover, in the nineteenth century, British officials such as Browne had deplored the existence of *baithka*s as impedi-
ments to the education and "moral improvement" of Indians, implying
that these schools were flourishing at the time.

The Memorandum, however, does mention the desire of the "better
class Indians" to have their children taught Indian languages privately,
pointing to a trend that would become significant in the future. At issue
here is the "discovery" of Indian languages as repositories of "culture"
by elite groups among the Indians. Resigning themselves to the fact that
formal education in Mauritius was organized along European lines, they
were instead convinced that supplemental learning and literacy in an
Indian language, above all Hindi, represent a "defense" of Indian cultural and religious traditions in the face of European, especially French,
hegemony in Mauritius. Later this view would be formulated as an ideology of ancestral languages, and from the Second World War onwards,
calls for instruction in these languages in the school system would be one
of the dominant issues in Mauritian education.

These emerging Indo-Mauritian elites who began to valorize Indian
ancestral languages received important official support from India in
1924. Kunwar Maharaj Singh, an Indian aristocrat, Oxford graduate,
and convert to Christianity, was sent by the Government of India to
Mauritius to report on the possibility of renewed emigration to Mauritius. This was in response to the government of Mauritius's request for
new immigrants due to a temporary labor shortage on Mauritian plantations. Maharaj Singh strongly advised against new emigration, which
had been halted since 1915, based on the deplorable conditions of employment on the sugar estates. Taking up another issue brought to his
attention by several Indo-Mauritians, however, he suggested that Indian
languages should be taught in the primary schools (Ramyead 1985, 56;
Beejadhur 1935, 79–82). Following Maharaj Singh's report to the Indian
government, Indian indentured migration to Mauritius was terminated
for good, and the teaching of Hindi and Urdu was started in some primary schools. This was the first time since the 1850s through 1880s,
when British administrators attempted yet failed to institutionalize vernacular or Anglo-vernacular education, that the British administration
officially included Indian languages in the primary school curriculum.
But the main difference, of course, is that in contrast to the earlier British
plans, which were rooted in some British officials' colonial experience in
India as well as in Victorian notions of "moral improvement" through
Protestant Christianization coupled with a desire for social control, this

time the demand for Indian languages in Mauritian education came from Indians and Indo-Mauritians. Even so, the medium of education was not at issue any more, since they were not demanding an Indian language as a medium of education, along the lines of the earlier projects. In principle accepting the established order of languages in Mauritian education, they claimed that Indian languages, above all Hindi, should be added to the school education of children of Indian background on an ethnic basis. That is, Indian languages should be taught at school not to facilitate general learning or enable socio-economic achievement, but as a gesture of cultural and political assertion by Indo-Mauritians in an emerging politics of recognition.

THE RISE OF INDO-MAURITIAN POWER AND THE INSTITUTIONALIZATION OF ANCESTRAL LANGUAGES

The Second World War, with its debilitating consequences for British colonialism, represents a turning point in the balance of political power among the ethnoreligious groups then present in Mauritius. Changes in British policies towards the expansion of suffrage in the concluding years of the empire strengthened the position of Indo-Mauritians.[30] The impact of Indo-Mauritian, especially Hindu, activists who were campaigning for universal suffrage and the teaching of Indian languages also became apparent, which highlighted the issue of ancestral languages. As Indo-Mauritians asserted themselves politically against Franco-Mauritian dominance Indian languages were valorized, largely as a reaction to their marginalization in education and their devaluation in the eyes of the Franco-Mauritians, also as a move to "defend" cultural traditions through the "defense" of language. In 1931, regulations stated that up to Standard V in primary school any language could be the medium of instruction, and that from that standard onwards instruction should be in English — a rule never strictly applied[31] — though French was allowed whenever it was found necessary.[32] This colonial linguistic order in education was never fundamentally challenged by the advocates of Indian languages; their demand was simply to add the teaching of Indian ancestral languages to it. This unleashed a political dynamic in which members of different ethnoreligious groups in Mauritius came to regard the institutional position of an ancestral language as iconic of the political power shared by the group claiming ownership of it.

In 1941, the British administration in Mauritius decided to officially establish an Education Department, the forerunner of the Ministry of

Education. The Department of Education (Constitution) Ordinance of 1941 was debated in the Council of Government in conjunction with another ordinance calling for the "more effective teaching of English and the spread of the English language in the colony." The positions taken by the various representatives on the Council provide a clear picture of the contrasting perspectives on language and linguistic differentiation in Mauritius and how they related to political claims made by those who saw themselves as representatives of the island's ethnoreligious groups.

In the course of this 1941 Legislative Council debate, the Franco-Mauritian delegates did not openly oppose the idea of improving the teaching of English in Mauritius, but rather stressed that the privileged position of French should in no way be impaired. Like their predecessors in the nineteenth century, they again made it clear that, according to them, French and not English was the language of Mauritius. "The French language is the current language of the country; a large number of Mauritians, to whatever community they belong, speak French, all speak the French *patois,* and they manage to understand French more easily than English."[33]

Reaffirming this point raised by a fellow delegate, A. Raffray also presented French as the language "uniting" all Mauritians. In his view, the spread and instruction of French could counterbalance the divisive forces in this plantation colony, whose inhabitants were officially classified according to their ethnoreligious or "racial" identities. Arguing against the teaching of Indian languages to Indian students, he suggested: "I think we should, or rather the authorities in charge of primary education in this Colony, should strive to unite, to unify rather than separate and to sever. . . . There is no doubt that education in this colony is based on the Western system, our civilization in this colony is the Western civilization . . . .Well, as all realise, it is a tricky problem, but at the same time if a medium had to be chosen that only should be chosen which would be the medium best suited to all the boys [*sic*] without distinction and it should be the vernacular, the Creole language, which is itself a corruption of the French language, and as the hon. member for Flacq has already stated, I think the basic medium of instruction is French and it has to remain so."[34]

Here once again, the crucial ideological assimilation of Creole to French, which from a Franco-Mauritian perspective justifies French as the language of Mauritius, is the guarantor of unity. This representation of the language situation is used to legitimize the view that the "civilization" present in Mauritius is Western, despite the fact that over two-thirds of the population is of Indian origin. It also serves to legitimatize Franco-Mauritian dominance in Mauritius and conceptually erase the presence of other "civilizations" on the island. One Franco-Mauritian delegate, Leclézio, even claimed that since according to the agreement following the British conquest of Mauritius from the French in 1810 the British promised to respect the Catholic religion and the traditions of the Franco-Mauritians, the British administration and its Director of Education were formally obliged not to "neglect" the French language.[35] The British Governor of Mauritius at the time, Sir Bede Edmund Hugh Clifford, responded by affirming that while according to the British government no such treaty obligation existed, British policy was friendly to such requests, but not only regarding those made by Franco-Mauritians: "We do respect and as far as possible maintain the laws, customs and habits not only of one but every community which comes under British rule."[36] Governor Clifford's view was in consonance with the policy called for by the Indo-Mauritian delegates, providing a context for their own claims for the promotion and teaching of Indian languages. According to them, every community was in possession of a distinct language and culture, and had the right to government support for their maintenance and cultivation. From this perspective, one Indo-Mauritian representative turned the Franco-Mauritians' pleas in favor of French into an argument for the teaching of Indian languages in schools: "It is quite natural that people of Indian origin who form two-thirds of the population of this colony may come and ask that the language in which they study their religion in this colony must be taught in the primary schools, or natural that the people of French origin who are some 10,000 and the coloured people [*gens de couleur*, elite Creoles] who may be from 10,000 to 15,000 who may be speaking French should like the French language to be taught in schools and thus allow them to keep their culture."[37]

Most of the themes of the ideology of ancestral languages, so important for politics in late-colonial and post-independence Mauritius, are evident here. The people of Mauritius are defined by specific spatial and cultural origins — India in the case of the Indo-Mauritians, France in the case of Franco-Mauritians, and so on. Their origin defines their culture, and it is by virtue of this origin that different groups in Mauritius also have languages of their own, supposedly spoken by their immigrating ancestors. This condition is represented as "natural." But most important, this condition enables groups to lay a political claim on the state to support the maintenance and promotion of such ancestral languages and cultures.

From this perspective, the "naturalness" of ancestral languages and cultures means that such political claims on the state are also naturally legitimated. In the 1941 debate analyzed here, Delegate Ramgoolam, who would later become the first Prime Minister of independent Mauritius, explicitly stressed the necessity for the state to intervene in order to "protect" the culture and ancestral language of Indo-Mauritians:

> I think the hon. member for Flacq or the hon. member for Moka has pointed out that it will be necessary to preserve the French customs and everything that goes with the French civilization, and I think it is only reasonable that this country and that we, Indians, will not be pushed further back into our scale of life [sic] in this country so that when our boys [sic] grow up they will not be able to speak properly their own language. I think, Sir, this is a state of affairs in which government must certainly try to draw its full weight, so that it is amended.[38]

Also evident in this statement is a conflation among culture, civilization, and language, which are represented as one interconnected, ethnicized whole, the property of a particular community. Further, there is the sense of competition between groups: if one group manages to "preserve" its ancestral language and culture, and another group is less successful, then the latter falls behind, and it is the task of the state to intervene in order to correct the situation.

What renders this 1941 debate particularly significant is that it marks the end of Franco-Mauritian hegemony in the cultural politics of the island. After their conquest of Mauritius in 1810, the British colonial administration had for a period in the nineteenth century challenged the very powerful position the Franco-Mauritian plantocracy enjoyed not only economically but also politically and in terms of cultural hegemony, though their attempts to anglicize the island failed. But they had never really questioned European cultural dominance on the island, as reflected in the shaping of the educational system. This time, however, the British governor sided with the Indo-Mauritian representatives against Franco-Mauritian claims for continued supremacy.

Notably, the debate discussed here took place in the shadow of the 1941 *Report on Education in Mauritius* by W. E. F. Ward,[39] the newly appointed Director of Education. Ward argued that since there were too many Indian languages whose teaching was argued for by Indo-Mauritians, and because it was already difficult enough to teach English and French to students whose first language was Creole, the teaching of Indian languages in government schools should be discontinued and left to the Indian community. The statements by Indo-Mauritian delegates in the Council of Government were partially intended as protests against Ward's suggestions. Ramgoolam in particular was fiercely opposed to Ward's views on the question of Indian languages at school and organized a mass walkout at a public talk given by Ward in the municipal theater of Port Louis. Unwilling to antagonize the leaders of the politically mobilizing Indo-Mauritians at a time of frequent strikes and labor unrest in 1940s Mauritius, the British government did not follow Ward's suggestions and instead proclaimed a policy of ethnic evenhandedness in matters of cultural policy.

In the ensuing years, the British administration became more and more accommodating to Indo-Mauritian demands in educational policy. This process reflected the rapidly growing power of political leaders such as Ramgoolam as the British Empire headed towards decolonization and Mauritius in particular moved closer to constitutional reform, which from 1947 onward enabled many Indo-Mauritians to vote in the elections to the Legislative Assembly for the first time. The 1944 Report on Education, for example, displayed an entirely new attitude towards Indo-Mauritian aspirations in educational policy when it concluded that "it seems wrong that the schools should ignore the available Indian culture and regard it as no part of their business to introduce it in the schools." It also deplored the fact that "no provision whatever is made for the religious or moral instruction of non-Christian pupils" and stated that if suitable teachers can be found, all government schools should provide instruction in "the Ramayana or the Mahabharata for Hindus and Tarikhe Islam for Moslems." [40] Religious instruction in schools for Christian students had been available from the very beginning of state-run primary education in Mauritius in the nineteenth century. At that time, the British administration had encouraged the conversion of Indians and Indo-Mauritians to Protestantism through schools run by missionaries, and had sometimes been hostile to self-organized efforts at education and non-Christian religious instruction in Indian communities through Hindu *baithka*s or Muslim *madrasa*s. Now the colonial administration, under the pressure of political changes in Mauritius as well as in the empire at large, began to regard non-Christian religious instruction in schools as falling within their responsibilities. In 1947, in order to improve the teaching of Indian languages, Mauritius officially requested the assistance of the Government of India in obtaining textbooks.[41] Two years later, the government of now-independent India sent an expert "tutor" for the teaching of Indian languages, Ram Prakash, to the Teachers Training College in Beau Bassin, which had opened in 1943.[42]

In rejecting Ward's 1941 suggestion, and in yielding to the demands for the teaching of Indian languages on an ethnic basis, the British evidently realized that the "language problem" in this "modern Tower of Babel"[43] represented a "problem not of a purely educational nature, but [having] political, social, racial and emotional aspects."[44] In fact, a close ideological connection between Indian languages and religion was clearly apparent. Hindu organizations such as the Arya Samaj since its foundation in Mauritius in 1910 and its Sanatanist, high-caste-led competitor the Hindu Maha Sabha from 1925 onwards had campaigned for Hindi instruction in Mauritius. Following Hindu nationalists in India, they promoted Hindi as the "language of the Hindus." Other pro-Hindi organizations, such as the Hindi Pracharini Sabha, founded in 1935 and linked to the Hindi Sahitya Sammelan in India, were in fact exclusively run by Hindus, had strong links with Hindu religious bodies, and extensively used Hindu imagery in their campaigns. All these organizations ran their own Hindi schools. In addition, starting in the 1940s after his return from university studies at Lahore and Calcutta, the Gandhian missionary Basdeo Bissoondoyal led an intense and successful movement of religious and political mobilization among Hindus in Mauritius, delivering sermons throughout the island. His campaigns culminated in the staging of large public Hindu rituals such as processions, the centralized celebration of Hindu festive holidays, and the performance of a *mahayajna*, the Vedic sacrificial ritual, attended by sixty thousand devotees in Port Louis in December 1943 (Ramyead 1985, 81). One of Bissoondoyal's central campaign issues was the propagation of Hindi. In fact he himself was active as a Hindi teacher. In 1946 he announced a plan to open three hundred additional part-time Hindi schools in Mauritius (Ramyead 1985, 83), and in 1951 the Education Department described his movement of Hindi evening schools to be "flourishing."[45] Although Bissoondoyal saw himself as representing all "Indians" in Mauritius, he was in fact a Hindu missionary who identified Indian culture and civilization with Hindu traditions. These missionaries and Hindu organizations effecting a "Hindu revival" in Mauritius in the first half of the twentieth century set the stage for later globally operating groups of Hindu nationalists who after independence would become important actors within the framework of a Hindu-dominated government and state apparatus, and would place ancestral languages at the top of their ideological agenda.

Besides the fact that the main spokesmen and organizations for the teaching and promotion of Indian languages, especially Hindi, were heavily involved in religious nationalism, in the immediate postwar period there were also institutional arrangements within the state school system favoring the close association of Indian languages with religion. In most schools in which Indian languages were specially being taught to Indo-Mauritian students, the teaching took place in the time slots for Christian religious instruction, when non-Christian students would normally sit idle, since Hindu or Islamic religious instruction was still not provided in schools.[46] Consequently, Indo-Mauritians themselves tended to view their learning Indian languages as equivalent to their Christian fellow students' study of catechism.[47] In addition, the contents of the Indian language lessons were often based on religious themes. This situation, which in principle has remained unchanged up to the present, was the case with not just Hindi but also the other three languages the teaching of which was institutionalized in state schools through the 1950s, namely, Tamil, Telugu, and Urdu. This was mainly because cultivation of these languages had previously been almost exclusively in the hands of religious bodies and many of the available teachers had taught at *baithka*s connected to Hindu temples or Muslim *madrasa*s. This connection was explicitly evoked when Labour Party delegate and later Prime Minister Ramgoolam complained in the Legislative Council about the low pay of Hindi teachers. He suggested that the Education Department was taking financial advantage of the teachers' religious virtue, implying that most of them were also religious specialists in their local communities. "Hindu priests and Moslem priests consider it a part of their duty to teach people, even without payment, and that is why these people have been going on famine pays, because Hindu philosophy and Hindu social outlook taught them to do so as a duty to their religion."[48]

Ramgoolam clearly took the identification of Hindi with Hinduism and the Hindu religious establishment in Mauritius for granted. Arguing during the same debates against plans to test senior Hindi teachers, he even conflated the two: "I am not against any test being made for people who are now joining us as Hindu [*sic*] teachers."[49] Ramgoolam played a crucial role in the establishment and expansion of Indian languages as regularly taught subjects in state schools in Mauritius. In addition to serving as a delegate in the Council of Government (Legislative Assembly after 1947), and leader of the Indo-Mauritian-dominated Labour Party, he was Liaison Officer for the Education Department and also had excellent relations with the first Indian High Commissioner to Mauritius, Dharam Yashdev, who was in charge of distributing the resources the Indian government provided for teaching these languages in Mauritius.

The link between an ancestral language and a particular ethnicized religious tradition was also highlighted by advocates for Telugu. They mobilized in the mid-1950s, after the teaching of Hindi and then Urdu and Tamil had been institutionalized in the school system. In the context of an ultimately successful petition for instruction in Telugu and the employment of Telugu teachers, the following argument was made: "The Telegus [sic] are in fact a minority in this island, but a minority that counts more than 30,000 souls according to the recent figures from the report of the committee on religious subsidization."[50] The government had decided in 1950 to extend religious subsidies, which the Catholic and Anglican churches in Mauritius had been benefiting from for a long time, to non-Christian religious bodies. Alongside longer-established Hindu organizations, such as the Arya Sabha (Arya Samaj) and the Hindu Maha Sabha, newer Tamil, Telugu, and Marathi temple organizations mobilized in order to obtain subsidies for running their places of worship. In the religion category on the census, Mauritians were encouraged to respond in detail offering sectarian or ethnic information, such as "Arya Samaji Hindu" or "Telegu [sic] Hindu," rather simply a generic term like "Hindu."[51] The results became guidelines for estimating the amount of subsidy given to the religious organizations claiming to represent these particular sectarian or ethnically defined religious groups. Crucially, these categories and numbers were in turn successfully used to justify the state-organized teaching of particular Indian ancestral languages, which were represented as corresponding to particular ethnoreligious labels, such as Telugu Hindu. In this way, the identification of ancestral languages with religious traditions was institutionalized in its most direct form — as language ideologies representing the emerging varieties of religious nationalism in Mauritius.

The proponents of Hindi and Urdu entered into conflict from the outset. This process has to be seen not only in connection with intense religious mobilization and the frequent arrival of both Hindu and Muslim missionaries from India that started in the 1930s, but also in the context of growing political tensions between Hindus and Muslims in Mauritius. Hindus at the time predominantly supported the Labour Party under the leadership of Ramgoolam, and most Muslims sided with the Comité d'action musulman (CAM) led by Abdul Razack Mohamed, the Indian-born leader of the local Kutchi Memon community. Making use of their strong ties through commerce, intermarriage, and religious networks with India, prominent members of this Gujarati trader caste had established themselves as the main sponsors and promoters of institutionalized

Islam in Mauritius, which at the time was still largely dominated by the Ahl-e Sunnat va Jama'at, or Barelwi, tradition (Eisenlohr 2006a, 2006b. Growing religious communalism among both Hindus and Muslims in Mauritius focused on the "defense" of the ancestral language, which in turn was closely identified with particular religious traditions. Mohamed complained in the Legislative Council that although Hindi was taught in numerous schools, the teaching of Urdu was obstructed. Claiming that Urdu was "discriminated" against in the Education Department, he suggested that the head of the section for Indian languages, Ram Prakash, sent as an expert by the Indian government in 1949, was probably responsible for this state of affairs, since he was both from India and a Hindu. Mohamed protested that it was inappropriate to place an Indian Hindu in charge of a language "which is considered to be an Islamic language or is considered as a language of an Islamic state [referring to the newly formed Pakistan]." [52] Delegate Gujadhur, at the time head of the wealthiest and most prominent Hindu family on the island, immediately protested, saying he was "defending my language" against such accusations and objecting to the "teaching of Urdu on a communal basis."[53] Delegate Millien, a Creole, then started to lament the destruction of the "unity" of the country through disputes about an increasing number of different languages to be taught in schools and ended with the suggestion: "Why not should Mauritius teach one language only?" The exchange that followed illustrates the contested nature of the language situation in Mauritius:

> Mr. Gujadhur: All right, and let that language be Hindi.
> Dr. Millien: No, it should be English.
> Dr. de Chazal: Rubbish.
> Dr. Millien: We have heard in this place and seen published that there are only 20,000 people writing and speaking French.
> Mr. Rault: No, 10,000.[54]

Different linguistic ideologies, linked to claims for political power by different ethnoreligious groups, Hindu, Muslim, Creole, and Franco-Mauritian, found expression in a dispute in which their sharply diverging views of the linguistic reality of Mauritius confronted each other. Franco-Mauritians like de Chazal had nothing but disdain for the growing number of Indian languages for which recognition and state-sponsored instruction was being sought. They were, however, concerned about the continued dominance of French, which they considered the "real" language of Mauritius, and felt it to be threatened by measures to strengthen the position of English in the educational system. "Very adroitly it has been arranged that the English language should gradually oust the lingua franca of this island, which nobody will gainsay is French. Very adroitly English is slowly ousting out [sic] the lingua franca of this island in our schools specially in our primary schools."[55] Franco-Mauritian delegate Koenig argued that French was the "*de facto* medium of instruction" anyway, and further suggested, claiming to quote an unnamed former British governor of Mauritius, that in reality "Mauritius is a French colony governed by the British."[56] According to him, far more than a mere 10,000 people knew and used French, which was spoken whenever people of different communities on the island met. Indo-Mauritian delegate Osman replied: "How many people in Mauritius do understand French? A very small proportion."[57] The representatives of the different ethnoreligious groups disagreed sharply over the "facts" of the linguistic situation in Mauritius because they held conflicting views over which group should dominate the island politically. They drew on different perceptions of linguistic differentiation to support opposing claims for political power.

Against the view of French as the lingua franca and dominant colonial language of Mauritius, the Hindu Tamil delegate Seeneevassen sought to recontextualize French as just one of several "mother tongues" with a limited number of speakers in Mauritius: "I think there is no harm in a child whose mother tongue is French, learning French, in a child whose mother tongue is Hindi learning Hindi, in a child whose mother tongue is Urdu learning Urdu, in a child whose mother tongue is Tamil learning Tamil, and so on."[58] Central to Seeneevassen's comment, of course, is the identification of "mother tongue" with ancestral language — in contrast with the sense of "mother tongue" as the main language of childhood socialization, which was never the case for Urdu or Hindi in Mauritius.[59] However, while Hindus tended to represent Hindi as the main language of the "Indians," Muslim leaders strongly insisted on a distinct identity, claiming that the position of Urdu in Mauritian schools was unfairly overshadowed by Hindi.

Along the same lines, the inferior position of Urdu in the schools system vis-à-vis Hindi was presented by Mohamed as iconic for the political marginalization of Muslim Indo-Mauritians by the numerically superior Hindus. The same semiotic process was involved in most of the disputes regarding Indian languages in education. Based on the strong indexical connection established between a particular ancestral language and a given ethnoreligious tradition, the relative status of the language in the colony's educational system was perceived as iconic of the power and influence of the community that to a large measure was created by cultivation of that language. If this status was not considered as satisfactory, it was made the basis for complaints and political claims against the colonial state, often by pointing to supposedly excessive favors enjoyed by other groups.

In another 1954 example, Delegate Sookdeo Bissoondoyal, the missionary Basdeo Bissoondoyal's younger brother, presented a demand for radio programs in Tamil in the Legislative Assembly. Referring to the 1952 census, in which 19,000 persons had declared their "mother tongue" as Tamil, he claimed that "19,000 persons speak Tamil" and therefore deserve broadcasting in Tamil. Again referring to the census, he concluded: "Now, only 31,000 people speak French and we know what is the number of hours devoted to broadcasting in the French language."[60] On the one hand, this again represented an attempt to conceptually reduce the status of French from its dominant position to the level of just one more language among several in Mauritius, on a par with the Indian languages, by presenting census figures for Tamil as "mother tongue" — commonly interpreted by Mauritians as ancestral language — as figures for Tamil speakers. On the other hand, based on this conceptual slippage between Tamil as "mother tongue" and Tamil as language spoken, Bissoondoyal made a political case for the presumed injustice of depriving Tamils of radio programming compared to French as the dominant broadcasting language. Again, the struggle over the representation of the language situation in Mauritius was at the core of these debates, because the position and "strength" of a language was interpreted as an image of the political position of the particular community associated with it.

This general trend of ethnoreligious communalization of debates about language in education continued after the establishment of Indian ancestral languages as regular subjects in Mauritian schools. The colonial positions of French and English remained entrenched, but the teaching of ancestral languages was gradually expanded until independence in 1968, and assistance from the Indian government increased. In 1967, for example, Indian Education Officers were present to teach Hindi, Tamil, Urdu, and Telugu at the Teachers Training College and to "supervise the teaching of these subjects throughout the island."[61] Echoing the Ward report of 1941 and similar views voiced by British administrators in the nineteenth century, the 1961 Meade report, commissioned by the British colonial government, concluded that the educational system of the colony was seriously deficient because of the multiplicity of languages children were required to learn on the primary level (Meade 1961). English, French, and for most students an Indian language were compulsory from Standard I, even though none of these was familiar to the great majority of children when they began schooling, a situation that has remained unchanged until the present day. Along the lines of earlier recommendations, the Meade report urged the reduction of the number of languages to be studied on this level. However, given the importance of politically charged ideas about language, highlighting the link between languages and ethnoreligious identity, such proposals have had little chance of political acceptance in Mauritius.

PLURICULTURAL MAURITIANISM
AND ANCESTRAL LANGUAGES

Mauritius became independent from the British Crown in 1968, a date that signified further important political power shifts on the island and the beginning of Hindu political dominance. Universal suffrage having finally been introduced in 1959, the 1967 elections were principally fought over the issue of independence, represented as a struggle between two ethnically defined political camps. An alliance centered around the Parti Mauricien and its leader, Gaëtan Duval, was backed by the Creole, Franco-Mauritian, and Sino-Mauritian ethnic groups, and most members of the Muslim community as well. They represented an alliance of all the ethnic "minorities," who wanted continued association with Great Britain out of fear of Hindu hegemony. However, the Labour Party alliance, led by Seewoosagur Ramgoolam and backed by the Hindus, campaigned for full independence from Britain and won the elections. The British government was entirely satisfied with the result, since they had no interest in holding onto this island colony characterized by ethnic antagonism — riots between Muslims and Creoles had left an estimated one hundred persons dead in January 1968 — as well as widespread poverty, a demographic explosion, and a vulnerable monocrop economy. In fact, Britain had pressed for Mauritian independence since the first constitutional conference held in London in 1961, but the process had been delayed by profound disagreements among the leading political figures in Mauritius over a future constitution and fundamental political arrangements of power sharing among the different ethnoreligious groups (Simmons 1982).

The 1970s, during which Mauritius was ruled by a Labour government under Ramgoolam, were characterized by a rapid expansion of schooling and the abolition of school fees for secondary schools. The position of the colonial languages in the educational system was left untouched. English remained the official medium of instruction and French maintained its otherwise dominant position in the curriculum. However, the teaching of Indian ancestral languages was greatly increased, so that these languages were now taught in practically every school frequented by Indo-Mauritian students. The issue of these languages at school became important in Mauritian elections, where voting has frequently been informed by ethnic or "communal" considerations.

Ramgoolam's government invested in the teaching of Indian languages based on the view that the new postcolonial era of Hindu political dominance offered an opportunity to finally "correct" a historic wrong: the long political disenfranchisement and marginalization, often coupled with cultural contempt from the Franco-Mauritian plantocracy, of the Indo-Mauritian majority under colonial rule. This strategy, very popular with Hindu voters, was effective because of the perceived link between the official position of an ethnoreligious group's ancestral language, such as Hindi, and the group's share of power in the island's political affairs. The improvement of the facilities to teach Hindi was thus appreciated by Hindus, even though knowledge of Hindi offered few economic or professional rewards in Mauritius, with one notable exception — the educational sector itself. Providing instruction in an ancestral language involves a whole apparatus of state-paid functionaries and specialized teachers who are without exception recruited exclusively from the particular ethnic group that "owns" the ancestral language in question. Therefore, strengthening the position of an ancestral language in the educational system functions as a form of ethnic patronage in a quite tangible way. When Ramgoolam realized that the survival of his government in the first post-independence elections of 1976 was at stake, he hired a large number of Hindi teachers just before the elections to increase his popularity with the Hindu electorate. Furthermore, many of these Hindi teachers were also leading figures in village *baithka*s and temple committees, often holding key positions in Hindu religious bodies and voluntary associations in the localities where they lived. In keeping these persons in pay and satisfied, the Hindu-dominated Labour government had a powerful tool of political patronage at its disposal. At the same time, the government was able to claim that they were "protecting" Hindu culture and religion in Mauritius. Since the main non-Indian eth-

nic group in Mauritius, the primarily Catholic Creoles, do not claim an
ancestral culture or ancestral language originating outside Mauritius, the
benefits of this system of political patronage with its economic and legitimizing ideological aspects are only available to Indo-Mauritians.[62] Thus,
in the context of formal decolonization in Mauritius, changes in the balance of power among what had become established as ethnoreligious
groups under the dual legacies of British and French plantation colonialism further enhanced the political significance of ideologies of ancestral
languages.

On a transnational level, independence opened up new possibilities
for increased official ties between Mauritius and India in which a discourse of cultural and ancestral links, stressed by both the Mauritian
government and Indian diplomacy, plays a crucial role. As mentioned
earlier, official support for the promotion of Indian ancestral languages
began at the time of India's independence in 1947. After Mauritius
became independent, this cultural policy cooperation reached a new
level, culminating in the foundation of the Mahatma Gandhi Institute in
Moka as a joint venture between Mauritius and India in 1970. This institute, comprising a secondary school, an institute of higher education, and
a cultural center, is officially a center of study for non-European cultures
and languages in Mauritius but is mainly focused on Indian traditions
and the ancestral languages claimed by Indo-Mauritians. Despite its
claims and actual efforts to promote all Mauritian cultural traditions, it
is widely perceived on the island as a Hindu-dominated institution. One
of the responsibilities of the institute is to oversee the production of
Indian ancestral language textbooks and teaching materials, which were
first imported from India but are now locally produced. Indian diplomacy and foreign cultural policy have seized on these connections in
order to increase their political influence in the Indian Ocean region. The
Mauritian governments since independence, in turn, have been able to
claim that they are serious about promoting "Indian culture" through
these networks.

Officially, the Mauritian government promotes the cultural and linguistic heritage of all ethnic groups in Mauritius in the educational system, but actually its support is unevenly distributed. The issue is not so
much that an ideologically explicit promotion of French and English is
not a undertaken by the state, since the continued dominance of these
colonial languages in the Western-oriented school curriculum of
Mauritius is taken for granted and never questioned. The crucial point is
that the main non-Indian ethnic group, the Creoles, do not have recog-

nized claims on an ancestral language and ancestral culture. This is because the institutionalized ideology of ancestral languages suggests that for a language and cultural tradition to count as ancestral, it has to be linked to a putative place of origin outside Mauritius. Therefore, in contrast to Indo-Mauritians, Creoles have little access to the state-supported ancestral language apparatus in the educational system. The system of political patronage and lobbying, which the ancestral language sector provides in Mauritius, is hardly available to Creoles either. And in the contest over which group holds a superior claim on the nation, Creoles are widely represented as "having no culture," especially by Indo-Mauritians, and this tends to marginalize them politically and economically. In postcolonial Mauritius, government policies privilege diasporic ancestral languages and cultural traditions over those that might provide a basis for claims of indigenous authenticity, such as the Creole language, implying that full membership in a Mauritian nation is achieved through the cultivation and public display of diasporic cultural and linguistic traditions.

Another crucial consequence of the politics of promoting ancestral languages and cultures is the privileging of standardized, homogenized views of such ancestral traditions. The institutionalization of ancestral languages and ancestral cultures is based on the erasure of the great diversity of regional origins, religious or sectarian affiliation, and linguistic diversity that characterized the original immigrants, who later were classified as belonging to the same community. For example, Mauritian Muslims are officially a community, recognized in the constitution, whose constituting immigrants mainly belonged to two markedly distinct groups: indentured Bihari agriculturists and laborers and freely immigrating Gujarati traders (Kalla 1987). These two groups were very different in terms of regional origin in India, linguistic and ethnic affiliation, and of course class position. The great majority are Sunni Muslims, but there are also two Shi'ite minorities among the Gujarati Muslims. Yet they are all officially considered a single community, sharing the same ancestral culture defined through Islam, and the same ancestral language, Urdu — which in fact was unknown to the vast majority of these immigrants. However, the Muslim case also demonstrates how the promotion of ancestral languages can lead to the creation of new boundaries within such homogenized communities. In the late 1970s, a group of Muslims supported by the Egyptian and Libyan governments successfully campaigned for the additional recognition of Arabic as an ancestral language of Mauritian Muslims, and since then Arabic has been taught to Muslim students in a number of schools, to the detriment of Urdu. The identification with Arabic, which was known by practically no immigrants at all, is related to religious disputes among the Sunni majority (Eisenlohr 2006b). In the context of this rivalry, Urdu and Arabic as Muslim languages of identification have become associated with two different modern South Asian Islamic traditions in Mauritius, reinforcing a religious division within the Muslim community.[63] This recent split between the advocates of two competing ancestral languages has no immediate relation to any of the numerous criteria dividing Muslims at the time of their immigration but represents a new differentiation in the context of the promotion of different ancestral languages.

CHAPTER 5

Performing Purity

Television and Ethnolinguistic Recognition

GENRE, INTERTEXTUALITY, AND LANGUAGE SHIFT

Hindu activists in religious organizations and state and para-state bodies, some of whom are also involved in the network of Hindu nationalist organizations that operate in both India and Mauritius, are concerned about the rapid language shift from Bhojpuri to Mauritian Creole among Hindu Mauritians. Interpreting the decreasing use of Bhojpuri as a threat to the reproduction of Hindu difference in Mauritius, and making use of their close connections to state institutions, they are trying to reverse the shift to Creole by arranging for the use of Bhojpuri on national television and radio. As I will discuss below, the use of Bhojpuri on Mauritius Broadcasting Corporation (MBC) television has to be analyzed against the contemporary salience of electronic media for language activism and movements promoting ethnolinguistic recognition. Moreover, opening up the state-controlled sector of mass media to Bhojpuri has gone hand in hand with the promotion of a new linguistic model, characterized by purism and sanskritization as well as erasure of the lexical items of Creole origin that are very common in Mauritian varieties of Bhojpuri. The new linguistic model also shows structural novelties, especially the frequent use of honorific pronouns and verbal suffixes — even as Mauritian Bhojpuri in everyday speech is undergoing a wholesale loss of honorific forms in the process of shifting towards Creole. The project to promote Bhojpuri by using it on television has thus become an attempt to turn a purist register associated with Hindu religious discourse and sermons into a broadcast standard.

As I seek to show, this project is failing because it ultimately accelerates the language shift it is intended to stop. The changes on the lexical level in particular are locally interpreted as assimilating Bhojpuri to Hindi, the ancestral language of Mauritian Hindus claiming north Indian origins. By thus "hinduizing" Bhojpuri, the new standard not only excludes non-Hindu users of Bhojpuri, most notably Muslims, but also identifies Bhojpuri with the established category of ancestral languages, thereby turning it into an entity to be venerated but not used on a regular basis.[1] The project of purist standardization also devalues the linguistic practices of most speakers of Mauritian Bhojpuri, which now appear as "mixed" and unsophisticated because of the high frequency of words derived from Creole and other stigmatized features discussed below. This discourages, above all, young speakers from continuing to use Mauritian Bhojpuri, since most of them already feel more at ease using Creole than Bhojpuri.

The problem of genre plays a central role in the outcome of this process. Building on the work of Mikhail Bakhtin (1986), anthropologists have explored the links between genre, performance, and politics in various ethnographic contexts, particularly the role of genre in the constitution of political authority through public performance (Briggs and Bauman 1992, Bauman and Briggs 1990, Hanks 1987, Kuipers 1990). In Mauritian Bhojpuri, the problematic of genre emerges as vital for questions of power and stratification inherent in processes of language standardization. The purist register, which provides the linguistic model for the projected standard of Mauritian Bhojpuri, is indexically linked to the local genre of Hindu religious discourse *(pravacan)*, which in turn is associated with social authority and legitimacy. Therefore, the question of whether particular utterances drawing on the purist register can be recognized as fitting the genre of Hindu religious discourse is important for their recognition as relatively sophisticated, powerful speech. Playing on the indexical and other links between the purist register promoted as a standard and the genre of Hindu religious discourse is a strategy to present the new broadcast standard as authoritative and to naturalize the arbitrariness of its imposition. Yet highlighting these links in fact undermines the success of the standardization project. The perceived generic fit between the new broadcast standard and Hindu religious discourse results in an ideological hinduization of Mauritian Bhojpuri, which only further contributes to the language shift to Creole.

Let us look at the following example of Hindu religious discourse on the occasion of a Ramayana reading sponsored by a widow in memory of her late husband, and attended by family members and neighbors. The reading took place in the widow's home in a town a few kilometers from La Nicolière, and the chanting of the Ramayana was followed by a long *pravacan* by the invited pandit. In the sermon, the pandit explicated lessons for moral conduct that can be drawn from the Ramayana. As outlined in chapter 3, pandits are known for the purist, "hindiized" Bhojpuri they use on such occasions, often accompanied by code switches to Hindi and even entire stretches of discourse in Hindi. While the purist quality of the pandit's discourse is rather evident, especially in the avoidance of Creole loans, the most striking aspect of the following excerpt is the brief switch to Creole in lines 14–16.

EXAMPLE 5.1 *

Sab ke bula kareke Ramchandraji apan sabha men paas mein baithelan, dekha samip bhaithare, jab bhi koi ke kuch boleke rahela, kaise bolal jala ih sikheke, shiksha deyke rahela, kuch bhi ke.	1 Calling everybody, Ramchandraji sat down next to them in his assembly, look, sit down nearby, whenever there was someone there to talk, he 5 taught how to speak, he gave instruction, about anything.
Aajkal maa baap apan ghar men bhi apan beṭwa se dur se batyala, beṭi se, nai, accha gun batawela ki ya to unkar pas jaakar baithke batyala, ya to unkar apan paas bula karke jagah men thik baitha karke shanti se oke bola, sikhawa, nai ki daante lagah. . . . **Kifer to pa fin al lekol? Ki fin arrive, kot to ti ete, kifer ton tarde?**	Nowadays even in their own homes parents talk to their sons from afar, to their daughters, no, you 10 should tell them in a good way, whether you go and sit next to them, or whether you call them to you, have them sit down properly talking to them calmly, teach them, don't 15 scold them . . . . **Why didn't you go to school? What has happened, where were you, why were you late?**
. . . Yeh sab nai chahi kareke, jo pehela chahiye uska, usko kya chahiye, usko bhi maan chahiye. Ketno bhi maa-baap khai-piyeke dei apan laika ke, lekin oke **respe** nai kari oke pyar nai dei, tah u laika baghi ho jay . . . konchi men? Na okar parivaar ke kaam aay, osan	. . . One should not do all this, what one should do first, what one 20 should do, one should accept them. How many parents give their children to eat and to drink, but do not **respect** them, do not give them love, so that child runs away . . . 25 where? It will come to help neither in

*Bhojpuri is unmarked; Creole is boldfaced.

laika, nah apan desh ke kaam aay.
Uhise ego shiksha batawat hawan
hiya ki priti samip baithare, apan
bhiri pyaar ke saath baithela, aur
bhagat sugat mridu vachan uchare
mitha boli men bollat hawan Ramji,
ih hawan Ram ke shiksha.

the family's work, this child, nor in
the work of one's country. This way
he [Ram] gave education, he made
them sit down nearby with affection,
30 he sat down close to them with
affection and spoke to the devotees
with sweet voice, with sweet words
he spoke, Ramji, this is Ram's way of
instruction.

This stretch of discourse provides a good example of the generic model for the purist standard that advocates of Bhojpuri seek to popularize via electronic media. The large-scale avoidance of Creole lexical items coincides with the expression of what are presented as Hindu values of ideal conduct. However, the pandit also uses a Creole "voice" to underline the moral point he is trying to make. He employs Creole to animate an anonymous parent scolding and pressuring his child, not only making the voice of the parent maximally distinct from his own voice by switching to another language, but also using Creole to exemplify the sort of behavior he morally condemns in his sermon. Thus, purist Bhojpuri and Creole are contrasted here as opposed social voices, one very explicitly representing moral authority, the path of action that the deity Ram himself would have taken, the other representing moral aberration and directly opposed to the example of Ram.

Continuing his sermon, the pandit again uses purist Bhojpuri and Creole as contrasting, morally loaded social voices.

EXAMPLE 5.2*

Khali sab kaam chorke, "hé Ram, hé
Ram, hé Ram," nai apan kam karya
jab, lekin niyam anusar kabbo kabbo
okar naam bhi le liyaja, ih bollak
niyampurvak . . . niyampurvak.

1 Just abandoning all work, [chanting]
"Hé Ram, hé Ram, hé Ram," not
doing one's work, but [one should]
from time to time invoke his [Vishnu/
5 Ram's] name, according to the
proper rules, this is what is called
lawful . . . lawful.

Ek bar Naradmuni gal Vishnu
se puche "Narayan, Narayan,
Narayan" bollal karele, u tah
jab bhi dekhba ta bina bajayte

Once Naradmuni went to Vishnu
and asked chanting "Narayan,
10 Narayan, Narayan" [one of the
names of Vishnu], as soon as the

*Bhojpuri is unmarked; Creole and Creole loans are boldfaced. All-uppercase indicates vocal emphasis.

"Narayan, Narayan" bolal kare,
gal Vishnu se bole, hé Vishnu
bollatah tohar sabse param bhakta
keh hah? Bolle hau gauwa men jayah
torah ego kisan lauki u hamar param
bhakta ha. Bolle, apan man men
sochat hawan dekhat hawan, ham
roj Narayan, Narayan bolte rahila
aur ih dusar bagal bata delak, hamra
nai bollak ki tuhi hawa.

Yeh tah **sertifikat**-wa apne khatin
khojata. [laughter]
Tah gal jake dekhe tah dekhatah
un vyakti jab uthata tah bollak ha
"hé Ram" phajir ke nam lelak phir
apan hal lelak jake khet jot ke aal,
halchalake, phir sham ke samay jab
haath pao dho delak tah phir se "hé
Ram" karlak.

Bhojan kareke age do baar, ari
duhi baar, **de fwa** aha, **li fin gayn sa
de minit lin dir lin gayn premier
grad?**
[laughter]

Aur ham roj roj aise hola koi
pustak ke kira rahela parhte rahela
parhte rahela aur sab kuch bhulake.
Bad men pagla ho jala! Lekin jon
NIYAM anusar parhela, sab kaam
karte hue parhela, u **reissi** howela.

latter saw that he was constantly
chanting "Narayan, Narayan,"
Naradmuni went to Vishnu and said,
"Hé Vishnu, who is your greatest
devotee?" Vishnu said, "Go to this
village, you will see a farmer there,
he is my greatest devotee."
Naradmuni thought and said to
himself, "I keep on chanting
'Narayan, Narayan' every day, and
on the other hand [Vishnu] tells me,
'I did not say it was you.'"
He was looking for a **certificate**
for himself. [laughter]
So he went off and saw, when this
person [the farmer] got up, he said,
"Hé Ram," he took Ram's name in
the morning, then he took his plough
and went to the field, ploughing,
then in the evening when he washed
his hand and feet he again chanted,
"Hé Ram."
While eating two times, yes just
[exactly] two times, just two times,
**two times aha, he [only] had these
two minutes, and he [Ram] said he
got the best grade?**
[laughter]
And I am being a bookworm
every day, reading, reading, and
forgetting everything. Later he
went mad! But he who reads
according to the PROPER RULES,
while doing all his work, he will be
successful.

In this moral narrative performed in purist Bhojpuri, a character aspiring to become the deity Vishnu/Ram's foremost devotee is thwarted and surpassed in his efforts because he concentrates only on the formulaic chanting of the deity's name while neglecting his other duties. The pandit switches entirely to Creole in lines 35–37 to animate the conversation that this morally inadequate character is reported as having with himself, voicing incomprehension of his own shortcomings. In this way, the pandit performatively reinforces the moral guidance the devotees should take from reading and chanting the Ramayana by the skillful use of two linguistic registers linked to contrasting moral images and values (compare Hill 1995, McIntosh 2005).

In both examples, the performance of moral and religious purity is supported by the use of purist Bhojpuri and explicitly contrasted with the values that now characterize social voices performed in Creole. The moral contrast performatively established between Creole and Bhojpuri as social voices in the context of the religious event underlines the ethnoreligious value ascribed to purist Bhojpuri while at the same time justifying the exclusion of Creole elements in moral terms. The purism characterizing the speech genre of Hindu religious sermons with its ideologically motivated avoidance of Creole elements is now extended to a new standard promoted by state-controlled electronic media in Mauritius.

BHOJPURI AND INDO-MAURITIANS

Originating from what are today Bihar and Eastern Uttar Pradesh in northern India, the majority of Indian migrants destined for the sugar plantations of colonial Mauritius are known to have been speakers of varieties of Bhojpuri (Baker and P. Ramnah 1985, Baker and A. Ramnah 1988). In Mauritius they created a new variety of Bhojpuri, described as a koine by linguists examining other colonies where indentured north Indian laborers settled (Barz and Siegel 1988, Gambhir 1988, Mesthrie 1993). Bhojpuri in Mauritius has mainly been associated with north Indians from Bihar and neighboring regions who left for Mauritius via the port of Calcutta. However, large numbers of Mauritians who trace their origins to the Tamil- and Telugu-speaking lands of south India also learned and used Mauritian Bhojpuri. In this way, Bhojpuri became the predominant language of the Mauritian countryside in the second half of the nineteenth century, a lingua franca overshadowing other north Indian dialects (Gambhir 1986). Most people on the sugar estates and in the newly established predominantly Indo-Mauritian villages knew and used Mauritian Bhojpuri, which led to it becoming firmly associated with sugarcane agriculture.[2] Known in Mauritius as both *moṭiya* (the coarse one) and *kalkattiya*, pointing to the Indian port of departure for most of its speakers' ancestors, the practice of Bhojpuri came to be evaluated as a social and spatial indicator, standing for a rustic, unsophisticated medium of humble indentured laborers in the sugarcane fields but also indicative of a particular point of origin, a homeland in India. While Mauritian Bhojpuri was thus evaluated as unquestionably Indian, it was brought into relation with multiple spatial differences. On one hand, it became associated with a rural-urban divide in Mauritius between the Indian-dominated countryside and the towns where Creoles were initially more numerous; on the other hand, it evoked a north-south differentiation relative to India with respect to the north Indian places of origin of the great majority of its users.

Whereas speaking Bhojpuri indexed rural life and agriculture, Creole was associated with lower government offices and schools, even if English was officially used in those settings. Today, many Mauritians point out that even children who grow up in one of the decreasing number of families where Bhojpuri is still in daily use stop using it when they start going to school. Hindu activists in Mauritius, on the other hand, have more recently considered the abandonment of Bhojpuri as a continuation of an earlier history of oppression and cultural contempt by the Franco-Mauritians and upper-class Creoles, who are remembered as having exploited and mistreated the Indians during the colonial period, as well as having had an interest in their conversion to Christianity and their assimilation to the Creole ethnic group. This fear of what members of an emerging Indo-Mauritian elite referred to as "deculturization" is what led to the demand for instruction in Hindi and other Indian languages considered ancestral in state schools from the 1940s and 1950s onward. In the period after independence, when Hindus started to gain dominance in the government and state apparatus, state-sponsored valorization of Indian ancestral languages intensified, with greatly expanded teaching of Hindi, training and employment of large numbers of "Oriental language" teachers, and increasing air time for programming in Hindi on the national radio and television network. However, Bhojpuri was not linked to celebrations of belonging until recently, and did not attract attention by state institutions in order to further its practice.

This situation changed in the late seventies as a result of the campaign for Creole as the national language of Mauritius, waged at the time by the Mouvement Militant Mauricien and several leftist intellectuals and writers. While they did not explicitly take a position against Creole, some Hindu activists saw the move towards official recognition of Creole as a denigration of Hindu heritage in Mauritius and reacted by calling for a state-sponsored valorization of Bhojpuri. A group of Hindu activists under the leadership of Sarita Boodhoo, whose husband, Harish Boodhoo, was Vice Prime Minister at the time, founded the Bhojpuri Institute in 1982. Making the most of their excellent connections to various sectors of the state apparatus, the proponents of Bhojpuri were successful in having the state-controlled mass media produce programs in Bhojpuri for the first time, one series of which, titled *Bhojpuri Bahaar,* had the promotion of Bhojpuri as an explicit goal. Hindu activists engaged in championing Bhojpuri continue to see themselves as primarily involved in a struggle to stop and even reverse the language shift towards Mauritian Creole. It is Hindus almost exclusively who are involved in pro-Bhojpuri activism.[3] As in the projects of the Bhojpuri promoters in the state-controlled mass media, there is a bias towards Hindu themes in the work on Mauritian Bhojpuri by the Mahatma Gandhi Institute, such as the recording and editing of Bhojpuri folk songs with Hindu religious themes performed at Hindu weddings.

Bhojpuri television programs of the MBC constitute the main source for the linguistic model I discuss in this chapter. These programs often refer to the necessity to speak and "preserve" Bhojpuri and discuss the "loss" of Bhojpuri as a threat to Hindu identity. At the time of my research there were two regularly scheduled programs on MBC television advertised as Bhojpuri language programs. One was the amateur folk song contest program named *Bhojpuri Bahaar* (translatable as either "Bhojpuri spring [the season]" or "Bhojpuri merriment"); the other was *Chingari* (spark). *Bhojpuri Bahaar* was clearly presented as a celebration of Indian rural folklore in Mauritius, and participants were exclusively Hindu. *Chingari* was consciously modeled on Western-style talk-show programs, with the host interviewing and conversing with invited guests and also taking questions from people who call in. The themes discussed were general social issues and problems rather than content associated with a particular ethnic group. Both Bhojpuri programs were hosted by the same person, who is also fluent in Hindi and trained at All India Radio.[4]

THE NEW BROADCAST BHOJPURI

Let us start with an example from the Bhojpuri-language television talk and call-in show *Chingari,* specifically, the final words of the host as he concludes the program by thanking the audience and other participants. His speech shows a number of striking parallels to the purist Bhojpuri used by pandits in the genre of *pravacan* described earlier, including the avoidance of Creole loans and the prominent presence of sanskritized Hindi words not normally used in Mauritian Bhojpuri. Finally, the speaker employs various forms of grammaticalized honorification, such as in pronouns of address *(ap)* and verbal suffixes, which in present-day Mauritius rarely occur in everyday conversations in Bhojpuri.

EXAMPLE 5.3*

Ta accha, matlab hamni ke <u>samay</u> chalal ba te aur hamni ke chahin ke apan **program** rokeke aur kafi <u>prashn</u> karla*ja ap* log aur kafi matlab *ap* log ke <u>pratikriya</u> rahal ih par hamni jon <u>darshak</u> bhai aur behen log hawan*ja* aur kafi behes karli*ja* u shayad eker se aur hal saki nikli. Aur jaisse dekhni*ja* hamni ke matlab hamni ke ek daur ha eh ih daur chahinala pura kareke keusno karke kahi ke ego admi jaisse hamni bat karli*ja* ke bich men ki hal chahin kareke konoke <u>samasya</u> hoi ta aukar hal chalte chalte mili. Aur *ap* log aila*ja ap* sabhi ke hamni <u>dhanyavad</u> dewatai*ja* aur sath men hamni ke du go <u>sahyogi</u> hawan*ja* u log kafi matlab date ke <u>prashn</u> le lane*ja* aur kafi aile bhi u log ke hamni ke **kamera** ke piche bhi hawan*ja* matlab u log ke bhi kaam ha. Ta *ap* sab log ke <u>namaskar</u> aur hamni ki taraf se *ap* sab ke <u>namaskar</u>.

1 Well, our <u>time</u> has run out and we have to end our **program,** and *you* people have asked quite a lot of <u>questions</u>, and there has been quite 5 a lot of <u>reaction</u> by *you*, our <u>viewers</u>, and we have discussed a lot and perhaps you can join us again. And as you see, that is, we have one round [of programming] and 10 we should complete it by whatever means, so if there is somebody like the person we spoke with in between, about how he is doing and what <u>problems</u> there are, so we will learn 15 about it. And *you* who have come we give our <u>thanks</u> to all of *you*, and with me there are the two <u>assistants</u> and they took a lot of <u>questions</u> from you, and a lot have also come [here], 20 and it is also the work of our people behind the **camera.** So <u>greetings</u> to all of *you* and my <u>greetings</u> to all of *you*.

Some of the most striking features of the purist register of Mauritian Bhojpuri adopted by the government-controlled Mauritian Broadcasting Corporation are elements taken directly from standard Hindi usage. These are almost never encountered in the everyday Mauritian Bhojpuri, as they are normally restricted to the genre of Hindu religious discourse, for which the use of a purist register of Bhojpuri or standard Hindi is pre-supposed. Therefore, the project to turn a purist register of Bhojpuri into a new standard in Mauritius is a twofold operation. On one hand, it is centered on presenting one particular register as the true standard, ignoring, for example, all registers recognizable as pertaining to forms of

---

*Bhojpuri is unmarked; Bhojpuri honorific verb suffixes and pronouns of address are italicized; Creole loans are boldfaced; Hindi and hindiized terms are underlined.

everyday discourse. On the other hand, the broadcast standardizers draw freely on standard Hindi in order to construct a standard Mauritian Bhojpuri, since the purist register used as a model for the new broadcast standard features numerous elements calqued on or otherwise influenced by Hindi. This is evident in the following example, also taken from an episode of *Chingari,* in which the host introduces the day's discussion topic to the audience at the beginning of the program.

EXAMPLE 5.4*

Hamni ke i jon <u>karyakram</u> ha tani buṛha jan, hamni ke jon <u>purwaj</u>, matlab jon saṭh sal ke upar ho gaylan*ja*, unkar bare men hamni charcha karab*ja*. Waise janela <u>sanjukt</u> <u>rashthra</u> ke taraf se jon pahla oktobar ha okra hamni ke jon buṛha jan hawansa unlog ke khatir ke jon <u>antarashtriya</u> <u>diwas</u> <u>ghoshit</u> karal gal. Aur hamni hiya toulog ke bol dewa*ja* ki hamni ke <u>desh</u> men i <u>samay</u>, i <u>samay</u> ketna hamni ke <u>vridh</u> ba.

    Waise <u>vridh</u> ta saṭh sal tak jite rahab*ja* ta ho jab *ja*, hamni ke <u>desh</u> men is <u>samay</u> ek lakh sat hajar ek sau <u>vridh</u> ba. Aur i sab jetna <u>vridh</u> hawan*ja* ulog ke hamni ke <u>desh</u> ke age baṛhawe men kafi <u>sahiyog</u> ba. Ta in log ke bare men hamni charcha karab*ja* lekin in log ke bare men kaise hamni charcha karab*ja* matlab in logon ke kon rakh rakhawa ba, <u>mantralay</u> ke taraf se, <u>sarkar</u> ke taraf se konchi ho tare aur sath men ketna.

1 In our <u>program</u> we will talk a little about old people, our <u>ancestors</u>, that is, those who have passed over the age of sixty. As you know, an 5 <u>international</u> <u>day</u> has been <u>declared</u> by the <u>United</u> <u>Nations</u> on the first of October for our old people. And we will here speak to you about how many of our <u>elderly</u> there are in our 10 <u>country</u> at this <u>time</u>, this <u>time</u>.

    About <u>elderly</u> <u>people</u> who have passed the age of sixty, there are at this <u>time</u> in our <u>country</u> one hundred seven thousand one hundred <u>elderly</u> 15 <u>people</u>. And all these <u>elderly</u> <u>people</u> have <u>supported</u> the progressing of their, of our <u>country</u> quite a lot. So we will talk about these people, but how will we talk about them, that is 20 who is in charge of their living, what is offered from the <u>ministry</u>, from the <u>government</u> and how much.

In the following exchange between the program host and an invited guest, a pandit, from another episode of *Chingari,* the similarity between the linguistic purism performed by the two speakers and the generic model of Hindu religious discourse is also striking. Here the two speakers discuss the widespread practice of public gambling at wakes.

*Bhojpuri is unmarked; Bhojpuri honorific verb suffixes and pronouns of address are italicized; Hindi and hindiized terms are underlined.

EXAMPLE 5.5*

H: Ek <u>prashn</u> *ap* se poochti ki samaj-   1   H: I have one <u>question</u> for *you*: you
   la ke kahin par marni ho gal ba te   know when there has been a
   aur huwan par admi log tash   death somewhere and if people
   <u>itiyadi</u> nai khelai, jaise ego <u>pratha</u>   there would not play cards <u>and so</u>
   ban gal bate, ego **tradisyon** ban   5   <u>on</u>, as if it had become a <u>custom</u>,
   gal bate, ego <u>parampara</u> ban gal   a **tradition**, become a <u>tradition</u> in
   ba ek tarah se. Ta shayad admi   a way. So maybe people would
   log itna nai jutyan*ja* bahar men.   not gather so much outside.
G: Ih zaruri nai ha ke huwa mela   G: It is not necessary that there is
   lagi.   10   such a [merry] gathering.
H: Lekin bahar men bhi bhaiteke   H: But sitting together outside
   ramayan karyan*ja*. Hamni ke   people also do Ramayana
   Mauritius <u>ki</u> jon <u>istithi</u> ba ekar   [i.e., chant from the Ramayana].
   bare men bat *kara*.   What the <u>situation</u> is like in our
                                               15   Mauritius, talk about it.

Let us consider the characteristics of the purist broadcast register in greater detail by examining other broadcast excerpts. A salient example of a standard Hindi element in the purist register is the introduction of *ap* as the second person honorific pronoun of address, analogous to Hindi usage, instead of the formerly nonhonorific and now neutral *tou* or *toulog* common in Mauritian Bhojpuri.

EXAMPLE 5.6†

Hamni ke <u>sahayogi</u> hawan*ja ap* ke   1   There are our <u>assistants</u>, whatever
jon bhi sawaal kareke hoi jon bhi   questions *you* ask, in whatever
bhasha men hamni i sawaal yahaa   language, we will ask the <u>present</u>
par <u>upasthit</u> mehmaan se puchab*ja*.   guest these questions.

EXAMPLE 5.7‡

S: *Ap* ke pati haw*an*?   1   S: Do *you* have a husband [literally,
                                                         is your husband (present)]?
M: Nai haw*an*, guzar gayel*an*.   M: No [literally, he is not (present)].
                                                         He has died.

*Bhojpuri is unmarked; Bhojpuri honorific verb suffixes and pronouns of address are italicized; Creole loan is boldfaced; Hindi and hindiized terms are underlined,
†Bhojpuri is unmarked; Bhojpuri honorific verb suffixes and pronouns of address are italicized; Hindi and hindiized terms are underlined.
‡Bhojpuri is unmarked; Bhojpuri honorific verb suffixes and pronouns of address are italicized.

The introduction of *ap* has to be understood in relation to the fact that no honorific second-person pronouns are employed in contemporary Mauritian Bhojpuri usage. *Tou* and *toulog*, as singular and plural, are the only forms of second-person address used. The honorific *raur*, akin to *raura* in Bihari varieties of Bhojpuri, is still understood by some older speakers and seems to have been a common second-person honorific form of address in the past (cf. Domingue 1971, 38), but it is definitely considered archaic today. The loss of honorific pronouns of address in Mauritian Bhojpuri appears to be a consequence of the long-standing process of language shift among Indo-Mauritians from Bhojpuri to Creole, which has gone hand in hand with a functional contraction of registers of Bhojpuri. Even before the Second World War, Creole emerged as indexing social mobility, schooling, and nonagricultural professions and has, among many other functions, taken over the role of a register among Bhojpuri-Creole bilinguals indicating relative social distance between the parties interacting. Simultaneously, Mauritian Bhojpuri registers of honorification for everyday contexts have fallen out of use, since using Bhojpuri has become an index of local in-group solidarity in bilingual Indo-Mauritian communities. The loss of *raur* and the uniform use of *tou/toulog* is a consequence of this process of "register stripping" due to the functional contraction in the context of language shift. Thus, the reintroduction of a honorific second-person pronoun by advocates of the new standard in the form of the hindiizing *ap* represents a conscious effort to regain register functions indicating prestige and respect in Bhojpuri. In fact, as I will demonstrate below, one of the consequences of the broadcast standardizers' project to overcome the present-day stigmatization of Bhojpuri and its exclusion from prestige and deference functions is the frequent use of honorific forms, as a presupposed component of a purist register, in the new broadcast Bhojpuri on MBC television.

Pronouns of address are not the only grammatical elements linked to the indexing of distance or deference in Mauritian Bhojpuri. Verbal suffixes, as well, can be divided into honorific and nonhonorific forms (compare Neerputh 1986: 50). Similar to pronouns, verbal endings can function as grammaticalized indexical categories of deference, the object deferred to being a function of both the grammatical category used and the interactional context (Agha 1993, 1994). There is often an overt link in Mauritian Bhojpuri between grammatical categories and the focus of deference, as in the case of a pronoun or a verb in the second person indicating respect for the addressee in an interaction, as in the classic discussion of honorification and pronouns of address by Brown and Gilman

(1972 [1960]). However, the focus of deference cannot be always derived from the particular grammatical category used, as when the presence of an interlocutor perceived as being of high status prompts a speaker to use honorific Mauritian Bhojpuri forms throughout the interaction. The use of honorific forms is also considered a sign of distinction and thus socially and morally elevating for the speaker himself, so that the use of honorific pronouns and verbal suffixes turns out to be simultaneously addressee-focused *and* addressor-focused. In this sense, honorification in purist Mauritian Bhojpuri bears some resemblance to the social semiotics of Javanese speech levels, where a similar ambiguity is at issue. While honorifics in Javanese are used as signs of deference to an interlocutor, full command of the entire complex and stratified range of honorific speech levels in Javanese at the same time indicates the refinement and exemplary status of the performer, since the highest speech levels are associated with precolonial Javanese court cultures (Errington 1985, Smith-Hefner 1988).

This evoking of distinction and refinement largely accounts for the prominent status of honorific forms in the purist register of Mauritian Bhojpuri, which some middle-class Hindus closely connected to the state apparatus seek to elevate to the status of a linguistic standard. In the purist register, the use of the second-person singular honorific verbal suffix -*la* (instead of -*le,* which is not marked for deference) and the third-person singular honorific verbal suffix -*lan* (instead of -*la* or -*lak*), as well as the plural honorific verbal suffix -*ja,* is now expected. Consider these two samples from the *Chingari* program:

EXAMPLE 5.8*

Abhi dekhi*ja* Mauritius desh men ketna buṛha log hawan*ja* ekar men ego chota soun documentary tayar karlan*ja* tani dekh*la*.	1 Now we see how many old people there are in Mauritius, on this they have prepared a small documentary, just have a look.

EXAMPLE 5.9†

Ulog bhag leilan*ja* waha par sab mililan*ja* ta ulog apne ap ke alag nay mehesus kariyan*ja*.	1 They take part and they all meet there so they do not feel separated from one another.

---

*Bhojpuri is unmarked; Bhojpuri honorific verb suffixes and pronouns of address are italicized.
†Bhojpuri is unmarked; Bhojpuri honorific verb suffixes and pronouns of address are italicized.

Apart from the striking use of an entire construction adopted from Hindi, *apne ap ke alag,* in example 5.9, the most noteworthy aspect of such a widespread use of honorifics in the new broadcasting standard is that it neatly fits the linguistic conventions of the genre of Hindu religious sermons and addresses in Mauritius, where both Mauritian Bhojpuri and Standard Hindi honorific forms are expected. Religious sermons in temples and public speeches delivered at religious festivals, as well as formal explications and comments on Hindu ritual in homes performed by Hindu pandits, all feature the frequent use of Mauritian Bhojpuri honorific pronouns and verbal suffixes.

This particular use of grammatical forms indexing deference in Mauritian Bhojpuri represents an interesting parallel to the Mexicano (Nahuatl) case discussed by Jane and Kenneth Hill (Hill and Hill 1978, 1986), in which language shift from Mexicano to Spanish in Central Mexico has resulted in a decrease of the use of honorific forms due to functional contraction and the valuation of Mexicano as a language of *indígenista* solidarity on one hand, and the emergence of a purist register characterized by the avoidance of Spanish lexical items and a very high frequency of honorific forms on the other. The advocates of purist Mexicano are often people who are better off and very much socially involved in the dominant Spanish-speaking world outside the Mexicano communities, and also normally speak the most hispanized Mexicano. The purist register of Mexicano is linked to a discourse of nostalgia for the past, when people presumably were more honest and spoke to each other in properly respectful ways (Hill 1998). The Mauritian case discussed here represents an analogous scenario in several ways. The middle-class advocates of the new "standard" are those who are least likely to use Bhojpuri in their homes, and none of them are employed as manual workers in the sugar industry, the social category most associated with Bhojpuri in Mauritius. They are often middle-rank state functionaries or employees on a similar level in para-state institutions, such as the Mauritian Broadcasting Corporation. The celebration of the purist register of Bhojpuri is performed in the wider framework of a state-supported valorizing of ancestral cultures as a key way to shape and reproduce ethnic groups and establish their places in a Mauritian nation.

A further grammatical difference between the purist register and everyday registers of Mauritian Bhojpuri is the avoidance of the noun suffix *-wa.* This suffix, grammatically indexing a diminutive quality of the noun and a slightly disrespectful stance of the speaker towards the noun's referent in Bihari varieties of Bhojpuri (Tiwari 1960, 104), is used as a marker of endearment and familiarity in Mauritian Bhojpuri,[5] as well as a marker of definiteness of the noun in question (Baker and P. Ramnah 1985, 218–20; Baker and A. Ramnah 1988, 51). The reasons for the exclusion of this otherwise common feature from purist Bhojpuri seem to be twofold. First, this way of grammatically marking definiteness is unknown in Hindi. Second, this suffix is linked with emotions of familiarity and endearment, which conflict with the purist register's associations of deference and respect on one hand, and distinction on the other. Another feature of purist broadcast Bhojpuri is the avoidance of interjections *re* (indicating a male speaker) and *ge* (indicating a female speaker), which are frequently used in colloquial Bhojpuri in order to interpellate someone or finish an utterance (see also Neerputh 1986: 15). Since these forms are absent in standard Hindi and are also locally considered linguistic stereotypes of "rough," uneducated speech, their exclusion from the purist register aspiring to a standard is not surprising. The co-occurrence of these interjections with honorific forms of address and verbal endings is seen as highly inappropriate, since they have become iconic of "undeveloped" speech.

Finally, the most salient feature of the new purist broadcast Bhojpuri concerns the lexicon. This register is characterized by relentless sanskritization and the avoidance of lexical items of Creole and Perso-Arabic origin. Creole loans in Mauritian Bhojpuri are so common, however, that many of them are not recognized as "foreign." In fact, one of the slogans under which the Bhojpuri Institute started its campaign for the revitalization of Bhojpuri in the early 1980s was *Bhojpuri joli ba* (Bhojpuri is beautiful), *joli* being, of course, of Creole and ultimately French origin. Many in Mauritius do indeed concede that their practice of Bhojpuri is very much mixed with Creole. Yet out of concern for what they consider the linguistic and ancestral purity of Mauritian Bhojpuri, the standardizers are eager to suppress all items they recognize as derived from Creole, and substitute them with sanskritized equivalents adopted from standard Hindi. In table 3 are some examples of sanskritized Hindi terms introduced into the new broadcast Mauritian Bhojpuri, replacing words or expressions now recognized as derived from Creole.

For a comparison, here is a counterexample, taken from the speech of an invited guest on the *Chingari* program, that does not follow the purism of the new standard. This sample shows the extent to which Creole words are used in contemporary Mauritian Bhojpuri in unmarked ways. The lexical items that would be targeted the purists are in boldface.

TABLE 3   Some sanskritized Hindi terms and the Creole terms
they replace in broadcast Mauritian Bhojpuri

Hindi sanskritisms	"Ordinary" version	English translation
sanyukt rashtra	*nasyon ini*	United Nations
swasthya mantralay	*minister lasante*	ministry of health
antararashtriya diwas	*lazurne enternasiyonal*	international day
sanstha	*lenstitisiyon*	institution/institute
svatantrata	*landepandans*	independence
yogdan	*kontribisyon*	contribution

EXAMPLE 5.10*

Me moris men kale **swasant an**	1	**But** in Mauritius only until [the age
parski hamni ke ego **zaffer form** ha		of] **sixty years**, because we have a
ki jab koi kaam karela oke **swasant**		**kind of regulation** that when some-
an hogal ta **oblize** parela **retret** leyke		one has worked until he has become
	5	sixty years old he is obliged to retire.

This example not only demonstrates how far removed the new projected standard is from the ways of speaking with which most Mauritian
Bhojpuri speakers are familiar, but is also a good example of the lexical
mixing abhorred by purists. By seeking to purge words recognized as
Creole or suspected of really belonging to Urdu, the broadcast standardizers again follow the conventions of the genre of Hindu religious discourse in Mauritius, for which the use of either a sanskritized register of
Bhojpuri, or standard Hindi is expected.

Finally, Bhojpuri activists have adopted the Devanagari script for
Mauritian Bhojpuri alongside the roman alphabet, which is occasionally
used. This is a very important step, since Mauritian Bhojpuri was previously an unwritten language. It still is rarely written, and the vast majority of its users have never bothered to write it, since in the context of the
Mauritian educational system they are striving above all for literacy in
English and French and, to a lesser degree, Hindi. However, the purists
are eager to demonstrate that Bhojpuri can be written in the Devanagari
script used for Sanskrit and Hindi, not just in Latin script, which most
Mauritians read. While the use of the Latin writing system is not consid-

*Bhojpuri is unmarked; Creole loans are boldfaced.

TABLE 4 Main features of purist Mauritian Bhojpuri

Phonology	Substitution of [š] for [s] where standard Hindi usage would prescribe it *(deš* for *des,* *šakti* for *sakti)*
Lexicon	Avoidance of common Creole loans
	Use of sanskritized Hindi vocabulary
Grammar/morphology	Honorification: frequent use of Mauritian Bhojpuri honorific verb suffixes and the Hindi honorific personal pronoun of address, *ap;* occasional use of Hindi honorific verb morphology *(khaiye* for *khala)*
	Avoidance of noun suffix -*wa/wa*
	Occasional use of Hindi verb morphology *(jata* for *jaila)*
	Occasional use of Hindi gendered postpositions *(ka/ki* for *ke)*

ered problematic by the purists, the crucial point here is the exclusion of the Arabic-derived Nasta'liq script otherwise used for Urdu. For example, one Urdu teacher voiced his disappointment with the Bhojpuri language essay contests held by the Bhojpuri Institute because entries in Nasta'liq, written by Muslim users of Mauritian Bhojpuri who had studied Urdu at school and had not learned Devanagari, were rejected. Another example of this policy is the Bhojpuri folk tale collection written in Devanagari script with roman transliteration and translations by a Hindi teacher and sponsored by the Human Service Trust (Mohit 1994). Also, the announcements and programs for the annual Bhojpuri drama competition organized by the Mauritian Ministry of Arts and Culture are printed in roman and Devanagari letters, but not in Nasta'liq. This official use of Devanagari but not Nasta'liq links Mauritian Bhojpuri, originally spoken by most of the Hindu and Muslim Indian indentured laborers who immigrated to Mauritius, to Hindi and to a Hindu identity. It recalls the key role that disputes about writing systems played in the Hindi-Urdu conflict in nineteenth- and twentieth-century India (Brass 1974, King 1994). Sanskritization and the use of the Devanagari script on the one hand, against the rejection of Nasta'liq on the other, supports the widespread notion among Mauritians that Bhojpuri is a dialect of Hindi. As a consequence of the link established between Mauritian Bhojpuri and a Hindu identity, rural Muslims are conceptually erased as speakers of Mauritian Bhojpuri,[6] even though they represent a sizable number of Mauritian Bhojpuri-Creole bilinguals.

ACCELERATION OF LANGUAGE SHIFT
AS AN IRONIC CONSEQUENCE OF PURISM

So far I have argued that a purist register, linked to the genre of Hindu religious discourse, is the linguistic model that some middle-class Hindus in Mauritius are seeking to turn into a broadcast standard for Mauritian Bhojpuri. These state-sponsored efforts to promote Bhojpuri in the mass media in order to stop and even reverse the language shift to Creole have resulted in the appropriation of Bhojpuri as a "Hindu language." I argue that for this reason the project to stop the language shift away from Bhojpuri in Mauritius is likely to fail. The hinduizing and hindiizing of Bhojpuri effected through the adoption of the new broadcasting standard is convincing Bhojpuri speakers of non-Hindu and non–north Indian background that Bhojpuri is above all for Hindus.

Bhojpuri used to be both the most common language of the country-side and the lingua franca shared by speakers of different religious and regional origins, a role filled by Creole these days. Nevertheless there are still many users of Mauritian Bhojpuri who are not Hindus of north Indian origin, above all rural Muslims and Hindu south Indians. The ancestors of most Hindus and Muslims of north Indian background are known to have migrated to Mauritius from what is today the state of Bihar (Carter and Deerpalsingh 2000). Their families can often be traced back to the same districts (Deerpalsingh 2000), and often they know their ancestors were Bhojpuri speakers. In present-day Mauritius, however, Bhojpuri is largely considered a Hindu language. Numerous Muslims are also speakers of Bhojpuri, combined in the usual bilingual situation with Mauritian Creole. However, they are much less interested in laying a claim on Bhojpuri and are also less concerned about the language shift to Creole in their community. The communal appropriation of linguistic elements coalescing into a purist register, while indexing one ethnoreligious group, has been followed by a rejection of the same elements by other groups. The language shift away from Bhojpuri among non-Hindu Bhojpuri users is accelerated, and their children are unlikely to be encouraged to use Bhojpuri at all.

ELECTRONIC MEDIA
AND ETHNOLINGUISTIC RECOGNITION

The promotion of languages with a historically subordinate status in electronic media, intended to "save" the language from abandonment by its users while supporting claims of ethnolinguistic recognition, exhibits a number of parallels with previous strategies of language standardization and their social and political consequences. The construction of a new standard for radio or television broadcasting necessarily involves selection among several possible linguistic varieties and registers. And since linguistic varieties and registers are very frequently indexically linked to particular groups of persons among the speakers of a language, the choices made have social and political implications and consequences. For example, language standardizers, activists, and litterateurs involved in what Benedict Anderson has called a "lexicographic revolution" in nineteenth-century Europe (Anderson 1991, 71) played a crucial role in defining and shaping the European standard vernaculars while turning them into national languages (Hobsbawm 1990, 54–63). That process of excluding and including linguistic material had profound consequences for the shape and internal setup of the national communities imagined through the prism of national languages and putative "mother tongues," since the choices privileged certain regional or religious groups or social classes while marginalizing or excluding others from claiming full membership in a newly fashioned national community. Thus, the making of new standards, by the lexicon, grammar book, or collection of folk tales, through either what Anderson (1991) has called print capitalism or the use of a language in electronic media is rarely a politically innocent act, since the choices involved also suggest which categories of persons are central to the community for which ethnolinguistic recognition is sought. This problematic is also salient in the new use of Mauritian Bhojpuri on state-controlled television. By privileging linguistic forms and registers indexically linked to Hindu religious practice and the category of persons typically using them, the institutionalization of a purist, hindiized Bhojpuri suggests a new ethnicization of Bhojpuri. Bhojpuri is now turned into a Hindu language, implying that non-Hindu users of Bhojpuri are not centrally important users of the language, while suggesting that purist Bhojpuri, with its perceived resemblance to the linguistic medium of Hindu religious discourse, is superior to other varieties and registers of Bhojpuri used by Mauritians.

In recent decades, language activists and ethnolinguistic movements worldwide have made increasing use of electronic media to promote particular linguistic varieties in attempts to stop and even reverse language shift. Very often, the use of such languages in electronic media is linked to notions of ethnic community and identity in a politics of recognition (Silverstein 2003). The problem of intertextual gaps (Briggs and Bauman

1992) also emerges as a key issue in these projects to promote languages previously excluded from use in electronic media. These gaps arise when new genres of linguistic entextualization introduced as part of electronic media practices appear at odds with preexisting genres of public speaking in particular settings. For example, attempts to stop language shift from Navajo to English by setting up a Navajo-language radio station have led to the emergence of a new genre of "broadcast Navajo" (Peterson 1997), which some Navajo consider as conflicting with traditional Navajo linguistic practices. Similarly, recontextualizing the linguistic model of purist Bhojpuri from pandits' sermons in Hindu devotional settings to a television program in which a host interviews and converses with invited guests while viewers call in with questions on the topics discussed involves a bridging of the gap between the discourse genre of *pravacan* and a new mass-mediated genre where Mauritian Bhojpuri has never been used before.

The attempt to champion the use of a minority or other historically subordinate linguistic variety also frequently raises the issue of the appropriate variety to be used in the new context. Such has been the case with Irish (Hindley 1990) and Breton (Jones 1998b, McDonald 1990), where a new standard, oriented toward language activism and revitalization associated with ideologically committed urban middle-class second-language learners, contrasts with a range of dialectal varieties used by predominantly rural, working-class first language speakers, many of whom consider the new standard inauthentic and artificial. The use of Irish and Breton on radio and television has accentuated such conflicts, which may ultimately divide and weaken movements for ethnolinguistic recognition. Similarly, in Catalonia, a state-appointed "commission of linguistic normalization" supervising the use of Catalan on state television has had to negotiate between the tendency of television producers to favor "light" Catalan, exhibiting greater tolerance towards the use of Castilian Spanish elements, and the pressure by linguistic nationalists for more purist, "heavy" varieties of Catalan (Gardner et al. 2000, Vallverdú 1995). In contrast, producers of Welsh-language radio and television have sought a compromise between the Welsh standard established in the 1970s and the range of dialectal varieties in Wales while deciding on which varieties of Welsh should be used for broadcasting (Jones 1998a, 273–78). Also, Corsican language broadcasters have resisted the claims of language activists for using a standard Corsican presumably purified of "foreign" influences and distant from spoken dialectal varieties in Corsica by incorporating both the dialectal variation and frequent code-switching to French that is characteristic of everyday linguistic practices on the island (Jaffe 1999). Purist strategies of language activism for ethno-linguistic recognition that insist on the supremacy of a single linguistic norm and thus imply an institutionalized hierarchization of varieties of a previously unstandardized language often lead to conflicts around competing linguistic norms. This sometimes alienates large numbers of users of the language to be "revitalized" who do not identify the new purist standard as "theirs" in a socially meaningful way (Dorian 1994, Hornberger and King 1999). This of course is the case we see in Mauritius, where the purist strategy of promoting Bhojpuri as a strongly hindiized and Creole-avoiding variety in television and radio broadcasts carries the risk of alienating considerable numbers of bilingual users of Bhojpuri for whom there is no obvious link between the new standard variety oriented toward the genre of Hindu religious discourse and their own practice of Bhojpuri.

For example, the widespread use of honorific forms in the purist model constitutes a dilemma for Muslim users of Bhojpuri because of the register-bound connection to Hindu religious settings and activities, as well as the association of frequent use of the honorific forms with the high-caste Babuji-Maraz, especially the Maraz, the Brahmin caste group of Mauritius, who constituted the first social elite among Hindus. Until 1986, the Babuji-Maraz held a near monopoly on the state-subsidized temple priest positions,[7] and members of this group often had some knowledge of standard Hindi even before it was generally taught in schools to all Hindu students. The Bhojpuri spoken by high-caste Hindu families was considered refined and hindiized, and most of the purist structural and lexical characteristics mentioned earlier are still seen by many as indexing the Babuji-Maraz as a social group. However, the ethnic elite among the Muslims of Mauritius are to a large extent Gujaratis, who were never Bhojpuri speakers. Therefore, many Muslim users of Bhojpuri consider the generalized use of the honorific pronouns and verbal suffixes in the new "standard" for Mauritian Bhojpuri as linked to a particular Hindu social group and symptomatic of the Hindu bias of pro-Bhojpuri language activism.

The contradictions of this project become even more evident if one pays attention to the role of genre. I have discussed the indexical link between the purist register and the local genre of Hindu religious discourse, or *pravacan*. Invoking such a connection represents a strategy of entextualization of particular utterances designed to render them powerful and authoritative. Keeping in mind that generic forms are never permanently fixed, and that the actualization of a particular genre always remains a problematic performative achievement (Hanks 1987), perfect matches between particular utterances and historically defined generic forms are rare. Rather, the linking of particular texts to generic forms is better understood as a process of imperfect entextualization, which frequently results in a disjuncture between the utterance and the presupposed generic form in its historical context. Bridging or minimizing such disjunctures then becomes an exercise of social power, common in projects of codifying history, nationhood, ethnicity, and identity, while their highlighting may constitute an ironic subversion of such projects.

In the Mauritian scenario, the minimizing of the distance between purist utterances presented as tokens of a new linguistic standard and the Hindu religious discourse genre presents the new standard as authoritative. Nevertheless, the attempt to minimize that distance alienates non-Hindu speakers of Bhojpuri in a society characterized by interethnic rivalry. Muslims in Mauritius often read the purist Bhojpuri used on MBC television as evidence that Hindus connected to state institutions are using the promotion of Bhojpuri for political gains. As Fauwzee, an Urdu teacher put it: "At first, we liked the idea of protecting Bhojpuri very much. But then it became clear that Hindus turned this into a political issue, after the MMM [Mouvement Militant Mauricien] tried to push for Creole in 1982. I also often have trouble understanding what this one guy [the talk show host] who you see in the Bhojpuri programs says. This is communalizing Bhojpuri, and it has nothing to do with the way we speak it." Shareef, a civil servant, remarked that initially his three children found the Bhojpuri programs interesting, but once they realized that Muslims are hardly ever invited to talk on the programs and that Hindus monopolize it, they stopped watching it. Also, not having studied standard Hindi in school, they were unfamiliar with the sanskritisms frequently used by the program host and his assistants.

The Mauritian Bhojpuri standardization project has implications not only for non-Hindu users. By implicitly devaluing most Mauritian Bhojpuri speakers' linguistic practices, which do not measure up to the purist standard, the standardizers' strategy also discourages young Hindus from using Bhojpuri. Hindu Mauritians below approximately the age of thirty are often insecure about their command of Bhojpuri and already use Creole in most daily contexts. Except in conversations with older people, many of these younger speakers are now most likely to use Bhojpuri when joking among social intimates, and these contexts of use are experienced as greatly at odds with the purist register promoted on television. Thus the outcome is not only the exclusion of non-Hindu Bhojpuri speakers or potential speakers; the introduction of the broadcast standard also risks making Hindu Mauritian Bhojpuri users insecure about the appropriateness of their linguistic practices. In the end, the authorization strategy for the new purist standard does not stop the language shift to Creole but rather contributes to the abandonment of Bhojpuri registers in the linguistic repertoire of Hindu Mauritians.

TELEVISION, TEMPORALITY,
AND ETHNOLINGUISTIC RECOGNITION

Why have Hindu activists chosen electronic media for promoting Bhojpuri? And what makes the circulation of purist Bhojpuri on television different in its social effects from other ways of using a hindiized register of Bhojpuri? The circulation of discourse through electronic mediation has been described as a powerful practice in the creation of a sense of community, since it provides a large public with common linguistic reference points that can be appropriated and reworked for purposes of face-to-face interaction (Spitulnik 1996). In this regard, electronic mediation at first glance may not seem much different from, for example, print capitalism as analyzed by Benedict Anderson. After all, mass mediation of discourse by print has been credited with "integrating" populations through enhancing communication between previously weakly connected regions and populations (Deutsch 1953) — specifically by creating a reading public with an awareness of anonymous others consuming the same print products (Anderson 1991). One way to start investigating the question of what the electronic medium uniquely offers is to pay attention to how practices of electronic mediation reconfigure experiences of spatial and temporal distance. Much of the appeal of electronic mediation lies in its ability to minimize experiences of spatio-temporal distance to an extent not achievable by the circulation of print (Harvey 1989, Tomlinson 1999). This has interesting implications for contemporary struggles around ethnolinguistic recognition, since such activism often seeks to counter what Ralph Grillo has called "ideologies of contempt" (Grillo 1989), which justify the supremacy of certain languages over others by relegating presumably inferior linguistic varieties and the people indexed by them to peripheral positions in space and time, away from geographical centers and the temporal present, by casting them as "backward," rustic, and unsuitable for modernity. The presentation of such historically subjugated language varieties through electronic mediation, with its potential to mitigate experiences of spatiotemporal remove, may thus represent a strategy to rework the mapping of linguistic differences effected by such "ideologies of contempt." In recent years, activists seeking the revitalization of lesser-used languages have made increasing use of audio-visual and digital media in ways that clearly seek to counter perceptions of a spatiotemporal "lag" on the part of dominant ideologies of language (Browne 1996, Cazden 2003, Kroskrity 2002, Warschauer 1998, Williams 2000). Implicit in this is a highlighting of allochrony (Fabian 1983) as a mechanism of inequality and power. In particular, one of the assumed properties of practices of electronic mediation per se seems to be their ability to counter denials of temporal coevalness (Cotter 2001) for lesser-used languages and the populations indexed by them.

The use of languages such as Mauritian Bhojpuri, associated with rural margins and obsolescent positions in time "without a future," on television can be seen as a way to counter such "ideologies of contempt" and to find alternative ways to map linguistic differentiation on space and time. The chronotopes (Bakhtin 1981) of distancing and removal through which subordinate linguistic varieties are often described and represented are undercut not only because of the emblematic status of audio-visual media as icons of modernity and globalization but also in more concrete ways. For instance, in the context of shaping authentic, diasporic Hindus, the Hindu activists engaged in the promotion of Bhojpuri aim to portray the language as after all not confined to unsophisticated, tradition-bound persons in the Mauritian countryside but linked to practices of electronic mass mediation, which are in turn connected to geographical and political-economic centers. Thus, the goal is to present the practice of Bhojpuri as fully relevant to the present and future concerns of Hindus in Mauritius. The broadcast standardizers hope this might motivate viewers not to abandon usage of Bhojpuri, which is represented as a key feature of Hindu heritage in Mauritius. Hence, the manipulation of spatial and temporal indexicality plays a key role in such performances of diasporic purity on television.

Yet the use of purist Bhojpuri on MBC television play a crucial role in the ethnicization of Bhojpuri as a "Hindu language," which makes its continued use in Mauritius problematic in other ways. While the promotion of Bhojpuri on Mauritian television as part of a Hindu nationalist agenda demonstrates the affinity between the use of purist, essentialist notions of culture, on one hand, and contemporary strategies of media and advertising industries (Mazzarella 2004) as well as electronically mediated political struggles of recognition (Ginsburg et al. 2002), on the other, the consequences of ethnicizing Bhojpuri on state-controlled television are ambiguous. While it certainly effects a performative recognition of Bhojpuri as Hindu diasporic heritage, the purism of the broadcast standard alienates not only non-Hindu users of Bhojpuri but also many Hindus who do not consider the new broadcast standard to be meaningfully linked to their linguistic practices.

CHAPTER 6

Calibrations of Displacement

Diasporization, Ancestral Language, and Temporality

In this chapter I examine the creation and transformation of diasporic "Indianness" in Mauritius through alternative understandings of temporal remove and simultaneity in relation to an Indian homeland. The purpose is to interrogate temporality as a mode of building ethnic and national communities with an eye to how the category of diaspora is thus turned into a malleable entity. In this way, I seek to contextualize diasporization in Mauritius through practices that shift diasporic allegiances, preventing them from being permanently tied to a certain homeland. Language plays a central role in the production and transformation of the relations diasporic communities entertain to changing homelands, thus producing shifting "counter-geographies" (Appadurai 1996b). Here I focus on how language shapes the temporal and spatial relationships between Indo-Mauritians and the assumed homeland that constitute the diasporic experience. In this sense, thinking about diasporic communities as mediated by linguistically produced regimentations of temporality intersects with theorizing nationalism, since in that study too the problem of language-mediated concepts of time in the creation of large-scale communities has played a central role (Anderson 1991).

The significance of apprehensions of temporal remove and simultaneity with respect to a homeland for understanding diaspora raises two issues. First, experiences of the temporality of community in diaspora often provide the ground for characterizing diasporic cultures as hybrid, on the assumption that these cultures are the result of mixing cultural traditions that have been dislocated from their assumed origins in a different spatiotemporal frame (García Canclini 1995; Gilroy 1993; Tomlinson 1999, 141–49). Thus, cultural hybridity in the diaspora can also be described as the experiencing of a variety of places at a single moment of time. In a paradoxical way, the concept of cultural hybridity embraces cultural change over time as well as a re-inscription of the origins of cultural traditions in space and time. On one hand, the creation of hybridity in the diaspora is often understood as a process of cultural fusion and creation unfolding in time, indicating an increasing sense of temporal distance from the world of the ancestors. This is especially the case when cultural hybridity is expressed in discourses of creolization (Hannerz 1987, 1996). On the other hand, hybridity as a concept remains fixated on origins against which diasporic culture can be described as hybrid and mixed (Khan 2001), thus conjuring up the simultaneous presence of multiple cultural pasts in a single instant.

Second, the sense of spatiotemporal distanciation from a homeland, which is what ultimately accounts for the diasporic experience, may be shaped by different or even conflicting senses of how to locate a diasporic community in time. That is, varying temporalities may interact in shaping the relationship between the diaspora and the homeland, projecting alternative histories and forms of diasporic belonging. Following the argument that linguistic ideologies shape such understandings of temporality and that different temporalities imply different conceptions of diaspora, the question then is how language mediates divergent temporal orders. At the same time, it is important to realize that linguistically mediated temporality interacts with other modes of producing diasporic consciousness. In this chapter I analyze how the shaping of diasporic community through linguistic ideology converges with religious ritual and performance by showing how the Shivratri pilgrimage in Mauritius becomes a resonating context for the cultivation of Hindi as the language of the ancestors. Viewed against the background of a history of internal antagonisms and fragmentation into a number of separate ethnic groups and communities, the Shivratri pilgrimage demonstrates the potential for ideological homogenization inherent in creating the concept of a common Indian homeland for the otherwise very heterogeneous group known as Hindus in Mauritius. Religious performance interacts with the propagation of Hindi as the ancestral language of Hindus in order to point towards a Hindu homeland in India. This scenario also offers a description of how images and discourses of language and linguistic differentiation are coordinated with other elements of "Indianness" in

Mauritius, such as religious festivals and spatial imaginations, together producing a diasporic consciousness. It also points to a tension in the Indo-Mauritian diasporic identity between two opposing dynamics evident in Indo-Mauritian politics and self-imagination. While ethnoreligious elites have succeeded in building separate minority communities around the concept of an ancestral language, the way the pilgrimage is organized and performed resonates with the purist and unifying vision of Hindu nationalists, who downplay the awareness of profound cultural change while seeking to be the spokesmen of all Hindus in Mauritius. The conflict between these positions is expressed in divergent diasporic concepts of homeland which are connected to divergent visions of linguistic differentiation in Mauritius.

CONCEIVING DIASPORA IN TIME:
"OVERSEAS INDIANS" AND LANGUAGE

Writings on the social and cultural aspects of Indian diasporas and writings on language in the Indian diaspora have traditionally constituted separate bodies of literature. Nevertheless, these two literatures share two important themes, namely, a focus on "transplanted" entities and their origins, and concerns about the preservation or erosion of what has become dislocated, whether Indian languages or other cultural traditions. The older anthropological literature on Indian diasporas is dominated by concerns for cultural retention and attenuation, especially with regard to religious practice and those social institutions long considered essential features of Indian society: caste and the joint family. Describing Indian diasporas in terms of cultural retention or attenuation also implicitly locates people of South Asian origin in different temporal positions in terms of either convergence with the world of the ancestors or cultural transformation over time. Overall, one of the dangers of the category of diaspora in its more common, wider sense, as describing people with an allegiance to a more or less distant homeland, is that it may induce a view of diasporic groups as extensions of their assumed homelands.

This problem is present in much of the earlier anthropological work on Indian indenture diasporas in the former sugar colonies, with its preoccupation with "transplanted" culture and the persistence and survival of Indian customs, and debates regarding the degree to which Indian cultural traditions have been maintained in the new setting (Jayawardena 1966, Klass 1961, Nevadomsky 1980a, 1980b, Niehoff 1959). The anthropology of caste among overseas Indians can be seen as symptomatic of this tendency (Schwartz 1967). Taking an idealized Indian caste system, in the tradition of Louis Dumont (1970), located in the presumably self-sufficient Indian village community as the starting point of comparison, anthropologists attempted to determine how far the practices of "overseas Indians" deviated from the ideal. That is, particular attention was paid to whether people of South Asian descent in these locales had successfully "preserved" the world of their immigrant ancestors or whether there had been significant cultural change.

Interestingly, the literature on Indian languages abroad, especially on "overseas Hindi," has conceptually followed a very similar route. Writers in this tradition focus on the survival and viability of such languages in diasporic locales, attempting to measure linguistic change in terms of linguistic difference in relation to an assumed point of departure in India. The study of these varieties has largely been conducted within a paradigm of the study of "transplanted languages" (Barz and Siegel 1988, Bhatia 1982), comparing the linguistic situation in India at the time of emigration with the present diasporic varieties. Siegel's work on Fiji Hindi (1987) focuses on how different linguistic varieties of Avadhi and Bhojpuri were brought by Indian indentured laborers to Fiji, where these varieties became the basis for the creation of what Siegel analyzes as a koine, a uniform Fiji Hindustani or Fiji Hindi. In order to analyze the process of koineization, Siegel seeks to identify the linguistic origins of this Fijian variety by trying to determine the home districts of most immigrants in present-day Uttar Pradesh and Bihar. He then infers the linguistic varieties spoken from the places of origin of the immigrants and correlates the relative influences of particular north Indian dialects on Fiji Hindi with the numbers of immigrants to Fiji from certain districts. Mesthrie (1991, 1993) takes a similar approach regarding koineization in the Indian diaspora of South Africa in seeking to determine the origins of South African Bhojpuri. He follows a procedure akin to Gambhir's work on Guyanese Bhojpuri (1981, 1988), in which detailed lists of linguistic features of South African Bhojpuri are established and then linked to corresponding features in Indian varieties associated with particular locales in India. The underlying assumption in these approaches is that knowing an immigrant's place of origin means knowing the language he or she used at the time of settling in an overseas colony.

Such isomorphism of language and place, coupled with an overriding concern for linguistic origins, is also evident in the study of Mauritian Bhojpuri. In Gambhir's comparison of Mauritian Bhojpuri with other "transplanted" varieties of "overseas Hindi," the occurrence of certain linguistic features in Mauritian Bhojpuri as opposed to other "overseas" Hindi or Bhojpuri varieties is explained in an analogous fashion. The study is guided by the assumption of a direct link between linguistic varieties, certain places in India, and particular linguistic features characteristically used by persons migrating from the areas in question (Gambhir 1986). The reason proposed for the presence of such features in Mauritius is the relative prevalence of migrants from those districts of north and northeast India regarded as the location of linguistic varieties containing such forms. In contrast, the relative absence of such characteristically Mauritian features in other former plantation colonies is linked to the smaller number of migrants from such districts and the greater number of immigrants originating from other places associated with alternative linguistic forms. Regarding the origins of Mauritian Bhojpuri, Domingue (1971) as well as Baker and A. Ramnah (1988) have likewise sought to relate particular features of Mauritian Bhojpuri to varieties of Bhojpuri in certain areas of Bihar and Uttar Pradesh, though without necessarily suggesting that an immigrant's place of origin determines his or her native language. The origins of a number of salient linguistic features in Sarnami, or Surinamese Hindustani, have been accounted for in a similar manner (Damsteegt 1988). Given the prominence of Creole issues in writings on the linguistic situation of Mauritius, and also the "mixed" quality of Mauritian Bhojpuri, some scholars whose work is primarily focused on French and Mauritian Creole have mistakenly concluded that Mauritian Bhojpuri is a Creole language (Chaudenson 1979: 34; Stein 1982: 131), a claim refuted by Baker and P. Ramnah (1985).

A central assumption in these approaches to the study of "overseas Hindi" is that linguistic varieties are bounded entities spatially rooted in certain locales or areas. When these objectified entities are taken out of their normal place and "transplanted" overseas, they undergo transformations because they now exist in a different environment and in close contact with other non-Indian linguistic varieties, even while they retain linguistic features identifiable in languages in India. The parallel between the methods and assumptions of this linguistic tradition of research on the Indian diaspora with earlier work on other, social and cultural aspects of Indian diasporic communities is striking. The latter body of literature also presupposes the existence of bounded Indian traditional cultural forms, tied to particular locales of South Asia, that are either retained or transformed under conditions of diasporic dislocation. Both the varieties of "overseas Hindi" and the Indian cultural traditions in the diaspora are defined by and seen as new extensions of their origins in India. At the same time, these origins are temporally marked, constituting the "before" of the act of migration. Analyzing diasporic language in terms of transformation or continued sameness also involves the positing of temporal relationships to such points of departure.

A set of newer writings addressing the problematic of the Indian diaspora has described the formation and transformation of Indian diasporic communities in a manner sensitive to its colonial context and the politics of new nation-states. In this way, more recent work on religion in Indian diasporic communities, for example, has largely resisted the temptation to cast "overseas Indians" in terms of the persistence and attenuation of cultural traits. Instead, these authors have drawn attention to how cultural traditions such as religion or understandings of purity and pollution (Khan 1994) are constantly reproduced and transformed in changing historical circumstances that are fundamentally different from the Indian context (Vertovec 1990, 1992, 1994, van der Burg and van der Veer 1986, van der Veer and Vertovec 1991). However, these studies pay less attention to the process of diasporization, that is, to the production of a diasporic relation of these groups to India, and focus more on changes in religious organization and practice (Hollup 1994, 1995). The question thus remains how diasporic imaginations of assumed homelands, and therefore diasporic communities as such, are created. This necessitates an interrogation of the category of India as a homeland in relation to which the diaspora has suffered a kind of displacement, stressing how concepts of locality in the diaspora are produced (Appadurai 1996a).

Investigating this diasporic relationship is best done by treating it as a dynamic concept, as an orientation that is potentially flexible and constantly being reworked, rather than as a classification necessarily determined by the fact of migration. Diasporic orientations are not to be presupposed by knowing the place of origin of migrants; rather, diasporas are produced through an ongoing reinterpretation of history, including temporal relationships with the world of the ancestors. In some of the most recent work on the Indian diaspora this problem is addressed by focusing on the colonial context of Indian migration and the formation of diasporic communities. These authors have demonstrated how colonial discourses on Indians in overseas colonies and the Indians' political consciousness as well as identity formations have been mutually constitutive (Kelly 1991, Kaplan and Kelly 1994). In this way, highlighting the colonial aspects of migration has accounted for both the shaping of

Indian communities overseas out of highly heterogeneous groups of immigrants, and the deep transformations they have undergone in the contexts of empire and indenture (Kale 1995). Also, the contemporary dynamics of Indian diasporic communities can only be made sense of in light of their postcolonial situation (Kelly 1995, Bates 2000).

These important advances in the study of the Indian diaspora notwithstanding, the focus on colonialism for the study of how diasporic allegiances and imaginations of homelands have become malleable has further implications. Certainly, existing studies have shown that Indian diasporic communities can by no means be considered extensions of India. In fact, more recent studies privileging the colonial aspects of the formation of Indian diasporic communities have emphasized the extent to which this context has resulted in deep cultural and political transformations while creating communities inscribed as Indian across the British Empire and, to a lesser degree, other colonial domains. However, the question remains: how have these processes affected and changed imaginations of diasporic belonging and constructions of homelands among people of Indian origin in such locales?

In Mauritius, these transformations of Indian diasporic communities in a colonial and postcolonial context, resulting in new relationships to an imagined homeland, have been mediated by ideas about language. The cultivation of ancestral languages with origins in India has significantly contributed to the creation of diasporic communities and their allegiances to homelands in South Asia. Images and discourses of linguistic differentiation thus provide a privileged way of representing such diasporic relationships, creating new localities defined in relation to shifting homelands (Appadurai 1996b).

The production and reworking of diasporic relationships through linguistic ideology often focuses on the regimentation of temporal and spatial distance and indexicality, placing the community thus imagined in a relation to the homeland in time and space. The concept of ancestral language is especially potent in this regard. At the same time, ancestral language can be cultivated in conjunction with ritual performance in order to construct a particular collective stance in time and space vis-à-vis the homeland. Rather than trying to read off the intensity of a diasporic link from the continued use or abandonment of Indian linguistic varieties in the diaspora, the task is to analyze how the use of such varieties contributes to the creation of communities defined by a spatiotemporal remove from a diasporic homeland.

DIASPORIZATION, DIASPORIC REORIENTATION, AND THE CREATION OF HOMELANDS

The transformation of what the British colonial administration classified as the Indian community in Mauritius into a number of separate groups has also resulted in new kinds of diasporic allegiances to South Asia. A principal driving force in this process has been the building of communities around the concept of Indian ancestral languages indexing places of origin in India. The state-assisted proliferation of imagined language communities in Mauritius can be considered the result of a policy of disciplinary multiculturalism (initiated by the colonial authorities after the Second World War and intensified by the Hindu-dominated postcolonial governments) in the sense that such classifications appear inescapable and there is little possibility for Mauritians assigned to one particular ethnolinguistic community to legitimately develop allegiances to ancestral languages and cultures other than those associated with this group. The Hindu-dominated state apparatus of Mauritius has actively encouraged the formation of ethnolinguistic communities built around the notion of Indian ancestral languages. Hindus within the group once known as Indians or Indo-Mauritians, who use Mauritian Creole and to a lesser extent Bhojpuri in their daily lives, have been officially subdivided into "Hindi-speaking," "Tamil-speaking," "Telugu-speaking," and "Marathi-speaking" people (roughly 41 percent, 6 percent, 3 percent, and 2 percent of the population, respectively). The formation of such ethnolinguistic communities in the diaspora around ideologies of ancestral languages has also resulted in a diasporic reorientation, expressed through identification with new homelands linked to particular ancestral languages.

Modern standard Hindi as an ancestral language in Mauritius demonstrates how changing language ideologies engender shifts in diasporic loyalties among a population over time, indicating how diasporic imaginations of an origin in India can change while supposedly constructed around the same ancestral language. The politics of ancestral language should therefore be understood within the context of a dialectics of de- and re-territorialization, in which migration and diasporic displacement engender a tendency to imagine new territorialized "homelands" (Appadurai 1996a). Significantly, this process often involves a transformation of the images and discourses of that homeland. For example, over the course of the twentieth century, the significance of Hindi in Mauritius has shifted from an index for a larger Indian Hindu identity to a link to a more narrowly conceived notion of a north Indian, Bihari Hindu origin. The earlier view of Hindi as a necessary component of a pan-Indian Hindu identity is claimed by many Hindu nationalists both in Mauritius and India, but is largely rejected by those Indo-Mauritians claiming south Indian origin. The development and institutionalization of Tamil, Telugu, and Marathi ethnicities, involving claims to corresponding ancestral languages, out of the larger category of Hindus in Mauritius has been responsible for the shrinking diasporic scope of Hindi in Mauritius, especially after the Second World War.

Mauritians were officially counted and categorized as three groups during most of the British colonial period: "Indo-Mauritians," who comprised slightly over two-thirds of the population from the 1860s onward; "Sino-Mauritians"; and the "General Population," comprised of everyone who did not belong to the other two categories: de facto Catholic Creoles and Franco-Mauritians. Processes of diasporic community formation among Indo-Mauritians, comprising both Hindus and Muslims of diverse regional and ethnic origins in India, have to be understood in the context of their highly heterogeneous backgrounds. Also, even though the vast majority of Indian immigrants arrived as indentured laborers for the sugar plantations, some of them, mostly Gujarati Muslims, settled in Mauritius as free immigrants engaged in trade (Kalla 1987), and an ethnic and class cleavage often persists between the descendants of the two groups.

Led by wealthy Gujarati merchant groups such as the Kutchi Memons, Indo-Mauritian Muslims had already developed their own religious organizations and institutions by the Second World War. In particular, the religious networks of the Sunni reformist movement Ahl-e Sunnat va Jama'at, otherwise known as the Barelwi school in India (Sanyal 1996) and supported by the Kutchi Memons throughout the Indian Ocean region, enabled frequent visits by missionaries. These were received as bearers of religious authority and authenticity, similar to the role the Arya Samaj and Sanatan Dharm missionaries played among Hindus. The principal language used in these networks was Urdu, which after the Second World War became institutionalized as the ancestral language of Muslims in Mauritius.

Political pressure led by the Hindu Labor Party politician and future Prime Minister Seewoosagur Ramgoolam prompted the colonial government to permanently establish the teaching of Indian ancestral languages in state schools and to support the training of Hindi and Urdu teachers at the island's new Teachers Training College with the help of experts from India after 1950. This institutionalization of ancestral languages meant opportunities for employment in state schools and subsidies for Indian language teaching in temples and mosques at a time of widespread poverty and unemployment in Mauritius, which encouraged claims for recognition by other Indian ancestral languages in the two decades before independence in 1968.

At the same time, the colonial government changed its policy of subsidies for religious bodies, agreeing to grant state subsidies to non-Christian religious associations in 1950. This led to the emergence of religious organizations among Indo-Mauritians in order to claim and distribute the subsidies to temples and mosques, prompting both a higher degree of religious organization and an increased ethnic fragmentation especially among Hindus. In a refusal to be subsumed under a larger category of "Hindu," Tamil, Telugu, and later also Marathi Hindu organizations were founded. Claims for Tamil, Telugu, and Marathi as separate ancestral languages to be recognized and to be taught in state schools played a key role in this ethnic breakup of the category "Hindu." Tamil, Telugu, and Marathi Hindus, who if they had previously studied an Indian language would most likely have learned Hindi at the local temple or school, were now provided with instruction in their own ancestral languages.

Migrants from India and their descendants were often known as "Kalkattiya," "Bombai," or "Madras," after their port of embarkation in India (the label "Kalkattiya" is still used to distinguish Muslims of indenture background from those among the Gujarati trader communities); however, the solidification of these labels into ethnicities with demarcated ancestral cultures and ancestral languages is a more recent phenomenon. For example, Tamils were among the first Indian migrants in Mauritius during the French colonial period (1715–1810), Tamil temples are the oldest on the island, and a trading diaspora of Tamil origin played an important role in the commercial life of nineteenth-century Port Louis (Sooriamoorthy 1977). Nevertheless, the concept of a Tamil community as clearly distinct from other Indo-Mauritians only took hold after the Second World War, in a period characterized by the growing importance of ethnic politics and awareness of imminent decolonization (Simmons 1982). The Hindu Maha Jana Sangam as a Tamil Hindu organization was established in 1944, but it was mainly in the context of establishing the Tamil Temple Federation in 1952 that the notion of a separate Tamil community spread among both Tamil Mauritians and other Indo-Mauritians. This federation, today considered the main representative of Tamils in Mauritius, controls most Tamil places of worship and was founded in order to receive state funds after the government changed its policy concerning religious subsidies. The institutionalization of Telugu as an officially recognized ancestral language, which went hand in hand with the establishment of a Telugu community, is similarly a relatively recent development. The Mauritius Andhra Sabha, the principal organization controlling Telugu temples in Mauritius, was established in 1947 in a context similar to the creation of the Tamil temple organization. The development of an infrastructure for the teaching of Telugu, such as the training of teachers and the production of teaching materials, continued until the early 1960s. Apart from the founding of the Sabha, and the official recognition implied in the government's granting of subsidies and support for the teaching of Telugu in schools and temples, a key event in the coalescing of the Telugu community was the return of Pandit Ootoo (1913–1971) in 1960 after a thirteen-year stay in what had recently become the state of Andhra Pradesh in India. He had studied Sanskrit and Telugu and learned about Andhra regional traditions of Hindu worship, which he popularized with the support of the Sabha after his return. The pandit is widely regarded as the restorer of a "forgotten" Telugu tradition in Mauritius. The most recent split-off from the larger category of Hindus is the Marathi community. The Mauritius Marathi Mandali Federation, also designed as a recipient of government subsidies for temples, was only established in 1960, and instruction in Marathi was institutionalized in schools shortly before independence. Only a few Indo-Mauritians of Marathi identification know Marathi well. Many of them previously learned Hindi as an ancestral language, since the Arya Samaj was very influential among Mauritian Hindus originating from what is today Maharashtra.

The question of the ancestral status of these standardized Indian languages is further complicated by widely acknowledged and long-standing patterns of intermarriage between rural Tamils and Telugus, as well as between Marathis and Hindi-associated north Indian Hindus. Although it is clear that Muslims of south Indian background migrated to Mauritius in the nineteenth century (Carter and Govinden 1998), the south Indian ethnolinguistic categories have become exclusively Hindu, so that identification as a Tamil, Telugu, or Marathi Muslim in Mauritius is unheard of today. South Indian Muslims have become part of the larger Muslim community of Mauritius, which is not defined by regional or ethnic origin, and their ancestral languages are held to be Urdu and, more recently, also Arabic.

The formation of diasporic communities in Mauritius leading to the reconfiguring of Indo-Mauritian understandings of community has historically proceeded in the following way: By the 1940s, the distinction between Hindus and Muslims grew to be so marked that Indo-Mauritians became either Hindu or Muslim. The intense interaction with religious nationalist organizations and missionaries from the subcontinent and the institutional patronage of local elites, starting with the Kutchi Memon and Sunni Surtee Gujarati trading communities among Muslims for whom there was initially no Hindu counterpart, played vital roles in this process. In everyday discourse, the label "Indian" *(endyen)* has become a synonym for "Hindu" but is never applied to Muslims despite their Indian background. Finally, the Hindu community became further divided into Hindus of north Indian, mainly Bihari, background, and the smaller Tamil, Telugu, and Marathi groups.[1]

Ideologies of ancestral language have played a crucial role in the fragmentation of the Hindu community and the formation of additional ethnolinguistic communities in Mauritius and diasporic attachments to new homelands. The awareness of an ancestral language, never used in daily life and often not mastered at all, not only is constitutive for ethnonational group formation in Mauritius but also establishes links between these groups in Mauritius and nationalist projects in South Asia associated with the ethnoreligious communities in question.

What, then, accounts for the power of ancestral language in the establishment and reworking of diasporic links? I suggest that the answer lies in how ideologies of ancestral language mediate between different apprehensions of spatiotemporal distanciation from the homeland that are at the base of diasporic experiences. In doing this, they intersect with other forms of cultivating relationships with the land of the ancestors, such as the Shivratri pilgrimage in Mauritius.

LANGUAGE IDEOLOGIES AND TEMPORALITY

Politically charged representations of language and its use are inescapably implicated in the temporality inherent in social life. On the one hand, they are the complex products of the historical contexts in which they arise; on the other hand, these representations themselves contribute to the temporal structuring of social worlds by establishing relationships between linguistic forms, communicative practices, and sociocultural valuations. There are few instances in which this double-faced embeddedness is as apparent as in the modes of linking experiences of time and nationhood through language that figure prominently in contemporary theories of nationalism.

The connection between temporality and ethnonational community through language is also evident in the case of Indian ancestral languages in Mauritius. The nostalgic use of ancestral languages for creating ethnolinguistic identities represents a different way of figuring community through language-mediated chronotopes (Bakhtin 1981) compared to the notion of "empty, homogenous time" proposed by Benedict Anderson.[2] Indo-Mauritian ancestral languages as a mediating base for national and diasporic communities among Hindus in Mauritius are presented as providing a strong link to ancestors who left a homeland in India in order to settle in Mauritius. One of the ways Hindi is involved in processes of group identification is through the projection of notions of a Hindu community through a particular regime of temporalization. Cultivating Hindi does so by locating the meaning of Hindu-ness in Mauritius in an ancestral time, combining ideas about language with ritual performance evoking an ancestral homeland in India.

At the same time, ideologies of ancestral language represent an answer to questions of historical consciousness among Hindus in Mauritius. In several ways, identification with ancestral Hindi addresses questions of historical change, which can be located along the axis of Anderson's empty, homogenous — that is, linearly progressing — time, measurable in uniform units. In constituting themselves as a diasporic community concerned with questions of ethnolinguistic authenticity, Hindu Mauritians are aware of their profoundly transformative history, rising from a community of poor indentured laborers in the sugarcane fields under colonialism to the politically dominant group of the country, now on average enjoying reasonable prosperity. Hindu activists and their followers in Mauritius cast what they regard as the heroic maintenance of Hindi under the pressure of new historical circumstances as part of the story of Hindu success in the diaspora. The triumph over adversity and hardship during and after the period of indenture is the leading theme of a historical interpretation of the past, which many Hindus remember not just in terms of economic exploitation and political repression, but as displaying the successful "preservation" of religious traditions and ethnoreligious group identity. Ancestral Hindi, then, negotiates the differences between two chronotopes of community, closely resembling the contrast Benjamin (1968) draws between "empty, homogenous" time and "messianic," sanctified simultaneity across time: Hindus in Mauritius as one with their ancestors versus the Hindu community as progressing through time in a narrative of political and economic rise and heroic preservation of ancestral traditions in dramatically changing circumstances.

The interplay between these processes of temporal reckoning is especially evident in the relationship between ideologies of ancestral language and Hindu pilgrimage in Mauritius. My analysis of the Shivratri pilgrimage later in this chapter, which highlights the parallels between the celebration of ancestral Hindi and this event as a reenactment of Hindu pilgrimage to sacred bodies of water in India in a reconstituted sacred geography in Mauritius, focuses on the semiotic processes enabling the negotiation of the spatiotemporal disjuncture between diasporic Hindus and the world of their Indian ancestors. Inspired by Michael Silverstein's discussion of "nomic calibration" (1993, 48–53), I argue that the pilgrims' performance of iconic likeness between the world of the ancestors and the world of their diasporic descendants can be understood as a *calibration of displacement*. This particular form of indexical-iconic regimentation of signs facilitates a ritual experience of temporal equivalence between the contexts of diaspora and the ancestors' India on the occasion of Shivratri.

Hindi is involved in the production of the Hindu community in Mauritius in a double way. It provides a discursive field through which ideologies of a shared ancestral language contribute to processes of group identification, resulting in the imagining of a Hindu community in Mauritius. It also plays an important role in public performances of Hindu belonging, which combine religious ritual with a collective enactment of a link to an ancestral homeland of Mauritian Hindus in India.

At the same time, the ideology of Hindi as an ancestral language ties the notion of a Hindu community in Mauritius to particular notions of temporality. The celebration of the ancestral language constitutes a chronotope that locates the idea of a Hindu community in Mauritius within a temporal order centered on the collapse of the world of the Indian ancestors into the world of present-day Hindus in Mauritius. The annual Shivratri pilgrimage combines the celebration of an important Hindu festival and the performance of a diasporic relationship to a homeland with the celebration of Hindi as the language of the ancestors and founders of the Hindu community. As I will explain, an indexical order is established in which a Hindu homeland in India, a Hindu community, and Hindi as the emblem of Hindu group identification in Mauritius point to one another through the performance of pilgrimage. The integration of these disparate elements is then naturalized through a particular temporal regime.

CHRONOTOPES OF COMMUNITY

Benedict Anderson (1991) has suggested a close interrelationship between the rise of nationalism and changes in the linguistic mediation of concepts of community. Anderson claims a direct link between widened processes of literary communication under print capitalism, resulting in expanding publics of "co-readers," and the emergence of national consciousness. However, this is not the only language-based argument in Anderson's influential model of nationalism. Equally central to his account is his analysis of new literary genres, such as the realist novel, as enabling a new conception of time: "empty, homogenous" time. This new form of experiencing time — as linearly moving forward and measurable by clock and calendar — provides an abstract yardstick on which otherwise disparate and disconnected events can be conceived as linked by virtue of simultaneity relative to that axis of time. Anderson argues that this way of conceptualizing time also enables modern subjects to imagine a national community as progressing forward through history in a manner somewhat analogous to characters in a novel, whose disparate lives and actions are connected by virtue of being locatable on the same temporal measure of an unfolding plot (1991, 26). This chronotope of empty, homogenous time underlying Anderson's model of nationalism is borrowed from Benjamin and stands in contrast to the latter's concept of "messianic time," a sacred simultaneity across past, present, and future that always contains the potential for revolution and redemption.[3] In the European context, messianic time is often associated with the historical consciousness of the Middle Ages, when people lived with the certainty of an imminent doomsday (Auerbach 1953; Koselleck 1985, 241–42). Benjamin specifically alludes to Jewish traditions in coining the term messianic time, since "every second of time was the straight gate through which the Messiah might enter" (Benjamin 1968, 264). Against this background, Anderson sees the rise of the conception of empty, homogenous time as a hallmark of modernity, engendered by the genre of realist reportage in the novel. Through this new regimentation of time, subjects can experience themselves as existing in a synchronized manner together with other subjects in temporally and spatially bounded yet homogeneous units of nations.

There are other ways language works in order to create ethnonational consciousness in a particular temporal mode. The link between language and the national imagination is also mediated by varying cultural ideologies as they make use of linguistic images and tropes, and there is no

inevitable link between the national community and the particular
language-mediated sense of time described by Anderson. Silverstein
(2000) has shown how a Whorfian "Standard Average European" conception of Newtonian space-time — homogeneous, mensurable, and creating the effect of "unisonance" or "one voice" for the subjects inhabiting
it — underlies the Andersonian model of nationalism. But Andersonian
"Standard Average European" space-time is not the only possible, nor
even the most plausible, chronotope of a nation (Kelly 1998a). Indo-
Mauritian engagements with ancestral languages as the mediating base for
national and diasporic communities in Mauritius, with strong links to
immigrating ancestors, show a mode of joining experiences of time and
nationhood through language that is rather different from Anderson's
model. The cultivation of ancestral languages as a way of feeling "one
with the ancestors" is not so different from what Benjamin described as
"messianic" simultaneity across linear time. I suggest that ideologies of
ancestral languages evoke a vision of the present "which is shot through
with chips of messianic time" (Benjamin 1968, 265) and characterized by
an "explosion" of the continuum of history (Benjamin 1968, 263). The
emphasis here is not on the synchronized progression through homogenous time with other national co-subjects but on the ever-present quality
of heroic and virtuous ancestors. Yet since these languages with ascribed
ancestral qualities like Hindi nevertheless form the basis for new ethnonational solidarities, Anderson's claim that the experience of nationality is
dependent on one particular form of temporal regimentation needs to be
reconsidered. Not just empty, homogenous time but also messianic modes
of temporal structuration can be conducive to the formation of ethnonational communities. That is, while nationalism is a modern phenomenon,
it does not necessarily rest on the kind of radical modernist reorientation
of experiencing time highlighted by Anderson.

In her recent critique of Anderson, Kathryn Woolard has argued that
the transformation from a "messianic" to a modernist and progressivist
understanding of historical time did not originate in the context of the
eighteenth-century rise of nationalism (Woolard 2004). Instead, it can be
traced to the European Renaissance and sixteenth-century humanist
scholarship — an argument also suggested by Erich Auerbach, on whose
work Anderson draws, and who describes a transformation away from
medieval "messianic" concepts of time already at the time of the Renaissance (Auerbach 1953; Woolard 2004; see also Koselleck 1985, 241–
42).[4] In her analysis of linguistic ideologies in sixteenth- and seventeenth-
century Spain, Woolard argues that in this early period of Spanish nation

building a developmentalist notion of history coexisted with "messianic" notions of time. I would like to add to Woolard's critique that an emphasis on a plurality of modes of temporal regimentation also recalls the phenomenological critique of what Benjamin called the "empty, homogenous" time of historicism, according to which historical events and epochs follow each other in an objective sequence of "nows." Historicists such as Leopold von Ranke postulated that such events and epochs have to be understood in their own terms in order to be apprehended — as Ranke famously stated, "the way it really was" — deliberately leaving behind the perspective and interpretative horizon of the those who came later. Since "every epoch is immediate to God" (Ranke 1973, 53), the historian's task is to arrive at an interpretative and intuitive understanding approximating a standpoint within the historical formation to be analyzed, thus doing justice to the irreducible individuality of historical events and epochs. In contrast, phenomenological approaches to historicity have stressed how remembered and anticipated events are constantly reshaped and inevitably reconfigured from the shifting horizon of the present. It is only in relationship to this ever-changing horizon of the present that remembered events can be organized into meaningful narratives, which at the same time point to future anticipated events (Husserl 1964, Ricoeur 1988).[5] This implies a plurality of modes of temporality, which are always subject to contestation and reformulation, and which may also be manifest in a tension between a particular reading of progressive, historical time and Benjamin's messianic time.

Further, a phenomenological perspective can also account for how the empty, homogenous time of historicism rejected by Benjamin is subject to very different formulations and narrative structuring, thus not being homogenous, after all. The way historicists have engaged with past events and epochs attests to this plurality within presumably empty, homogenous time. For example, Ranke saw more in history than a recounting of events. According to him, the historian's task is to grasp the causal nexus *(Zusammenhang)* that links events in a way that elucidates what he assumed to be the ideational unity behind every cultural and historical context (Ranke 1973, 40–44). That is, as the historian's task is constructive in establishing relationships between events, in the search for a particular inner *Zusammenhang,* their representation involves different modes of temporal structuration. Further, Ranke, drawing on the theory of ideas *(Ideenlehre)* of Wilhelm von Humboldt (1973, 22–23), combined an emphasis on the individuality of historical events and epochs, to be understood on their own terms, with a general theory of human progress through the ages. Progress in history is manifest in the increasing realization of original ideas. However, one of the preconditions for the experience of progress is a particular temporal reckoning in connecting events and conditions, which is "rooted in the knowledge of the noncontemporaneities which exist at a chronologically uniform time" (Koselleck 1985, 248). In the practice of historical narration, Ranke thus arranged events and epochs in a particularly meaningful succession, one in which the significance of remembered events only fully reveals itself in the present or in a future anticipated in a certain progressivist mode. Nevertheless, Ranke always left open the possibility of historical "decline" as an alternative temporality through which events can be connected in a storyline imbued with meaning, a temporality that sometimes interacts in complex ways with narratives of progress. Along with Hegel, he considered progress in history an essentially European matter and believed that the societies of Asia had long ceased to be spiritually and intellectually "developing," being subject to historical "decline" from their glorious earlier days (Ranke 1973, 56). The work of pioneering historicists such as Ranke shows that a historical conception of time, as opposed to messianic temporalities, need not consist of an "empty" addition of successive events "like the beads of a rosary" (Benjamin 1968, 263). They may instead be subject to very different temporal regimentations, thus investing remembered events with varying degrees of significance, contrary to the accusation Benjamin leveled against the historicists that they fail to distinguish between more significant and less significant events and epochs (Benjamin 1968, 263). Such different temporalities, in turn, project different communities and solidarities when they become part of socially shared memory.

Benjamin highlighted another aspect of the tensions between what he called "empty, homogenous" and "messianic" time that is of importance for my analysis in the remaining part of this chapter. According to him, ritual practice is also of great significance for understanding how varying modes of temporality produce different experiences of community. While discussing the new regimentation of time of the French revolutionary calendar, Benjamin suggested that festivals and sacred days represent instances of messianic time, since "basically, it is the same day that keeps recurring in the guise of holidays, which are days of remembrance" (1968, 263). This also attests to the fundamentally cyclical character of messianic time, which is nowhere as apparent as on such ritual occasions.

THE SHIVRATRI PILGRIMAGE

The particular instantiation of an ancestral trope of community that I would like to discuss here is the annual Hindu pilgrimage to Grand Bassin, a mountain lake in the southwest of Mauritius known to Hindus as Ganga Talao (Ganges pond) on the occasion of the Hindu festival of Shivratri. The Shivratri pilgrimage to Grand Bassin is one of the two main Hindu festivals in Mauritius — the other being Divali — and is unrivaled in the scale of public religious performance on the island. Shivratri is an official national holiday in Mauritius. Every year around three hundred thousand pilgrims, out of a total population of slightly over 1.2 million, make the pilgrimage to the sacred mountain lake, many of them in processions on foot, from distances of up to forty miles, staying in Hindu temples along the way. Official figures for the 2002 pilgrimage even reached the mark of four hundred thousand participants.[6] The main ritual consists in the collecting of sacred water from the lake, which is then offered to *shivlings*, phallic representations of the deity Shiva. This is performed in the two Shiva temples at Grand Bassin, as well as in temples of the pilgrims' home communities after their return, especially at the all-night prayers and worship dedicated to Shiva during the night of Shivratri known in Hindi as *cār pehar kī pūjā* (worship of four vigils, or three-hour time periods, i.e., of one whole night). The Mauritian state is heavily involved in the organization of the pilgrimage, from regulating traffic and providing public transport to the site and providing infrastructural amenities to pilgrims at Grand Bassin to the arrangement for extensive media coverage through the government-owned and government-controlled Mauritius Broadcasting Cooperation. Since independence, the state has also played a pivotal role in turning Grand Bassin into a major and well-endowed site of Hindu pilgrimage, working hand in hand with Hindu activists and organizations based in both Mauritius and India.

Perhaps the most striking aspect of the pilgrimage to Grand Bassin / Ganga Talao is the performative and spatial re-creation of a sacred geography resembling that of the Hindu pilgrimage sites on the sacred river Ganges in north India. Steps leading down to the lake have been built in the manner of bathing *ghāṭs* common at Hindu places of pilgrimage located at sacred bodies of water *(tirtha)*, which pilgrims use when they perform *pūjā* (ritual worship) on the banks of the lake and collect amounts of the sacred water *(jal)*. The *ghāṭs* are overlooked by four main temples and other shrines whose roof architecture resembles what is con-

sidered the shape of a typical Indian temple roof. Grand Bassin / Ganga
Talao is primarily a Shaivite place of pilgrimage, but the distinction
between Shaivism (worship of the deity Shiva) and Vaishnavism (worship
of the deity Vishnu in its various forms) is not very meaningful for
Mauritian Hindus. In fact, Hindu temples *(shivala)* throughout Mauritius feature images and statues *(murti)* of all the major sanskritic deities
within their precincts for worship. This is also true for the four main temples at Ganga Talao, two of which are primarily dedicated to Shiva, one
to Ganga, Yamuna, Sarasvati, and the remaining one to Hanuman,
respectively. In addition to these four larger temples, there are also five
smaller shrines. The two *shivmandirs* (Shiva temples), however, feature
prominently at Grand Bassin / Ganga Talao with respect to both their
location and their significance for the Shivratri pilgrimage. Both are also
centrally involved in the re-creation of a sacred Hindu geography in
Mauritius, and each features a large *shivling* brought from India.

One of the two temples dedicated to Shiva is the oldest and largest temple structure at Grand Bassin, directly overlooking the most elaborate
part of the *ghāṭs* leading to the shore of the sacred lake. This temple,
established in 1964, is named Kashi Vishvanath Mandir after the most
prominent temple of the holy city of Banaras, on the Ganges in north
India. The other temple, more recently built and located directly on the
lakeshore, is officially known as Mauritiuseswarnath Mandir. The name
of this second Shiva temple likewise signals a claim of religious authenticity by postulating a direct link to prominent centers of Hindu worship in
India. According to the keepers of the temple, the government-subsidized
Mauritius Sanatan Dharm Temples Federation, the sacred *shivling* in the
temple is on a par in religious significance with twelve other famous
lingams, or manifestations of Shiva, in India. A table in the temple lists the
trayodash jyotir lingam — the twelve *lingams* located in places of Hindu
pilgrimage across India as prominent as Kedarnath, Banaras, Somnath,
Ujjain, and Nasik, while the thirteenth reads: "Mauritiuseswarnath ji: On
the bank of Ganga Talab, Mauritius" (*talab* being the Hindi equivalent of
Bhojpuri *talao*).

This explicitly formulated claim of continuity with the sacred Hindu
landscape in India is echoed by the location of the Hanuman Temple on
top of a hill directly overlooking the lake of Grand Bassin / Ganga Talao.
Hanuman, a very popular deity among Bihari immigrants, is famous in
the epic Ramayana for his supreme strength as one of the divine com-
panions of the god Ram in his struggle against the demon king Ravan.
According to the epic, he is associated with mountains in a particular

FIGURE 1. View across Grand Bassin from the Kashi Vishvanath Mandir.
Photograph by the author.

way: When Ram's brother Lakshman was mortally wounded in battle
against the forces of Lanka, Hanuman was sent to fetch a curative herb
from Mount Kailash in the Himalayas. Unsure about which herb to collect, he lifted the entire mountain and brought it to the battle scene. The
location of the Hanuman temple on the steep hill overlooking the lake is
understood to be an allusion to this mythical deed. Atal Bihari Vajpayee,
later Prime Minister of India, in his former function as Minister of
Foreign Affairs, is reported to have suggested the construction of a
Hanuman temple on the top of the hill for this reason during his visit to
Mauritius in 1977. He also arranged for the donation of a large statue,
or *mūrti,* of Hanuman. The *mūrti* was eventually sent by the Sanatan
Dharm Sabha of New Delhi.[7] The hill, marked as Piton Grand Bassin on
the French-made road map of Mauritius, is known to Hindus as Nil
Parbat, or Nilgiri (blue hill), which is also the name of a mountain range
in south India.

Another important element in the re-creation of an Indian Hindu
sacred geography in the uplands of Mauritius is the fact that this mountain lake has long been imagined in local Hindu folklore to be an extension of the sacred river Ganges in India. Soon after the discovery of the
site and its establishment as a place of ritual in 1898 by a group of pil-

FIGURE 2. View from the Hauman Temple across Grand Bassin towards the
Kashi Vishvanath Mandir. Photograph by the author.

grims led by the Brahman Pandit Sajiwon of the northern village of
Triolet, stories circulated to the effect that this remote lake, at that time
known as Pari Talao (fairies' pond) among Indians, was in fact linked to
the river Ganges by a subterranean connection beneath the ocean.
According to another legend, the origin of Grand Bassin / Ganga Talao is
due to a tear the goddess Ganga shed when she saw her children, the
Indian emigrants, leave for far-away Mauritius. Vayu, the god of the
winds, then carried the tear to this place in the uplands of southwest
Mauritius. This version of the creation of Ganga Talao, highlighting the
link of consubstantiality to the sacred Ganges river, here represented by
the goddess Ganga herself, is endorsed by the Hindu Maha Sabha, the
government-subsidized high-caste Hindu organization in charge of most
of the temples at Grand Bassin. At the hundredth anniversary celebration
of the pilgrimage in February 1998, the first item visible to visitors as
they entered the educational display in the Kashi Vishvanath Mandir
was a text posted on a board retelling the legend.[8] And in 1972, a public
ceremony headed by the Indian pandit Vidya Nidhi Pandey officially
and performatively proclaimed the existence of a concrete link between
Grand Bassin and the river Ganges. A vessel of Ganges water *(gangā jal)*,
flown in from the pilgrimage city of Hardwar with the assistance of the

Indian government, was ritually worshipped and then discharged into the lake, officially consecrating the latter as Ganga Talao.

To conclude, the pilgrimage to Grand Bassin / Ganga Talao in Mauritius, during which Hindus from all over the island converge on the mountain lake, represents in a variety of ways a local reenactment of the important Hindu pilgrimages to sacred sites along the river Ganges, such as Kedarnath, Hardwar, and Banaras. The most prominent of these, Banaras, is located in eastern Uttar Pradesh, the home region of large numbers of immigrants to Mauritius, while the Ganges river also runs west to east through Bihar, the area from which most indentured immigrants departed for Mauritius. The site of Grand Bassin / Ganga Talao has been spatially arranged to resemble such sites of pilgrimage. Hindu activists in the Mauritian state apparatus, with help from the Indian government as well as Hindu organizations in India, have played a crucial role in this project. Ganga Talao, with *ghāt*s on its shores, is presented to Hindus as a direct extension of the sacred Ganges river in India. The two main temples are dedicated to the worship of Shiva, as at the Indian sites of pilgrimage along the Ganges. Also, their names evoke the sacred landscape of these Indian pilgrimage sites. Further, another temple is dedicated to the river goddesses Ganga, Yamuna, and Sarasvati (the latter two are tributaries of the Ganges and Sarasvati is also the goddess of learning), and at a pond in front of this temple pilgrims can bathe in the sacred waters.

In other words, Grand Bassin / Ganga Talao as a site of pilgrimage stands in iconic relation to a sacred religious geography in India, while the Shivratri pilgrimage to the site can be seen as a diagrammatic reenactment of Hindu pilgrimages to sacred sites along the river Ganges. This iconicity is manifest in multiple kinds of similarities. It is evident in the assumed consubstantiality of the water of Grand Bassin / Ganga Talao with the Ganges in India, in the location of the temples by a sacred lake overlooking *ghāt*s rimming the shore, as well as in the functions and names of the temples, some of which directly embody a claim of continuity with particular sites of the sacred Gangetic homeland. Finally, the annual movement of pilgrims from all over the island to the mountain lake can be considered a diagrammatic icon (Peirce 1932, 157–60) of similar itineraries followed by Hindu pilgrims on *tirth yatra*s in India, that is, on their way to and from holy sites situated at sacred bodies of water, especially the Ganges. Grand Bassin / Ganga Talao and the Shivratri pilgrimage are not just sites of Hindu religious practice, they embody a particular diasporic orientation toward a Hindu homeland.

HINDI AND THE SHIVRATRI PILGRIMAGE

The annual Shivratri pilgrimage to Grand Bassin / Ganga Talao, which represents an attempt to project a unified Hindu community through a strategy of temporalization focused on ritual performance and the use of Hindi as reenactments of ancestral practices, is one of the most important occasions for the celebration of Hindi as the language of the ancestors of Mauritian Hindus. It provides a privileged and presupposed context for the use and celebration of Hindi in religious songs *(bhajan)*, sermons, and speeches, which are at the same time broadcast on national television and radio. The role of Hindi in mediating between Mauritian Hindus and the homeland of their ancestors is highlighted regularly in the context of religious rituals and events, speeches, and the teaching of Hindi in state schools and temples throughout Mauritius. However, no other event provides such a centralized and nationwide focus on the ancestral qualities of Hindi as the annual Shivratri pilgrimage, which is itself understood to have been initiated by the immigrating ancestors from India.

Nevertheless, the simultaneous celebration of the pilgrimage and of Hindi as instances of Hindu ancestral culture is subject to contradictions and always remains a problematic performative achievement. The propagation and use of Hindi by a network of Hindu organizations and representatives of Mauritian state authorities combined in a Shivratri "task force" appear strangely at odds with the linguistic practices of the pilgrims, who are mostly Creole-speaking, and is confined to official performances of Hindu belonging in the context of the event. However, these events feature prominently in state-controlled television and radio reporting of the pilgrimage.

The aim of the organizers to both unite all Hindus in Mauritius and have them reenact what are represented as the actions of their ancestors is also in permanent conflict with the fragmented nature of the Hindu community. Hindus of south Indian background, such as Tamils and Telugus, have their own sociocultural organizations, which are not engaged in the Shivratri pilgrimage, and they are also involved in the propagation of different ancestral languages. In contrast to the massive participation among Hindus of north Indian background, far fewer Tamil and Telugu Hindus join in the pilgrimage. Tamils and Telugus in La Nicolière sometimes expressed suspicion about the close relationship between north Indian–dominated Hindu organizations and prominent members of the government, and rejected their claim to represent a united Hindu ancestral culture. The emblematic use of Hindi in the context of the pilgrimage was also interpreted as a political act, calculated to justify the political dominance of Bihari Hindus over the rest of the Hindu community. Furthermore, the celebration of ancestral culture and ancestral language stands in a relationship of potential disjuncture with the everyday projects that motivate people to join the pilgrimage. While showing their devotion to Shiva by fasting and undertaking the long march to Grand Bassin / Ganga Talao, usually termed a "sacrifice" (*fer sakrifis* in Creole), the pilgrims I knew spoke about the benefits they hoped for — improved health, professional success, the passing of crucial school exams — rather than a desire to reenact the deeds of the ancestors or to cultivate Hindi.

On the other hand, several residents of La Nicolière affirmed the linkage between Hindi and Hindu identity as they undertook the pilgrimage. Although he did not know Hindi well, Rakesh, a man in his mid-forties, referred to Hindi as "our language," thereby engaging in an act of identification shared by numerous other people in the village. After returning from the pilgrimage, Sadna, a woman in her late sixties, declared herself offended by the fact that a pandit in a neighboring village did not always use Hindi in the temple, saying, "What will become of our religion if everybody speaks Creole while worshipping?" Another middle-aged male pilgrim, Vinod, expressing his concern about the loss of Hindu tradition in conversations with me, approvingly quoted the motto of the Hindi Pracarini Sabha: "When the language [Hindi] is gone, the culture [*sanskriti*] is also gone," switching from Creole to Hindi to do so. He was also concerned that his children showed little interest in Hindi classes at school and made sure that they attended Hindi Sunday school in the local *baithka*.

The attempt to project a unified Hindu community emphasizing the copresence of Mauritian Hindus and the world of the ancestors through ritual performance and ancestral language has to gloss over such contradictions and diversity of views in order to be successful. This strategy of temporalization represents a denial of both everyday Hindu linguistic practices and the internal differentiation in the Hindu community in Mauritius. Hindu organizations, in conjunction with transnationally operating Hindu nationalists, seek to impose a vision of what is understood to be Hindu ancestral culture in Mauritius, yet it is a vision in which north Indian traditions predominate and their own central position as guardians of tradition is affirmed.

HOW ARE HINDUS PERSUADED
THAT HINDI IS "THEIR" LANGUAGE?

I have described the pilgrimage to Grand Bassin / Ganga Talao as a complex sign in which pilgrims engage in a reenactment of Indian sacred relations and where Hindi functions to emphasize the diagrammatic relationships between the ancestors' sacred practices in the homeland and the annual Mauritius event. How is an ancestral language not used in daily interactions made relevant to the experience of being Hindu in Mauritius and the mediation of diasporic belonging? More particularly, given the potential disjuncture between the participants' concerns during the Shivratri pilgrimage and the official representation of a diasporic relationship to a homeland and ancestral world as effected in the pilgrimage, how are so many Hindus in Mauritius persuaded that Hindi is finally "their" language? As discussed in the previous chapters, following similar patterns of mobilization in India since the late nineteenth century, Hindu activists in Mauritius, now well connected to state institutions, have championed standard Hindi as the emblem of an emerging Hindu identity in Mauritius for over ninety years. Yet for many Mauritian Hindus, there is also a different level of awareness, apart from the institutionalized promotion of Hindi, on which Hindi can be experienced as their own.

In order to explain this dynamic, it is useful to refer again to the ethnicization of Bhojpuri as a Hindu language discussed in chapter 5. Bhojpuri, the only Indian vernacular language still used in Mauritius (though in a bilingual situation with the dominant Mauritian Creole), is subject to attempts at purification in which the boundaries between standard Hindi and Mauritian Bhojpuri are blurred. This is particularly evident in linguistic practices in which frequently used lexical items of Creole origin are replaced by sanskritized Hindi items. This practice not only ethnicizes Bhojpuri by representing this Indian language spoken by both rural Muslims and Hindus as Hindu property but also makes ancestral Hindi conceptually accessible as part of everyday linguistic practices.

Here I want to draw on a particular example from La Nicolière. As described in chapter 2, becoming a member of the temple board and taking a leading role in temple activities such as the celebration of major Hindu festivals are alternative routes to social recognition for men who otherwise lack the credentials of an education in the state education system or the higher-paying jobs in the government service that such credentials provide. Leadership roles in the temple association involve the directing of devotional activities, which cannot entirely be left to a pandit, who only comes to the temple once a week from another village. An important part of such duties of directing worship is the delivery of an address or brief speech at the opening of the two main regular Hindu devotional activities in the temple: singing devotional songs *(kirtan)* and chanting from the Ramcaritmanas. This kind of performance calls for speaking in purist Bhojpuri, while the use of Creole or "ordinary" Bhojpuri is frowned upon. The ability to speak purist Bhojpuri is in turn usually contingent on some training in Hindi, through either the school system or a temple school.

The setting for the following example is the home of a retired *sirdar* (an overseer in the sugar industry) in his sixties (speaker 2) who is known in the village for his involvement with the temple. The *sirdar* had invited worshippers to his home for a *kirtan,* which normally takes place in the temple on Friday nights. While the devotees were sitting on the floor of the living room of the *sirdar's* house, the principal of the temple board, a man in his forties who is also employed as a *sirdar* by the nearby sugar mill (speaker 1), opened the gathering by thanking the members of the temple society for coming and thanking the host for opening his home to the worshippers. Toward the end of the host's response, a woman in her thirties (speaker 3) sitting in the audience joined in, interrupts in order to thank him on behalf of the worshippers for his involvement with the temple.

The switch from Creole and ordinary Bhojpuri to purist Bhojpuri at the beginning of the following excerpt marked the change to a new speech genre, signaling the beginning of a performance of address embedded in Hindu moral discourse. A central situational focus emerged and the audience fell silent.

EXAMPLE 6.1*

(A mother to her children in the background: Olog bhitre hawansa, assize twa, assize twa, bizin alle dan grup.)

S 1: Hamni mandir ke **sadasya** ke **taraf** se abhi Beharry **parivar** ke, ke **dhanyavaad** dewat haija ke hamni ke aaj ego esan

1 (A mother to her children in the background: They are inside, sit down, sit down, you have to go in a group.)

5 S 1: On **behalf** of the **members** of the temple we now give **thanks** to the Beharry **family** that today they gave us such an

*Hindi lexical items are boldfaced; Creole is italicized; Bhojpuri is unmarked.

mauka delak ke aake unke lage
bhagwan ke **sewa** kareke awsar 10
milal ta suk ke din hamni ta
kirtan *abitye* haisa shivala men.

Aaj mamu ke **kripa** se aaj
hija hogal itne tadad toulog
ailaja ek ghanta hamni ke sange 15
bitailaja. **Isse liye** hamni toulog
ke **koti dhanyavad samarpan**
karat haija **kyonki is samay,** ih
ghatawa sakta kucho bhi kare,
television dekhe, koi butik lage 20
rahi, koi ghumat hoi, koi
parhat hoi, to kucho karat hoi.
Ta ek ghanta nikalke baba,
bhagwan ke kaam men toulog
hamni ke saath delaja. **Isi liye** 25
hamni **hirday se dhanyavad
samarpan** karat haija.

Ta ab mamu boli, mamu?
Bolah, tu ab ka bolbah.

S 2: Ham ihi bolat hay: accha, jetna 30
upastitha sajan ba sab **parivar
bahut dhanyavad aaplog** ke,
dinon bahut **aasha** rakhle rahan
ke u din kirtan karyan, to aaj
u din u kam pura hoi. Aaplog 35
okra **ashirvad** dah aur **aplog**
ke **dhanyavad** hoi apan apan
ghar se etna **samai** nikalke,
aaplog padharla aike. Kirtan
karla, bhajan karla, prabhu 40
ke naam sunlija in ta bahut
kritarth hoi hamni. Sabke
dekha ketna hamar natin ba,
beti ba, pato ba ailanja aake
kasta uthake aaj elog ke ghar 45
men, **bahut bahut utsah** milal
bahut bahut dhanyavad
bhagvan ke. Bhagvan **sahaita**
ba, aur **parampita paramatma**
ke **daya** se toulog ke **jiwan** men 50
ham esne sukh santi aur kushi
aur har **parivar** man kushi
chaile rahi bhagvan ke
ashirvad par **paripurna** rahi
toulog ke man **hamesha utsah** 55

opportunity to come to their
place to **serve** god, we got the
chance as Friday we are *used* to
kirtan at the shivala.

Today through mamu's[9]
kindness, today it has taken
place here so many of you
have come to spend one hour
together with us. **Therefore our
distinguished thanks we present**
to you **because at this time,** this
hour, one could do whatever,
watch television, hang around
at a bar/store, wandering
around somewhere, study
something, do whatever. So you
have taken an hour to join us in
the work of god. **Therefore we
present heartfelt thanks.**

So mamu, speak, mamu?
Speak, now what will you say?

S 2: I say this: well, how many
gentlemen are **present,** all
families, thanks a lot to you,
for quite some time there has
been **hope** that one does kirtan
that day, so today this work has
become completed, give your
blessings. And **thanks to you** for
taking so much **time** from your
home, **you have graced us by
coming.** Do kirtan, do bhajan,
when we hear the name of god,
we are very much **indebted.**
Look at all, how many grand-
daughters and daughters are
there, how many daughter-in-
laws are there who have taken
the trouble to come today may
there be in the home of these
people, **a lot, a lot of enthusiasm thanks a lot, a lot** to god.
God is **relief,** and through
the **grace** of **parampita
paramatma**[10] may there
be in your **lives** such joy and
peace and happiness and in

hoi aur jaike bahut **aasha** rahi
ki ham kab mandir men jai
jab puja karab dekha ih ego
ghar ba La Nicolière men esan
ego choṭa ghar ba ki jane sab   60
parivar milke ego choṭa san
mandir banayan jaha koi **aasha**
nai rahal **andhkar** rahal aaj ego
hawja par choṭa sun mandir ba.
. . . .   65

every **family** happiness and may
it be **replete** with the **blessings**
of god, may there be **always**
enthusiasm in your spirit and
when you go may there be
much **hope** that when I go to
the temple when I worship I
see there is such a home in La
Nicolière, there is such a small
home that somehow when all
families meet becomes a small
temple where there is no **hope**
there is **darkness** today there is
a small temple there.
. . . .

Ab bar bar **namaskar** karat hai   70
toulog ke jo koi hiya ailaja
sabke **namaskar bahut**
dhanyavad aaj hamra **asra**
milalke aaj etna hamar **parivaar**   75
chal aal baki bhagwan **ki daya**
se sab kuch pura hoi. . . .

Now many times I **greet** you
people who have come here,
greetings and many thanks.
Today we gain **reassurance**
today so many of our **families**
have come only through the
grace of god will **everything**
be achieved. . . .

S 3: Hamni tohar puja karilasa,   80
chacha.

S 2: Ka karab, beti, in ta toulog ke
sahas ha.

S 3: Tohro gor hath niman se rahi.
Tu mandir men sabakan karba   85
athi.

S 2: Hamar barka maa **ashirvad**
devat hawan, han, barka
ashirvad dewat hoi ki tohar gor
hath niman rahi aur. . . .   90

S 3: Nahi, hamni bahut tohar tohar
puja path karlisa parski tu sab
ka kam karela u mandir ke.

S 3: We pray for you, chacha.

S 2: What should I do, daughter,
this is you people's **greatness.**

S 3: May you remain healthy. You
do so much for the temple.

S 2: Our great mother gives
blessings, yes, she gives great
blessings so that you remain
healthy and. . . .

S 3: No, we respect you very much
because you do everything in
that temple.

This opening to the main activity of the evening involves a mutual giving of thanks among participants in the context of a moral discourse invoking the blessings of the deity. The main marker of performance is code choice, the switch to purist Bhojpuri, which is especially evident in the speech of speaker 2, the older *sirdar*, who is also the host for the evening. Speaker 1, the younger *sirdar* and a senior member of the temple committee, uses purist Bhojpuri as a marker of performance signaling the beginning of the devotional event, at which point the devotees ended their individual conversations, which had continued while everyone gathered in the house and found their seats on the floor. Speaker 1's speech includes only one instance of a Creole loan, the use of *abitye* in line 12. After thanking the older *sirdar* and his family on behalf of the temple committee for hosting the event and thanking the devotees present for coming, speaker 1 asks the host to give an opening address (lines 28–29). The host, speaker 2, also thanks the devotees gathered and, to a greater degree than Speaker 1, frames his remarks as a discourse of religious devotion. Hindi lexical elements are used frequently, especially in lines 46–50, when the blessings of God are invoked repeatedly as a desired compensation for the devotees' presence and acts of worship.

The host's performance is met with approval by speaker 3, who is one of the regular worshippers in the temple. She expresses her deep appreciation for the older *sirdar*'s commitment to the temple (line 80 ff.). She in turn asks for divine blessings to be bestowed on the host. Speaker 3 also tries to speak for the entire audience, as evident in her use of the first-person plural pronoun *hamni* in lines 80 and 91, to convey the feelings of thankfulness she assumes all the worshippers share.

One of the most salient effects of such performances is that they demonstrate a blurring of linguistic boundaries between Mauritian Bhojpuri and Hindi that is all the while interpreted by local speakers as Bhojpuri. This is because they consider a Bhojpuri with fewer words of Creole origin to be more "pure," that is, showing less influence from non-Indian sources and being more clearly linked to the practice of Hindu traditions. In fact, several of the Hindi lexical elements in example 6.1 refer to religious concepts, or are otherwise used in explicitly religious contexts, such as *ashirvad* (blessing, lines 36, 54, 87, 89), *sahaita* (relief, line 48), *parampita paramatma* (supreme father and soul, line 49), *daya* (grace, mercy, lines 50, 76) and *asra* (reassurance, line 74).

The hindiization of Mauritian Bhojpuri effected here is not confined to the level of the lexicon. There are also grammatical elements of Hindi characteristic of this purist register, such as demonstrative pronouns in the oblique case, which Mauritian Bhojpuri lacks (e.g., *is samay*, 'at this time," line 18; *isi liye* or *isse liye*, "therefore," lines 16, 25). The use of gendered possessive postpositions, as in *bhagwan ki daya* (the grace/ mercy of god, line 76) is a feature of standard Hindi, while in Mauritian Bhojpuri only a single form, *ke*, is used. Similar to several examples in chapter 5, speaker 2 even uses a honorific pronoun of address, which is lacking in contemporary Mauritian Bhojpuri, referring to the audience gathered as *aplog* (line 36). Nevertheless, these grammatical features of Hindi are primarily segmentable surface items, and lexical choice remains the focus of awareness for most people when classifying the performances as hindiized (cf. Silverstein 2001 [1981]).

The point here is not to arrive at a simple categorization of lexical items as Hindi or Bhojpuri. Rather, the items highlighted in the example above represent choices that strike speakers as uncommon because in other contexts Creole items would be preferred in their place. Also, certain items have phonetic shapes that make them sound like Hindi, such as the substitution of [s] by [š] in *ashirvad* (lines 36, 54, 87, 89) as opposed to Mauritian Bhojpuri *asirvad*, since [š] is not used in ordinary Mauritian Bhojpuri (compare with example 5.14 in the previous chapter). These choices have a certain in-between quality that make them intermediaries between Bhojpuri and Hindi — local speakers identify them as Hindi but they are not counted as clear code switches to Hindi, and the overall discourse is still understood to be Bhojpuri.[11] The intermediary characteristic of these purist items greatly contributes to the overall effect of blurring the linguistic boundaries between Hindi and Mauritian Bhojpuri.

In addition, in certain institutional contexts Hindi is regularly conflated with Bhojpuri, for example, in Hindi classes in the school system. Students in Hindi classes are often told that Hindi is their "mother tongue" (*matṛbhāṣā* in standard Hindi). While visiting Hindi classes in state and state-funded schools, I several times heard a Hindi teacher assert that "Hindi is your mother tongue" — and heard a student respond that his mother spoke Bhojpuri. On several occasions the Hindi teacher took this as a starting point for a lecture about the diversity of Hindi, stressing that Bhojpuri is a form of Hindi *(bhojpuri hindi ka ek rup hai)*, a dialect of Hindi, like Braj, Avadhi, Maithili, and even Hindustani. This view is based on a slippage between two different notions of "Hindi": standard Hindi and Hindi as a cover term for a chain of cognate dialects stretching across northern India from Rajasthan in the west to Bihar in the east (Gumperz and Naim 1960; Siegel 1988, 2). Standard Hindi, like Urdu, draws on varieties of Hindi in the second sense known as Khari Boli, which is spoken in the western part of Uttar Pradesh (east and northeast of Delhi), whereas Bhojpuri forms part of the Bihari group at the eastern end of this chain of linguistic varieties.

The relationship between Hindi and Bhojpuri, however, is not only one of nearly opposite poles on a linguistic continuum stretching west to east across the Gangetic plain; it is also a matter of politics. Attempts to standardize Bhojpuri have not been successful, whereas standard Hindi has the status of a national language in India and is the official language of administration and education all the way from Rajasthan across the Gangetic plain to the border with West Bengal, including the state of Bihar. The slippage between these two senses of Hindi, because of which Bhojpuri can be conceived as a kind of Hindi, interacts with that other shifty term, "mother tongue," the invocation of which portrays Hindi simultaneously as an ancestral language and the language Hindu children supposedly grow up with in Mauritius. *Matribhasha*, as outlined in chapter 1, is generally identified with the institutionalized concept of ancestral language, providing a link to the ancestors immigrating from India. At the same time, the idea of mother and motherhood refers to the Hindu concept of divine motherhood, manifested by the Goddess in her various forms. In the context of pro-Hindi activism, the image of the divine mother who is worshipped and protected by her children also provides a connection to the history of social and political conflict in India, resonating with other gendered representations of Hindi present in Hindu nationalist politics since the late nineteenth century (Dalmia 1997, King 1989, 1994). At the same time, *matribhasha* is often simply translated as "mother tongue" or *langue maternelle* in Mauritius, implying that Hindi is a language of childhood socialization in Mauritius. The slippage between these two understandings of *matribhasha* — revered language of the ancestors of Mauritian Hindus and language of childhood socialization — is employed to establish the "indigenousness" of Hindi in Mauritius, and the subsumption of Bhojpuri under the more prestigious category of Hindi represents an attempt to resolve this contradiction. Likewise, local Hindu organizations represent Bhojpuri as inseparable from Hindi, often using organic imagery,[12] or a particular reading of the history of Indian immigration to Mauritius,[13] a view even shared by the head of the Hindi department of the Mahatma Gandhi Institute.[14]

As far as the attempts to indigenize Hindi are concerned, extensive explicit ideological discourses by Hindu activists, nationalists, and Hindi teachers are not the only means. Crucially, the use of purist, hindiized Bhojpuri at religious community gatherings as illustrated above provides a context in which Hindus appropriate and experience Hindi as "theirs" by making the language of the ancestors part of linguistic practices central to local processes of Hindu group identification. Hindi is the object of a discourse about ethnicized heritage in the diaspora yet it also represents the pure and authentic end of a linguistic continuum, in use alongside Creole among rural Hindu Mauritians, stretching from ordinary Bhojpuri with its often remarked frequency of use of Creole lexical items to purist Bhojpuri-Hindi and sanskritized standard Hindi.

HINDI, THE ANCESTORS, AND THE PILGRIMAGE

Generally, the Hindu institutions involved in organizing the pilgrimage and running the temples at Grand Bassin / Ganga Talao see the propagation of Hindi as one of their goals, and Hindi classes are regularly offered in most temples across Mauritius. In a conversation with me, a former secretary of the Mauritius Sanatan Dharm Temples Federation said that the Federation considers itself the "main movement of the Hindi-speaking people" and also organizes and funds visits of prominent Hindi writers to Mauritius.

The religious significance of Hindi in Mauritius is affirmed at Grand Bassin / Ganga Talao by the fact that most sermons *(pravacan)* delivered during the festival, by pandits visiting from India as well as by local Hindu priests, are in Hindi. In 1998, a stage was built next to the Mauritiuseswarnath Temple where local Hindu pandits and swamis from India delivered speeches in Hindi to an audience that included leading political figures — the Prime Minister and several ministers and the Indian High Commissioner. Hindi *bhajan*s were played from tape in the temples, and pandits and *pujari*s instructed worshipping pilgrims in Hindi — in salient contrast to the conversations in Creole among the pilgrims themselves. This emblematic use of Hindi in the midst of a Creole-speaking crowd was also evident in slogans often repeated in speeches and sermons, such as *hindī ṛṣiõ kī bhāṣā hai* (Hindi is the language of the ancient sages). This particular claim that Hindi is both ancient and connected to religious authority was displayed in Devanagari script on the large tent of the Human Service Trust, the Hindu nationalist body founded by Swami Krishanand, which maintains links with the RSS and the VHP, at Grand Bassin / Ganga Talao in February 1998. The slogan, exhorting Hindus to learn and cultivate Hindi, was first coined in Mauritius by the Hindu missionary and political activist Basdeo Bissoondoyal, who used it in a song in his highly successful campaign for religious mobilization in the 1940s. Central to this movement was a Hindi basic literacy campaign in the context of the struggle for Hindu voting rights, since after a constitutional change in 1947 Indo-Mauritians were required to pass a simple literacy test in order to be eligible for the franchise. The second line of the song is the beginning of the Hindi alphabet (Verma 1984, 91):

All Hindus study Hindi	*sab hindū paṛho hindī*
a, ā, i, ī	*a ā i ī*
This is the language of the gods	*yeh devtāõ kī bhāṣā hai*
This is the language of the ancient sages	*yeh ṛṣiõ kī bhāṣā hai*

The last line of the song, recontextualized as a slogan in the setting of the pilgrimage, served to cast Hindi as a language of great antiquity, presumably already used by gods and ancient sages, the study of which is a religious duty for Hindus. This echoes the call of Mauritian writer Jay Narain Roy, a leading figure of the Hindi Pracarini Sabha (Society for the propagation of Hindi) as well as a member of the Legislative Council, that "learning and teaching our mother tongue *(matṛbhāṣā)* is our first religious duty."[15] Hindi thus becomes a central part of a project of missionizing and religious purification through which Hindu nationalists want to turn Indo-Mauritians into good Hindus in the diaspora.

The pilgrims also frequently and emblematically use Hindi in Devanagari script to indicate the name of their home village or town and the name of their community group or local religious association on the decorated *kanvars* — colorfully decorated structures of bamboo carried by members of local Hindu associations or temple committees toward and on the way back from Grand Bassin / Ganga Talao. Brass vessels *(loṭa)* in which sacred water from the lake is carried home to be offered in the shrines of the pilgrims' villages, are traditionally fixed to the ends of the bamboo poles of these structures. *Kanvars* often resemble the shape of Hindu temples and display images of Hindu deities or representations of the sacred sound *om*, while the pilgrims carrying them chant Hindi *bhajans* as they head to the mountain lake. This is another instance of a presupposed indexical link between Hindi and Hindu religion in Mauritius.

Many Hindu Mauritians remember the discovery of remote Grand Bassin by a small group of devotees travelling on foot as an act of sacrifice and renunciation and therefore as based in Hindu traditions emphasizing these virtues. As one Hindu activist involved in the state-assisted development of Grand Bassin / Ganga Talao as an important site of Hindu pilgrimage put it in an interview with me: "They [the Hindu ancestors] could go without food, water, clothes, but not without their *dharma*, not without their rituals." Furthermore, the sacrifice and efforts of the original pilgrims are recalled as symptomatic of their general living conditions as indentured immigrant laborers in Mauritius, characterized by hardship, deprivation, and political repression.[16] Hindu activists frequently pointed to the example of the ancestors in overcoming difficulties as an inspiration for Hindus in the present and emphasized the necessity to continue to honor them for the sacrifices they made. In this way, the pilgrimage to Grand Bassin / Ganga Talao, undertaken by many devotees on foot from places across the entire island, can be understood not only as a religious performance but simultaneously as a collective reenactment and commemoration of the past sufferings of the immigrant ancestors. The pilgrimage in 1998 in particular, being the centenary observance of the pilgrimage, exhibited the perceived ancestral quality of this event by honoring the achievements of the pioneer pilgrims who found this remote lake in the upland forests of southwest Mauritius and started turning it into a site of Hindu pilgrimage. The sacrifices made by those resilient ancestors in order to maintain their Hindu religion in an alien and oppressive environment are thus extolled in a conservative discourse focused on the perpetuation of ancestral Hindu culture.

Despite the fact that few Indian immigrants had knowledge of standard Hindi when they reached Mauritius, representations of Hindi in the school system, in discourses of Hindu activists, and in the context of the pilgrimage depict it as the language of these ancestors. Indeed, the metaphor of the ancestor as the origin of tradition, understood as ancestral culture, is an essential element that binds together the pilgrimage to Grand Bassin / Ganga Talao, Hindi as the ancestral language, and the faraway Hindu homeland.

The Shivratri pilgrimage to Ganga Talao constitutes a multilayered performative enactment of a diasporic link to Hindu India. The creation of a sacred geography iconically resembling the holy sites of Hindu pilgrimage along the river Ganges, such as Hardwar and Banaras, provides the context, and the waters of the Ganga Talao in Mauritius are literally consubstantial with the Ganges in India. The pilgrimage also supports the propagation of Hindi as the language of the ancestors whose heroic deeds in preserving Hindu traditions under the harsh circumstances of indenture on sugar plantations the Shivratri pilgrimage celebrates. And the pilgrimage and its celebration of Hindi take place in ancestral time, a spatiotemporal framework in which the ancestors and their Hindu descendants are simultaneously present.[17] The presence of the ancestors is evoked by both the celebration of "their" language and the recreation of a sacred Indian geography. Moreover, the very structure and rhythmic temporality of the annual pilgrimage highlights the larger theme of the cyclical return of the ancestor's world, including "their" language, to the present. While Hindu forms of collective belonging in Mauritius thus become tied to a spatiotemporal order emphasizing the copresence of Hindus and the world of their ancestors, the propagation of Hindi is also linked to questions of historical consciousness and change. From the perspective of Hindu nationalists, a diasporic population in Mauritius needs to be transformed into authentic Hindus through Hindi in order for the assumed copresence with the ancestors to take place. That is, those who see a Hindu community in Mauritius as constituted through a regime of temporality, evoking Benjamin's messianic time, also implicitly recognize the importance of change and progress along the dimension of empty, homogeneous time in order to become one with their ancestors.

CALIBRATIONS OF DISPLACEMENT AND TEMPORALITY

As I have outlined here, the cultivation of Hindi as the language of the ancestors in Mauritius is part of a larger process of establishing a diasporic relationship to a homeland in India. This relationship is then naturalized by the presupposed and performative use of shared metaphors, which establish iconic relations of likeness between Hindi, the pilgrimage, and the homeland. The semiotic mediations involved in establishing a diasporic link to the homeland constitute a particular metapragmatic regimentation or indexical alignment. Here I draw on Michael Silverstein's (1993, 48–53) analysis of the metapragmatic function of different types of pragmatic calibration, that is, different ways of establishing indexical relationships between sign-events. In demonstrating how sign-events become interpretable by relating them to other, antecedent sign-events, thus providing a "context," Silverstein distinguishes between three ways of indexically uniting (laminating) layers of events, enabling their pragmatic contextualization — "reportive," "reflexive," and "nomic" calibration. Reportive calibration is characteristic of a more or less explicit marking that the ongoing sign-event is a representation of a previous discursive sign-event, as in reported speech. Reflexive calibration refers to the more implicit process of making sense of discursive interaction by relating the stream of indexicals to "event-frames" (socially recognizable types of events) and vice versa. Nomic calibration concerns the relation between two sign-events as defined by their location in ontically separate realms. The anterior sign-event, for example, is presented as inhabiting a religious otherworld, a mythical realm, the world of the ancestors or a world of abstract generalization, while the presently unfolding sign-event is understood to be the available and often privileged experience of that realm.

I suggest that the performatively established link between Hindi, the pilgrimage, and the homeland bears some similarities to what Silverstein has termed nomic calibration, and I expand Silverstein's concept of nomic calibration to better capture the relationships of spatial and temporal displacement and convergence between the different worlds brought into relation during the Mauritian Shivratri pilgrimage. Understood as sign-events, both the celebration of Hindi as the ancestral language and the reproduction of a sacred Hindu geography in Mauritius in the context of the pilgrimage to Ganga Talao are located in a different realm from the homeland they strongly point to. However, the difference between realms is not of an ontic kind, but rather one imagined to be characterized by a spatial and temporal remove that is then minimized in the context of the pilgrimage. This type of indexical calibration of displacement, which in the case discussed here might also be called diasporic calibration, involves the regimenting of indexicals as pointing towards a diasporic source conceived as a spatially removed homeland, which is furthermore invested with ancestral qualities.

Such processes of indexical calibration also constitute orders of temporality. The creation of relationships between sign-events, as through reported speech or by performing a mythical narrative, also creates relationships in time, such as temporal sequence and temporal difference or convergence. In particular, a calibration of displacement bridges the temporal and spatial remove between events, therefore suggesting a relationship of temporal equivalence.

I have stressed how the regimenting of indexicals results in making the pilgrimage and the cultivation of Hindi interpretable as instances of invoking an ancestral Hindu homeland. The lamination of the sign-events in the diaspora on the one hand and in the homeland on the other is also effected by iconicity, so that diasporic sign-events become available experiences of the homeland. That is, the metaphors that are perceived as shared between Hindi, the pilgrimage in its setting, and the homeland create a dense set of indexical-iconic links between these three. This semiotically regimented diasporic connection appears natural because of the effect of inherent likeness produced by the metaphors underpinning the diasporic link.

This also has implications for constructing a temporal order of collective belonging. Ideologies of ancestral language mediate between the ancestral and linear temporal dimensions outlined in this chapter. Calibrations of displacement are ways of laminating sign-events from different realms in a way that downplays the spatiotemporal difference between those events. That is, the world of the homeland and the ancestors is presented as inhabiting the world of diasporic Hindus in Mauritius, emphasizing the themes of sacred simultaneity and cyclical return central to the Shivratri pilgrimage. However, being one with the ancestors in Mauritius also depends on particular achievements in the dimension of linear time. Diasporic Hindus need to be made authentic through Hindi on several levels of activity, such as collective religious performance, explicit nationalist discourse, and particular forms of linguistic practice. The purifying qualities of ancestral Hindi for transforming Indo-Mauritians into diasporic Hindus are crucial in constituting community in this mode of temporality. In the case discussed here, such a linear dimension of temporality comprises both the authenticating purification of diasporic subjects and a historical narrative of the heroic political and socio-economic rise of a community of Hindus in Mauritius, who managed to preserve their ancestral traditions under difficult circumstances. At the same time ideologies of Hindi as the ancestral language of the Hindus contribute to concepts of community based on allegiance to an ancestral origin, which can be made present through religious performance and the voicing of an ancestral world in the cultivation of Hindi.

CONCLUSION

In this chapter I have sought to demonstrate how ideologies of ancestral language interact with the performance of Hindu pilgrimage in Mauritius to create a sense of diasporic belonging based on an experience of ancestral time. In other words, the ideology of Hindi as an ancestral language also represents an indexical order of temporality in which the temporal and spatial disjuncture between Mauritian Hindus and the world of their Indian immigrant ancestors is negotiated and momentarily minimized. Instead of presenting diaspora as a hybrid cultural ensemble, such temporal regimentation emphasizes the theme of cultural purity, while Mauritian Hindus constantly struggle with the obvious impact of profound cultural and social transformations.

What are the implications of the process I have called a calibration of displacement for the question of language and community? In his case for the radical modernity of nationalism Benedict Anderson has argued that a fundamentally new experience of time, referred to as empty and homogenous and mediated by a new literary genre, has crucially enabled the experience of national community. In this he has raised an important issue: the fact that the creation of language-mediated imagined communities often involves a reorganization of temporality. However, Anderson's narrowing of the temporal dimension of the production of language-mediated imagined communities to linear, empty, homogeneous time fails to capture certain forms of time reckoning that are at the heart of modern ways of ethnonational identification. As Anderson and other scholars of nationalism have pointed out, the objects of national devotion and identification — the nation and its people — are often represented as possessing considerable antiquity, despite their often manifest novelty. Conceptualizing a community of nationals as being on a linear march through history is not the only way to relate to the imagined antiquity of such communities; equally important are ritualized moments of communion with the ancestors that suspend the spatiotemporal remove of the present from their imagined national forebears. Instead of postulating the superseding of one dimension of temporality by another, an analysis of the complex interplay and coexistence of multiple dimensions of temporal regimentation represents a more promising approach to the problem of temporality, language, and community.[18]

Conclusion

Time, Technology, and Language

In this book I have sought to account for the emergence of diaspora in practical, phenomenological, and ideological terms by analyzing how a sense of being in diaspora is produced by language and its uses among Hindus in Mauritius. In this, I have focused on the indexical and iconic values of linguistic practices whose deployment in everyday social interaction and metapragmatic discourse results in ethnolinguistic forms of belonging pointing to a diasporic homeland. To be meaningful, these practices depend on a whole range of other linguistic practices and valuations among Hindu Mauritians that are not immediately concerned with issues of diaspora or even ethnic marking. In a more formal manner, I have also examined the formation of diasporic community as centered on the theme of spatio-temporal displacement while describing how linguistic ideologies in conjunction with other ritual practices negotiate and shape the experience of temporal and spatial remove that is central to being in diaspora.

In chapter 6 I made reference to how the question of the phenomenology of time is fundamental to the creation of national community in the work of Benedict Anderson. In this context, I sought to demonstrate that Anderson's narrowing of temporality to a single dimension under modern conditions of nation formation is unwarranted, and claimed that linguistic practice creates national communities by mediating between a plurality of modes of experiencing time. Nevertheless, Anderson, like others before him, has addressed an important problem in pointing to how particular semiotic technologies through their formal properties may regiment our sense of being in time. While for Anderson the particular technology was the novel as a literary genre, a similar question had already been asked by Marshall McLuhan in his comparison of the effects of print cultures and electronic media on our sense of being in the world, including our experiences of temporality (McLuhan 1964, 4). Here the introduction of new semiotic technologies, such as new literary genres or new technical means of mass mediation, also result in new dominant forms of experiencing time, which also imply a new organization of social relations, such as the nation for Anderson or the interconnected "global village" for McLuhan. McLuhan's work has provided inspiration for new materialist perspectives on media and time, such as the work of Friedrich Kittler. Against the background of a theory of culture shaped by technologies of data processing, Kittler also seeks to demonstrate how new semiotic technologies, in particular digital media, determine a phenomenology of time (Kittler 1993, 200–201; see also Sandbothe 1996).

These approaches have important implications for my discussion of time and diasporic community because they raise the following questions: If temporality is crucial for the making of national and diasporic communities, are semiotic technologies not the most appropriate site of investigation for such regimentations of temporality? Should an analysis of how a shared sense of being in diaspora emerges through the mediation between different temporalities be focused on semiotic technology such as literary genres or forms of mass media, instead of on language and linguistic ideologies? In concluding this study, I want to address the problem of time and semiotic technology raised by Anderson and briefly sketch some of the implications of my ethnography of language and diaspora among Hindu Mauritians for contemporary debates on time and media technology. I argue that my findings suggest a critique of privileging the material and formal dimensions of such technologies over situated linguistic practice.

Contemporary work on the philosophy of time is characterized by a growing interest in new media technologies, especially among those writing from a poststructuralist perspective. Nevertheless, compared to the work of Kittler, other poststructuralist approaches to the question of time have tended to be more skeptical of a materialist reading of how semiotic technologies shape temporality. Jacques Derrida, for example, has argued that a conception of writing modeled on the primacy of the spoken word, dominating Western intellectual traditions since Plato, is also linked to a "linearist concept of time" (Derrida 1976, 72). Consequently, a future deconstruction of such a "metaphysics of presence" centered on the spoken word as the locus of truth would also imply a transition to a "delinearized temporality" (87). However, Derrida does not accord to a particular semiotic technology a key role in bringing about such a transition, since according to him a delinearized and plural concept of time is an irreducible dimension of the actual workings of language and signification. Nevertheless, several scholars sympathetic to Derrida's deconstructive rejection of any dominant form of controlling time take the impact of new semiotic technologies on phenomenologies of time quite seriously. For them, the fact that time also takes material forms subject to a particular structuring raises the question of a link between temporality and technology. Concurring with Derrida's thesis that any conceptual approach to defining the nature and functioning of time is doomed to failure, David Wood nevertheless insists that material orders of time do exist and that they have a crucial impact on social life (Wood 2001[1989], xii–xvi). Jean-François Lyotard is more willing to speculate about particular links between semiotic technologies, especially digital media, and changing experiences of time. Along the lines of Derrida's view of the indeterminacy of time implied in the play of *différance,* he also rejects the possibility of one single overarching form of temporality, whether metaphysically founded or produced as the effect of a particular semiotic technology. Nevertheless, Lyotard suggests that "telegraphic" technologies of electronic mediation do have a transforming impact on apprehensions of time, particularly as they "destroy presence, the 'here-and-now' of the forms and their 'carnal' reception" (Lyotard 1991, 118; see also Sandbothe 1996, 144–46). Along similar lines, Bernard Stiegler seeks to account for the constitution of temporality through technics and consequently accords to formal dimensions of contemporary media technologies the power to shape a distinct form of time experience he calls "light-time." According to him "light-time forms the age of the différance in real time" (Stiegler 1998, 276). Mike Sandbothe takes a related position in evaluating how the modalities of mediation prevalent on the Internet also provide its users with a multiplicity of ways of experiencing time, dissolving the linearity of what Benjamin has called empty, homogenous time into a pluridimensional array of different mutually coexisting temporalities (Sandbothe 1999).

In contrast to these recent approaches in the philosophy of time, the ethnographic scenario I have outlined does not privilege a particular semiotic technology. Nor does it imply a privileged relationship between a particular semiotic technology, such as a literary genre or a certain form of mass media, and a particular phenomenology of time. Instead, I have described a plurality of modes of experiencing time as linked to particular kinds of historical consciousness and memory rather than particular media techniques. In this, I have found Paul Ricoeur's approaches to the problem of temporality, identity, and community more useful than Marshall McLuhan's or Friedrich Kittler's technicism or more recent post-modern attempts to connect an undoing of linear modes of time to particular electronic media technologies. Ricoeur has demonstrated how the challenge of navigating a plurality of temporalities arises independently of any particular semiotic technologies used. Whenever subjects are engaged in the work of identifying themselves and locating themselves and others in social collectives, they negotiate the gap — or, frequently, disjuncture — between subjective and cosmic times. The products of this work of iden-tification are senses of being in time with others, that is, particular social and historical times. Ricoeur has not only shown how changing circum-stances of the present lead to different remembered pasts and anticipated futures, thus making sure that, pace Anderson, temporalities come in the plural; he has also pointed to the crucial mediating role of linguistic prac-tices such as narrative in accomplishing this negotiation of different senses of being in time (Ricoeur 1988, 245–47). Thus negotiating between dif-ferent temporalities is always a part of making identities and communi-ties, and their particular shapes and contexts can tell us much about the circumstances and dilemmas characterizing the historical present. While narrative could also be characterized as a semiotic technology in the broadest sense, its wide poetic possibilities do not as such entail formal constraints regimenting temporality in the way a particular literary genre might do, such as the novel in Anderson's reading.

The formal and material dimensions of semiotic technologies as in new forms of media are doubtlessly important and need to be taken into account whenever such technologies become sites of temporal structura-tion. Nevertheless, my analysis of diaspora as a form of historical con-sciousness shaped by particular temporalities cautions against any privi-leging of the formal and material dimensions of such technologies over the capacities of subjects to construct meaningful story lines and to reshape memories and anticipations in articulation with an experienced situation of the present. While not denying that the formal dimensions of semiotic technologies may motivate certain temporalities over others, one conclusion of this study is that situated actors are likely to transform and subvert any such technology-induced regimentations of temporality. If the mediation between different temporal perspectives through linguistic practice is a key dimension of processes of personal and collective identification, any normalization of temporal experience through semiotic technologies, such as proposed in Anderson's theory of nationalism, or Frederic Jameson's account of postmodernity (2003), is likely to be incomplete and undercut by an irreducible plurality of time. Future research about semiotic technologies and temporality will then have to take account of how the formal dimensions of such technologies are unable to fully encompass the practices of historically and socially situated actors — such as the practices of Hindu Mauritians, who make the world of the ancestors part of their place in a Mauritian nation as they mediate between different times while narrating a history informed by the politics of the present.

Notes

1. *Cités* are public housing projects in Mauritius whose residents are predominantly poor Creoles.

2. The figure of $50 million was given in the 1999 report on Human Rights Practices on Mauritius, released by the U.S. State Department in 2000. The indirect economic damage from the riots through the disruption they caused to the country's vital garment and tourism industries was considerable.

3. Of course both diasporic and "indigenous" cultural practices and symbols have to be understood as largely locally created. My concern here is to highlight the differences in their ideological representations as direct continuations of traditions essentially imagined to be elsewhere or as uniquely particular to the island.

4. *Le Mauricien,* 9 November 1998.

5. Philip Baker (1972) proposed the spelling "Kreol" for Mauritian Creole, ostensibly not only to emphasize a symbolic break with French but also to avoid identification of the language with the ethnic group known as Creoles. However, since this spelling is rarely used in Mauritius and so far remains confined to the writings of a few scholars and activists, I have chosen to retain the most widespread English spelling, "Creole," using the term "Mauritian Creole" where confusion with the homophone ethnic label is possible.

6. "Ancestral culture" is the term used by the Mauritian state bureaucracy; *culture ancestrale* is the term used in the French-language press. Throughout this book I have used the term "ancestral culture" without quotations marks in order to avoid unnecessary cluttering of the text. As should be clear from the context, ancestral culture is an official construction by the Mauritian state and ethnoreligious organizations. My use of the term "culture" in this respect is not intended to evoke earlier notions of cultures as organic wholes.

7. Strictly speaking, Wilhelm Dilthey (d. 1911) was not part of a phenome-

nological engagement with historicism; however, he anticipated important phenomenological insights into the creative nature of temporality, especially in his treatment of autobiography as a struggle for the "coherence" *(Zusammenhang)* of a life story (Dilthey 1958; Carr 1986, 74–75). In this, he profoundly influenced Heidegger's account of temporality as the meaning of existence (Bambach 1995, Carr 1986).

8. Jameson's description of a reduction to the present as characterized by an aesthetic of suddenness (2003: 712) differs from Benjamin's "messianic time" in its lack of metaphysical or redemptive dimensions, both of which are central to Benjamin's concept.

CHAPTER I. CREOLE ISLAND OR LITTLE INDIA?

1. The Mauritian term for ethnic politics, "communalism" *(communalisme* in French and *kominalis* in Creole), follows Indian usage, where "communalism" is a label for the predominance of ethnic and religious communities as actors in colonial and postcolonial public spheres (Freitag 1996).

2. Eriksen (1994, 557–58) highlights similar tensions between the official goal of this performative genre and the local interpretations of its significance.

3. Stein (1980, 377) comments on the contrast between state support for ancestral languages and the corresponding lack of such support for Creole in the following terms: "But present politics rather play the strategy of communalism, and therefore privilege the ancestral or ethnic languages. At the same time one refuses Creole the status of fully counting as a language, and thus Creole is excluded from many domains, including education."

4. According to the 1990 census, a total of 28.58% of Mauritians stated that Bhojpuri was their "language usually spoken at home," including those respondents who also listed a second language other than Bhojpuri in this category and those claiming to speak either Hindi or Urdu — neither of which is actually used as a language of everyday interaction — at home (Mauritius 1990). The corresponding figure from the 2000 census is 19.61% (Mauritius 2000). De Robillard, who himself advances the figure of 18–26% for those having acquired competence in Bhojpuri in their homes (de Robillard 1989, 136), provides a survey of all estimates of the number of Bhojpuri speakers in the scholarly literature on Mauritius (de Robillard 1989, 135–36); these range from 18.7% to 43.0%.

5. According to the 2000 census, the figure for French in the category "language usually spoken at home" is 3.38%, and 6.40% if those are included who claim to use it alongside another language, here mostly Creole. Stein claims an unlikely figure of 21% for French used at home (Stein 1982, 545), a finding strongly disputed by Baker (Baker 1984, 394), who points to the 1972 census figure of 4.8%. De Robillard states that 50–60% of the population have a reasonable competence in French, by virtue of being exposed to it in the school system and the mass media (de Robillard 1989, 140–41). Stein states that 65.1% out of his sample of 720 persons claimed to have a "good knowledge" of French (Stein 1982, 361).

6. The 2000 census (Mauritius 2000) gives the following figures:

	Language of forefathers (%)	Language usually spoken at home (%)
Creole	49.02	80.53
Chinese (all varieties)	1.93	0.88
English	0.09	0.09
French	3.51	6.40
Arabic	0.07	0.07
Bhojpuri	38.71	18.16
Gujarati	0.17	0.17
Hindi	5.52	1.63
Marathi	1.64	0.31
Tamil	4.57	0.59
Telugu	1.87	0.43
Urdu	4.19	0.47

Percentages refer to the total resident population of the Republic of Mauritius. The columns do not add up to 100% because answers stating bilingualism in the respective categories were possible.

7. The lack of state support for Kutchi and Hakka, and the minimal state support in the case of Gujarati, are striking, since these languages, unlike any of the officially promoted ancestral languages, are actually used in everyday conversation by small numbers of Mauritians. The situation can be explained by the fact that the people using these languages are members of ethnic groups officially associated with ancestral languages different from the "ethnic" languages they still use. Almost all speakers of Kutchi and the majority of users of Gujarati are Muslims, whose ancestors migrated to Mauritius as free traders, and who still maintain very active networks of trade, kinship, and marriage with Gujarat and other parts of India. Muslims in Mauritius, however, regardless of their regional origins in India, are supposed to claim Urdu (and also, increasingly, Arabic) as their ancestral language (Eisenlohr 2006b). Only the minority of Hindus of Gujarati origin, who mainly came to Mauritius as employees of one of the trading companies owned by Muslim Gujarati families, place any official claim on Gujarati as their patrimony. Apart from occasional television and radio programs by the government-controlled Mauritius Broadcasting Corporation, there is no policy of supporting Gujarati. The case of Hakka, the predominant Chinese vernacular among Sino-Mauritians (Baker 1969, 83), is complicated by the fact that only Mandarin, which never had any native speakers in Mauritius, is officially assigned as the ancestral language of this ethnic group. There is an interesting parallel to this situation in Singapore, where the varieties of Chinese actually in use are of southern provenance, but the government is intent on promoting only Mandarin and has launched "Speak Mandarin" campaigns (Bokhorst-Heng 1999). In Mauritius, of course, the predominant language of everyday interaction among Sino-Mauritians is Creole.

8. Bhojpuri has been subject to language revitalization efforts by Hindu community activists; however this is often accompanied by attempts to present Bhojpuri as a local form of Hindi, with consequences that are laid out in detail in chapter 5.

9. It is important to realize that the Mauritian census category of "language of the forefathers" has not always corresponded to the concept of an officially recognized and promoted ancestral language as discussed here. This has particularly been true since the census of 1983, when Bhojpuri was admitted for the first time as a valid response to the question of "language of the forefathers" (Mauritius 1983). In the 2000 census, Creole and Bhojpuri together accounted for 68.72% of all answers to this census question, 38.58% for Creole and 30.14% for Bhojpuri (if one takes stated bilingualism in this category into account, the figures are 87.73%, 49.02%, and 38.71%, respectively) (Mauritius 2000). However, in contrast to the standardized "Asian" and especially Indian ancestral languages discussed, these two languages are hardly supported or officially promoted by the Mauritian state. Nevertheless, Hindu organizations concerned about the ancestral languages promoted by the state take the census very seriously. They publish ads in newspapers before the census is taken, publicly asking members of the ethnoreligious communities they represent to give appropriate answers regarding "language of the forefathers" (Hookoomsing 1986). There was substantial overlap between the categories "language of the forefathers" (Mauritius 1972) and "mother tongue" (Mauritius 1962) in the census until 1972 and the notion of officially recognized and supported ancestral languages, at least as far as answers from Indo-Mauritians were concerned. It appears that many of those listing Bhojpuri as "language of forefathers" from 1983 on had stated either Hindi or Urdu in this category up to the 1972 census. In 1962, 36.44% of the population claimed Hindi and 13.54% claimed Urdu in this category (then labeled as "mother tongue"); for 1972, the figures were 38.84% and 8.67%, respectively (Mauritius 1962, 1972). The changes in the interpretation of the census category "language of forefathers," involving a clear shift away from a link between this census category and the language of ethnolinguistic identification, are apparent when compared with the 2000 results for Hindi and Urdu, which are 3.04% and 2.89%, respectively (5.52% and 4.19% if stated bilingualism is included) (Mauritius 2000).

10. The proportion listed as Urdu was negligible. The proportion of airtime for Indian languages has increased substantially over the last three decades (compare to Baker 1969, 92; 1972). In the sample mentioned, the proportion of English-language programming is somewhat inflated, since between 24:00 and 7:00 the second MBC channel broadcasts mostly English-language programs, fed by satellite, which are watched by very few people. If these hours on the MBC2 channel are taken out of the calculation, the proportion of French increases to 38% and that of Indian languages to 36.9%, of which Hindi and Hindustani account for 31.9% of total airtime on Mauritian television. RFO (French state-controlled) television from the neighboring French overseas département Réunion can be received in most areas of Mauritius and is rather popular, which significantly increases the availability of French-language programming to Mauritian television viewers. Also, although very few television programs are announced as Creole-language, most locally produced shows, primarily those listed as being in French, feature a large amount of de facto use of Creole in interviews, live coverage of events, and political speeches.

11. Digest of Educational Statistics 1994, Ministry of Education, Port Louis, Mauritius.

12. According to the Mauritian constitution, the population is divided into four communities: Hindus, Muslims, Sino-Mauritians, and the General Population, comprised of everyone not belonging to the three other groups, in effect, Creoles and Franco-Mauritians.

13. The Franco-Mauritian MMM leader Paul Béranger became Prime Minister in September 2003 — succeeding Anerood Jugnauth, who had held the post from 1982 to 1995 and from 2000 to 2003 — as part of a coalition agreement with Anerood Jugnauth's MSM party. Despite his notorious past as a leftist pro-Mauritian Creole *militant* and labor organizer in the 1970s and early 1980s, Béranger has become known as a neoliberal in economic policy, and as a conservative promoter of ethnicized ancestral traditions and "cultural centers." He has often been mocked for his habit of wearing formal Indian dress when attending functions related to the celebration of Indo-Mauritian "ancestral cultures." Hindus do not expect him to challenge the ethnic composition of the state apparatus, and he is widely respected among Mauritians for his skill in managing the country's economy and state finances. In this, his ancestry is seen as a crucially contributing factor, facilitating contacts with the country's Franco-Mauritian business elite, based on the widely shared racial stereotype of whites as having superior management and organizational skills. Franco-Mauritians, approximately 1% of the population, are widely considered an ethnically "invisible" community and not part of the competition over state power often defined by Mauritians in ethnic terms. With the exception of Béranger, who started his career as a leftist rebel against the Franco-Mauritian establishment, Franco-Mauritians do not enter official politics in postcolonial Mauritius, knowing that their overwhelming economic power is sufficient to safeguard their interests. Thus, the implications of a Prime Minister of Franco-Mauritian ancestry for Mauritius are very different from those of a Creole or Muslim Prime Minister. The latter two scenarios would indeed constitute a severe challenge to the political status quo. In July 2005, the coalition headed by Béranger lost the general elections to the Labour Party, and Navin Ramgoolam, who had already held the post from 1995 to 2000, again became Prime Minister.

14. *Communauté majoritaire* is a common way to refer to Hindus in political discourse and the press.

15. This contrasts with some Afro-Creole communities in the Caribbean, such as in Trinidad, where Islam is recognized and cultivated as an African heritage by a relatively small but apparently growing number of Afro-Trinidadians. Unlike in Mauritius, in Trinidad, Islamic traditions crosscut racial and ethnic boundaries between people claiming African and Indian origin. This has added a new dimension to ongoing disputes about the authenticity of Islamic traditions on what is experienced as the periphery of the Muslim world (Khan 2004).

16. Carroll and Carroll (2000b) analyze the actual as well as perceived dominance of Hindus of north Indian background in Mauritian state institutions as one of the main challenges to interethnic peace in the country, and as having contributed significantly to the outbreak of riots in February 1999. According to

them, this is particularly the case with regard to the situation of the Creoles, who view themselves as largely excluded from these domains, an issue also repeatedly raised by the Catholic Church in recent years.

17. In a profound irony for a reform movement famous for its rejection of the caste system, two organizations split off on a caste basis from the Arya Sabha, the representative of the nationalist Hindu reform movement Arya Samaj in Mauritius. Since the split-offs were carried out by members of low castes (known in Creole as *ti nasyon*), this in effect leaves the Arya Sabha dominated by the mid-ranking Vaish caste, which is also dominant in Mauritian politics. The Arya Ravived Pracharini Sabha established itself as the main religious organization of Hindus of the low-ranking Ravived caste, formerly known by the stigmatized name *chamar*, a common designation for untouchables in India. Subsequently, members of the also-low-ranking Gahlot Rajput caste, who adopted this more prestigious label to replace their old name *dusadh*, established a Gahlot Rajput Sabha. On the transformation of the caste system among Hindus in Mauritius see Hollup (1994).

18. *Le Mag,* 28 May 1995. See Basu (1996, 40–41, 92–93) and Jaffrelot (1996 [1993]) on the Ram Shilan Puja as a campaign of the VHP to force the temple issue in Ayodhya on a political agenda, and the communal rioting associated with it. The consecrated bricks, from different parts of India as well as other countries such as Mauritius, were brought by the VHP to Ayodhya for the laying of the foundation stone of the Rama temple on 9 November 1989.

19. Hindu Council of Mauritius, Souvenir Magazine, All Africa Hindu Conference, Nairobi, 7–9 August 1998. The magazine features a message on official stationery on the first page by Deputy Prime Minister of Mauritius Kailash Purryag lauding the "golden opportunity for the establishment of a Hindu Council of Africa to uphold the status of the Hindu community in the Continent [sic]." This is followed by another official message from the High Commission of India, Port Louis, in which Acting High Commissioner K. V. Bhagirath states, five and a half years after the demolition of the Babri Masjid, "I am very happy to learn that the Hindu Council of Mauritius is issuing a special souvenir magazine on the occasion of All Africa Hindu Conference to be held in Nairobi, Kenya next week. The Hindu Council of India [here obviously referring to the VHP] has, since its inception, persistently worked for the promotion of values that are important to promote peace and harmony in plural societies such as we have in Mauritius and India." Finally, the president of the Vishva Hindu Parishad / Chinmaya Ashram in Mauritius, in his contribution entitled "We Believe in Action," makes the following observation about the conference: "I understand that it has the blessings of the Rashtriya Swayamsevak Sangh, the largest organization catering for the welfare of Hindus living in and outside Bharat." The Souvenir Magazine also features a sponsoring full-page advertisement for the state airline Air Mauritius on the back cover. Prior to the conference, the chairman of the Hindu Council of Kenya made a visit to Mauritius, during which he met representatives from all the major Hindu organizations at the Hindu House, followed by a press conference. The Vishva Hindu Parishad then convened a meeting of the Mauritian conference delegates at the headquarters of the more mainstream Hindu Maha Sabha in Port Louis, where they were addressed by the Kenyan

president of the Hindu Council. VHP Bulletin no. 11, a newsletter published by the VHP of Mauritius, July 1998.

20. *Le Mauricien,* 29 January 1997.

21. *Le Mauricien,* 27 January 1997. I thank Trilo Gujadhar for this point.

22. *Hindu Vishva (New Delhi),* March-April 1979, p. 21. See also McKean (1996, 104–5).

23. *Hindu Vishva (New Delhi),* March-April 1979, p. 39.

24. *Hindu Vishva (New Delhi),* March-April 1979, pp. 39–40.

25. *Hindu Vishva (New Delhi),* March-April 1979, p. 40, emphasis in original.

26. *Hindu Vishva (New Delhi),* November-December 1976, p. 46.

27. *Hindu Vishva (New Delhi),* November-December 1976.

28. *Le Mauricien,* 3 August 1998.

29. *Sangh parivar* (Sangh family) is a cover term for the main Hindu nationalist organizations, such as the Bharatiya Janata Party (BJP), the Rashtriya Svayamsevak Sangh (RSS), and Vishva Hindu Parishad (VHP), as well as the Bajrang Dal (the VHP youth organization) and the Hindu Maha Sabha, referring to the "parental" role of the RSS in relation to the others (Ludden 1996, 15).

30. *Le Mauricien,* 3 November 2001.

31. *Weekend,* 4 November 2001. The newspaper reported Joshi's statements in the following words: "Avant de terminer sa conference de presse, le Dr. Joshi dira, sur une note philosophique, qu'il a constaté deux facteurs unificateurs entre l'Inde et Maurice: l'océan Indien — les deux pays sont en fait baignés par cet océan et la langue hindi."

32. In political discourse and the press, *organisations socio-culturelles* is a common way to refer to religious organizations with an ethnic or "communal" agenda.

33. Eightieth Anniversary of Arya Samaj in Mauritius, Souvenir Magazine, 20 October 1990, p. 7.

34. *Le Mauricien,* 17 April 2003.

35. *Le Mauricien,* 26 August 1998.

36. *Le Mauricien,* 28 August 1998.

37. The fact that the Mauritian state apparatus is not monopolized by one ethnic group but rather members of all communities are found in the government and among the political elite has been read as an indication of "relatively even integration" (Eriksen 1998, 184) into state institutions favoring interethnic cooperation (Carroll and Carroll 2000a, 133). However, this perspective does not take the crucial transnational aspects of Hindu political power into account, nor the very widespread assessment among non-Hindus, especially Creoles and Muslims, that state institutions are grossly and unfairly dominated by Hindus. This stance is even shared by many individuals from certain Hindu subgroups, such as Tamils, who think that Hindus of north Indian origin systematically deprive them of what they see as their "fair share" of state jobs. Compare this to recent calls by Hindu organizations about a perceived danger of Hindus losing political power in Mauritius, leading a coalition of organizations gathered at the Hindu House, including the Arya Samaj and the Mauritius Sanatan Dharma Temples Federation, to publicly demand that "Hindus must keep the political power." The president of the Mauritius Sanatan Dharma Temples Federation was quoted

as having declared in Creole: "We are governing [this country]. And despite this we are witnessing a kind of Hindu-bashing in the country. We cannot allow this" (*Nou qui faire gouvernement. Et pourtant zordi nou pé assisté ene genre de hindu-bashing dans le pays. Nou pas capave permett ça!*) (*Le Mauricien*, 23 April 2001). The presumption here of course is that from a Hindu perspective it is legitimate and taken for granted that Hindus dominate the politics of post-independence Mauritius.

38. Second International Arya Youth Conference, 8–10 December 1995, Souvenir Magazine, special issue of *Āryoday*, p. 54.

39. Basdeo Bissoondoyal announced a plan to open three hundred such schools in 1946 (Bissoondoyal 1990, 119; Ramyead 1985, 83).

40. The contribution of Hindu activism to the cause of Hindi as an ancestral language and emblem of identity was also pointed out by the president of the Mauritius Hindi Lekak Sangh (Mauritius Union of Hindi Writers), when he thanked the Arya Sabha of Mauritius for the decades of support their Hindi-language periodical *Āryoday* has contributed to the cause of Hindi in Mauritius (Second International Arya Youth Conference, 8–10 December 1995, Souvenir Magazine, special issue of *Āryoday*, p. 27). In December 1997, the Arya Sabha Mauritius invited the Indian poets Surendra Sharma and Alok Chakradhar, the latter having previously been invited by the Mauritius Sanatan Dharm Temples Federation, to a *kavi sammelan* (poetry meeting) at its headquarters in Port Louis There the poets recited poems together with the president of the Hindi Lekak Sangh, an event also covered on national television, while the two Indian poets were introduced by the cultural secretary of the Indian High Commission.

41. William F. S. Miles is right in stating that the CPE issue of 1995 "revealed that politicians cannot automatically count on ethnic languages in mobilizing local political support" (Miles 2000, 227). However, the crisis is less likely to signal the demise of ancestral languages in general, or language "tipping" (Miles 2000, 227), since their significance as signs of communal identity does not depend on their use in everyday conversation. Also, despite Jugnauth's defeat at the polls after thirteen years in power for numerous reasons, the CPE issue being only one among them, the connection of ancestral languages to ethnicity in Mauritius was reaffirmed in the end. In 2004, the proponents of ancestral language finally accomplished their goal of having the exams in ancestral languages counted as part of the overall CPE results.

42. In their speeches at the national Shivratri ceremony in 2004 Vice Prime Minister Parvind Jugnauth and Minister of Telecommunications and Information Technologies Pradeep Jeeha prided themselves on this accomplishment and called for vigilance so the events of 1995 would not repeat themselves. A speaker for the Mauritius Sanatan Temples Federation rejected the comments by members of other communities opposing the inclusion of ancestral languages into the CPE results as anti-Hindu and declared: *Nou patience éna limite: si parole pas suffi et si bizin servi coup de pied, nou va servi li* (Our patience has a limit: if words are not enough and one has to have recourse to a kick with the foot, we are ready to do it). *Le Mauricien*, 16 February 2004.

43. See Errington (1998) on the somewhat parallel case of Javanese in New Order Indonesia. In a way recalling the place of Mauritian ancestral languages in

official visions of development, the Indonesian government under Suharto planned for the development and cultivation of Javanese as a medium of "tradition" to be "protected" from the ravages of modernization and the spread of "modern" Indonesian.

44. Second International Arya Youth Conference, Mauritius, 8–10 December 1995, Souvenir Magazine, special issue of *Āryoday*, p. 52.

45. *Le Mauricien,* 3 August 1998.

46. The idea of Hindus as inherently "tolerant" can be traced to Orientalist scholarship on India, and was in turn adopted by early Hindu nationalists. The latter used it especially to express their animosity toward Islam, which they considered doctrinal and intolerant (Hansen 1999: 70). Turned into a discourse of "hierarchical relativism" (van der Veer 1994a, 68), *hindutva* was presented by Hindu nationalists as "tolerant" of ethnic and religious diversity and in favor of national unity, on the assumption that Hindus would dominate the Indian nation and would be central to official representations of Indian identity. While the Orientalist genealogy of discourses of Hindu tolerance as an instance of "cultural collusion" (Burghart 1996, 278–99) can be regarded as well established, the concept of "tolerant" hierarchical inclusivism also recalls a more ancient theme in Indic political representation, described in terms of "galactic polities" by Stanley Tambiah (1976; 1992, 173–77). Here, the polity is conceived of as a representation of the cosmos — as deeply inclusivist and having fuzzy and potentially limitless boundaries. However, it is also indicative of a hierarchical cosmology, characterized by a continuum of purity, in which subjects inhabiting the polity are thought of as progressively more impure and barbarous the further away they dwell from its apex and center (compare also Burghart 1996, 285–86).

47. Hindu Council of Mauritius, Souvenir Magazine, All Africa Hindu Conference Nairobi, 7–9 August 1998, p. 2.

48. Second International Arya Youth Conference, 8–10 December 1995, Souvenir Magazine, special issue of *Āryoday*, p. 54.

49. *Pankaj,* special issue, *Caturth viśva hindī sammelan ke avsar par prakāśit viśeṣānk* (Hindī pracāriṇī sabhā, Long Mountain, Mauritius, December 1993).

50. For example, during the electoral campaign of 1995, which was dominated by the CPE issue, Anil Baichoo, a member of the cabinet, declared in a speech at Belle-Mare on the occasion of the Hindu festival Ganga Asman: "The day when the Oriental languages will disappear, the name of the Hindus will also disappear." *Le Mauricien,* 7 November 1995.

51. Report of the Select Committee on the Ward Report of Education, sixth meeting, 29 December 1942, Port-Louis, Government Printing 1943. Quoted in Bhuckory (1988 [1967], 86).

52. Second International Arya Youth Conference, 8–10 December 1995, Souvenir Magazine, special issue of *Āryoday*, p. 40.

53. *Nasyon* is a polysemic concept in Mauritian Creole that, apart from meaning "nation," in everyday usage is more often taken to mean "caste" among Hindus, or as synonymous with "African" or "person of African phenotype," or "Creole," depending on the context. See Eriksen (1994) on the confusion this reportedly caused during the 1982 campaign.

54. Jean Houbert has summed up the political conflict of 1983 in the follow-

ing way: "Nevertheless, a régime dominated by the M.M.M. having abandoned its radical class position would put the stress on the 'nation' and that — objectively — favored the creole fraction of the petty bourgeoisie. The stake was high: no less than the reversal of the whole ethnic political balance which had structured the régime of independence" (Houbert 1982/83, 254).

55. This possibility has an interesting parallel in Trinidad, where there is a tradition of portraying Creoles of African descent as the creators of local, national culture, in contrast to Indo-Trinidadians, who are cast as "bearers" of an essentially foreign culture (Munasinghe 1997).

56. In fact, perceived racial differences constitute a deep divide among Creoles, pitting those of African phenotype *(ti-creole)* against the light-skinned *gens de couleur,* which are to a larger proportion of French descent. This cleavage very frequently overlaps with a class difference, the *ti-creole* constituting probably the most disadvantaged and poorest group in Mauritius, while many of the *gens de couleur* are francophone members of the middle class, often employed in Franco-Mauritian-owned enterprises.

CHAPTER 2. AN INDO-MAURITIAN WORLD

1. *Endyen* literally translates as "Indian" but is nowadays used to refer exclusively to Hindus. Muslims, who are also of Indian background, are never labeled *endyen* but are known as *misilman.*

2. See Sewtohul (1990, 29–31) for an account of this process with regard to one large village in northern Mauritius, which in the meantime has developed into a sizable town.

3. This process is reminiscent of recent developments in the Weyewa language of Eastern Indonesia (Kuipers 1998).

4. While the language of the Ramcaritmanas at the time of its composition has been described as especially close to village vernaculars, and is still quite comprehensible to rural north Indian audiences, the role of more standardized varieties of modern Hindi in mediating the text has become increasingly important, not just in Mauritius, but also in India (Lutgendorf 1991, 415–20). On the role of the Ramcaritmanas in political mobilization among Hindus in colonial Fiji see Kelly (2001).

5. The white paper issued by the Ministry of Education in 1997 strikes a similar note: "The liberalisation of the audio-visual landscape and the availability of global instant information bring in their wake a form of cultural neo-colonialism that may place great stress on our complex social fabric. How successful we are in checkmating the alien effect depends on our Education System." White Paper on Pre-Primary, Primary and Secondary Education. Port Louis, September 1997. Specifically with regard to "ancestral languages" Prime Minister Navin Ramgoolam stated: "It is inconceivable that any of our ancestral languages will be cast aside in a development process which focuses only on economic growth" Address to the Hindi Pracharini Sabha, Montagne Longue, 14 December 1997.

6. A British pop music group popular at the time.

7. Roots certainly are one of the organic and in particular arboreal meta-

phors featuring prominently in talk about national communities across a wide array of ethnographic contexts (Malkki 1992).

8. Contrary to what one might infer from the party's name, its agenda is not oriented to socialism in any way.

9. See Hansen (2002) on the similar experiences reported by middle-class South Africans of Indian origin traveling to India in search of "roots."

10. See also Burn (1996, 58).

11. Jean-Claude Lau Thi Keng (1991, 88–91) has also described the historical memory of past oppression and the pro-independence stance as the main justification for contemporary Hindu political dominance given by the Hindu interlocutors in his study. His finding of contrasting Muslim attitudes rejecting Hindu dominance in Mauritian politics is especially interesting, since most Muslims lived under very similar conditions under colonialism and especially the period of indenture. Lau Thi Keng's findings support what might be called an ethnicization of past experiences of suffering, which were in fact shared across what are now perceived as communal boundaries.

12. Car brands in Mauritius are an illustrative example of how globally circulated commodities can acquire a particular ethnic sign value in local contexts. In Mauritius this applies to new automobiles, since the ethnicity of the person or family owning a particular car franchise in Mauritius is public knowledge, and most people in Mauritius purchasing a new automobile prefer to buy from someone of their own community. Therefore, Toyota in Mauritius has become the "Hindu" brand since the importer of Toyota automobiles in Mauritius is a Hindu. French brands such as Renault and Citroën are available from a Franco-Mauritian company; thus these brands are preferred by many Franco-Mauritians and upper-middle-class *gens de couleur* and Creoles. Nissan used to be the "Muslim" car in Mauritius until the franchise was sold to a Sino-Mauritian company. Since then, Muslims have tended to purchase Proton automobiles from Malaysia, as the importer is Muslim. The luxury brands Mercedes and BMW are exceptions, since the relatively few Mauritians who can afford them (import duties add between 100% and 200% to the purchasing price of new automobiles) buy them from the Franco-Mauritian company that also imports the French brands, regardless of ethnic background. It seems, then, that at the very top of the automobile market, class prestige overrides concerns for the ethnic identity of the importer. The striking relationship between car brands and ethnicity does not apply to the second-hand car market.

13. Such concerns about the sexual morality of Indian women in postindenture settings among both Indians and non-Indians have a colonial genealogy, not only in Mauritius (Carter 1994, 1995), but also in Fiji (Kelly 1991, Lal 1985) and Guyana and Trinidad (Faruqee 1996, Kale 1995). Reports about sexual assaults on Indian women in overseas colonies (Lal 1985; Kelly 1991, 46–51) and the protests this generated in India significantly contributed to the termination of the indenture system by the Government of India in 1920 (Kelly 1991, 86–120).

14. Thomas Blom Hansen describes a similar dynamic in postapartheid South Africa, where the racially conceived overall category of "Indians"

imposed by the apartheid regime is becoming less and less relevant for processes of identification among those claiming origins in India. In a manner closely resembling the situation in Mauritius, differences along boundaries of religion and sectarian affiliation, ethnicity, and language are becoming increasing institutionalized (Hansen 2002). However, unlike in Mauritius, this is occurring in a context in which people of Indian origins are often denied full membership in a new postapartheid nation often imagined through the lens of African autochthony.

15. A related incident in fact took place in Port Louis in March 1995, when the weekly *l'Indépendant* reprinted a controversial article from the French news magazine *Le Point* on the life of the prophet Muhammad. A week later the vice president of the Jummah Mosque of Port Louis and several imams associated with the Sunnat Jama'at led a protest demonstration at which copies of the paper were publicly burned. Also, the newspaper's chief editor received death threats, and the printing facilities of the paper were attacked with Molotov cocktails. However, the underlying dynamics had more to do with internal disputes among Muslims, and the desire of some among the Sunnat Jama'at, by protesting against the newspaper article, to publicly present themselves as more pious and therefore endowed with greater religious authority than their competitors, especially the Tablighi Jama'at (Jahangeer-Chojoo 1997, 177–78). Indeed, in recent years the latter has made considerable inroads into the constituency formerly dominated by the Sunnat Jama'at (Eisenlohr 2006a, 2006b). That is, the intended audience of the protesters was primarily Muslim. The protest was not aimed at demonstrating Muslim unity to a wider Mauritian public; however, this is how it was interpreted by many non-Muslims Mauritians.

16. See the discussion of the colonial history of "cultural collusion" (Burghart 1996, 278–99) behind the widespread assertion of Hindus as inherently tolerant in chapter 1.

17. *Ras* is a polysemic concept in Mauritian Creole, literally denoting "race" but more frequently used as a shorthand for ethnoreligious community, and thus used as a synonym for *kominote*.

18. The idea of a "golden Vedic age" was already central to the reformist politics of the Arya Samaj, and was then incorporated into modern Hindu nationalism by V. D. Savarkar, president of the Hindu Mahasabha from 1937 to 1942 and author of the foundational manifesto *Hindutva: Who is a Hindu?* (1923) (Gold 1991; Jaffrelot 1996 [1993], 20–27).

19. According to Oddvar Hollup, "After the 1983 election . . . Muslims felt so persecuted that many of them became hawkers or opened small businesses" (Hollup 1996, 294).

20. See Kelly (1995) for a related assessment of new Hindu missions, including the Sai Baba movement in Fiji.

21. In the early 1990s there was a dispute in a *shivala* in Mahébourg when a pandit objected to the presence of images of Satya Sai Baba placed in the temple by devotees. The Mauritius Sanatan Dharma Temples Federation, to which the temple belongs, eventually decided in favor of the devotees. Images of Sai Baba are now commonplace in *shivala*s throughout Mauritius.

CHAPTER 3. SOCIAL SEMIOTICS OF LANGUAGE

1. I use the concepts of style and register to refer to linguistic formations such as those known as *Creole fransise* or purist Bhojpuri. With the notion of register I highlight their link to particular stereotypic social activities (i.e., Hindu worship) and images of persons engaging in these. The focus here is on the indexical links between the linguistic entity, social practices, and types of persons, also suggesting that these links are to some degree institutionalized (Agha 2004). With style, I pay attention to interconnected processes of social and linguistic differentiation, a "social semiosis of distinctiveness" (Irvine 2001, 23). I thus do not use the concept of style in the traditional sociolinguistic sense — as slight individual speaker variation relative to the speech situation at hand (as opposed to switching between registers or varieties) (Labov 1972). Rather, following Irvine, I use the notion of style to point to the processes by which social distinctions among activities and people are mediated by differentiation between registers and varieties, and vice versa. In this sense, style as a theoretical concept also points to the social process of enregisterment of linguistic forms and social values, which makes registers with their indexical loading appear distinct from other such formations (Agha 2004, 37).

2. General Malartic was the French governor of Mauritius from 1792 to 1800. He sided with the locally dominant colonists when the French National Assembly declared slavery abolished in 1794, a move that was fiercely resisted by the French colonists. He is remembered for a flexible, even opportunistic, style of politics, always ready to change principles in the face of a superior power.

3. The French-lexifier Creole of St. Lucia (Kwéyòl) does not fully fit the Creole continuum paradigm, since the dominant European standardized language in St. Lucia is English and it would be difficult to describe basilectal Kwéyòl, "High" or anglicized Kwéyòl, and English in terms of a linguistic continuum (Garrett 2000). Nevertheless, as in the other examples, the emerging "high," or formal, variety or register of Kwéyòl exhibits extensive influence from the dominant standard language with which it coexists in the same sociolinguistic system, even if the latter was not the lexifier language at the time Kwéyòl was created.

4. In his pioneering work on Mauritian Creole, Charles Baissac speculates on the origins of Mauritian Creole as the imperfect acquisition of French by African slaves in early eighteenth-century Mauritius in the following terms:

> The slave had to learn the language of the master and to speak it instantly. But, less even than the Germanic barbarians at the time when their conquest led them to establish themselves on Roman land, our slaves were not able to make use of the delicate instrument, which a twelve-century-old civilization had slowly perfected for its use. These exact relations between words, this luxury of modifications in their form or their inflexion following their place or their function, these subtle as well as varied articulations between different parts of the clause or phrase, all these means, all this machinery, so many fetters which they necessarily had to break, and which they did break. . . . One sees, as a method of construction, this is rudimentary, we have to do with a wall built of dry stones, with the pure and simple juxtaposition of materials more or less impaired during their fall. Could such a system allow the erection of any building? Alas! Hardly a humble one, a quite humble construction, and

still under the explicit condition that it had no ambition to reach more than a few
feet above the ground. (Baissac 1880, iii–v)

Baissac establishes a series of metaphoric links between the grammatical complexity and richness of the French language and what he sees as the high stage of
French civilization. In contrast, he compares African and Malagasy slaves in
Mauritius to barbarians, suggesting a direct relationship between their presumed
lack of civilization and what he sees as the lack of structural complexity of Mauritian Creole. Note especially the use of the building metaphor for bringing
together the themes of "civilization" and language, and for "explaining" how
civilizations and languages are constructions differing in the "height" they are
able to achieve. The imagining of an iconic correspondence between the structural simplicity of Creole and the state of civilization of its speakers inherent in
these images has had a powerful effect in justifying the subordination of Creole
under French.

5. The Franco-Mauritian Baissac provides us with a fully formulated theory
of "clarity" with respect to French and Creole. In this, he mainly focuses on the
idea that French is a medium highly suitable for expressing "abstract" ideas, a
feature he claims is completely absent in the case of Creole:

> From barbarism, where the slave-ships *(négriers)* went to take them, abruptly placed
> through slavery in the presence of the new world of ideas inherent in the French lan-
> guage, our blacks boldly stopped their ears and shut their eyes, and, beyond the nar-
> row circle of the material life, they wanted to ignore everything, feeling themselves
> incapable to understand anything. Above all abstraction encountered them as invin-
> cibly rebellious, to the point that the abstract verb *par excellence,* the essential verb
> "to be" does not exist in Creole, where it is impossible to say: God is. Descartes was
> lucky to have another language at his disposal. . . . The conquests in this field are al-
> ways and everywhere the slowest, one knows it, and only in Mauritius the Catholic
> religion has opened to these coarse spirits a few glimpses of the world of the pure idea
> through its ardent proselytism in the last thirty-five years. (Baissac 1880, viii–ix)

Here we are presented with another key ideological element often used to
establish the inferiority of Creole vis-à-vis French: the assumed superior capacity
of French for clearly expressing abstract ideas. This again is presented as in stark
contrast to Creole, seen as unable to convey the world of "pure ideas" because of
its crudeness and its inherent lack of clarity, while ideas of "clarity" have been
central to the myth of the superiority of the French language since the French
Revolution (Swiggers 1990). The crucial point, however, is once again the imagination of shared qualities of simplicity and crudity ascribed simultaneously to
the Creole language and its stereotypic speakers. This perceived isomorphism
makes the assumption of Creole as a language for "coarse spirits" seem natural
and its hierarchically determined relation to French appear self-evident.

6. The term "legitimate language" evokes Pierre Bourdieu's discussion of language as a particular form of symbolic capital (Bourdieu 1991). However, the
Mauritian scenario I analyze is obviously very different from Bourdieu's model of
the sociolinguistic situation of France. The latter is predicated on the dominance
of a single "legitimate language" over a single, integrated "linguistic market,"
largely denying the importance of the covert prestige of substandard varieties

highlighted by sociolinguists such as Trudgill (1983). In contrast, I highlight the plurality and contested nature of linguistic norms in Mauritius.

7. Viranjini Munasinghe notes the prevalence of a very similar pattern of residence in Indo-Trinidadian villages (Munasinghe 2001, 159).

8. The "redundant" form of the Bhojpuri noun, such as in *raja-wa* (versus "short" *raja*) often indexes either familiarity or slight contempt with regard to the noun.

9. *Samachar* is also the name of the Hindi news bulletins on Mauritian Broadcasting Corporation television, which is probably the context of use for this term most familiar to many Mauritians.

CHAPTER 4. COLONIAL EDUCATION, ETHNOLINGUISTIC IDENTIFICATIONS, AND THE ORIGINS OF ANCESTRAL LANGUAGES

1. The colonial specificity Chatterjee ascribes to a "reactive" nationalism centered on the celebration of an "inner, spiritual" sphere as the focus of difference is doubtful, since its dynamic is also familiar from some strands of German nationalism, based on a distinction between a (Western) *Zivilisation* of external technical trappings and *Kultur* as a sphere of superior spiritual values and orientations. In Germany, this binary distinction was mobilized by nationalist intellectuals, especially during the First World War and its aftermath (Sontheimer 1990).

2. In this chapter my main concern is with Indian immigrants and Indo-Mauritians in a wider sense, as opposed to the focus on Hindu Mauritians in other chapters. There are two reasons for this. First, colonial authorities whose policies I analyze in this chapter did not treat Hindus and Muslims of indenture background in markedly different ways. Second, the antagonism between Hindus and Muslims so important for contemporary Mauritian politics and "communalism" only developed in the first half of the twentieth century, and therefore the distinction only becomes important towards the end of this chapter's discussion.

3. With respect to India, Sumathi Ramaswamy (1997) and David Washbrook (1991) also stress that colonial linguistic knowledge was often appropriated and used by groups among the colonized in ways opposed to the interests and intentions of those who had produced it.

4. Minute by Governor W. Nicolay on the expenses of the colony. In Recueil des Lois, Ordonnances, Proclamations, Notes et Avis du Gouvernement, Publiés à l'Ile Maurice l'Année 1838, p. 42–43.

5. Despatch of 12 Aug 1856 of Mr. Labouchère, Secretary of State for the Colonies, to Governor Higginson. In *Official Documents*, edited by the Catholic Union, series I, 1844–1887 (Port Louis: Imprimerie Engelbrecht, 1891).

6. Annual General Report on the Government Schools of Mauritius for the Year 1870, Browne to Edward Selby Smyth (Major General).

7. "The mental capabilities of a malabar child are of no inferior order. Quite the reverse. The intellectual, rather than the reflective faculties, predominate. Their perseverance is remarkable, and what they lack in talent they make up in tact. They are found to be affectionate and confiding, when properly managed;- cunning, vindictive, and sly, when ill treated. They possess vices inherent to their

nationality, but they are not destitute of virtues which would do credit to any race." Annual Report on Elementary Schools in Mauritius Supported or Assisted by the Government During the Year 1864 by J. Comber Browne, Superintendent of Schools. "Intellectually speaking, the Indian is perhaps superior to the Creole, whilst in generosity and affection, somewhat his inferior. The attachment of the one mostly arises from motives either selfish or mercenary; whilst that of the other springs spontaneously from a naturally warm heart." Annual General Report on the Government and Elementary Schools of Mauritius for the Year 1869, Browne to Governor Barkly.

8. "Every one familiar with the social habits of the Indian knows well how necessary it is that he should be placed under incessant supervision." Annual General Report on the Government and Elementary Schools of Mauritius for the Year 1869, Browne to Governor Barkly. See also Report on Elementary Schools in Mauritius. Supported or Assisted by Government During the Year 1865 by J. Comber Browne.

9. Annual General Report on the Government Schools of Mauritius for the Year 1870.

10. Report on Elementary Schools in Mauritius. Supported or Assisted by Government During the Year 1865 by J. Comber Browne.

11. Report on Elementary Schools in Mauritius Supported or Assisted by Government During the Year 1865 by J. Comber Browne.

12. Report on Elementary Schools in Mauritius 1868. Browne to Sir Henry Barkly, Governor.

13. Report on Elementary Schools in Mauritius. Supported or Assisted by Government During the Year 1865 by J. Comber Browne.

14. Browne's career and political concerns provide a very clear example of the mutual influences that policies of colonial control and bourgeois policies directed towards the lower classes and marginal groups in the European metropole had on each other. In this way, Browne's interests represent a vivid illustration of what Dirks has described as bringing colonialism "back home" (Dirks 1992).

15. Report on Primary Instruction in Mauritius for the Year ending 31.12.1876. By J. Comber Browne. These concerns also provide further evidence for Marina Carter's argument that in coexistence with the harshly oppressive indenture system, which has been likened to a "new system of slavery" (Tinker 1974), Indian settlement in Mauritius with its family and kin group recruitment also displayed similarity to the *sardari* or *kangani* style of migration prominent in the export of Indian labor to Ceylon and Malaya (Carter 1995). In contrast to slavery, this type of migration enabled the reproduction of religious and folk-educational institutions, which could be found all over Mauritius from the earliest days of indenture.

16. "I venture to submit that if children were trained to speak, read and write correctly in their own language — the usual language of the colony, adopted like, in a pure or corrupted form, by the European, the African, the Asiatic — a more real development of the moral and intellectual faculties would be more easily obtained." Extract from Annual Report of the Inspector of Roman Catholic Aided-Schools for the Year 1883. In Minute Papers of the Council of Education

1878–84. The "language of the colony" meant here, spoken by everyone in either a "pure" or "corrupted" form, is of course French.

17. Minute by Governor A. P. Phayre, 10 December 1878. In Report on Primary Instruction in Mauritius for the Schoolyear 1877–1878 by the Superintendent and Inspector of Schools.

18. Charles Bruce was also Rector of the Royal College, Mauritius's most prominent and for a long time only secondary school. He later became Governor of Guyana and was knighted.

19. Memorandum on Primary Education in Mauritius. By the Hon. C. Bruce, Colonial Secretary, 1 December 1883. In *Education in Mauritius, Official Documents*, edited by the Catholic Union, series I, 1844–1887 (Port Louis: Imprimerie Engelbrecht, 1891).

20. Minute of 17 February 1875 by W. H. Ashley to Edward Newton, Colonial Secretary, in answer to the latter's minute of 29 January 1875. Annex to Report on Primary Instruction in Mauritius for the year 1874, by J. Comber Browne, Esquire.

21. Report of the Superintendent of Government Schools on Primary Instruction in Mauritius for the year 1882. W. H. Ashley to Governor F. Napier Broome.

22. Report on the Roman Catholic Aided Schools for the year 1885, by A. de Boucherville, Inspector of Roman Catholic Aided Schools.

23. Council of Education Papers. Annexure I to Minutes of Council of Education no. 5 of 11th June 1891.

24. Council of Education Papers. Annexure I to Minutes of Council of Education no. 5 of 11th June 1891. My emphasis.

25. Colony of Mauritius. Annual Report of the Education Department for the year ending 31st Dec. 1950.

26. Colony of Mauritius. Annual Report on Education for 1911.

27. Memorandum on Education in Mauritius, 1913, by W. T. A. Emtage, Director of Public Instruction. Port Louis, Government Printing Office.

28. Colony of Mauritius. Education Code. Mauritius, Government Press, 1916.

29. Memorandum on Education in Mauritius, 1913, p. 13.

30. This was certainly far from a linear development, free from setbacks. British plans to give citizenship and voting rights to Indians in the empire already existed in the 1920s. When white settlers in Kenya resisted this policy, the colonial authorities gave in because they feared a secession of Kenya from the empire. After the attempts to introduce these reforms in Kenya had failed, the reforms were abandoned in Mauritius and other colonies, too (Tinker 1976; Kaplan and Kelly 1994, 138).

31. See for example Ministry of Education and Institutions. The New Education Code 1958, Mauritius Government Publicity, p. 9–10.

32. Colony of Mauritius. The Annual Report of the Superintendent of Schools for the Year 1931.

33. Delegate Leclézio, in Colony of Mauritius. Debates of the Council of Government 1941, Session of 27 May 1941.

34. Delegate A. Raffray, in Colony of Mauritius. Debates of the Council of Government 1941. Session of 27 May 1941.

35. Delegate Leclézio, in Colony of Mauritius. Debates of the Council of Government 1941, Session of 27 May 1941.

36. Governor Sir Bede Edmund Hugh Clifford, in Colony of Mauritius. Debates of the Council of Government 1941, Session of 27 May 1941.

37. Delegate Osman, in Colony of Mauritius. Debates of the Council of Government 1941. Session of 27 May 1941. According to the census of 1944, the population of Mauritius numbered 419,185.

38. Delegate Ramgoolam, in Colony of Mauritius. Debates of the Council of Government 1941. Session of 27 May 1941.

39. Report on Education in Mauritius. Port Louis, Government Printer 1941.

40. Colony of Mauritius. Report of the Education Department for the Year Ending 30th June, 1944.

41. Colony of Mauritius. Report of the Education Department for the Year Ending 30th June, 1947.

42. Colony of Mauritius. Annual Report of the Education Department for the Year Ending 30th June, 1949.

43. Colony of Mauritius. Annual Report of the Education Department for the Year 1952.

44. Colony of Mauritius. Annual Report of the Education Department for the Year Ending 31st December, 1953.

45. Annual Report of the Education Department for the Year Ending 31st December 1951. Port Louis, Government Printers 1952.

46. Annual Report of the Education Department for the Year Ending 31st December 1950. See also the statements of delegates Ramgoolam and Seeneevassen in Colony of Mauritius. Debates of the Legislative Council, 4 July 1950.

47. During my fieldwork, several of my older Indo-Mauritian interlocutors stressed this point, remembering their school days in the 1940s and 1950s.

48. Colony of Mauritius. Debates of the Legislative Council, 11. April 1950.

49. Colony of Mauritius. Debates of the Legislative Council, 11. April 1950.

50. Delegate Venkatasamy. in Colony of Mauritius. Debates of the Legislative Assembly, 4 December 1956.

51. Colony of Mauritius, Central Statistical Office. Census of Mauritius and its Dependencies 1952.

52. Delegate Mohamed, in Colony of Mauritius. Debates of the Legislative Council, 9 March 1954.

53. Delegate Gujadhur, in Colony of Mauritius. Debates of the Legislative Council, 9 March 1954.

54. Colony of Mauritius. Debates of the Legislative Council, 9 March 1954.

55. Delegate de Chazal, in Colony of Mauritius. Debates of the Legislative Council, 9 March 1954.

56. Delegate Koenig, in Colony of Mauritius. Debates of the Legislative Council, 30 March 1954.

57. Delegate Osman, in Colony of Mauritius. Debates of the Legislative Council, 30 March 1954.

58. Delegate Seeneevassen, in Colony of Mauritius. Debates of the Legislative Council, 9 March 1954.

59. See the more detailed discussion of the problematic of "mother tongue" in Mauritius in chapter 1.

60. Delegate S. Bissoondoyal, in Colony of Mauritius. Debates of the Legislative Assembly, 30 November 1954. According to the 1952 census, the total population of Mauritius at the time was 501,415.

61. Annual Report on Education for 1967. Port Louis, Government Printers, 1968.

62. Mandarin is also taught in schools having a significant presence of Sino-Mauritian students, though the ideological and political ramifications are quite different from the Hindu case. The small but economically very significant Sino-Mauritian community keeps a low profile politically in Mauritius, and is much less concerned about state support for their ancestral language than Hindus, who draw an ideological link between the state support for Indian languages and their claim to be the politically dominant group in the country.

63. The promoters of Urdu tend to be followers of the still dominant Sunnat Jama'at, the local representative of the Ahl-e Sunnat va Jama'at, one of the movements of Islamic reformism that emerged in the second half of the nineteenth century in colonial India. Established by the 'alim Ahmad Riza Khan Barelwi (1856–1921) (Sanyal 1996), this movement is also known as the Barelwi tradition after the North Indian town of Bareilly known as a seat of Islamic learning and as the residence of the movement's founder. The advocates of Arabic as the ancestral language of Mauritian Muslims often belong to the local Tablighi Jama'at and the Islamic Circle, both descended from the famous Deoband school. One of the key points of contention in the debates between the Deobandi and Barelwi reform movements in the nineteenth century, continuing until the present day, is the issue of spiritual intercession by the prophet Mohammad and Sufi saint-teachers on behalf of believers. The Ahl-e Sunnat va Jama'at strongly advocates practices aimed at such intercession, while the Deobandis intensely oppose such practices, castigating them as illicit innovation *(bid'a)*. The debates between followers of the two traditions in Mauritius strongly resemble those conducted in India and Pakistan. The Islamic Circle of Mauritius was founded in the late 1950s by a Pakistani follower of Mawlana Mawdudi, the founder of the Jama'at-i Islami, today the most prominent Islamist political party in Pakistan.

CHAPTER 5. PERFORMING PURITY

1. Richard Barz's analysis of the relationship between Standard Hindi and Mauritian Bhojpuri also suggests such a "hinduization" of Mauritian Bhojpuri. Barz claims that the relationship between the two languages is "symbiotic" (Barz 1980, 7), because Mauritian Bhojpuri supplies Standard Hindi with "living roots" in Mauritius, represented by a "large and linguistically healthy body of speakers of Mauritian Bhojpuri" (Barz 1980, 11). L. P. Ramyead also endorses this perspective (1985, 267). Barz does describe the presence of Muslim speakers of Bhojpuri and concludes that such a "symbiotic" relationship could in principle also link Urdu and Mauritian Bhojpuri. Other authors, in order to underscore what they see as the close relationship between Hindi and Mauritian Bhojpuri, have gone as far as claiming Bhojpuri to be a kind of Creole Hindi. "Bhojpuri is

to Hindi what Creole is to French" (Bhuckory 1988 [1967], 9). Peter Stein, too, suggests that Mauritian Bhojpuri is a Creole language (Stein 1982, 131). However, he differs from Bhuckory in describing Bhojpuri as standing in a diglossic relationship with respect to both Hindi and Urdu (135–36).

2. During my field research, older interlocutors repeatedly stressed that especially before the Second World War it was common for even Franco-Mauritian overseers in the plantation economy and rural Sino-Mauritian retail merchants to be competent in Mauritian Bhojpuri.

3. Sarita Boodhoo established the Mauritius Bhojpuri Institute in 1982. This institution, which also houses a small library, holds organized folklore festivals, poetry recitals, and public talks aimed at promoting the use of Bhojpuri in Mauritius. The activities of the Bhojpuri Institute cast Bhojpuri as deeply linked to Hindu traditions. The Mahatma Gandhi Institute, an academic institution originally set up as a joint venture with the Indian government, is dedicated to both research in and the promotion of Asian and African cultures and languages in Mauritius, its main emphasis being Indian traditions. This institution plays an important role in the training of teachers and the production of teaching materials for ancestral languages and also has a department of Bhojpuri and Oral Traditions whose members are working on the documentation of Bhojpuri verbal art, as well as on a dictionary of Mauritian Bhojpuri. Suchita Ramdin, head of the department, has published a major collection of Mauritian Bhojpuri folksongs performed at Hindu rites of passage (sanskar), principally weddings, with analysis and commentary in Hindi (Ramdin 1989).

4. Compared to television, Mauritian Broadcasting Corporation radio features a somewhat greater variety of Bhojpuri language programming, ranging from folklore programs in which Bhojpuri folktales and jokes are transmitted and programs with Hindu religious content to radio call-in shows in which listeners can ask for Hindi film songs to be played.

5. For a literary reference on this function of the noun suffix -wa in Mauritian Bhojpuri with regard to names, see the memoirs of the writer, lexicographer, and school inspector Goswami Sewtohul, who grew up in Rivière-du-Rempart (Sewtohul 1996, 172).

6. The semiotic process of erasure is often part of representations of social differentiation through language ideology (Irvine and Gal 2000).

7. In 1986, a secretary of the Mauritius Sanatan Dharm Temples Federation and the Indian pandit Acharya Ravindra Nagar together started to offer training courses leading to the priesthood open to all Hindus with a minimum level of education. The Babuji-Maraz members of the association, until then dominating the organization, immediately protested and sought the removal of the secretary responsible for this innovation. The latter countermobilized and was elected president in a "coup," leading to a shift in power from the higher castes to the mid-ranking Vaish caste in Mauritius's largest Hindu organization. Temples dominated by the Babuji-Maraz subsequently split off from the Mauritius Sanatan Dharm Temples Federation, whereas in the Federation access to becoming a pandit was opened to the Vaish caste group, the numerically largest and politically most influential in Mauritius. The temples of the Arya Sabha, the local branch of

the Hindu reformist movement Arya Samaj, were never under the leadership of the Babuji-Maraz, since this movement rejects the privileges of higher castes.

CHAPTER 6. CALIBRATIONS OF DISPLACEMENT

1. Burton Benedict's monograph on the Indians in Mauritius, based on research in the late 1950s, provides a vivid account of the "Indian revival" after the Second World War. Benedict stresses that this cultural and political revival by no means led to a homogenization of the Indian community but rather provided the impetus for the strengthening of separate ethnoreligious identities among Indo-Mauritians (Benedict 1961, 36–38).

2. Following Bakhtin (1981, 84), I use the term "chronotope" as referring to types of temporal-spatial relationships, acknowledging that temporal relations necessarily involve spatial relations and vice versa. While Bakhtin used the concept of chronotope to analyze literary genres, I extend its use to distinguish different ways of forming ethnonational communities.

3. Drawing on the work of Ricoeur, Joel Robbins analyzes a similar temporal contrast in his work on "everyday millenarism" among the Urapmin in Papua New Guinea (Robbins 2001).

4. Reinhart Koselleck has located the shift away from a sense of temporality shaped by the certainty of an imminent doomsday towards a sense of history "open to the new and without limit" in the aftermath of the devastating religious wars that followed the Reformation in sixteenth- and seventeenth-century Europe. The change occurred when these wars failed to bring about the end of times they were initially believed to herald (Koselleck 1985, 241–42).

5. In this context, the phenomenological critique of historicism is also consonant with Gadamer's philosophical hermeneutics. Gadamer argues that any sort of intuitive or unmediated transposition of oneself into the mind of an interlocutor or an author of times past is impossible. According to him, the rapprochement of interpretative horizons is only feasible on the basis of one's own "prejudgment" *(Vorverständnis)*, which plays a constructive and essential part in any hermeneutic process. In an approach similar to the phenomenological critique of historicism, Gadamer emphasizes how the interpretation of the past is thus necessarily shaped by the situation of the present. In this regard, he also stresses the importance of understanding the *Wirkungsgeschichte,* or "history of effects," of a text, analyzing how a particular text or representation of an event has accumulated additional layers of meaning or been transformed by previous interpretations through interpreters located in different historical contexts and finally by interpretations in terms of our own historical position and knowledge interests (Gadamer 1982).

6. *Le Mauricien,* 11 March 2002.

7. Hindu Maha Sabha. Souvenir Magazine 1998, 100th Anniversary of Maha Shivratri Pilgrimage to Ganga Talab, p. 39.

8. On a table, a newspaper article entitled *Le lac mystique* from the daily *L'Express* dated 21 February 1971 retelling the legend was reproduced: *Grand Bassin naquit d'une larme versée par la déesse Ganga lorsqu'elle vit s'expatrier*

ses enfants pour l'île lointaine et que Vaayu, le dieu des vents a précieusement recueillie et emportée pour la laisser tomber dans un creux sur les hauteurs mauriciennes afin qu'elle puisse refraîchir le front brûlant et le cœur meutri des générations futures. Cette larme s'est multipliée et emplit maintenant Grand Bassin, le lac mystique profond et silencieux, qui fascine l'âme et lui fait connaître une étrange plénitude et ou les descendants des premiers émigrants venues des bords de Ganga vont chaque année pour puiser l'offrande à Siva.

9. A kinship term referring to mother's brother. Here it is used as a respectful term of address somewhat less associated with patriarchal authority than *chacha* (father's brother).

10. Two terms for God, translatable as "supreme father" and "supreme soul."

11. Recalling the qualities of *Creole fransise* discussed in chapter 3, the "intermediary" quality of these purist items also bears some resemblance to what Kathryn Woolard has termed bivalency, "the use by a bilingual of words or segments that could 'belong' equally, descriptively and even prescriptively, to both codes" (Woolard 1998, 7), since these elements could be identified as either Hindi of Bhojpuri. What is different, however, is that in contrast to the Catalan-Castilian case described by Woolard, this use of bivalent words does not lead to discourse impossible to define as either Bhojpuri or Hindi. Also in contrast to Woolard's case, where the bilingual phenomenon blurring linguistic boundaries is also associated with the voicing of dual identities, the use of intermediary Hindi-Bhojpuri elements becomes part of a purist perspective on Hindu identity in Mauritius.

12. According to the preface to a recent collection of Mauritian Bhojpuri folk songs, proverbs, and stories written by a Hindi teacher and sponsored by the Human Service Trust, the two languages are so close as to be virtually interdependent: "In Mauritius the relation between Bhojpuri and Hindi is like that between soul and body. If in the body, Hindi, the soul, Bhojpuri, will remain alive, then Hindi will be on the road of progress. If Hindi remains alive, then the culture *(samskṛti)* will remain alive and we can be proud to call ourselves Hindus" (Mohit 1994, 7).

13. In a commemorative publication dedicated to the efforts of various Hindu organizations for the propagation and dissemination of Hindi in Mauritius, a former minister and senior official of the Hindi Speaking Union states that "Hindi in the form of Bhojpuri used to be the link language among Indians of the entire island of Mauritius." Ravindra Garbaran in *Pankaj: Hindī pracāriṇī sabhā kī sahityik traimāsik patrikā* (Pankaj: Literary quarterly journal of the Society for the Propagation of Hindi), 4:10 (1997), 5.

14. Keshvadutt Chintamani in Pankaj: *Pankaj: Hindī pracāriṇī sabhā kī sahityik traimāsik patrikā* (Pankaj: Literary quarterly journal of the Society for the Propagation of Hindi), 2:4 (1995), 42.

15. *apni matṛbhāṣā ko sīkhna aur sīkhāna hamārā pratam dharmik kartavya hai* (Roy 1970: 139).

16. The writings of Abhimanyu Unuth, the most prominent Hindi writer of Mauritius and winner of several literary prizes in India, focus on the suffering of the Indian indentured laborers during the colonial period, as in his first major novel, *Lāl pasīnā* (Red sweat). In an essay entitled "Hindi's Journey of Struggle in

Mauritius" *(Mariśas mẽ hindī kī sangarṣ yātrā)*, he sets out by graphically describing the toil and abuse the indentured ancestors of the Hindus in Mauritius were submitted to: "While mingling blood and sweat in the cane fields not even the chance of a little rest was given to those Indian laborers" (Unuth 1988, 139). He then goes on to depict how Hindi, especially in the form of collective reading and chanting of the Ramcaritmanas, became a form of resistance against the oppression by the planters, who, he claims, tried to suppress the learning of Hindi among the Indian laborers. Unuth's particular version of remembering the situation of the Indian indentured immigrants in colonial Mauritius ends with the claim that the cultivation of Hindi represents the greatest and most crucial achievement in the "preservation" of Indian culture in Mauritius. "The biggest reason for the greatness of Indianness and of Indian culture in Mauritius has been the creative process in Hindi" (Unuth 1988, 143).

17. In some ways this situation recalls Keith Basso's analysis of ancestral place names among the Western Apache, where these names serve as vehicles of ancestral authority (1988, 110–13) and evoke the mental presence of a spatially and temporally removed world in communicative encounters. Among the Western Apache, "speaking with names" not only affirms the value of ancestral traditions and knowledge but is also used to express charitable concern for other peoples' worries (1988, 114–15).

18. Frederic Jameson's thesis of an "end of temporality," superseding a sense of "deep time" in which past, present, and future mutually constitute each other, postulates another normalization of temporality, here traced to the workings of postmodern capitalism.

References

Agha, Asif. 1993. Grammatical and Indexical Convention in Honorific Discourse. *Journal of Linguistic Anthropology* 3(2): 131–63.

———. 1994. Honorification. *Annual Review of Anthropology* 23: 277–302.

———. 2004. Registers of language. In *A Companion to Linguistic Anthropology*, ed. Alessandro Duranti. Malden, MA: Blackwell.

Alladin, Ibrahim. 1993. *Economic Miracle in the Indian Ocean: Can Mauritius Show the Way?* Rose-Hill: Editions de l'Océan Indien.

Allen, Richard B. 1984. Indian Immigrants and the Beginnings of the Grand Morcellement (1860–1885). In *Indians Overseas: The Mauritian Experience*, ed. U. Bissoondoyal. Moka: Mahatma Gandhi Institute.

———. 1999. *Slaves, Freedmen, and Indentured Laborers in Colonial Mauritius*. Cambridge: Cambridge University Press.

Anderson, Benedict. 1991. *Imagined Communities: Reflections on the Origin and Spread of Nationalism*. London: Verso.

———. 1994. Exodus. *Critical Inquiry* 20 (winter 1994): 314–27.

Appadurai, Arjun. 1996a. *Modernity at Large: Cultural Dimensions of Globalization*. Minneapolis: University of Minnesota Press.

———. 1996b. Sovereignty without Territoriality: Notes for a Postnational Geography. In *The Geography of Identity*, ed. Patricia Yaeger. Ann Arbor: University of Michigan Press.

Auerbach, Erich. 1953. *Mimesis: The Representation of Reality in Western Literature*. Princeton: Princeton University Press.

Axel, Brian Keith. 2001. *The Nation's Tortured Body: Violence, Representation, and the Formation of a Sikh "Diaspora."* Durham: Duke University Press.

Baissac, Charles. 1880. *Étude sur le patois créole mauricien*. Nancy: Berger-Levrault.

Baker, Philip. 1969. The Language Situation in Mauritius with Special Reference to Mauritian Creole. *African Language Review* 8: 73–93.

———. 1972. *Kreol: A Description of Mauritian Creole*. London: C. Hurst.

———. 1982. On the Origins of the First Mauritians and of the Creole Language of Their Descendants: A Refutation of Chaudenson's "Bourbonnais" Theory. In *Isle de France Creole: Affinities and Origin*, by Philip Baker and Chris Corne. Ann Arbor: Karoma.

———. 1984. Review of *Connaissance et emploi des langues à l'Ile Maurice*, by Peter Stein. *Language in Society* 13: 390–96.

Baker, Philip, and Amarnath Ramnah. 1988. Recognizing Mauritian Bhojpuri. In *Language Transplanted: The Development of Overseas Hindi*, by Richard K. Barz and Jeff Siegel. Wiesbaden: Harrossowitz.

Baker, Philip, and P. Ramnah. 1985. Mauritian Bhojpuri: An Indo-Aryan Language Spoken in a Predominantly Creolophone Society. Papers in Pidgin and Creole Linguistics no. 4, *Pacific Linguistics* A-72: 215–38.

Baker, Philip, and Vinesh Y. Hookoomsing. 1987. *Morisiyen — English — Français: Diksyoner kreol morisyen*. Paris: L'Harmattan.

Bakhtin, Mikhail M. 1981. *The Dialogic Imagination*. Austin: University of Texas Press.

———. 1986. *The Problem of Speech Genres*. In *Speech Genres and Other Late Essays*. Austin: University of Texas Press.

Balibar, Etienne. 1991. The Nation Form: History and Ideology. In *Race, Nation, Class: Ambiguous Identities*, ed. Etienne Balibar and Immanuel Wallerstein. London and New York: Verso.

Bambach, Charles R. 1995. *Heidegger, Dilthey, and the Crisis of Historicism*. Ithaca: Cornell University Press.

Baptiste, Espelencia Marie. 2002. A Nation Deferred: Language, Ethnicity, and the Reproduction of Social Inequalities in Mauritian Primary Schools. Ph.D. diss., Johns Hopkins University.

Barz, Richard K. 1980. The Cultural Significance of Hindi in Mauritius. *South Asia*, n.s., 3(1): 1–13.

Barz, Richard K., and Jeff Siegel, eds. 1988. *Language Transplanted: The Development of Overseas Hindi*. Wiesbaden: Harrassowitz.

Basso, Keith H. 1988. "Speaking with Names": Language and Landscape among the Western Apache. *Cultural Anthropology* 3(2): 99–130.

Basu, Amrita. 1996. Mass Movement or Elite Conspiracy? The Puzzle of Hindu Nationalism. In *Contesting the Nation: Religion, Community, and the Politics of Democracy in India*, ed. David Ludden. Philadelphia: University of Pennsylvania Press.

Bates, Crispin. 2000. *Communalism and Identity among South Asians in Diaspora*. Heidelberg Papers in South Asian and Comparative Politics, Working Paper no. 2. Heidelberg: South Asia Institute, University of Heidelberg.

Bauman, Richard, and Charles L. Briggs. 1990. Poetics and Performance as Critical Perspectives on Language and Social Life. *Annual Review of Anthropology* 19: 59–88.

Beejadhur, Aunauth. 1935. *Les indiens à l'Ile Maurice*. Port Louis: Typographie Moderne.

Benedict, Burton. 1961. *Indians in a Plural Society: A Report on Mauritius*. London: Her Majesty's Stationery Office.

Benjamin, Walter. 1968. *Illuminations*. New York: Harcourt, Brace & World.

Benoist, Jean. 1985. Les îles créoles: Martinique, Guadeloupe, Réunion, Maurice. *Hérodote* 37–38 (2–3): 53–75.

———. 1989. De l'Inde à Maurice et de Maurice à l'Inde: La reincarnation d'une société. *Carbet* 9: 163–84.

Bernabé, Jean, Patrick Chamoiseau, and Rapaël Confiant. 1993. *Eloge de la Créolité*. Edition bilingue. Paris: Gallimard.

Bhabha, Homi. 1990. DissemiNation: Time, Narrative and the Margins of the Modern Nation. In *Nation and Narration*, ed. Homi Bhabha. London: Routledge.

———. 1994. *The Location of Culture*. London: Routledge.

Bhatia, Tej K. 1982. Transplanted South Asian Languages: An Overview. *Studies in the Linguistic Sciences* 11(2): 129–34.

Bhuckory, Somdath. 1988 [1967]. *Hindi in Mauritius*. 2d ed. Rose-Hill: Editions de l'Océan Indien.

Bissoondoyal, Uttam. 1990. *Promises to Keep*. New Delhi: Wiley Eastern.

Blom, Jan-Petter, and John J. Gumperz. 1972. Social Meaning in Linguistic Structure: Code-Switching in Norway. In *Directions in Sociolinguistics*, ed. John J. Gumperz and Dell Hymes. Oxford: Basil Blackwell.

Blommaert, Jan, ed. 1999. *Language Ideological Debates*. Berlin: Mouton de Gruyter.

Bokhorst-Heng, Wendy. 1999. Singapore's Speak Mandarin Campaign: Language Ideological Debates in the Imagining of the Nation. In *Language Ideological Debates*, ed. Jan Blommaert. Berlin: Mouton de Gruyter.

Bonniol, Jean-Luc. 1985. L'aire créole: Du modèle historique aux enjeux politiques actuels. *Hérodote* 37–38 (2–3): 77–89.

Borneman, John. 1992. *Belonging in the Two Berlins: Kin, State, Nation*. Cambridge: Cambridge University Press.

Bourdieu, Pierre. 1977. *Outline of a Theory of Practice*. Cambridge: Cambridge University Press.

———. 1991. *Language and Symbolic Power*. Cambridge: Harvard University Press.

Bowman, Larry. 1991. *Mauritius: Democracy and Development in the Indian Ocean*. Boulder: Westview.

Brass, Paul R. 1974. *Language and Politics in North India*. London, New York: Cambridge University Press.

Briggs, Charles, and Richard Bauman. 1992. Genre, Intertextuality and Social Power. *Journal of Linguistic Anthropology* 2(2): 131–72.

Brown, R., and A. Gilman. 1972 [1960]. The Pronouns of Power and Solidarity. In *Language and Social Context*, ed. Pier Paolo Giglioli. Harmondsworth: Penguin.

Browne, D. R. 1996. *Electronic Media and Indigenous Peoples: A Voice of Our Own?* Ames: Iowa State University Press.

Brubaker, Rogers. 1992. *Citizenship and Nationhood in France and Germany*. Cambridge: Harvard University Press.

Bunwaree, Sheila S. 1994. *Mauritian Education in a Global Economy*. Rose-Hill: Editions de l'Océan Indien.

Burghart, Richard. 1996. *The Conditions of Listening: Essays on Religion, History and Politics in South Asia.* Delhi: Oxford University Press.

Burn, Nalini. 1996. Mauritius. In *Gender and Industrialization: Mauritius, Bangladesh, Sri Lanka,* ed. Uma Kothari and Vidula Nababsing. Rose-Hill: Editions de l'Océan Indien.

Butler, Judith. 1990. *Gender Trouble: Feminism and the Subversion of Identity.* London and New York: Routledge.

———. 1997. *Excitable Speech: A Politics of the Performative.* London and New York: Routledge.

Carr, David. 1986. *Time, Narrative, and History.* Bloomington: Indiana University Press.

Carroll, Barbara Wake, and Terrance Carroll. 2000a. Accomodating Ethnic Diversity in a Modernizing Democratic State: Theory and Practice in the Case of Mauritius. *Ethnic and Racial Studies* 23(1): 120–42.

———. 2000b. Trouble in Paradise: Ethnic Conflict in Mauritius. *Commonwealth and Comparative Politics* 38(2): 25–50.

Carter, Marina. 1994. *Lakshmi's Legacy. The Testimonies of Indian Women in Nineteenth Century Mauritius.* Rose-Hill: Editions de l'Océan Indien.

———. 1995. *Servants, Sirdars, Settlers: Indians in Mauritius 1834–1874.* Delhi: Oxford University Press.

Carter, Marina, and Saloni Deerpalsingh. 2000. Bihar: The Migratory State. In *Across the Kalapani: The Bihari Presence in Mauritius,* ed. Marina Carter and Saloni Deerpalsingh. Port Louis: Centre for Research on Indian Ocean Societies.

Carter, Marina, and Vishwanaden Govinden. 1998. The Construction of Communities: Indian Immigrants in Mauritius. In *Coloring the Rainbow. Mauritian Society in the Making,* ed. Marina Carter. Port Louis: Centre for Research on Indian Ocean Societies.

Cazden, C. B. 2003. Sustaining Indigenous Languages in Cyberspace. In *Nurturing Native Languages,* ed. J. Reyhner, O. Trujillo, R. L. Carrasco, and L. Lockhard. Flagstaff: Northern Arizona University.

Chatterjee, Partha. 1993. *The Nation and Its Fragments: Colonial and Postcolonial Histories.* Princeton: Princeton University Press.

Chaudenson, Robert. 1979. *Les créoles français.* Paris: Nathan.

———. 2001. *Creolization of Language and Culture.* London and New York: Routledge.

Clifford, James. 1997. *Routes: Travel and Translation in the Late Twentieth Century.* Cambridge: Harvard University Press.

Cohn, Bernard S. 1985. The Command of Language and the Language of Command. In *Subaltern Studies IV,* ed. R. Guha. Delhi: Oxford University Press

———. 1987. The Census, Social Structure and Objectification in South Asia. In *An Anthropologist among the Historians and Other Essays.* Delhi: Oxford University Press.

Comaroff, Jean, and John Comaroff. 1991. *Of Revelation and Revolution: Christianity, Colonialism, and Consciousness in South Africa.* Vol. 1. Chicago: University of Chicago Press.

Cooper, Frederick, and Ann L. Stoler, eds. 1997. *Tensions of Empire: Colonial Cultures in a Bourgeois World.* Berkeley: University of California Press.

Cotter, C. 2001. Continuity and Vitality: Expanding Domains through Irish-Language Radio. In *The Green Book of Language Revitalization in Practice,* ed. L. Hinton and K. Hale. San Diego: Academic Press

Coupland, Nikolas. 2001. Dialect Stylization in Radio Talk. *Language in Society* 30(3): 345–75.

Dalmia, Vasudha. 1997. *The Nationalization of Hindu Traditions: Bharatendu Harishchandra and Nineteenth-Century Banaras.* Delhi: Oxford University Press.

Damsteegt, Theo. 1988. Sarnami: A Living Language. In *Language Transplanted: The Development of Overseas Hindi,* ed. Richard K. Barz and Jeff Siegel. Wiesbaden: Harrassowitz.

Deerpalsingh, Saloni. 2000. The Characteristics of Bihari Recruits. In *Across the Kalapani: The Bihari Presence in Mauritius,* ed. Marina Carter and Saloni Deerpalsingh. Port Louis: Centre for Research on Indian Ocean Societies.

de Robillard, Didier. 1989. Développement, langue, identité ethno-linguistique: Le cas de l'Ile Maurice. In *Langues, économie et développement,* Tome 2, ed. Francis Jouannet, Laurent Nkusi, Michel Rambelo, Didier de Robillard, Rada Tirvassen. Aix-en-Provence: Institut d'Études Créoles et Francophones / Didier Erudition.

Derrida, Jacques. 1976. *Of Grammatology.* Baltimore: Johns Hopkins University Press.

———. 1991. Signature, Event, Context. In *A Derrida Reader: Behind the Blinds,* ed. Peggy Kamuf. New York: Columbia University Press.

Deutsch, Karl W. 1953. *Nationalism and Social Communication: An Inquiry into the Foundations of Nationality.* Cambridge: MIT Press; New York: Wiley.

DeVotta, Neil. 2004. *Blowback: Linguistic Nationalism, Institutional Decay, and Ethnic Conflict in Sri Lanka.* Stanford: Stanford University Press.

Dilthey, Wilhelm. 1958. Der Aufbau der geschichtlichen Welt in den Geisteswissenschaften. *Gesammelte Schriften* VII. Band. Stuttgart, Göttingen: Teubner/Vanderhoeck & Ruprecht.

Dirks, Nicholas. 1992. Introduction. In *Colonialism and Culture,* ed. Nicholas Dirks. Ann Arbor: University of Michigan Press.

Domingue, Nicole Zuber. 1971. Bhojpuri and Creole in Mauritius: A Study of Linguistic Interference and Its Consequences in Regard to Synchronic Variation and Language Change. Ph.D. diss., University of Texas at Austin.

Dorian, Nancy. 1994. Purism vs. Compromise in Language Revitalization and Language Renewal. *Language in Society* 23: 479–94.

Dumont, Louis. 1970. *Homo Hierarchicus: An Essay on the Caste System.* Chicago: University of Chicago Press.

Eagleton, Terry. 1991. *Ideology.* London: Verso.

Eisenlohr, Patrick. 2004. Temporalities of Community: Ancestral Language, Pilgrimage, and Diasporic Belonging in Mauritius. *Journal of Linguistic Anthropology* 14(1): 81–98.

———. 2006a. As Makkah Is Sweet and Beloved, So Is Medina: Islam, Devotional Genres, and Electronic Mediation in Mauritius. *American Ethnologist* 33(2): 230–45.

———. 2006b. The Politics of Diaspora and the Morality of Secularism: Muslim Identities and Islamic Authority in Mauritius. Journal of the Royal Anthropological Institute, n.s., 12(2): 395–412.

Embree, Ainslie T. 1994. The Function of the Rashtriya Swayamsevak Sangh: To Define the Hindu Nation. In *Accounting for Fundamentalisms: The Dynamic Character of Movements,* ed. Martin E. Marty and R. Scott Appleby. Chicago: Chicago University Press.

Eriksen, Thomas Hylland. 1990. Linguistic Diversity and the Quest for National Identity: The Case of Mauritius. *Ethnic and Racial Studies* 13(1): 1–24.

———. 1992. Containing Conflict and Transcending Ethnicity in Mauritius. In *Internal Conflict and Governance,* ed. Kumar Rupesinghe. Houndmills, U.K.: Macmillan.

———. 1993. *Ethnicity and Nationalism: Anthropological Perspectives.* London: Pluto.

———. 1994. Nationalism, Mauritian Style: Cultural Unity and Ethnic Diversity. *Comparative Studies in Society and History* 36(3): 549–74.

———. 1997. Mauritian Society between the Ethnic and the Non-Ethnic. In *The Politics of Ethnic Consciousness,* ed. Cora Govers and Hans Vermeulen. Houndmills: MacMillan.

———. 1998. *Common Denominators: Ethnicity, Nation-Building and Compromise in Mauritius.* Oxford: Berg.

———. 2003. Creolization and Creativity. *Global Networks* 3: 223–38.

Errington, J. Joseph. 1985. On the Nature of the Sociolinguistic Sign: Describing the Javanese Speech Levels. In *Semiotic Mediation,* ed. Elisabeth Mertz and Richard Parmentier. New York: Academic Press.

———. 1998. *Shifting Languages: Interaction and Identity in Javanese Indonesia.* Cambridge: Cambridge University Press.

———. 2001. Colonial Linguistics. *Annual Review of Anthropology* 30: 19–39.

Fabian, Johannes. 1983. *Time and the Other: How Anthropology Makes Its Object.* New York: Columbia University Press.

Faruqee, Ashrufa. 1996. Conceiving the Coolie Woman: Indentured Labor, Indian Women, and Colonial Discourse. *South Asia Research* 16(1): 61–76.

Fischer-Tiné, Harald. 2003. Inventing a National Past: The Case of Ramdev's *bharatvarṣ kā itihās* (1910–14). In *Hinduism in Public and Private: Reform, Hindutva, Gender and Sampraday,* ed. A. Copley. Oxford: Oxford University Press.

Foucault, Michel. 1978. *The History of Sexuality.* Vol. 1: *An Introduction.* New York: Vintage Books.

———. 1980. *Power/Knowledge.* New York: Pantheon.

Fox, Richard G. 1990. Hindu Nationalism in the Making, or the Rise of the Hindian. In *Nationalist Ideologies and the Production of National Cultures,* ed. Richard G. Fox. Washington, D.C.: American Anthropological Association.

Freitag, Sandria B. 1996. Contesting in Public: Colonial Legacies and Contemporary Communalism. In *Contesting the Nation: Religion, Community, and the Politics of Democracy in India,* ed. David Ludden. Philadelphia: University of Pennsylvania Press.

Friedman, Jonathan. 1994. *Cultural Identity and Global Process.* London: Sage.

Friedrich, Paul. 1972. Social Context and Semantic Feature: The Russian Pronominal Usage. In *Directions in Sociolinguistics,* ed. John J. Gumperz and Dell Hymes. Oxford: Basil Blackwell.

Gadamer, Hans-Georg. 1982. *Truth and Method.* New York: Crossroad.

Gal, Susan. 1979. *Language Shift: Social Determinants of Linguistic Change in Bilingual Austria.* New York: Academic Press.

———. 1993. Diversity and Contestation in Linguistic Ideologies: German Speakers in Hungary. *Language in Society* 22: 337–59.

Gambhir, Surendra K. 1981. The East Indian Speech Community in Guyana: A Sociolinguistic Study with Reference to Koine Formation. Ph.D. diss., University of Pennsylvania.

———. 1986. Mauritian Bhojpuri: An International Perspective on Historic and Sociolinguistic Processes. In *Indian Labor Immigration: Papers Presented at the International Conference on Indian Labor Immigration (23–27 October 1984) Held at the Mahatma Gandhi Institute,* ed. Uttam Bissoondoyal and S. B. C. Servansing. Moka: Mahatma Gandhi Institute.

———. 1988. Structural Development of Guyanese Bhojpuri. In *Language Transplanted: The Development of Overseas Hindi,* ed. Richard K. Barz and Jeff Siegel. Wiesbaden: Harrassowitz.

García Canclini, Nestor. 1995. *Hybrid Cultures: Strategies for Entering and Leaving Modernity.* Minneapolis: University of Minnesota Press.

Gardner, N. M., Puigdevall i Serralvo, and C. H. Williams. 2000. Language Revitalization in Comparative Context: Ireland, the Basque Country and Catalonia. In *Language Revitalization: Policy and Planning in Wales,* ed. C. H. Williams. Cardiff: University of Wales Press.

Garrett, Paul. 2000. "High" Kwéyòl: The Emergence of a Formal Creole Register in St. Lucia. In *Language Change and Language Contact in Pidgins and Creoles,* ed. John McWorther. Amsterdam: Benjamins.

Gellner, Ernest. 1983. *Nations and Nationalism.* Ithaca, New York: Cornell University Press.

Gilroy, Paul. 1993. *The Black Atlantic: Modernity and Double Consciousness.* Cambridge: Harvard University Press.

Ginsburg, Faye, Lila Abu-Lughod, and Brian Larkin, eds. 2002. *Media Worlds: Anthropology on New Terrain.* Berkeley: University of California Press.

Goffman, Erving. 1974. *Frame Analysis: An Essay on the Organization of Experience.* New York: Harper & Row.

Gold, Daniel. 1991. Organized Hinduisms: From Vedic Truth to Hindu Nation. In *Fundamentalisms Observed,* ed. Martin E. Marty and R. Scott Appleby. Chicago: University of Chicago Press.

Grillo R. D. 1989. *Dominant Languages: Language and Hierarchy in Britain and France.* Cambridge, New York: Cambridge University Press.

Gumperz, John. 1982. *Language and Social Identity.* Cambridge: Cambridge University Press.

Gumperz, J., and C. M. Naim. 1960. Formal and Informal Standards in the

Hindi Regional Language Area. In *Linguistic Diversity in South Asia,* ed. C. Ferguson and J. Gumperz. Bloomington: Indiana University Press.

Gupta, Akhil, and James Ferguson. 1992. Beyond "Culture": Space, Identity, and the Politics of Difference. *Cultural Anthropology* 7(1): 6–23.

Haeri, Niloofar. 2003. *Sacred Language, Ordinary People: Dilemmas of Culture and Politics in Egypt.* New York: Palgrave.

Hall, Stuart. 1990. Cultural Identity and Diaspora. In *Identity: Community, Culture, Difference,* ed. J. Rutherford. London: Lawrence & Wishart.

———. 1991. Old and New Identities, Old and New Ethnicities. In *Culture, Globalization and the World-System: Contemporary Conditions for the Representation of Identity,* ed. Anthony D. King. London: Macmillan.

Hanks, William F. 1987. Discourse Genres in a Theory of Practice. *American Ethnologist* 14(4): 668–92.

Hannerz, Ulf. 1987. The World in Creolisation. *Africa* 57(4): 546–59.

———. 1992. *Cultural Complexity: Studies in the Social Organization of Meaning.* New York: Columbia University Press.

———. 1996. *Transnational Connections: Culture, People, Places.* Londonand New York: Routledge.

Hansen, Thomas Blom. 1999. *The Saffron Wave: Democracy and Hindu Nationalism.* Princeton: Princeton University Press.

———. 2002. Diasporic Dispositions. *Himal* 15(12): 12–20.

Harries, P. 1988. The Roots of Ethnicity: Discourse and the Politics of Language Construction in Southeast Africa. *African Affairs* 87: 25–54.

Harvey, David. 1989. *The Condition of Postmodernity: An Inquiry into the Origins of Cultural Change.* New York: Blackwell.

Hazaël-Massieux, Marie-Christine. 1996. Du français, du créole et de quelques situations plurilingues: Données linguistiques et sociolinguistiques. In *Francophonie: Mythes masques et réalités. Enjeux politiques et culturels,* ed. Bridget Jones, Arnauld Miguet, and Patrick Corcoran. Paris: Editions Publisud.

Heidegger, Martin. 1962. *Being and Time.* London: SMC Press.

Heller, Monica. 1988. Strategic Ambiguity. In *Codeswitching: Anthropological and Sociolinguistic Perspectives,* ed. Monica Heller. Berlin: Mouton de Gruyter.

———. 1992. The Politics of Codeswitching and Language Choice. In *Codeswitching,* ed. Carol M. Eastman. Clevedon: Multilingual Matters.

Herder, Johann Gottfried. 1968 [1784–91]. *Reflections on the Philosophy of the History of Mankind.* Chicago: University of Chicago Press.

Hill, Jane H. 1995. The Voices of Don Gabriel: Responsibility and Self in a Modern Mexicano Narrative. In *The Dialogic Emergence of Culture,* ed. Dennis Tedlock and Bruce Mannheim. Urbana and Chicago: University of Illinois Press.

———. 1998. "Today There is No Respect": Nostalgia, "Respect", And Oppositional Discourse in Mexicano (Nahuatl) Language Ideology. In *Language Ideology: Practice and Theory,* ed. Bambi B. Schieffelin, Kathryn A. Woolard, and Paul V. Kroskrity. Oxford: Oxford University Press.

Hill, Jane H., and Kenneth Hill. 1978. Honorific Usage in Modern Nahuatl. *Language* 54(1): 123–55.

———. 1986. *Speaking Mexicano*. Tucson: University of Arizona Press.

Hindley, R. 1990. *The Death of the Irish Language: A Qualified Obituary*. London: Routledge.

Hobsbawm, Eric J. 1990. *Nations and Nationalism since 1780: Programme, Myth, Reality*. Cambridge: Cambridge University Press.

Hollup, Oddvar. 1994. The Disintegration of Caste and Changing Concepts of Indian Ethnic Identity in Mauritius. *Ethnology* 33(4): 297–316.

———. 1995. Arya Samaj and the Shaping of "Egalitarian" Hindus in Mauritius. *Folk* 36: 27–39.

———. 1996. Islamic Revivalism and Political Opposition among Minority Muslims in Mauritius. *Ethnology* 35(4): 285–300.

Hookoomsing, Vinesh Y. 1980. Langue et littérature: Langue créole et littérature nationale à Maurice. *Notre Librairie* (C.L.E.F. Paris) 54–55 (julliet–oct.): 117–24.

———. 1984. Langue créole, litterature nationale et mauricianisme populaire. In *Koute pou tann! Anthologie de la nouvelle poesie créole*, ed. Lambert Félix Prudent. Paris: Editions Caribéennes / Agence de Coopération Culturelle et Technique.

———. 1986. Language et identité ethnique: Les langues ancestrales à Maurice. *Journal of Mauritian Studies* 1(2): 117–37.

———. 1987. L'emploi de la langue créole dans le contexte multilingue et multiculturel de l'Ile Maurice: Une étude de son importance en tant que langue commune et des implications sociolinguistiques de son elaboration en mauricien. Ph.D. diss.: Université Laval, Québec.

Hornberger, N. H., and K. A. King. 1999. Authenticity and Unification in Quechua Language Planning. In *Indigenous Community-Based Education*, ed. S. May. Clevedon: Multilingual Matters.

Houbert, Jean. 1982/83. Mauritius: Politics and Pluralism at the Periphery. *Annuaire des Pays de l' Océan Indien* 9: 225–65.

Humboldt, Wilhelm von. 1973 [1821]. On the Historian's Task. In *The Theory and Practice of History*, by Leopold von Ranke, edited with an introduction by Georg G. Iggers and Konrad von Moltke. Indianapolis and New York: Bobbs-Merrill.

Husserl, Edmund. 1964. *The Phenomenology of Internal Time-Consciousness*. Ed. Martin Heidegger. Trans. James S. Churchill. Bloomington: Indiana University Press.

Hymes, Dell, ed. 1971. *Pidginization and Creolization of Languages: Proceedings of a Conference Held at the University of the West Indies Mona, Jamaica, April 1968*. Cambridge: Cambridge University Press.

Inglehart, R., and M. Woodward. 1972 [1967]. Language Conflicts and the Political Community. In *Language and Social Context*, ed. Pier Paolo Giglioli. Harmondsworth: Penguin.

Inoue, Miyako. 2004. What Does Language Remember? Indexical Inversion and the Naturalized History of Japanese Women. *Journal of Linguistic Anthropology* 14(1): 39–56.

Irvine, Judith. 1993. Mastering African Languages: The Politics of Linguistics in

Nineteenth Century Senegal. In Nations, Colonies and Metropoles, ed. D. Segal and R. Handler. Special issue, *Social Analysis* 33: 27–46.

———. 2001. Style as Distinctiveness: The Culture and Ideology of Linguistic Variation. In *Style and Sociolinguistic Variation*, ed. P. Eckert and J. R. Rickford. Cambridge: Cambridge University Press.

———. 2004. Comments: Say When: Temporalities in Language Ideology. *Journal of Linguistic Anthropology* 14(1): 99–109.

Irvine, Judith, and Susan Gal. 2000. Language Ideology and Linguistic Differentiation. In *Regimes of Language: Ideologies, Polities, and Identities*, ed. Paul V. Kroskrity. Santa Fe: School of American Research Press.

Jaffe, Alexandra. 1999. *Ideologies in Action: Language Politics on Corsica.* Berlin: Mouton de Gruyter.

Jaffrelot, Christophe. 1996 [1993]. *The Hindu Nationalist Movement in India.* New York: Columbia University Press.

Jahangeer-Chojoo, Amenah. 1997. *La communauté musulmane de Port Louis: Une étude de géographie sociale.* Thèse de doctorat, Université Michel de Montaigne, Bordeaux III.

Jameson, Frederic. 2003. The End of Temporality. *Critical Inquiry* 29(4): 695–718.

Jayawardena, Chandra. 1966. Religious Belief and Social Change: Aspects of the Development of Hinduism in British Guiana. *Comparative Studies in Society and History* 8: 211–40.

Jones, M. C. 1998a. *Language Obsolescence and Revitalization: Linguistic Change in Two Sociolinguistically Contrasting Welsh Communities.* Oxford: Clarendon Press.

———. 1998b. Death of a Language, Birth of an Identity: Brittany and the Bretons. *Language Problems and Language Planning* 22: 129–42.

Kale, Madhavi. 1995. Projecting Identities: Empire and Indentured Labor Migration from India to Trinidad and British Guiana, 1836–1885. In *Nation and Migration: The Politics of Space in the South Asian Diaspora,* ed. Peter van der Veer. Philadelphia: University of Pennsylvania Press.

Kalla, Abdul Cader. 1984. The Language Issue: A Perennial Issue in Mauritian Education. In *National Seminar on the Language Issue in Mauritius,* ed. H. Unmole. Réduit: University of Mauritius.

———. 1987. The Gujarati Merchants in Mauritius C. 1850–1900. *Journal of Mauritian Studies* 2(1): 45–65.

Kaplan, Caren. 1996. *Questions of Travel: Postmodern Discourses of Displacement.* Durham: Duke University Press.

Kaplan, Martha, and John D. Kelly. 1994. Rethinking Resistance: Dialogics of "Disaffection" in Colonial Fiji. *American Ethnologist* 21(1): 123–51.

Kelly, John D. 1991. *A Politics of Virtue. Hinduism, Sexuality, and Countercolonial Discourse in Fiji.* Chicago: Chicago University Press.

———. 1995. *Bhakti* and Postcolonial Politics: Hindu Missions to Fiji. In *Nation and Migration: The Politics of Space in the South Asian Diaspora,* ed. Peter van der Veer. Philadelphia: University of Pennsylvania Press.

———. 1998a. Time and the Global: Against the Homogeneous, Empty Communities in Contemporary Social Theory. *Development and Change* 29(4): 839–71.

———. 1998b. Aspiring to Minority and Other Tactics against Violence in Fiji. In *Making Majorities: Constituting the Nation in Japan, Korea, China, Malaysia, Fiji, Turkey, and the United States,* ed. Dru C. Gladney. Stanford: Stanford University Press.

———. 2001. Fiji's Fifth Veda: Exile, Sanatan Dharm, and Countercolonial Initiatives in Diaspora. In *Questioning Ramayanas: A South Asian Tradition,* ed. Paula Richman. New Delhi: Oxford University Press.

Khan, Aisha. 1994. *Juthaa* in Trinidad: Food, Pollution, and Hierarchy in a Caribbean Diaspora Community. *American Ethnologist* 21(2): 245–69.

———. 2001. Journey to the Center of the Earth: The Caribbean as a Master Symbol. *Cultural Anthropology* 16(3): 271–302.

———. 2004. *Callaloo Nation: Metaphors of Race and Religious Identity among South Asians in Trinidad.* Durham: Duke University Press.

King, Christopher R. 1989. Forging a New Linguistic Identity: The Hindi Movement in Banaras, 1868–1914. In *Culture and Power in Banaras: Community, Performance, and Environment 1800–1914,* ed. Sandria B. Freitag. Berkeley: University of California Press.

———. 1994. *One Language, Two Scripts: The Hindi Movement in Nineteenth Century North India.* New Delhi: Oxford University Press.

Kittler, Friedrich A. 1993. *Draculas Vermächtnis. Technische Schriften.* Leipzig: Reclam.

Klass, Morton. 1961. *East Indians in Trinidad: A Study of Cultural Persistence.* New York: Columbia University Press.

Koselleck, Reinhart. 1985. *Futures Past: On the Semantics of Historical Time.* Cambridge: MIT Press.

Kroskrity, Paul. 2002. Language Renewal and the Technologies of Literacy and Postliteracy: Reflections from Western Mono. In *Making Dictionaries: Preserving Indigenous Languages in the Americas,* ed. W. Frawley, K. C. Hill, and P. Munro. Berkeley: University of California Press.

Kuipers, Joel C. 1990. *Power in Performance: The Creation of Textual Authority in Weyewa Ritual Speech.* Philadelphia: University of Pennsylvania Press.

———. 1998. *Language, Identity and Marginality in Indonesia: The Changing Nature of Ritual Speech on the Island of Sumba.* Cambridge: Cambridge University Press.

Labov, William. 1972. *Sociolinguistic Patterns.* Philadelphia: University of Pennsylvania Press.

Lal, Brij. 1985. Kunti's Cry: Indentured Women on Fiji Plantations. *Indian Economic and Social History Review.* 22: 55–71.

Lau Thi Keng, Jean-Claude. 1991. *Inter-ethnicité et politique à l'île Maurice.* Paris: L'Harmattan.

Lavie, Smadar, and Ted Swedenburg, eds. 1996. *Displacement, Diasporas, and Geographies of Identity.* Durham: Duke University Press.

Laville, Rosabelle. 2000. In the Politics of the Rainbow: Creoles and Civil Society in Mauritius. *Journal of Contemporary African Studies* 18(2): 277–94.

Lelyveld, David. 1993. The Fate of Hindustani: Colonial Knowledge and the Project of a National Language. In *Orientalism and the Postcolonial Predica-ment*, ed. Carol A. Breckenridge and Peter van der Veer. Philadelphia: University of Pennsylvania Press.

Ludden, David. 1996. Introduction. Ayodhya: A Window on the World. In *Contesting the Nation: Religion, Community, and the Politics of Democracy in India*, ed. David Ludden. Philadelphia: University of Pennsylvania Press.

Lutgendorf, Philip. 1991. *The Life of a Text: Performing the Rāmcaritmānas of Tulsidas*. Berkeley: University of California Press.

Lyotard, Jean-François. 1991. *The Inhuman: Reflections on Time*. Stanford: Stanford University Press.

Malkki, Liisa. 1992. National Geographic: The Rooting of Peoples and the Territorialization of National Identity among Scholars and Refugees. *Cultural Anthropology* 7(1): 24–44.

Managan, Jane Kathryn. 2004. Language Choice, Linguistic Ideologies, and Social Identity in Guadeloupe. Ph.D. diss., New York University.

Mauritius. 1944. *Final Report on the Census Enumeration in the Colony of Mauritius and its Dependencies, 11ᵗʰ June 1944*. Port Louis.

———. 1952. *Colony of Mauritius, 1952 Census of Mauritius and Its Dependencies, Pt. I*. Port Louis: Central Statistical Office.

———. 1962. *Colony of Mauritius, 1962 Population Census of Mauritius and its Dependencies, Vol. I*. Port Louis: Central Statistical Office.

———. 1972. *1972 Population Census of Mauritius, Vol. I (Preliminary Report)*. Port Louis: Central Statistical Office, Ministry of Economic Planning and Development.

———. 1983. *1983 Housing and Population Census of Mauritius*. Port Louis: Ministry of Economic Planning and Development, Central Statistical Office.

———. 1990. *1990 Housing and Population Census of Mauritius*. Port Louis: Ministry of Economic Planning and Development, Central Statistical Office.

———. 2000. *2000 Housing and Population Census of Mauritius*. Port Louis: Ministry of Finance and Economic Development, Central Statistics Office. http://statsmauritius.gov.mu/report/hpcenoo/Demogra/demofer.htm.

Mazzarella, William. 2004. Culture, Globalization, Mediation. *Annual Review of Anthropology* 33: 345–67.

McClure, Erica, and Malcolm McClure. 1988. Macro- and Micro-Sociolinguistic Dimensions of Codeswitching in Vingard (Romania). In *Codeswitching: Anthropological and Sociolinguistic Perspectives*, ed. Monica Heller. Berlin: Mouton de Gruyter.

McDonald, Maryon. 1990. *"We Are Not French!": Language, Culture, and Identity in Brittany*. London: Routledge.

McIntosh, Janet. 2005. Baptismal Essentialisms: Giriama Code Choice and the Reification of Ethnoreligious Boundaries. *Journal of Linguistic Anthropology* 15(2): 151–70.

McKean, Lise. 1996. *Divine Enterprise: Gurus and the Hindu Nationalist Movement*. Chicago: University of Chicago Press.

McLuhan, Marshall. 1964. *Understanding Media*. New York and Toronto: McGraw-Hill.

Meade, J. E. 1961. *The Economic and Social Structure of Mauritius*. London: Frank Cass.

Meeuwis, Michael. 1999. Flemish Nationalism in the Belgian Congo versus Zairian Anti-Imperialism: Continuity and Discontinuity in Language Ideological Debates. In *Language Ideological Debates*, ed. Jan Blommaert. Berlin: Mouton de Gruyter.

Mesthrie, Rajend. 1991. *Language in Indenture: A Sociolinguistic History of Bhojpuri-Hindi in South Africa*. London and New York: Routledge.

———. 1993. Koineization in the Bhojpuri-Hindi Diaspora with Special Reference to South Africa. *International Journal of the Sociology of Language* 99: 25–44.

Miles, William F. S. 1999. The Creole Malaise in Mauritius. *African Affairs* 98: 211–28.

———. 2000. The Politics of Language Equilibrium in a Multilingual Society. *Comparative Politics* 32(2): 215–30.

Ministry of Education, Arts, and Culture. 1984. *Let the Hundred Flowers Blossom*. Port Louis: Ministry of Education, Arts, and Culture.

Mintz, Sidney, and Richard Price. 1992 [1976]. *The Birth of African-American Culture*. Boston: Beacon Press.

Mohit, Dimlalah. 1994. *Moriśas kī bhojpurī mē pracalit lokoktiyā, muhāvare, gīt, paheliyā aur kahāniyā* (Current popular sayings, idioms, songs, riddles and stories in Mauritian Bhojpuri). Caroline, Bel-Air, Mauritius: published by the author.

Moorghen, Pierre-Marie, and Nicole Z. Domingue. 1982. Multilingualism in Mauritius. *International Journal of the Sociology of Language* 34: 51–66.

Munasinghe, Viranjini. 1997. Culture Creators and Culture Bearers: The Interface of Race and Ethnicity in Trinidad. *Transforming Anthropology* 6(1/2): 72–86.

———. 2001. *Callaloo or Tossed Salad? East Indians and the Cultural Politics of Identity in Trinidad*. Ithaca: Cornell University Press.

———. 2002. Nationalism in Hybrid Spaces: The Production of Impurity out of Purity. *American Ethnologist* 29(3): 663–92.

Myers-Scotton, Carol. 1993. *Social Motivations for Codeswitching: Evidence from Africa*. Oxford: Oxford University Press.

Neerputh, Naving Coomar. 1986. *Le système verbal du Bhojpuri de l'Ile Maurice*. Paris: L'Harmattan.

Nevadomsky, Joseph. 1980a. Changes in Hindu Institutions in an Alien Environment. *Eastern Anthropologist* 33(1): 39–53.

———. 1980b. Changes over Time and Space in the East Indian Family in Rural Trinidad. *Journal of Contemporary Family Studies* 11(4): 433–56.

Niehoff, Arthur. 1959. The Survival of Hindu Institutions in an Alien Environment. *Eastern Anthropologist* 12: 171–87.

Nirsimloo-Anenden, Devi A. 1990. *The Primordial Link: Telugu Ethnic Identity in Mauritius*. Moka: Mahatma Gandhi Institute.

Pandit, Ira. 1986. *Hindi English Code Switching: Mixed Hindi English*. Delhi: Datta Book Centre.

Parsuraman, Armoogum. 1988. *From Ancestral Cultures to National Culture: Mauritius*. Moka: Mahatma Gandhi Institute Press.

———. n.d. *Towards Green Horizons*. Beau Bassin: Mauritius Institute of Education / Curriculum Development Unit.

Peirce, Charles Sanders. 1932. *Collected Papers of Charles Sanders Peirce*. Vol. 2: *Elements of Logic*. Cambridge: Harvard University Press.

Peterson, L. C. 1997. Tuning In to Navajo: The Role of Radio in Native Language Maintenance. In *Teaching Indigenous Languages*, ed. J. Reyhner. Flagstaff: Northern Arizona University.

Price, Richard. 2001. The Miracle of Creolization: A Retroperspective. *Nieuwe West-Indische Gids* 75(1): 35–64.

Puri, Shalini. 2004. *The Caribbean Postcolonial: Social Equality, Post-Nationalism and Cultural Hybridity*. New York and Houndmills, U.K.: Palgrave.

Rafael, Vicente L. 1988. *Contracting Colonialism: Translation and Christian Conversion in Tagalog Society under Early Spanish Rule*. Ithaca: Cornell University Press.

Rai, Alok. 2000. *Hindi Nationalism*. New Delhi: Orient Longman.

Ramaswamy, Sumathi. 1997. *Passions of the Tongue: Language Devotion in Tamil India, 1891–1970*. Berkeley: University of California Press.

Ramdin, Suchita. 1989. *Sanskār manjrī: Mārisas ke bhojpurī sanskār gīt* (Bouquet of rites: Mauritian Bhojpuri ritual songs). Moka: Mahatma Gandhi Institute.

Ramdoyal, Ramesh Dutt. 1977. *The Development of Education in Mauritius 1710–1976*. Réduit: Mauritius Institute of Education.

Rampton, Ben.1999. Styling the Other: Introduction. *Journal of Sociolinguistics* 3(4): 421–27.

Ramyead, L. P. 1985. *The Establishment and Cultivation of Modern Standard Hindi in Mauritius*. Moka: Mahatma Gandhi Institute.

Ranke, Leopold von. 1973. *The Theory and Practice of History*. Edited with an introduction by Georg G. Iggers and Konrad von Moltke. Indianapolis and New York: Bobbs-Merrill.

Rickford, John R. 1987. *Dimensions of a Creole Continuum: History, Texts, and Linguistic Analysis of Guyanese Creole*. Stanford: Stanford University Press.

Ricoeur, Paul. 1988. *Time and Narrative*. Vol. 3. Chicago: University of Chicago Press.

Robbins, Joel. 2001. Secrecy and the Sense of an Ending: Narrative, Time, and Everyday Millenarianism in Papua New Guinea and in Christian Fundamentalism. *Comparative Studies in Society and History* 43: 525–50.

Roy, Jaynarayan. 1970. *Mārisas mē hindī kā sankśipt itihās* (A Concise History of Hindi in Mauritius). New Delhi: Sasta Sahitya Mandal.

Sandbothe, Mike. 1996. Mediale Zeiten. Zur Veränderung unserer Zeiterfahrung durch die elektronischen Medien. In *Synthethische Welten: Kunst, Künstlichkeit und Kommunikationsmedien*, ed. Eckhard Hammel. Essen: Die Blaue Eule.

———. 1999. Virtuelle Temporalitäten. Zeit- und identitätsphilosophische Aspekte des Internet. In *Identität und Moderne*, ed. Herbert Willems, Alois Hahn. Frankfurt: Suhrkamp.

Sanyal, Usha. 1996. *Devotional Islam and Politics in British India: Ahmad Riza Khan Barelwi and His Movement (1870–1920)*. Oxford: Oxford University Press.

Schiffman, Harold F. 1996. *Linguistic Culture and Language Policy*. London and New York: Routledge.

Schwartz, Barton M., ed. 1967. *Caste in Overseas Indian Communities*. San Francisco: Chandler.

Sewtohul, Goswami. 1996. *Schoenfeld Road: Reminiscences, Le Ravin, Rivière-du-Rempart*. Quatre-Bornes: Pandit Ramlakhan Gossagne Publications.

Sewtohul, Nivriti. 1990. *L'histoire du village de Triolet*. Port Louis: Proag Printing.

Shaery-Eisenlohr, Roschanack. 2005. *Constructing Lebanese Shi'ite Nationalism: Transnationalism, Shi'ism, and the Lebanese State*. Ph.D. diss., University of Chicago.

Sharp, H. 1965. *Selections from Educational Records, 1781–1839*. Reprint, New Delhi: Government of India Press.

Sheik Amode Hossen, Jacques. 1993. Colonisation française et linguistique à Maurice. *Culture et pédagogie* 10–11: 49–57.

Shukla, Sandhya. 2001. Locations for South Asian Diasporas. *Annual Review of Anthropology* 30: 551–72.

Siegel, Jeff. 1987. *Language Contact in a Plantation Environment: A Sociolinguistic History of Fiji*. Cambridge: Cambridge University Press.

———. 1988. Introduction to *Language Transplanted: The Development of Overseas Hindi*, ed. Richard R. Barz and Jeff Siegel. Wiesbaden: Harrassowitz.

Silverstein, Michael. 1976. Shifters, Linguistic Categories, and Cultural Description. In *Meaning in Anthropology*, ed. Keith Basso and H. Selby. Santa Fe: School of American Research.

———. 1979. Language Structure and Linguistic Ideology. In *The Elements: A Parasession on Linguistic Units and Levels*, ed. Paul R. Clyne, William F. Hanks, and Carol L. Hofbauer. Chicago: Chicago Linguistic Society.

———. 1993. Metapragmatic Discourse and Metapragmatic Function. In *Reflexive Language: Reported Speech and Metapragmatics*, ed. John A. Lucy. Cambridge: Cambridge University Press.

———. 1998. The Uses and Utility of Ideology: A Commentary. In *Language Ideologies: Practice and Theory*, ed. Bambi B. Schieffelin, Kathryn A. Woolard, and Paul V. Kroskrity. Oxford: Oxford University Press.

———. 2000. Whorfianism and the Linguistic Imagination of Nationality. In *Regimes of Language: Ideologies, Polities, and Identities*, ed. Paul V. Kroskrity. Santa Fe: School of American Research Press.

———. 2001. The Limits of Awareness. In *Linguistic Anthropology: A Reader*, ed. Alessandro Duranti. Oxford: Blackwell.

———. 2003. The Whens and Wheres — As Well As Hows — of Ethnolinguistic Recognition. *Public Culture* 15: 531–58.

Simmons, Adele Smith. 1982. *Modern Mauritius: The Politics of Decolonization*. Bloomington: Indiana University Press.

Singaravelou. 1976. La créolisation des Indiens à la Guadeloupe et à la Martinique. *Espace créole* 1: 95–107.

Smith-Hefner, Nancy J. 1988. Women and Politeness: The Javanese Example. *Language in Society* 17: 535–54.

Sontheimer, Kurt. 1990. *Deutschlands politische Kultur.* München: Piper.

Sooriamoorthy, Ramoo. 1977. *Les tamouls à l'Ile Maurice.* Port Louis: published by the author.

Spitulnik, Debra. 1996. The Social Circulation of Media Discourse and the Mediation of Communities. *Journal of Linguistic Anthropology* 6(2): 161–87.

Srebrnik, Henry. 2000. Can an Ethnically-Based Civil Society Suceed? The Case of Mauritius. *Journal of Contemporary African Studies* 18(1): 7–20.

Stein, Peter. 1980. Conflicts linguistiques et changements de langues dans une société plurilingue. In *Sprachkontakt und Sprachkonflikt.* Zeitschrift für Dialektologie und Linguistik, Beiheft 32, ed. P. H. Nelde. Wiesbaden: Franz Steiner Verlag.

———. 1982. *Connaissance et emploi des langues à l'Ile Maurice.* Hamburg: Helmut Buske.

Stiegler, Bernard. 1998. *Technics and Time, 1.* Stanford: Stanford University Press.

Swiggers, Pierre. 1990. Ideology and the "Clarity" of French. In *Ideologies of Language,* ed. John E. Joseph and Talbot J. Taylor. London and New York: Routledge.

Tambiah, Stanley Jeyaraja. 1976. *World Conqueror and World Renouncer.* Cambridge: Cambridge University Press.

———. 1992. *Buddhism Betrayed? Religion, Politics, and Violence in Sri Lanka.* Chicago: University of Chicago Press.

Tinker, Hugh. 1974. *A New System of Slavery: The Export of Indian Labor Overseas 1830–1920.* Oxford: Oxford University Press.

———. 1976. *Separate and Unequal: India and the Indians in the British Commonwealth 1920–1950.* Vancouver: University of British Columbia Press.

Tirvassen, Rada. 1989. Les langues d'enseignement à Maurice: Facteurs historiques du choix contemporain. *Journal of Mauritian Studies* 3(1): 35–58.

Tiwari, Udai Narain. 1960. *The Origin and Development of Bhojpuri.* Calcutta: Asiatic Society.

Tomlinson, John. 1999. *Globalization and Culture.* Chicago: University of Chicago Press.

Toussaint, Auguste. 1969. La langue française à l'Île Maurice. *Revue française d'Histoire d'Outre-Mer* 56(205): 398–427.

Troulliot, Michel-Rolph. 1998. Culture on the Edges: Creolization in the Plantation Context. *Plantation Society in the Americas* 5: 8–28.

Trudgill, Peter. 1983. Sex and Covert Prestige: Linguistic Change in the Urban Dialect of Norwich. In *On Dialect: Social and Geographical Perspectives.* New York: New York University Press.

Unuth, Abhimanyu. 1988. Mariśas mē hindī kī sangarṣ yātrā (Hindi's journey of struggle in Mauritius). *Mother India–Children Abroad (Research Journal of the Antar Rashtriya Sahayog Parishad, New Delhi)* 2(2): 139–143.

Urciuoli, Bonnie. 1996. *Exposing Prejudice: Puerto Rican Experiences of Language, Race, and Class.* Boulder: Westview.

Urla, Jaqueline. 1988. Ethnic Protest and Social Planning: A Look at Basque Language Revival. *Cultural Anthropology* 3: 379–94.

———. 1993. Cultural Politics in an Age of Statistics: Numbers, Nations, and the Making of Basque Identity. *American Ethnologist* 20(4): 818–43.

Vallverdú, F. 1995. The Catalan Used on Television. *Mercator Media Forum* 1: 65–76.

van der Burg, Cors, and Peter van der Veer. 1986. Pandits, Power, and Profit: Religious Organization and the Construction of Identity among Surinamese Hindus. *Ethnic and Racial Studies* 9(4): 514–28.

van der Veer, Peter. 1993. The Foreign Hand: Orientalist Discourse in Sociology and Communalism. In *Orientalism and the Postcolonial Predicament: Perspectives on South Asia,* ed. Carol A. Breckenridge and Peter van der Veer. Philadelphia: University of Pennsylvania Press.

———. 1994a. *Religious Nationalism: Hindus and Muslims in India.* Berkeley: University of California Press.

———. 1994b. Hindu Nationalism and the Discourse of Modernity: The Vishva Hindu Parishad. In *Accounting for Fundamentalisms: The Dynamic Character of Movements,* ed. Martin E. Marty and R. Scott Appleby. Chicago: University of Chicago Press.

———, ed. 1995. *Nation and Migration: The Politics of Space in the South Asian Diaspora.* Philadelphia: University of Pennsylvania Press.

van der Veer, Peter, and Steven Vertovec. 1991. Brahmanism Abroad: On Caribbean Hinduism as an Ethnic Religion. *Ethnology* 30(2): 149–66.

Verdery, Katherine. 1993. Whither "Nation" and "Nationalism"? *Daedalus* 122(3): 37–46.

Verma, Munindranath. 1984. *Morisas kā itihās* (History of Mauritius). Long Mountain: Hindi Pracharini Sabha.

Vertovec, Steven. 1990. Religion and Ethnic Ideology: The Hindu Youth Movement in Trinidad. *Ethnic and Racial Studies* 13(2): 225–49.

———. 1992. *Hindu Trinidad: Religion, Ethnicity and Socio-Economic Change.* London: Macmillan / Warwick University Caribbean Studies.

———. 1994. "Official" and "Popular" Hinduism in Diaspora: Historical and Contemporary Trends in Surinam, Trinidad and Guyana. *Contributions to Indian Sociology,* n.s., 28(1): 123–47.

Virahsawmy, D. N., and R. Pudaruth. 1984. From Pidgin to Morisiê. In *Proceedings of the 1982 National Seminar on the Language Issue,* ed. H. Unmole. Réduit: University of Mauritius.

Virahsawmy, Raj. 1984. A Form of Liberation—From the Camp to the Village. In *Indians Overseas: The Mauritian Experience,* ed. U. Bissoondoyal, pp. 348–56. Moka: Mahatma Gandhi Institute.

Warschauer, M. 1998. Technology and Indigenous Language Revitalization: Analyzing the Experience of Hawai'i. *The Canadian Modern Language Review / La revue canadienne des langues vivantes* 55: 139–59.

Washbrook, David. 1991. "To Each a Language of His Own": Language, Culture and Society in Colonial India. In *Language, History and Class*, ed. Penelope J. Corfield, pp. Oxford: Blackwell.

Wertsch, James V. 2002. *Voices of Collective Remembering*. Cambridge: Cambridge University Press.

Williams, C., ed. 2000. *Language Revitalization: Policy and Planning in Wales*. Cardiff: University of Wales Press.

Wood, David. 2001 [1989]. *The Deconstruction of Time*. Evanston: Northwestern University Press.

Woolard, Kathryn A. 1998. Simultaneity and Bivalency as Strategies in Bilingualism. *Journal of Linguistic Anthropology* 8(1): 3–29.

———. 2004. Is the Past a Foreign Country? Time, Language Origins, and the Nation in Early Modern Spain. *Journal of Linguistic Anthropology* 14(1): 57–80.

Woolard, Kathryn A., and Bambi Schieffelin. 1994. Language Ideology. *Annual Review of Anthropology* 23: 55–82.

World Bank. 1989. *Mauritius, Managing Success*. Washington, D.C.: World Bank.

———. 1992. *Mauritius, Expanding Horizons*. Washington, D.C.: World Bank.

Zerubavel, Eviatar. 2003. *Time Maps: Collective Memory and the Social Shape of the Past*. Chicago: University of Chicago Press.

Žižek, Slavoj. 1994. The Spectre of Ideology. In *Mapping Ideology*, ed. Slavoj Žižek. London: Verso.

Index

Activists, Hindu: on hardships of ances-
tors, 260–61; on ancestral languages,
35, 55, 280n40; on Bhojpuri, 208,
209, 224, 225; *hundutva*-affiliated, 43;
suffrage campaigns of, 186; ties with
Mauritian government, 35–44; view
of Creole, 208. *See also* Nationalists,
Hindu; Transnational organizations,
Hindu
Address, pronouns of, 112, 213
Afro-Creole movement, 64
Afro-Creoles, Caribbean, 28, 104,
277n15
Ahl-e Sunnat va Jama'at (Sunni movement), 235, 291n63
Ali Khan, Nusrat Fateh, 29
All India Radio, 209
Allochrony, 225
Ancestral culture, Mauritian, 273n6;
of Creoles, 33; and economic success,
100, 101; ethnic others and, 99–110;
Hindu, 5, 19; homogenized, 200; Indo-
Mauritian politics of, 12; official discourse on, 93; protection of, 173;
purity of, 58; of rural Hindus, 100,
110; in Shivratri festival, 261; state-
sponsored, 167; valorizing of, 215
Ancestral languages: African, 34; in diaspora formation, 9, 233; ideology of,
19; purity in, 12
Ancestral languages, Indian, 4–5, 6–7,
77–88; allegiances to, 234; colonial
genealogies of, 20–21; connection with
religion, 158, 191; conservative values
and, 82; contextualizing of, 29–32;
cultural importance of, 47, 80–81;

educational debates over, 168, 171–
73, 186–197; in ethnic communities,
171, 234; Hindu activists on, 35, 55,
280n40; ideologies of, 13, 188, 194,
238, 263; institutionalization of, 186–
97, 236; officially recognized, 31; political power and, 34, 186–97, 199; politics of, 19, 26–29, 234; in postcolonial
Mauritius, 200; purity in, 12, and religious nationalism, 192; role in belonging, 19, 30, 61–65; role in diaspora,
21, 46, 110, 229, 238, 267; role in
ethnic identity, 26, 197; role in Hindu
identity, 54, 55–56, 83–84, 88, 103,
251; role in nationhood, 6–7; state
support for, 29, 31, 46, 80, 188–89,
192–93, 200, 208, 274n3, 276n9;
sweetness of, 82; teaching of, 31, 34,
44–47; teaching subsidies for, 236;
valorization of, 185; in vernacular
practice, 88–90
Anderson, Benedict: on community, 241;
on lexicographic revolution, 220; on
linguistic homogenization, 169–70;
on temporality, 239, 264, 265, 267–
68, 270; theory of nationalism, 10–11,
20, 22, 24–25, 49, 169, 242, 264–65,
271; on vernacular languages, 23
Anglicists, 175. *See also* Mauritius, British
colonial: anglicization policy of
Apache, ancestral place names among,
295n17
Arabic language, 30; as ancestral, 200–
201, 237, 291n63; teaching of, 32
Arya Ravived Pracharini Sabha (organization), 278n17

Text 10/13 Sabon
Display Sabon
Compositor BookMatters, Berkeley
Cartographer Bill Nelson
Printer and binder IBT Global